Robert Cole's World

The publication of this book has

been supported by a grant from

the Maryland State Archives and

Hall of Records Commission.

Published for the Omohundro Institute of

Early American History and Culture

by the University of North Carolina Press

Chapel Hill and London

Robert Cole's World

· · · · · · ·

Agriculture and

Society in

Early Maryland

Lois Green Carr

Russell R. Menard

Lorena S. Walsh

FLIP

The Institute of Early American History and Culture is sponsored jointly by The College of William and Mary and The Colonial Williamsburg Foundation.

Library of Congress Cataloging-in-Publication Data

Carr, Lois Green.
    Robert Cole's world : agriculture and society in early
Maryland / Lois Green Carr, Russell R. Menard, Lorena S. Walsh.
        p. cm.
    Includes bibliographical references (p.   ) and index.
    ISBN 0-8078-1985-9 (cloth : alk. paper)
    ISBN 0-8078-4341-5 (pbk. : alk. paper)
    1. Chesapeake Bay Region (Md. and Va.)—Rural conditions.   2. Cole, Robert, fl. 1652–1660.   3. Cole family.
4. Maryland—Social life and customs—Colonial period,
ca. 1600–1775.   5. Virginia—Social life and customs—
Colonial period, ca. 1600–1775.   6. Plantations—Chesapeake Bay Region (Md. and Va.)—History—17th century.
7. Plantation life—Chesapeake Bay Region (Md. and Va.)—
History—17th century.   I. Menard, Russell R.   II. Walsh,
Lorena Seebach, 1944–   .   III. Institute of Early American
History and Culture (Williamsburg, Va.)   IV. Title.
HN79.M32C37   1991
306'.09752'09032—dc20   90-26168
                                                                    CIP

The paper in this book meets the guidelines for permanence and durability of the Committee on Production Guidelines for Book Longevity of the Council on Library Resources.

Manufactured in the United States of America
01 00 99 98 97   7 6 5 4 3

Publication of this book has been supported, in part, by a donation from FIGGIE INTERNATIONAL, INC., in memory of the former Governor of Virginia, JOHN N. DALTON.

This volume received indirect support from an unrestricted book publications grant awarded to the Institute by the L. J. SKAGGS AND MARY C. SKAGGS FOUNDATION of Oakland, California.

To

The Maryland State Archives

and the St. Mary's City Commission

with thanks for their role

in awakening interest in

Chesapeake history and

encouraging its recent flowering

Contents

. . . . .

Illustrations
and Maps

• • • • •

Illustrations

Maps

Tables

. . . . .

Preface

. . . . .

The region surrounding the Chesapeake Bay witnessed dramatic changes in the seventeenth century. The English invaded the area, wrested control of the territory from its aboriginal inhabitants, and wreaked havoc among those inhabitants in the process. By 1700 the tribal groups of the bay had been decimated by disease and warfare, their lands cultivated by the English and African slaves, their economies left in shambles, and their traditional beliefs strained and often shattered, as once independent peoples became tributary populations on the periphery of English settlement.

The nature of that English settlement also changed. Outpost colonies, beachheads along the bay, largely male and dominated by rugged, grasping entrepreneurs in Virginia and the younger sons of Catholic gentry in Maryland, soon became immigrant communities of small planters, communities in which a Chesapeake yeomanry worked owner-operated farms with the aid of their families and white indentured servants who aspired to become tobacco planters in their own right. By century's end this small and middling planter's age was itself on the wane. Class and race divided a once much-less-differentiated society as the patriarchal, gentry-dominated, and slave-based structure of the region's "golden age" began to take shape along the bay.

Agriculture—the process of farm making in particular—was a central, driving force in these transformations. Agricultural possibility—the chance to make tobacco and food crops while carving out a good life with a few comforts and some security on a farm of one's own—was the chief attraction of the Chesapeake colonies, drawing tens of thousands of young men and women from England to the bay colonies. Many came to early death, but the survivors transformed the landscape. They built farms, an activity that let many realize their dreams of independence and modest prosperity while at the same time it expanded the area of English settlement and put increased pressure on the Indians, who had to be "pacified" and pushed back to foster a sense of security among the colonists and to make room for still more farms.

Farm building was the central activity of the yeoman planter's age. Planters cleared land for tobacco and corn, erected housing and fences, raised stocks of cattle, swine, and horses, planted orchards, and set out gardens. The work was hard, but rewarding, for farms rapidly gained in value, living standards rose, assets accumulated, and levels of wealth and income grew at unprecedented rates for a preindustrial age. In the process Chesapeake planters developed a new system of agriculture—a blend of European and Native American techniques and methods of their own devising—through persistent experimentation as they learned by doing. There were limits to growth in the new system, limits partly grounded in costs of supervision, and for a while these limits helped to foster a small and middling planter society. Nevertheless, farm making in itself created inequality as some planters fared better than others (often by simply living longer), and as children inherited different amounts of property and thus began their own families with greater or fewer advantages. Furthermore, limits to growth were breachable. The Chesapeake system of agriculture could produce capital sufficient to finance expansion for those willing to take the risk. Such planters used accumulated wealth to acquire the necessary land and to purchase the laborers—increasingly slaves—to work it. The gentry-dominated, slave-based patriarchy of the eighteenth century did not simply replace the yeoman planter society of the early colonial period. Rather, it emerged as the result of farm making during the pioneering era.

These complex transformations have figured prominently in recent historiography, which has made small planters the central figures on the seventeenth-century Chesapeake scene. We now know a good deal about the basic demographic parameters that shaped their lives, the shifting fortunes of the international tobacco market that governed their incomes, their participation in public life, the sorts of houses they lived in, their diet and clothing, and their relationships with each other and with their family members and servants. Oddly, however, we know relatively little about a major aspect of their lives: the practice of agriculture and the process of building farms. This book begins to fill that gap. It does so through a focus on an especially well documented family, using the records of a single plantation to show how ordinary people tended their

fields, grew their crops, cared for their livestock—in short, made their living—along the tobacco coast in the early colonial period.[1]

That family was founded by Robert and Rebecca Cole, who migrated to Maryland from England in 1652. The Coles were not full and accurate representatives of the Chesapeake experience in the seventeenth century. No family or person was, for that experience was particular and varied, marked by individuality, accident, surprise, and difference. Still, the Coles were not unusual or remarkable, were not set apart from their neighbors by distinctive life histories. Further, despite the variety of life along the bay, there were shared activities and events—common processes, opportunities, aspirations, and disappointments—that touched most inhabitants and bound them together. Nor had regional differences begun to emerge that would make the Coles' experience atypical. The Cole family was distinctive in one fortunate respect, however. After Robert and Rebecca died in the early 1660s, their neighbor Luke Gardiner operated the family plantation for more than a decade until the children came of age and divided the assets among themselves. Gardiner kept detailed accounts of his administration, documents that survive in the records of the Maryland probate court. Those documents, printed as an appendix to this book, provide unique insight into the process of farm building, the practice of agriculture, and the activities of daily life along the bay during the early colonial period.

The agricultural practices of Chesapeake planters often earned the scorn of contemporary observers; their reputation has not fared much better at the hands of modern historians. Planters were charged with "exceeding Ill-Husbandry" and were portrayed as wasteful, slovenly farmers who abused the land and cared poorly for their livestock, accepted small yields and low incomes, used primitive tools, and resisted useful innovations.[2] This book challenges that view, on two counts. In the first place, the denigration of colonial agriculture is usually rooted in an inappropriate comparison with European farmers, who operated within much different constraints. Along the bay, where land was cheap and labor dear, it rarely made sense to follow the "best" Old World practices. Behavior that appeared slovenly and wasteful often reflected efforts to save labor in an economy where wages were high. "The aim of farmers in this country," George Washington explained more than a century after Robert and Rebecca Cole had died, "is not to make the most they can from the land, which is, or has been, cheap, but the most of the labour, which is dear, the consequence of which has been, much ground has been *scratched* over and none cultivated or improved as it ought to have been." Different factor prices required different farming methods.[3]

Second, those who hold colonial farmers in contempt underestimate their impressive accomplishments. Chesapeake tobacco planters created a new style of agriculture in the seventeenth century. Many particulars of that process are now lost, but the outcome is clear enough. Seventeenth-century Chesapeake families made plantations, accumulated wealth, built neighborhoods and communities, and acquired a measure of comfort and security. Those gains were bought at a frightful price in shortened lives, but they were accomplishments nonetheless.

This book explores those accomplishments through a study of farm building and agriculture on the Cole plantation. Chapter 1 sets the scene, offering a brief summary of the main developments in Chesapeake history through the middle of the seventeenth century and placing the Cole family and their plantation within Maryland society. Chapters 2 and 3 focus on agriculture, describing the process of farm building and the yearly cycle of work on the plantation in order to identify the main elements of the Chesapeake system of husbandry. Chapter 4 explores the results of that work by analyzing the accumulation of wealth and the standard of living supported by Chesapeake plantations. Chapter 5 studies relationships among family members and looks beyond the plantation to the networks that tied the Coles to their neighborhood and to the broader North Atlantic world. A concluding chapter follows the plantation and its inhabitants into the early eighteenth century and suggests how the small planter's world shaped by Robert Cole and his neighbors gradually became the slave-based "golden age" of the Chesapeake gentry.

Acknowledgments

. . . . .

This book has been many years in the making, and we are heavily indebted to many people and institutions that have helped us bring it into being. Two State of Maryland agencies, the St. Mary's City Commission (now part of the Department of Housing and Community Development, Division of Historical and Cultural Programs) and the Maryland State Archives, have nurtured the project from start to finish. The St. Mary's City Commission, established in 1966 to explore, preserve, and interpret the site of Maryland's seventeenth-century capital, has undertaken basic archaeological and historical research and publication on life in the Chesapeake tidewater. In the early days of the preparation of this book, all three authors were members of the commission staff, and the commission has continued to support the work through its Historian, Lois Green Carr. The Maryland State Archives has offered a home not only to the commission research staff but also to an array of scholars pursuing the history of the Chesapeake region, offering all of us intellectual stimulation as well as expert technical assistance. The splendid efforts of the archives over the years in collecting and preserving local records and making them accessible have helped to make possible a renaissance in Chesapeake studies. In addition, the archives has supported publications, including this one, with grants that help to bring the prices to reasonable levels. Our gratitude to these creative institutions is expressed in the dedication.

Many other institutions contributed to our work. We owe thanks to the National Science Foundation and the National Endowment for the Humanities, which financed parts of the research in its early stages under grants to the St. Mary's City Commission (GS32272; RO6228-72-468). Russell R. Menard acknowledges support from a National Endowment for the Humanities Fellowship for University Teachers and from the Graduate School and College of Liberal Arts of the University of Minnesota. Staff at the Folger Shakespeare Library, the Maryland Historical

Society, and the Georgetown University Library eased the task of locating essential records. Several friends contributed time and effort in finding materials. James P. P. Horn and Thomas L. Purvis researched the Coles' English background at the Greater London Record Office and other London repositories. Ronald Hoffman alerted us to the Carroll-Maccubbin Papers and their wealth of information on the later history of St. Clement's Manor. Garry W. Stone and Henry M. Miller, archaeologists for the St. Mary's City Commission, supplied information on a variety of topics for which evidence found in the ground is superior to that found in documents. They also read and criticized parts of the manuscript. We thank David O. Percy, former Director, National Colonial Farm, for sharing with us his knowledge of sources for studying Chesapeake husbandry, and Jack Larkin, Chief Historian at Old Sturbridge Village, for help in estimating the time required for land clearance. Portions of chapter 4 appeared in the *William and Mary Quarterly* of April 1983, giving us the benefit of Michael McGiffert's critical eye.

Over the years we have had the benefit of conversation with many colleagues besides those already mentioned. Morris L. Radoff (former State Archivist), Edward C. Papenfuse, Gregory A. Stiverson, Cary Carson, George Green, P.M.G. Harris, Allan Kulikoff, Gloria Main, John McCusker, and Stuart Schwartz have offered essential encouragement. Paul G. E. Clemens, Stanley Engerman, Jean B. Russo, and an anonymous reader read the whole manuscript, making shrewd comments. We must also thank Roger Ekirch, Thomas L. Purvis, and Fredrika Teute, editors in succession at the Institute of Early American History and Culture, for excellent suggestions. We did not always accept the advice of these various critics, but we highly valued the exchanges, and they surely improved our book. We alone are responsible for its errors.

On the technical side, we owe thanks to Emory Evans, who gave us part of his computer time on the mainframe at the University of Maryland; to Jean B. Russo, who handled our programming; to Nancy Bramucci, who keyboarded the tables and appendixes and other parts of the manuscript through a variety of transformations; to Gregory Chu of the Cartography Laboratory, Geography Department, University of Minnesota, who prepared the maps; and to Sandra Eisdorfer and her various colleagues at the University of North Carolina Press, who saw the book through its production. We must make special mention of our copyeditor,

D. Teddy Diggs, whose meticulous examination of the manuscript saved us from numerous errors and from the many inconsistencies to which coauthored books are prone.

On the personal side, we thank our families for living through the whole process with us.

1

· · · · ·

A Context
for the Cole
Plantation

Introduction

Robert Cole lived an ordinary life in a small corner of the English-speaking world. He left no diary nor any revealing personal letters. We know only the bare outlines of his career: when he was born and died, his wife's name and the ages of his children, his source of income and standard of living, who some of his friends were, the public offices he held and the religion he professed. Occasionally, we are provided fleeting insight into his personality, but his life remains skeletal, lacking the intimate detail needed to add flesh to a biography. We know, or at least could discover, as much or more about many other residents of the tobacco coast. But for a series of events that occurred after he died, there would be little reason to choose his family over several hundred others as the focus of a book on agriculture and society along the Chesapeake Bay in the seventeenth century.

Robert Cole's life as a Maryland tobacco planter was short. He planned a trip home, to England, in 1662, only ten years after he first set foot in the New World. Faced with the hazards of an Atlantic crossing, he made elaborate preparations for the care of his children and the management of his estate. Cole took a detailed inventory of his possessions in March and, in April, wrote a will. Within that brief interval, his wife of more than a decade, Rebecca, must have died: she is mentioned in the inventory but not in the will. Her death did not change Robert's plans. He charged two of his Maryland neighbors, Luke Gardiner and William

Evans, and a London cousin, Henry Hanckes, with the care of his children and property, and left for England, probably with the spring tobacco fleet. We know that by September 1663 he was dead, although the exact date and place of his death are uncertain. Cole left seven orphan children (two of them Rebecca's by a prior marriage) for his executors to raise and a small farm for them to operate.[1]

Ten years later, in 1673, Robert Cole's son, Robert Cole, Jr., and his son-in-law, Ignatius Warren, sued Luke Gardiner, the only surviving executor, over the management of the estate. Nothing suggests that this was a serious dispute reflecting real animosity between the executor and the heirs. Indeed, all parties may have thought the suit a convenient way to settle affairs and divide the assets. Judge Philip Calvert chastised Gardiner for careless record keeping and for failing to follow the letter of the law. In particular, Gardiner had not taken the executor's oath, had not appraised the estate, had on occasion failed to record the "Express time of the Delivery or to whome or for what account," and had not kept "such an Account . . . as hee dares absolutely Sweare to as an Executor ought to doe." Gardiner's errors were minor, however, and Calvert exonerated him from all charges of dishonesty or serious mismanagement. In fact, the children were fortunate in their father's choice of an executor, for the value of the estate increased substantially under Gardiner's supervision. In Philip Calvert's view, this was sufficient to override any technical shortcomings, and Gardiner escaped severe penalty.[2]

The documents generated by the suit are unique. The court ordered Gardiner to submit his accounts of the estate, which the Judge examined and "Rectifyed in many particulars."[3] A clerk then transcribed the accounts into the court record, a volume that is now at the Maryland State Archives in Annapolis. These documents detail income and expenditures on the Cole plantation for nearly twelve years, from Robert's departure for England in early 1662 until the initiation of the suit in mid-1673. Gardiner's bookkeeping may not have satisfied Philip Calvert, but the accounts provide more insight into the domestic economy of a seventeenth-century plantation than do any other single set of documents yet discovered. When combined with bits and pieces of evidence drawn from a variety of sources and interpreted with the help of some educated guesswork, the accounts reveal much about daily activities in colonial Maryland. Their survival elevates the Cole family to a central place in the historiography of the Chesapeake colonies in the seventeenth century.

The First Maryland Society

Robert Cole (c. 1628–c. 1662) was about twenty-five years old when he arrived in Maryland in June 1652 with his wife, Rebecca, four children (at least two were hers by an earlier marriage), and two servants. The Coles were Roman Catholics, which may explain the attraction Maryland held for them. Robert Cole also had a "kinsman," Benjamin Gill, who had lived and prospered in Maryland for a decade. Perhaps reports of Gill's success had reached Robert in England.[4]

We know little about Robert and Rebecca's life in England before they left for Maryland. His mother, Joan, was living in Heston, Middlesex, a rich farming region fifteen miles to the west of London, when he wrote his will. We suspect that Robert was born and raised in Heston, but the evidence is inconclusive. The parish records are spotty, so that what once may have been firm proof has since been lost; Cole was a common surname in the area, creating numerous opportunities for mistaken identification; and because of their Catholicism, the family were perhaps less dutiful in registering vital events than were people of the dominant Protestant faith. Most probably Robert was the son of William Cole, a yeoman (husband of one Joan Cole) who died in 1633 or early 1634 when Robert was only five or six years old.[5]

The family seems to have been prosperous. Some of the Coles in Heston had been doing well for more than seventy years. A William Cole was Heston's miller in 1576. A John Cole was constable in 1620, and a Solomon Cole was to be deputy steward of Heston Manor in 1664.[6] Robert's inheritance was apparently sufficient to finance the family's move to Maryland and the establishment of a plantation. Probably he sold land to help finance the trip: a Robert Cole sold land on Heston Manor in 1651. Cole's will implies that he still had a claim to property in England, presumably land or a lease in his mother's possession, and tax records of 1664 show that his mother lived comfortably, occupying a place in the top third of the Heston wealth structure.[7] It is likely that Robert was an only child, or at least the only surviving child when he died: his will mentions no brothers or sisters but instead makes a "couzin," Mr. Henry Hanckes of Holborne, London, his executor in England.[8] The fluent English of the will and inventory suggests that Robert had some formal education. He was almost certainly raised in the Catholic faith. He was clearly a Catholic by 1653 when his son and namesake was baptized by

Father Lawrence Starkey, and women of the Cole family had been prosecuted steadily for recusancy (failure to take communion or attend services in the Church of England) by the Middlesex County quarter sessions since the late 1500s. Among these was Joan Cole, wife of William when indicted in 1632 and a widow when indicted again in April 1634.[9]

We know less about Rebecca. She married Robert Cole between 1649 and their departure for Maryland. She had been married to a man named Knott and had had at least two and perhaps four children by him. She was probably older than Robert: he was at most twenty-four when they married, and she would have had to have married Knott at an unusually early age to have been younger than twenty-four and a widow with at least two children when she wed for the second time. It is also likely, judging from the inheritances later received by the Knott children, that she and her first husband were considerably poorer than the Cole family. Perhaps Robert, a Catholic in a region where Catholics were few, had "married down" to find a wife who shared his faith.[10]

It is likely that Robert and Rebecca Cole's Catholic faith was critical to their choice of Maryland. There, a Catholic proprietor offered people of any Christian religion the freedom to worship and to participate in public life. In principle, Catholics in Elizabethan and early Stuart England faced "severe financial penalties, exclusion from most official positions, and difficulties of various kinds." But as John Bossy has noted, during Robert and Rebecca's childhood "the actual situation was not quite as it appeared." Charles I (1625–49) was, if not a closet Catholic, as some believed, at least a sympathizer, as were many powerful men and women at the court. Moreover, at the local level, accommodations had often been worked out that permitted Catholics to practice their faith quietly without overt, sustained harassment and with some sense of security.[11] As a consequence, the English Catholic community, although tiny—about 1 percent of the total population—grew steadily during the early Stuart years, from about forty thousand people in 1600 to about sixty thousand by 1640, keeping pace with overall population growth.[12] On the other hand, Catholics in the area around London may have suffered more severely. From 1595 through 1642, of the twenty people from Heston indicted for failing to attend Church of England services, only three were men, a clear suggestion that a man who wished not to conform had to leave.[13] Conditions, furthermore, shifted rapidly with the outbreak of the Civil War, as Catholic sympathizers fell from office and militant Protestants seized power. Although it is not clear that persecution of Catholics (as distinct from Royalists) increased, it is certain that many Catholics were frightened and that their sense of security diminished.

The Coles arrived with some capital, probably enough to purchase land and begin a plantation immediately. They apparently moved to St. Clement's Manor in St. Mary's County and bought a 300-acre freehold there soon after arriving in Maryland. Robert also surveyed 350 acres of unimproved land in 1654 on the Nanjemoy River in the area that later became Charles County, but he sold the tract within four years and seems to have done nothing to develop it. He chose instead to keep his manor freehold, even though he had thereby to attend manor courts and suffer other, albeit very minor, feudal restrictions.[14]

The second Lord Baltimore's charter permitted him to grant manors, which had rights to hold courts having minor peacekeeping and civil jurisdiction. The manor, a feudal institution dying out in England, was seen by developers of early seventeenth-century colonies as a useful tool for establishing orderly settlements. The Maryland proprietor offered each of his first investors a 2,000-acre manor for every five settlers they imported, but in 1634 he reduced the land so granted to 1,000 acres. Under these "conditions of plantation," Dr. Thomas Gerard had patented St. Clement's Manor in 1639.[15]

The manor occupied a broad neck of land on the Potomac between the Wicomico River and St. Clement's Bay. Originally it contained only 1,030 acres, but Gerard enlarged and repatented it as a 6,000-acre tract in 1641. In 1678, when Gerard's heirs had the manor resurveyed, it was found to contain 11,400 acres, eloquent testimony to the amateurism of Maryland's first surveyors. By the time Cole arrived at St. Clement's, Gerard was beginning to emerge as one of Maryland's most successful estate developers, perhaps the only man to provide more than a fleeting substance to Lord Baltimore's manorial vision. Beginning with a little capital of his own and about £175 sterling borrowed from a brother-in-law, Gerard used intelligent management, a judicious credit policy, the marriages of his several daughters, and the force of his personality to build an impressive landed empire.[16]

Two circumstances may have affected Cole's decision to live on St. Clement's Manor. First, it was not far by water to the Jesuit mission at Newtown, across St. Clement's Bay (see map 1.1), and others had already taken up the land that was closer. Second, coming from Heston, he may

1.1 Aerial Photograph of St. Clement's Bay, 1988. Most of the area is still farmed, but much less of it was under cultivation in the seventeenth century. (United States Department of Agriculture, Agricultural Stabilization and Conservation Service)

have found manorial organization especially comfortable. Farmers on the Manor of Heston raised grain on open fields subject to regulation by the manor court. The area was preeminent for its fertility and its high-quality wheat. According to the Elizabethan surveyor John Norden, the queen had "the most part of her provision from that place." Evidently the extraordinary productivity averted pressures for enclosure. As late as 1818, two-thirds of the manor was still unenclosed. And the culture of manorial life must have been strong: the manor court convened until late in the

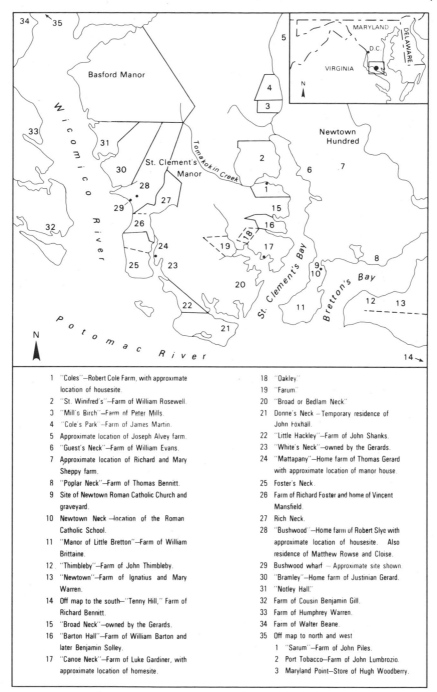

Basford Manor

Newtown
Hundred

Wicomico River

Tomakokin Creek

St. Clement's
Manor

Potomac River

St. Clement's Bay

Bretton's Bay

N

1 "Coles"—Robert Cole Farm, with approximate
   location of housesite.
2 "St. Winifred's"—Farm of William Rosewell.
3 "Mill's Birch"—Farm of Peter Mills.
4 "Cole's Park"—Farm of James Martin.
5 Approximate location of Joseph Alvey farm.
6 "Guest's Neck"—Farm of William Evans.
7 Approximate location of Richard and Mary
   Sheppy farm.
8 "Poplar Neck"—Farm of Thomas Bennitt.
9 Site of Newtown Roman Catholic Church and
   graveyard.
10 Newtown Neck—location of the Roman
   Catholic School.
11 "Manor of Little Bretton"—Farm of William
   Brittaine.
12 "Thimbleby"—Farm of John Thimbleby.
13 "Newtown"—Farm of Ignatius and Mary
   Warren.
14 Off map to the south—"Tenny Hill," Farm of
   Richard Bennitt.
15 "Broad Neck"—owned by the Gerards.
16 "Barton Hall"—Farm of William Barton and
   later Benjamin Solley.
17 "Canoe Neck"—Farm of Luke Gardiner, with
   approximate location of homesite.

18 "Oakley."
19 "Farum."
20 "Broad or Bedlam Neck."
21 Donne's Neck – Temporary residence of
   John Foxhall.
22 "Little Hackley"—Farm of John Shanks.
23 "White's Neck"—owned by the Gerards.
24 "Mattapany"—Home farm of Thomas Gerard
   with approximate location of manor house.
25 Foster's Neck.
26 Farm of Richard Foster and home of Vincent
   Mansfield.
27 Rich Neck.
28 "Bushwood"—Home farm of Robert Slye with
   approximate location of housesite. Also
   residence of Matthew Rowse and Cloise.
29 Bushwood wharf – Approximate site shown.
30 "Bramley"—Home farm of Justinian Gerard.
31 "Notley Hall."
32 Farm of Cousin Benjamin Gill.
33 Farm of Humphrey Warren.
34 Farm of Walter Beane.
35 Off map to north and west
   1 "Sarum"—Farm of John Piles.
   2 Port Tobacco—Farm of John Lumbrozio.
   3 Maryland Point—Store of Hugh Woodberry.

Map 1.1. The Cole Farm and Its Surroundings c. 1660–c. 1675

nineteenth century. Where Robert Cole grew up, the manor was still an exceptionally solid institution.[17]

It is not certain what effect Cole's choice of St. Clement's Manor had on his life in Maryland. Since open-field agriculture was not the practice, the manor court did not concern itself with land use. Business was chiefly confined to problems of land boundaries, livestock depredations, minor breaches of the peace, and attempts to enforce the manor lord's rights. Perhaps the existence of a functioning manorial organization created a more integrated neighborhood with a stronger sense of community than had yet emerged elsewhere in the province, although a high rate of population turnover suggests that this was not the case.[18] The manor had other attractive features, but they could be found elsewhere in Maryland as well. There were several men living on St. Clement's who could loan the capital needed to begin a plantation. Robert Slye, the son-in-law of the manor lord and perhaps the wealthiest merchant in Maryland, offered adequate marketing and supply facilities and linked local planters to the larger Atlantic economy. Although the soil was not the best in the county for tobacco, a good portion was more than adequate. Since the manor occupied a peninsula drained by several creeks, even interior locations offered the easy access to water transport sought by tobacco planters. Cole's residence on St. Clement's burdened him with a few minor duties, but it did not sharply distinguish him from the majority of planters who avoided manorial obligations.

Wherever Cole might have settled in Maryland, he was bound to raise tobacco, not wheat. Long before Cole arrived, tobacco had become "the only solid Staple Commodity of this Province," thoroughly dominating exports and tying planters to a wider world. It paid for servants, slaves, manufactured goods, and commercial services. It attracted immigrants and capital, shaped settlement patterns and income distributions, structured work routines, channeled investment, and limited occupational choices. Over the whole colonial period, so central was the crop to life in Maryland and Virginia that it is possible to identify a distinct "culture of tobacco," to trace the impact of the staple on the values, attitudes, and worldviews of the people who cultivated it.[19]

The political and social organization of Maryland was not so immediately determined. Lord Baltimore had envisioned a colony structured around manors like that of St. Clement's. But by the time Robert Cole arrived in Maryland, less than two decades after the landing of the first adventurers in the *Ark* and the *Dove*, the manor was already becoming something of a dinosaur, an institution of the colony's past. In fact, despite determined efforts of the early investors to develop large estates worked by tenants and governed by manorial arrangements, St. Clement's was the only manor that clearly functioned as such for more than a few years. There had been a time when the manor could have emerged as a central institution in Maryland's history. However, political instability joined with abundance of land and rapid economic growth to undermine the social relationships under which the manorial system might have flourished.[20]

Baltimore's colonization plan was designed to do two things: create a hierarchical, stratified, "well-ordered" community of landlords and tenants in Maryland, a structured world that evoked images of England's feudal past; and ease the financial burden of establishing a new settlement and sustaining it through its infancy. The manorial system was central to the design. Lord Baltimore hoped that the prospect of large landed estates, complete with titles, feudal trappings, and rents from a New World peasantry would attract well-born Englishmen of substance to the colony. Such men would finance the passage and supply of large numbers of ordinary settlers and provide a distinguished, qualified leadership. The recruitment campaign conducted around this plan in 1632 and 1633 was not an outstanding success. It turned up little money and few settlers. Nevertheless, a look at the passengers on the *Ark* and the *Dove* suggests that Cecilius Calvert's initial optimism was justified. "I have," he wrote Sir Thomas Wentworth in early 1634, "sent a hopeful Colony to Maryland, with a fair and probable Expectation of good success."[21]

The shipboard society was rigidly stratified: with one possible exception, all the first adventurers were either gentlemen or their servants. There were 17 men "of good birth and qualitie" among the roughly 140 passengers, including several members of English ruling-class families. Two of Baltimore's younger brothers, Leonard, who was appointed governor, and George, accompanied the settlers. The expedition included several others from families at least as prominent as the Calverts, "noble welborne and able gentlemen that know by experience both how to obey and command."[22] Thomas Cornwallis, for example, was the son of a member of Parliament and grandson of an ambassador to Spain. Jerome Hawley, Edward and Frederick Winter, Thomas Greene, Henry Wiseman, and Richard Gerard were also members of distinguished, well-connected families. The first adventurers formed a firm foundation on which to build a hierarchical, well-ordered community along the Chesapeake Bay. The nucleus of a New World gentry and a successful manorial system sailed for Maryland on the *Ark* and the *Dove*.[23]

With a few possible exceptions, the rest of the passengers were indentured servants. Indentured servitude had developed during the early years of Virginia as a way to move impoverished workers from England to its New World colonies. Poor men and women could in effect borrow the funds needed for transportation across the Atlantic and could repay the sum with several years of labor—labor desperately needed to develop the estates of those who financed their passage. The great majority of immigrants to Maryland and Virginia during the seventeenth century arrived as servants, some fleeing misery and hunger at home, others seeking opportunity in a place where land was cheap and labor dear. The servants on the *Ark* and the *Dove* were similar to those who were to arrive in the Chesapeake region for the rest of the century—young, mostly male, from a variety of social levels in English society, but with little hope of prosperity at home.[24]

This initial society of gentlemen and servants persisted through the first decade of settlement. Maryland was dominated by a few men with a claim to gentry status in England. They held the most important government positions and directed the spread of settlement. They owned the factors of production—land, capital, and most of the unfree labor—and they dominated local marketing and credit networks. They were distinguished from the majority of colonists by the titles that graced their names and by the quality of their educations. They controlled the trade of the province, maintained their English connections, and linked humbler colonists into a wider world. To a point, the manorial system operated according to plan: most of the wealthier gentlemen took up manors, and most of the more ordinary settlers lived on those manors as servants or as freedmen—that is, ex-servants—who were laborers, sharecroppers, and tenants.

Nevertheless, there were severe limits to manorial development in early Maryland. And contrary processes foreshadowed social relationships that would soon structure life differently in the colony. The local gentry were rich by frontier standards, but not rich enough for the task at hand. Even Thomas Cornwallis, perhaps the wealthiest of the early investors, complained that his "poore younger brothers fortune" had been run "allmost

out of breathe" in efforts to build a Maryland estate.[25] Manorial lords
could not import sufficient servants to develop their property, and rents,
in a region where land was cheap and easy to come by, provided only
meager incomes. Opportunity, furthermore, was already beginning to
erode the manorial structure, although its full effect would not be apparent until later, after mid-century. Servants gained their freedom, and
some free immigrants of modest means arrived in the colony. A few poor
men, after short stints as hired hands or tenant farmers, acquired land
and set up as independent farmers, and the crude material conditions of
frontier life imposed a rough-hewn equality on the inhabitants. Still, most
settlers remained in a dependent, subordinate position; the colony's hierarchy and structure allowed a clear distinction between the local gentry
and the great majority of colonists.

Lord Baltimore had recruited a distinguished leadership for his new
colony, but the anticipated consequence—an orderly, well-governed community—did not follow. The politics of the first decade were tumultuous
and ended in disaster for this fragile outpost of English colonization.[26]
Maryland's neighbors, the Virginians far more than the Indians, were
hostile to the entire enterprise and did their best to undermine it. The
colonists, instead of uniting against the threat, bickered among themselves over religion, constitutional issues, the fur trade, and Indian policy.
Most of the men "of good birth and qualitie" proved more willing to
"command" than "obey." They generally left the province within a few
years, died, or pursued personal aggrandizement with a single-minded
willfulness that disrupted public life and denied the colony effective
leadership.

Finally, in late February 1645, the English civil war reached Maryland and nearly undid Lord Baltimore's colony. Richard Ingle, a vet-
eran ship captain long employed in the tobacco trade, invaded St. Mary's
City, claiming that the government there exercised "a Tyrannical power
against the Protestants, and such as adhered to Parlyament."[27] The details of what followed are now obscure. Baltimore's supporters apparently
surrendered without a fight: Leonard Calvert abandoned the province
for refuge in Virginia. Ingle and his men ("most rascally fellows of desperate fortune," one colonist called them)[28] burned some houses, looted
others, and returned to London with several priests in chains and a few
other Catholic prisoners. The settlement was left in the hands of a small
group of mercenaries, recruited by Ingle in Virginia, and a few Protes-

tant collaborators, who fortified Governor Calvert's house to make a stronghold. For nearly two years Maryland was without stable government: the colonists were terrorized, their lives disrupted, their estates despoiled. The population fell sharply, from more than five hundred in 1644 to well under two hundred in 1646, when Leonard Calvert reestablished his authority. Settlers who remained referred to the period as the "time of troubles" or "the plundering time."[29]

Maryland survived Richard Ingle, but the attempt at a manorial system and the hierarchical, stratified society on which it was supposed to be based did not. However, the social relationships that Baltimore had envisioned had already been doomed. Ingle only hastened their passing. Processes in England and the Chesapeake, processes beyond Calvert's ability to control, joined to make Maryland a good poor-man's country in the middle of the seventeenth century and to transform the incipient manorial society, based on lords and their tenants and laborers, into a community made up largely of more ordinary planters and of men on their way to being planters.

Toward a New Social Order

Tobacco was the driving force behind this social transformation. Tobacco was "king" in the Chesapeake colonies, more so than cotton would become in the antebellum South. Any effort to understand social change in Maryland during the middle decades of the seventeenth century must begin with an expansion that took place in the tobacco economy, with the immigrants that this expansion attracted to the colony, and with the opportunities it offered poor men to accumulate property and achieve respectability in a New World community.

Tobacco played a small role in the early efforts to promote the colony. It was, in fact, treated as an afterthought, mentioned as only one of several crops in a diversified agriculture. Given that the Virginia economy was already organized around the export of tobacco, this is surprising. Perhaps the late King James's well-known aversion to "that Stincking Weede of America" (an aversion shared by Thomas Cornwallis, a key backer of the Maryland enterprise) had led to a decision to deemphasize the crop in the recruitment campaign.[30] Further, the price of tobacco had fallen sharply in the years just before the settlement of Maryland. The luxury prices that Virginia planters had commanded in the early 1620s had not lasted. By the end of that decade, tobacco prices had fallen so low that the Virginia economy was severely depressed, and the assembly took steps to restrict production. Tobacco did not look promising in the early 1630s. Perhaps the promoters of Maryland hoped to avoid dependence on a crop with so uncertain and unsatisfactory a price history.

Whatever the intentions of the Lords Baltimore, the colonists were soon engrossed in producing the "sot-weed." The adventurers did not grow tobacco at St. Mary's during the first year of settlement, but the crop quickly emerged as the mainstay of the Maryland economy. By 1637, only three years after the *Ark* and the *Dove* sailed up the St. Mary's River, tobacco had become the money of the province. Colonists traded with it, paid taxes with it, reckoned their worth in it, settled accounts with it, and priced other goods according to its value. By one estimate, Maryland exported 100,000 pounds of tobacco in 1639, an average of more than 600 pounds for each male old enough to work in the crop. Given that a man could make only about 700 to 750 pounds of tobacco a year during the 1630s, this was a thorough commitment to the staple.[31]

There is little mystery why Marylanders turned to tobacco production with such enthusiasm. Although promoters may have expected the successful export of a wide variety of products, tobacco was the only crop with a fully developed marketing network extending from the Chesapeake Bay to England. If the colonists were going to purchase English manufactures and thus achieve some semblance of the good life by their standards, they had to make tobacco. Further, even though tobacco prices fell over the seventeenth century and fluctuated sharply to produce recurrent booms and busts, gains in productivity were sufficient to sustain adequate profits over the long run. The first Marylanders found a readily available market for the weed with English and Dutch merchants who were already trading with Virginia tobacco growers, and these early planters found rising prices. By 1635, planters earned four to six pence for a pound of tobacco, up from the penny a pound of a few years earlier. So dramatic a jump in prices was a powerful incentive to concentrate on tobacco.

The boom of the 1630s proved short-lived. By 1638 the price of tobacco had fallen to three pence per pound, and it continued to fall for the next

several years. The Maryland economy slid into a depression and remained sluggish until Ingle's Rebellion. Paradoxically, that sluggishness,
while a major source of friction among the first settlers and between them
and Lord Baltimore, permitted the persistence of the structured, hierarchical society of manorial lords and their dependents through the first
decade of the colony's history. As servants became free, they could not
easily obtain the credit necessary to establish their own plantations. Many
remained as laborers or tenants on the manors. But a twenty-year boom
was to follow that would provide excellent opportunities for ex-servants
to become planters.

The tobacco boom that transformed Maryland society began in the
middle 1640s. Although there were occasional sharp, short-term rever-
sals and a tailing off in the pace of expansion toward the end of the period, it lasted until the industry collapsed into a profound depression in
the middle 1660s. The dimensions of the boom are impressive. According
to the earl of Clarendon, the Chesapeake region "was more improved in
people and in stock" during the late 1640s and early 1650s "than it had
been from the beginning to that time."[32] Hyperbole to be sure, but if the
period is extended only slightly, exaggeration becomes understatement.
Tobacco production, insofar as English imports serve as a guide, increased more than tenfold between approximately 1640 and the late
1660s. The population of the region also grew rapidly. Taxables in Virginia and Maryland, roughly white males of working age and black adults
of both sexes, more than tripled between 1645 and 1665, from about
forty-six hundred to more than sixteen thousand. Total population grew
even faster, from about eight thousand in 1645 to nearly thirty-four thousand in 1665, an average annual growth rate of 7.5 percent. Thousands
of acres of new land were surveyed and brought into production, and the
area of European settlement expanded substantially, both around the
edge of the bay and inland along the major rivers. The growth of local
government provides a convenient summary index of the pace of expansion: between 1648 and 1665, fifteen new counties—an average of nearly
one each year—were erected in the two colonies to accommodate the
spread of settlement and to serve the inhabitants' needs for justice and
social services.

Growth during this twenty-year boom was especially rapid in Maryland, at that time a Chesapeake frontier. Lord Baltimore had established

only a tenuous foothold along the bay in the first decade of the province: in 1644, something less than six hundred people inhabited the small settlements at St. Mary's and on Kent Island. Ingle's Rebellion revealed just how tenuous a foothold it was: in 1645, the colony could claim fewer than two hundred settlers. By 1665, there were thirty-seven hundred taxables and a total population of nearly eight thousand people in Maryland. The settled area had spread to the northern reaches of the bay, across the Chesapeake to the Eastern Shore, and well into the interior along the major rivers, particularly the Potomac and the Patuxent. By 1665, Baltimore's claim was secure.[33]

This remarkable growth was accompanied with an equally remarkable social transformation. The society established in Maryland by the 1660s little resembled the manorial community that had been envisioned by the Lords Baltimore and that had begun to emerge, at least in crude outline, in early St. Mary's before Richard Ingle. There were, of course, still indentured servants, free laborers, sharecroppers, and tenant farmers in more or less subordinate, dependent positions in the colony. There were also men much wealthier than most of their neighbors. In the main, however, Maryland society after mid-century was a relatively open community of farmers, a good small-man's country in which poor men could aspire to own land. By 1660, most free adult males in Maryland, like Cole, worked their own small plantations. Men who did not own land, if they based their judgment on the experience of neighboring planters, could expect to acquire farms soon. Planters of humble origins, furthermore, played a major role in Maryland's politics, frequently winning seats in the assembly and thoroughly dominating government at the local level. We might call these small landowners *yeomen*, although this term would encompass a wider range of wealth and status in the colony than in England. Sometimes they were distinguished in the Maryland records as "ordinary" planters.[34]

One source of this new social structure lay in a change in immigration, in the types of people attracted to Maryland by opportunities in tobacco. Before the mid-1640s, almost all settlers who came to the province were either indentured servants or gentlemen. Free colonists of modest means and origins were rare, and the society of early St. Mary's reflected the composition of the immigrant group. With the exception of the mid-1650s, when few new settlers arrived, immigrants from the mid-1640s to

the late 1660s differed markedly from those who came before Ingle's Rebellion (and from those who came in the last third of the century, for that
matter). Servants remained dominant—they now accounted for three-
fifths of the total—but this was a substantial decline from the years before
1645. Gentlemen, particularly members of the Calvert family, also continued to migrate to Maryland, but they were no longer a majority among
free immigrants. Men from landed families, such as Thomas Cornwallis,
were replaced as the most prominent immigrants by men with mercantile
backgrounds, men such as Edward Lloyd, Robert Slye, and William Stevens. Robert and Rebecca Cole and their children represent the most important change, however: the arrival of settlers in family groups. Family
migration was rare before 1645, but from 1646 to 1652 nearly half of the
immigrants arrived in family units, and from 1658 to 1667 nearly a third
did so.[35]

The new immigrants helped to expand the class of small, independent,
landholding planters in Maryland. Most of the families who came to the
province around mid-century were of middling status. Some, like the
Coles, came directly from England, but most were ex-servants who had
gotten a start in Virginia before striking out for the Chesapeake frontier.
Typically, they were recently married couples (with one or two small children) who brought enough capital to purchase land and begin farms as
soon as they arrived. These new immigrants helped to transform Maryland from a structured, manorial society into a community of households
mostly headed by small or middling planters.[36]

Good times enabled freed servants to join free immigrants as landowners and to contribute to the demise of the manors. Tobacco was a
good beginner's crop in the seventeenth century. It demanded little capital to start production: a cleared patch of land and a few simple tools were
all that was needed. And it earned few returns to scale: a man working
alone was nearly as efficient a producer as a large planter with many
servants or slaves.[37] Further, since wages were high and land was cheap
in early Maryland and since demand for the crop was growing rapidly,
the ex-servant who did not die too soon could obtain the sum needed to
purchase a tract or to pay fees for a land grant. He could save the sum
needed after a few years' work as a hired hand or a tenant farmer or could
borrow from a merchant or established planter.

As a consequence, those indentured servants who lived long enough—

no mean feat given the high death rates in the area—usually joined the ranks of small, landholding planters. Once they acquired land of their own, opportunities in tobacco production and farm building permitted many to accumulate additional property, create comfortable lives for themselves and their families, and become respected members of a New World community.[38]

Robert Cole's servants illustrate the opportunities. Of the four whose careers are traceable, three had success. Joseph Alvey, who arrived in 1657, owned two hundred acres and personal property worth £58 (including two servants) when he died in 1679, leaving a wife (also an ex-servant) and three minor children. John Johnson, also a 1657 arrival, took up the trade of cooper and died in 1687 with a wife, four minor children, one hundred acres, and a movable estate of £113. Robert Gates did even better. When he died in 1698 at about age fifty-five, he left his wife and six children nearly sixteen hundred acres of land and a personal estate appraised at £112. The appraisers called Gates "Mr." when they inventoried his estate, a rough index of the distance he had traveled since arriving on Cole's plantation as a twelve-year-old boy.[39]

The decades after 1650 can be labeled the Age of the Yeoman Planter. The era did not last long. In the older Maryland settlements, it was disappearing by the 1680s and 1690s.[40] But in Robert Cole's day, landowning planters of no great wealth were the dominant group in free male society. In this early stage of a land-abundant, labor-short economy, the yeoman planter and his farm building were a dynamic element in the development of a prosperous colony.

Sources of Disruption

Unfortunately, the social transformation worked in Maryland by middling immigrants and upwardly mobile ex-servants was not a painless, orderly process. To begin with, it was purchased with the lives of several thousand settlers who were the quick victims of a new disease environment, settlers who died before they had a chance to test the region's opportunities. Endemic malaria, dysentery, and typhoid reaped a repeated grim harvest among the settlers and left those who managed to survive weakened and often chronically ill. Typically, a man who came to Maryland in his early twenties could expect to live only about twenty more years, and women may have had even shorter lives.[41] Robert Cole and his wife died within eleven years of their arrival in Maryland.

Family life, furthermore, suffered severe disruption, and not just from high mortality. The formation of families was delayed by the nature of the immigrant population. Since the typical immigrant was young, single, and poor, most had first to complete a term of service during which they were not free to marry. Additional years were often required to accumulate the capital necessary to establish a household. Immigrant women in Maryland usually married in their mid-twenties, and most men were in their late twenties or early thirties. Moreover, because male immigrants outnumbered female by as much as three to one, many men never married at all; over one-quarter of the men who left estates in southern Maryland in the second half of the seventeenth century died unmarried.[42]

Late marriages and early deaths meant small families (although not necessarily small households). Most couples had only three or four children, and about half of these died in childhood. Of the 105 families in St. Mary's County in which one spouse left a will between 1660 and 1680, only 12 parents left more than 3 children behind, including those conceived but not yet born. The average number was 2.3, and the children were nearly always minors, some of whom might die before reaching maturity. Overall, population increase in Maryland did not result primarily from births in the colony before the late 1680s and did not produce a predominantly native population of adults before the first decade of the eighteenth century.[43]

Not only were families small, but the majority of children lost one or both parents before they grew up. In southern Maryland between 1658 and 1705, two-thirds of married or widowed men whose estates went through probate left all minor children, and only 7 percent left all adult children. The results for the children could be drastic. In the 1650s and 1660s, few had kin this side of the ocean to protect their interests. The courts assigned orphans to new families and tried to protect, from misuse by stepfathers or guardians, whatever property the children inherited. But many children doubtless suffered abuse to their persons as well as their property.[44] In this respect, as we shall see, the Cole children were very lucky.

Finally, political disruption did not disappear with the end of Ingle's

Rebellion. If the Coles came to Maryland in search of freedom to be Catholics, their timing was not the best. The 1650s were marked by severe, sometimes violent, political conflict as Virginia leaders fought Lord Baltimore for control of the northern Chesapeake. The result was several years in which Catholic civil rights were repressed.

Lord Baltimore had tried to forestall these problems. While Charles I was in power, Cecilius Calvert's influence at court equaled and perhaps surpassed that of the Virginia interest, but by 1645, the Virginia group, particularly the great London colonial merchants who supported Parliament, clearly held the upper hand and were pushing for withdrawal of the Maryland charter. Baltimore began to disassociate himself from his old Royalist-Catholic allies and to build links with merchants and radical Protestants. When Leonard Calvert died in 1647, the proprietor chose as governor William Stone, a Virginia Protestant and nephew of a prominent London tobacco merchant. Baltimore also actively recruited Protestant settlers, most successfully by offering refuge to a radical Protestant community suffering persecution in Virginia. At the same time he protected the position of his Catholic settlers by drafting, and insisting that the assembly pass, the famous Act Concerning Religion to guarantee religious freedom for all Christians. The success of the new strategy was soon apparent. By 1650 he could call on several leading London merchants, men who had worked against him as recently as 1647, to defend his cause before Parliament.[45]

Nevertheless, his position was insecure. In 1650, commissioners sent by Parliament to establish the authority of the new commonwealth in Virginia (where Governor William Berkeley had supported the Royalist cause) seized the opportunity to assert their authority in Baltimore's province. The next several years were an unsettled time in Maryland, marked by bickering between Calvert's supporters and the commissioners over who held ultimate authority in the colony. The dispute culminated in 1654, when the commissioners ousted Stone and Lord Baltimore's council and appointed a new council from the radical Protestant community, which had settled on the Severn River. Robert Cole and other Catholics must have been dismayed—and with good reason. The first assembly of the new regime abrogated the 1649 toleration act and prohibited Catholics from voting and holding office.

Governor Stone responded with an armed attack on the settlement at

Severn, but suffered a severe defeat. There were heavy casualties on the Calvert side, and the victors executed three of the Catholic leaders. The government also confiscated considerable property belonging to Stone and his supporters. However, the position of Catholics did not deteriorate further, perhaps because the new government was not certain of support from England. The Coles must have been thankful that there was no further violence and no general attack on Catholic property rights.

The next stages of the conflict were carried out in England, where Oliver Cromwell's government, without actually coming to a decision, showed no interest in backing the action taken by the Parliamentary commission. In 1657 the Virginia leaders gave up and made what could be called a treaty with Lord Baltimore. This agreement not only restored him to full authority but also stated that he would never permit a change in the religious policies laid down in 1649.

There was, however, a final episode in the struggle. This was known as Fendall's Rebellion, an incident in which some of Robert Cole's neighbors on St. Clement's Manor played a central role. Baltimore had appointed Josias Fendall governor in the aftermath of the battle at Severn River, and in the late 1650s, Fendall had worked hard and successfully to reestablish stable government and proprietary rule. Then, in early 1660, at a meeting of the assembly held on St. Clement's Manor, first at "Mr. Thomas Gerrard's howse" and later at Robert Slye's, Fendall attempted to "play the part in Maryland which Cromwell had just performed in England." He tried "to change the Government into the forme of a Commonwealth" and to "rayse a faction against his Lordship's Jurisdiction."[46]

Fendall's "pigmie Rebellion," as George Alsop called it,[47] did not amount to much, although as we shall see, it cut short Thomas Gerard's career in Maryland politics and thus had an effect on the development of St. Clement's Manor. With the backing of the newly restored Charles II in 1660, proprietary control was quickly reestablished. Calvert's cultivation of the London merchants and his long-standing Royalist connections had finally paid off, and the Virginia interest had lost. Lord Baltimore had at last achieved a firm hold on Maryland, a guarantee of toleration for Catholics, and a measure of political stability for his colonists. There was a bittersweet taste to Baltimore's success, however, for the society he governed little resembled his vision of a proper New World community.

Robert Cole's World

In 1660 some 2,300 people living on the lower Western Shore of Maryland were residents of Robert Cole's world.[48] The region, consisting of St. Mary's County and its two neighbors, Calvert and Charles, was sparsely populated—indeed, settlement was perhaps less dense in 1660 than it had been in the 1620s, before the English arrived. The colonists lived on "dispers'd Country Plantations" rather than clustered together in villages or towns.[49] Here "we have none That are called or cann be called Townes," Lord Baltimore explained in 1678. "In most places There are not fifty houses in the space of Thirty Myles." Even the capital, St. Mary's City, could "hardly be call'd a Towne." It was only a handful of buildings, badly overcrowded on court days or when the assembly was in session but with few year-round inhabitants.[50]

The 2,300 or so residents of the lower Western Shore lived in roughly 330 households, each of them home on average to perhaps 7 people.[51] The heads of those households, nearly all of them men, formed the backbone of the society. They made the basic entrepreneurial decisions. They chose where to settle and what and when to plant, decided what to purchase and what to forego, delegated and supervised work. They took responsibility for the behavior of their dependents and represented the household in public life.

There were social distinctions among these householders, but such distinctions were seldom firm or permanent. There was an identifiable cosmopolitan gentry[52]—merchants, planters, and a few professional men—who combined wealth with ties of trade, kin, and friendship extending beyond the limited, parochial environs of southern Maryland. Given that St. Mary's County contained the capital of the province, such men were probably more numerous there than elsewhere in the colony. Among the great majority of planters, who mostly tilled their own fields, there were many layers between the prosperous, comfortable, and secure men who had accumulated sizable property and might possibly reach high office and the poor, drab, and marginal planters still struggling to get established. Lower yet were most inmates, freemen who did not have their own households. But although such differences were clear and apparent to contemporaries, they were often crossed in the expanding economy and fluid society that Cole inhabited.

Furthermore, social differences were narrow by English standards. There were no great lords of the English aristocracy (with the possible exception of Cecilius Calvert's son Charles, who became the third Lord Baltimore in 1676 and was resident in Maryland from 1661 until 1684).[53] The great majority of immigrants arrived as indentured servants, and though their social origins and abilities varied, all started life in Maryland on the same terms. The status differences among them occurred chiefly after their arrival. In addition, the range of wealth represented was small. Over the seventeenth century on the lower Western Shore, the richest inventoried estate came to only £2,722 (constant value), whereas in England a nobleman might have this amount as a yearly income. The difference between the colony and mother country was also great at the bottom. In the English county of Essex in 1671, one-third of the householders were too poor to be charged for the hearth tax, the assessors explaining that they omitted those "that receves constant allmes," and other English counties recently studied for that period show a similar proportion of householders excluded from taxes. Complete dependence on poor relief did not reach so large a number, but James P. P. Horn has found that over the seventeenth century in the vale of Berkeley, about 10 percent of adult males received public charity, and in many areas of England enough paupers were able-bodied to induce the parishes to provide houses of correction and bridewells to exploit their labor. By contrast, in the Maryland counties of the 1660s and 1670s, with their severe labor shortages and high wages, there were no able-bodied paupers, and in any year at most one or two individuals—those who were too young or too ill or too old to work and who had no other means of support—were excused from taxes or needed a public allowance.[54]

Three kinds of sources provide insights that permit us to describe lower Western Shore society somewhat more precisely and follow changes in social structure: probate inventories, which in the Chesapeake valued all movable parts of a dead person's estate but not land and its improvements;[55] reconstructed censuses; and lists of residents (excluding bound laborers) for St. Clement's Manor. These records enable us to establish rough proportions for social groups and reveal extensive inequality. However, this evidence captures the society only at particular moments of time and hence misses the social fluidity that systematic studies of careers reveal.[56] The man who was a tenant in one period might be a landowner in the next, and the landowner might have become a gentleman justice of the peace.

We have divided the free adult male population into four groups: gentry, ordinary landowners (or yeoman planters), tenants, and inmates. Following the practice of the times, we based our definition of gentry on a combination of political position and wealth. We counted as gentry all justices of the peace, sheriffs, burgesses, councillors, and other important provincial officeholders. Only a handful of these men had the excellent educations and connections that would place them in the cosmopolitan gentry, but all performed functions reserved for gentlemen in England. In Maryland they were accorded the appropriate honorific titles, regardless of birth or education. We also included these officeholders' relatives who later inherited sizable estates and assumed high office and all others who owned fifteen hundred acres or more, including one widow of a manor lord. Almost all of the gentry group did in fact hold an office. Given the short supply of leaders in early Maryland, few men of wealth escaped service. When such men were unavailable, as frequently happened, lesser planters were elected or appointed.

Lower Western Shore gentry who left probate inventories between 1658 and 1665 numbered sixteen, of whom only three can be described as cosmopolitan. Two, John Bateman and William Batten, were merchants. One, Henry Sewell, was a member of a prominent English Catholic family and had recently arrived with an appointment from Lord Baltimore as the secretary of the province and a member of the council. These were the kinds of men the proprietor had hoped to attract as leaders but who over the seventeenth century remained in short supply.

Members of the gentry as a whole (about one-sixth of the total) held a wide range of wealth that reflected their varying origins, which stretched from propertied English gentleman to recently elevated former servant. The mean value of their movable assets at death, as shown in table 1.1, was about £195 and the median about £120; these were small estates by European standards. The range between the smallest and the largest was great—from just under £20 to more than £750. But whatever their movable property, most members of the gentry could be distinguished from yeoman planters by larger holdings in real estate (see table 1.2). Average landholding, whether measured by mean or median, was close to 1,000 acres. Although the smallest gentry estate was but a modest 100-acre

Table 1.1 Inventoried Wealth by Social Group, Lower Western Shore, 1658–
1665 (In Pounds Currency, Constant Value)

Group	N	Mean	Median	Mini-mum	Maxi-mum
Gentry	16[a]	196	120	18	754
Ordinary planters	48[b]	62	43	2	251
Tenants	11	21	17	8	63
Inmates	18[c]	13	9	3	45

Source: Lower Western Shore Inventory File, St. Mary's City Commission,
Maryland State Archives, Annapolis, Md.
[a]Includes one inmate and one widow.
[b]Includes two inmates with land and three planters whose landholding status
is unknown.
[c]Excludes inmates with land (N = 3).

Table 1.2 Landholdings by Social Group, Lower Western Shore Inventoried
Decedents, 1658–1665

Group	N	Mean Acres	Median Acres	Minimum Acres	Maximum Acres
Gentry	10	977	985	100	5400
Ordinary planters	28	300	300	50	1300

Sources: Surveys and patents from Patents, Maryland State Archives; deeds
printed in William Hand Browne et al., eds., *Archives of Maryland*, 72 vols. (Baltimore, 1883–1972), vols. 4, 10, 41, 49, 53, 60.
Note: Only decedents for whom size of landholding is known are included in
this table.

farm, all but two holdings were more than 800 acres, and the maximum
was 5,400 acres. Clearly most gentlemen hoped to profit not only from
farming but also from speculative sales or from leasing land to tenant
farmers.

Ordinary, or yeoman, planters, who owned land but held no high political office, were more than half of inventoried decedents.[57] Like the
gentry, they held a wide range of wealth, the result both of the differing
advantages with which they began life in the Chesapeake and of the varying stages they had reached in their careers when they died. Some of

these planters accumulated greater movable assets than some gentlemen (the highest ordinary planter estate was £251, and the lowest gentry estate was £18), but others had almost no movable property. Between 1658 and 1665, the mean value of ordinary planters' movables was about £60 and the median about £40. Mean and median landholdings were 300 acres, representing a good-sized family farm.[58] No decedents, and indeed very few living landowners, owned fewer than 50 acres, about the minimum size for a viable farm.[59] Some ordinary planters acquired additional tracts, either as a speculative investment or as an intended inheritance for their children. They did not, however, buy more land than what they or their immediate heirs could expect to develop.

Tenant farmers were much farther down the agricultural ladder, and in this early period, many were close to the beginning of their careers as freemen. Although tenant families could expect to raise their own food and make a profit from a crop of tobacco, rents cut heavily into the proceeds, and such planters would realize little profit from farm building until they acquired their own land. Among the handful of tenants who left inventories in the period 1658–65 (about one-eighth of all inventoried), movable assets ranged between about £10 and £60. The mean value of tenant estates was a third of that of ordinary landowners, and the median was less than half. Still, a tenant was head of a household and was responsible for his wife, children, and any others who lived in his house. He had status in the community, a status that inmates did not have.[60]

Inmates, who were one-fifth of the inventoried, occupied the bottom niche of the agricultural ladder. Some had just graduated from servitude; others, through a combination of fate, fortune, and character, had been unsuccessful either in winning a wife or in acquiring enough tools and livestock to begin farming on rented acreage. Many were contract laborers or worked for wages and had little say in how they would allocate their time and energy. All had to pay in part or full for lodging, food, washing and mending of clothes, and pasture for any livestock they might be lucky enough to acquire. Their estates were the most meager of all, with a mean of little more than £10.[61]

What were the relative sizes of these groups in the living population of free adult males? A reconstituted Charles County census for 1660 affords us some idea (see table 1.3).[62] We must use this source with caution. Although Charles County had much in common with the Potomac

River settlements of St. Mary's County, including St. Clement's Manor, English settlers had occupied the region for little more than a decade. In 1660, ordinary planters were predominant, making up two-thirds of the free adult males.[63] Most were either men who had immigrated with enough assets to buy a farm at the outset or men who had accumulated sufficient wealth in older-settled parts of Maryland or Virginia to permit a move up the agricultural ladder. Householding tenants accounted for 7 percent of free adult males, and inmates, 14 percent. As yet there were few indentured servants and fewer slaves.[64] In the older parts of St. Mary's and Calvert counties, bound labor was undoubtedly much more prevalent.[65]

Lists of St. Clement's Manor adult male residents who owed service in the manor court suggest a somewhat different picture of lower Western Shore society (see table 1.3). The numbers here are small but should not be ignored because the lists do not depend on estimations and are close to complete. They show a social composition of the manor quite different from that found among inventoried decedents or in the reconstituted Charles County male population. Relative to other groups, inmates on the manor were much more numerous. These inmates probably included not only bachelors who were boarding with manor landowners or tenants but also some householders who rented cabins and enough ground for gardens but did not have leases of farms. The position of the latter must have been similar to that of cottagers in England, except that the chances to move up were better. Probably there were proportionately more such folk on St. Clement's Manor—and perhaps on other large grants where owners were aggressive developers—than on the rest of the lower Western Shore. The high cost of labor suggests that many ordinary planters could not afford for long the pay that inmates could command.[66] Nevertheless, the manor evidence warns us that such men may have been a considerably larger group than our other sources reveal.

By the time Robert Cole, Jr., came of age, this social structure was beginning to change. Inventories show that wealth had increased for every group, but so had inequality.[67] The reconstituted Charles County census for 1675 (see table 1.3) shows proportionately fewer gentry and ordinary landowners among free adult males than in 1660, a decrease of one-third to one-half.[68] This decline was accompanied by a large increase in the bound labor force, although its percentage of the adult population is uncertain.[69] Equally dramatic was the larger share of inmates. Their

Table 1.3 Proportions of Free Social Groups from Various Sources

	N	Gentry (%)	Ordinary Planters (%)	Tenants (%)	Inmates (%)
Charles County, 1660	190	13	66	7	14
Lower Western Shore Inventories, 1658–65	93	17[a]	52[b]	12	20
St. Clement's Manor, 1659–61	44	7	14	36	43
Charles County, 1675–low estimate	568	5	37	5	53
Charles County, 1675–high estimate	723	6	47	6	40
Lower Western Shore inventories, 1671–77	308	16[c]	48[d]	15	21
St. Clement's Manor, 1670–72	84	11	15	8	67

Sources: Charles County reconstituted censuses and population estimates (Lorena S. Walsh); St. Clement's Manor biographical files and Lower Western Shore Inventory File, St. Mary's City Commission.

Notes: Among decedents whose landholding status is unknown for the 1671–77 group, householders (N = 22) are grouped with the known tenants (N = 23) and nonhouseholders (N = 17) with the known inmates (N = 49). For an explanation of the Charles County estimates for 1675, see Lorena S. Walsh, "Staying Put or Getting Out: Findings for Charles County, Maryland, 1650–1720," *William and Mary Quarterly*, 3d ser., 44 (1987): 90–91.

[a]Includes one inmate and one widow.

[b]Includes two widows, three planters whose landholding status is unknown, and two inmates with land.

[c]Includes one inmate.

[d]Includes ten inmates with land.

proportion was just under 15 percent of freemen in 1660, but somewhere between 40 and about 50 percent in 1675. This last change resulted first from a large increase in the number of servants imported into the county after 1660, servants who were free by the mid-1670s, and second from an influx of freedmen from older counties.[70] This rapid growth in the proportion of men who had not yet managed to move into the ranks of tenant farmers or to acquire land provides evidence that opportunity had begun to slow down, in part in Charles County itself and more in the older settlements from which many of the inmates came. The Charles County population of 1675 shows a 50 percent increase over 1660 in the number of landowners but a 75 percent increase in the number of inmates. St. Clement's Manor shows a similar change; in the years 1670–72, the already large proportion of inmates had increased by more than half since 1659–61.

Although inequality had grown by the early 1670s, social structure in southern Maryland was still fluid. It took longer to leave the status of inmate or tenant, increasing the risk that death would come first, but land was still available and cheap. Ex-servants could still hope to own land, and landowners could still expect to increase their wealth through farm building and perhaps to move into positions of power. However, for the poor the future of the region was less promising than it had been in Cole's day. The social groups of 1675 harbored signs of changes to come.

Robert Cole's Place

The fluidity of Maryland society over the third quarter of the seventeenth century makes it difficult to fix Cole's place in society with precision. When he left for England in 1662, he hovered about the vague line that separated the majority of planters from the county gentry. Cole was taking advantage of the opportunities that farm making presented to improve his estate and his social position when death stopped his progress. He had started in Maryland in 1652 with perhaps £50 to £60 (constant value) in land, labor, and equipment. In 1662, he had an estate in land and movables (including four servants) worth about £208, roughly four times larger.[71] With four sons who would soon be old enough to join the plantation work force, he had gone far toward realizing the hopes for prosperity that had helped persuade him to strike out for Maryland.

Cole never identified himself in a record as "mister" or "gentleman" and called himself "yeoman" in his will,[72] suggesting that he considered himself an ordinary planter; yet in this society he could have styled himself a "gentleman" had he so chosen. He was not a great planter, on the scale, say, of John Bateman with his more than five thousand acres and twelve field hands. Cole had only three field hands, and he undoubtedly still worked alongside them. Nevertheless, his estate was larger than most. Although his role in local government was limited to frequent jury service and an ensign's post in the militia, his wealth equaled and even surpassed that of many men with seats on the county bench and in the provincial assembly. He had also gained some recognition of his achievement. Beginning in 1658, he was occasionally but not usually called "mister" or "gentleman" in the public records, a clerical inconsistency reflecting the transitional stage he had reached in his career.[73] Had he lived, he might have joined his friends William Evans and Luke Gardiner on the county bench and assumed the designation of gentleman.

A comparison of Cole's assets with those of his neighbors helps to place him in his society. In the inventory Cole made of his possessions in 1662, he priced only a few items but estimated the total value of his personal property. By using data from other inventories taken in the early 1660s, we have been able to fill in the missing values.[74] Cole's movable estate was worth about £154, more than twice the mean estate probated on the lower Western Shore from 1658 through 1665 and nearly five times the median (see table 1.4).[75] Robert Cole, it is clear, died substantially better off than most other residents of his time on the tobacco coast. However, a different perspective is gained by looking at his place on the scale of wealth. He ranked eleventh in the whole group of ninety-three, or in the top 12 percent, but the ten above him owned 48 percent of the total wealth. On the scale of probated movable wealth, Cole was barely above the middle.

These figures omit land, a crucial component of wealth in an agricultural society. When land is included, Cole's distance from most other inventoried planters narrows a little.[76] His total wealth then comes to £208, less than twice the mean and less than three times the median. Among landowners, he was closer to the middle, his estate being less than twice the median and only just above the mean. He dropped to twelfth place in the whole group of ninety-three, and the eleven above him owned 49 percent of the wealth.[77]

Cole was young for the economic position he had attained. Among the inventoried dead of the lower Western Shore from 1658 through 1665, there were others like him, but 70 percent of the men who died before a child reached maturity were poorer. In general, of course, men who had spent years as servants fell behind those who, like Cole, began as freemen. Among the inventoried, many more ex-servants than free immi-

Table 1.4 Comparison of the Estate of Robert Cole with the Estates of All Lower Western Shore Inventoried Decedents, 1658–1665 (In Pounds Currency, Constant Value)

	Total Movables	Value of Land[a]	Total Estate Value	Acres of Land (N)
Cole	153.91	54.29	208.20	300.00
All estates[b] (N = 93)				
Mean	70.59	42.84	114.73	374.46
Ratio, Cole to Mean	2.18	1.27	1.81	.80
Median	33.96	36.28	70.17	150.00
Ratio, Cole to Median	4.53	1.50	2.97	2.00
All householders[b] (N = 73)				
Mean	85.89	54.58	140.89	460.62
Ratio, Cole to Mean	1.79	.99	1.48	.65
Median	47.71	41.72	89.38	150.00
Ratio, Cole to Median	3.23	1.30	2.33	2.00
All landholders[c] (N = 61)				
Mean	98.57	66.80	165.87	570.90
Ratio, Cole to Mean	1.56	.81	1.26	.53
Median	51.00	42.86	111.27	200.00
Ratio, Cole to Median	3.02	1.27	1.87	1.50
All gentry[d] (N = 16)				
Mean	196.38	119.77	316.16	1323.44
Ratio, Cole to Mean	.78	.45	.66	.23
Median	120.39	81.93	180.78	762.50
Ratio, Cole to Median	1.28	.66	1.15	.39

Sources: Lower Western Shore Inventory File and Career File of Seventeenth-Century St. Mary's County Residents, St. Mary's City Commission; Charles County Career File (Lorena S. Walsh); Cole Plantation Account, appendix 1.

[a]St. Mary's and Calvert county lands are valued at St. Mary's County prices, Charles County land at Charles County prices (see chapter 1, note 76).

[b]Includes two widows.

[c]Includes two inmates and two widows; excludes three planters whose land-holding status is unknown.

[d]Includes one inmate and one widow of a manor lord.

grants were still unmarried inmates, dead before they could establish households. Land belonged to slightly more than half the ex-servants, but to four-fifths of those who had paid their own way, although most of the latter had not reached Cole's level of wealth.[78] Cole's ability to transport his family and two servants and at the same time to acquire land gave him a head start over most immigrants.

What is most important to emphasize, however, is that the opportunities in tobacco production and farm building that had let Cole prosper put the possibility of owning land and gaining status in the community within reach of the poorest Maryland settler. Over the third quarter of the seventeenth century, social fluidity reached the bottom of white society. The newly freed servant might work for a man of beginnings similar to his and in future years might himself own land and servants. Not every poor immigrant achieved these goals. Early death, bad luck, poor judgment, or laziness could keep people down. But a good chance of success, if death did not intervene, was present and was visible to all.

These opportunities were tied to farm building. They diminished over time in early settled areas as the good lands filled up, but the process continued on new frontiers. In the mid-seventeenth century, southern Maryland was a frontier of Virginia. As the century progressed, these farm-building opportunities spread with settlement to other regions, on the upper Western Shore and the Eastern Shore of Maryland and into new areas of Virginia. Eventually, differing soil resources produced varying crop mixes and economies, but in the seventeenth century, settlers everywhere began with tobacco as their staple crop. The system of husbandry and the farm-building process were replicated in each region as it developed.

We can regard Cole's life in Maryland, then, as representative of opportunities for planters of a newly settled area. What distinguishes him from others occurred after he died. For eleven years following Robert's departure for England, from 1662 through 1672, Luke Gardiner administered the Cole plantation and kept a detailed account of income and expenditures. That rich record joins with the representative character of Robert Cole's career to make him, his family, and his farm a useful vehicle for exploring the yeoman planter's world along the Chesapeake in the seventeenth century.

2

. . . . .

Building
a Farm

Starting Out

How did an immigrant make his start in Maryland in the early 1650s?
When Robert and Rebecca Cole moved ashore with their children and
servants, they did not face the terrifying uncertainties encountered by
earlier colonists. English settlement in Maryland was eighteen years old.
On the St. Mary's Town Lands, where the Coles may have left ship, Bar-
naby Jackson had an inn—an "ordinary" in colonial usage—which offered food and shelter. However, the Coles would not have stayed long in
these meager and costly quarters. With so many people to house and feed,
Cole must have looked at once for a plantation with a house for rent.

By 1652 such accommodations were available. The large investors who
had taken up manorial grants had been leasing their lands to newly freed
servants to get improvements made. As freedmen moved away to property
of their own, the cleared land, fencing, and a cabin remained with the
landlord, who could then lease it at higher rents.[1] Plantations of dead
men could also be leased or purchased. Cole first set his family down
somewhere in the Newtown area, possibly on the Manor of Little Bretton,
where the Jesuits served the local Catholic community from the house of
William Brittaine.[2] Perhaps Cole's "cousin" Benjamin Gill, who lived
nearby, helped Cole arrange a move to rented land soon after the family's
arrival.[3]

Cole looked about before deciding on a permanent home. He needed
good tobacco soil, which in St. Mary's County was usually located near
the water. Waterfront was also desirable for access to the ships that took
the crop to European markets. By the early 1650s the best lands south of

William Brittaine's were already preempted. Some distance to the north was an area soon to become Charles County, on the extreme edge of English settlement. Cole patented some land there but never developed it and finally sold it. He chose instead to buy land and begin a farm on a site on St. Clement's Manor, a twelve-thousand-acre tract just across St. Clement's Bay from Brittaine's.[4] The manor was in an area about to be rapidly developed; it was not unsettled, but good unclaimed land was still available. An additional attraction for Cole must have been the location of his plantation not far from the Catholic mission (see map 1.1).

Cole could not patent his three-hundred-acre farm; Thomas Gerard, the lord of St. Clement's Manor, was the owner. But Gerard was eager to find settlers to develop his manor, and he sold freehold leases on excellent terms. Given what we know of these leases, Cole paid about ten pounds (constant value) for his land and owed a yearly rent of three barrels of shelled Indian corn. He also owed service at Gerard's manor court, probably the only manorial court that functioned for any length of time in Maryland. However, Cole could sell or devise his tract without interference from or further payments to the manor lord. In effect, he owned his land.[5]

Cole may have known that he could not carry on the kind of husbandry in which he had been trained in England. Differences in the supply of land, labor, and capital, in population density, in distance to markets, and in soils and climate between metropole and colonial outpost demanded different systems of agriculture. Heston, Cole's probable English home, was famous for its wheat (Queen Elizabeth's bread was made from Heston wheat),[6] but wheat was not a practical crop for food, much less export, where virgin forest had to be cleared for crops. Further, wheat was difficult to harvest, laborious to thresh, and plagued by a low grain-to-seed ratio. It also required a complex milling process that could be supported only by a relatively dense population. All told, wheat was a poor crop for "pioneer communities."[7]

The export crop in the Chesapeake was tobacco, and the staple food was Indian corn. Neither crop needed plowing, and hence neither required that the land be totally cleared. The Indians prepared fields for corn and tobacco by girdling the trees—that is, stripping away a band of bark and wood to prevent the sap from rising. Once the trees died, the Indians planted their crops in hills under the bare branches. These branches eventually fell down, and the Indians burned them, leaving the tree trunks or stumps. By the 1620s, Europeans in the Chesapeake had adopted these aboriginal crops and methods of cultivation.[8]

Little equipment was needed for this type of agriculture, a major advantage because tools had to be imported from England and capital was scarce. The Indians used Stone-Age tools—sticks and sharpened stones and shells. Englishmen used metal axes and hoes, but these were the only essentials. No animal power was required, with its attendant equipment and expense. Plows were not in use. Nor did corn or tobacco demand skilled processing with complex tools. An early observer noted with astonishment that a planter could raise his food and tobacco "without the help of man, horse, or oxe."[9]

On the other hand, tobacco demanded large amounts of land and labor time, and these facts affected every aspect of Chesapeake life. Both tobacco and corn were very demanding of nutrients and required long rotations to restore fertility in the absence of manure. The amount of land needed per hand in any one year was not great, but over a lifetime it was considerable. The minimum farm size was about 50 acres when land for forest and pasture was included, and if a man wanted to provide for more than one child he would need much more. In 1659 the median holding in St. Mary's County was 250 acres, and by about 1700 the number was still 200 acres. In most parts of England, by contrast, 50 acres was a large farm.[10]

Land in Maryland was plentiful and cheap, but it was not of much use without labor. Hundreds of acres availed little if no one was available to clear and hoe them. Labor shortages were severe and labor was expensive in a new land where the indigenous population was both sparse and unwilling to work for whites. Supposing, furthermore, that a planter had all the land and workers he wanted, tobacco required his full attention for a major part of every year, reducing the time available for other tasks. How best to make the most of his labor dominated the planter's decisions.[11]

These considerations must have affected Cole's choices as he started to develop his plantation. He needed, of course, to clear land for corn and tobacco at once and to build a dwelling house and a tobacco-curing house. Cole probably also planted an orchard immediately to have fruit for cider as soon as possible. This became standard policy in the Chesapeake. When planters let land to get it improved, they often required the tenant to plant and/or tend an orchard, usually specified to be seventy to one hundred trees.[12] The alternative to cider was beer, but beer made from corn was unpleasant, and growing barley for beer without plowing the land was difficult. Few planters wanted to take the time. Malting barley, furthermore, required skill and investment in a malthouse. By contrast, apple trees, once started, required little tending.[13] The general preference for cider over beer, and hence for orchards over barley fields, was a labor-saving decision.

Like other householders, the Coles doubtless purchased a sow and pigs, perhaps some chickens, and a cow or two to add milk, eggs, and meat to the family diet; but once more, the cost of labor determined how they cared for the animals. Cole would not have built housing for this livestock. Cattle and hogs ran freely in the woods, their ownership determined by marks on their ears. Cole probably built a cowpen, to which he brought the cows for milking, but otherwise he put no time into fencing in livestock. If he had fenced the animals, he would have had to feed them, and to feed them he would have had to raise the fodder. Let loose in the woods, the animals provided for themselves, although Cole may have offered them corn or corn husks during the barren part of winter. There were risks in this method of livestock care. Cattle died of starvation during the winter and got mired in swamps while looking for early grass in the spring. Wolves attacked them. But despite these hazards, livestock gradually multiplied in Maryland and Virginia, and planters did not think better care was worth their time.[14]

Clearing land was Cole's first major task. So far as we know, his land was entirely virgin forest, since Thomas Gerard had already settled on the part of the manor that Indians had recently cleared. For a house lot Cole needed about half an acre. This would provide enough land for his dwelling, a vegetable garden if he had one, and a cowpen. Adjoining, he needed, say, an acre for an orchard, the land required for about seventy trees.[15] For a corn patch he needed at least six acres. A rule of thumb in the early Chesapeake, expressed in Maryland law, guarded against shortages by requiring that two acres be put into corn for each hand that raised tobacco.[16]

This rule was a good one for ensuring self-sufficiency in corn. An acre of land produced fifteen to twenty bushels—or three to four barrels—of shelled corn, perhaps twice the yield of wheat. The standard annual ration was three barrels of shelled corn per adult male hand, which included seed for the following year.[17] Supposing women needed a three-quarter ration and small children a quarter, the eighteen to twenty-four barrels that Cole and two servants could raise on six acres were more than ample for the household of three men, one woman, and four small chil- dren. Still, for safety's sake after the first year, Cole probably planted an extra acre for the annual three barrels owed for rent, bringing his land in corn to seven acres. Any surpluses could be sold to new neighbors or could help winter livestock and fatten steers and hogs before butchering. Deficiencies could be made up by purchases from a more established planter.

More than an enough.

How much land Cole had to clear for tobacco is more complicated to determine. This depended first on the number of tobacco plants he set out and second on how closely he placed the plants. The number of plants he set out, of course, depended on how many he could tend. Evidence from the late seventeenth century suggests that by then, a laborer could handle 10,000 plants that produced 1,800 to 1,900 pounds of tobacco. In the early 1650s planters had not yet learned to handle this many plants. Mean production per hand was no more than 1,000 pounds of tobacco and, if the weight produced per plant was similar to that at the end of the century, probably came from 5,600 to 6,000 plants.[18] How far apart the plants were set depended somewhat on how many tree stumps had to be avoided, but contemporary accounts suggest that the distance was usually about four feet.[19] Six thousand plants set four feet apart would take up about 96,000 square feet, or two and one-fifth acres. Cole and his two servants needed six or seven acres for tobacco.

In all, then, Cole needed to clear approximately fifteen acres of land as soon as possible. There is no information about how long this process took in the seventeenth century. However, early nineteenth-century re- cords from the southern and western frontiers suggest that a man might take a month to clear an acre of forest completely but that if he girdled the trees first, he might save at least 40 percent of his time. Cole would have needed to chop down, rather than girdle, what trees he required immediately for housing, fencing, and firewood.[20] Perhaps an acre, in- cluding land for his house lot, had to be fully cleared, but otherwise he doubtless girdled the trees. If so, he and his servants would have spent nearly twelve weeks each, or close to three months, for clearing. If they chopped down all the timber, the process would take half again as long.

It is unlikely that Cole got into full production before the second year after he had purchased his land. Girdled trees would be clearer of dead branches by then and the sun better able to nurture plants. Furthermore, supposing Cole made his purchase soon after his arrival, he and his servants were doubtless unable to work with full efficiency at first. Everyone in his household must have been sick at least in the summer and early fall during the first year in Maryland.[21] And whether or not this "seasoning" was over by the time Cole moved to the manor, some effort had to go toward one-time activities, such as building a dwelling house, activities that took labor from the cultivation of crops.

In 1655, probably his third year of operation, Cole began to expand his labor force, evidence that his second year had been a success. He purchased a twelve-year-old servant boy, Robert Gates.[22] One so young was the equivalent of about half a hand for work in the fields[23] but could contribute in other ways—fetching wood and water for the house, pounding corn in preparation for cooking, or rounding up livestock and milking cows. With three children born since the family's arrival, Rebecca Cole could use such assistance. Two years later, in 1657, Cole's original servants finished their terms; he replaced them with two new men, Joseph Alvey, a servant, and Seth Tinsley, a freeman. He also added John Johnson, another twelve-year-old servant, and transported a kinswoman, Mary Mills, to help his wife, who late that year had her fourth child born in Maryland.[24]

It was probably the arrival of Mary Mills that enabled Rebecca Cole to add dairying to the plantation's activities. Milking, butter making, and cheese making were women's work, although young boys may also have milked.[25] By 1662 the Coles had twelve milk cows, a large herd, and were among the best-equipped families in the county for dairying, with six tubs for cooling milk, fifteen pans for raising cream, a churn and butter pots for butter making, and a cheese tub for making at least uncured cheese. In this, the household was exceptional. Most household inventories of the time show no equipment for dairying or at most pans or trays for raising cream. Probably Rebecca Cole had made butter back in Heston for the London market only fifteen miles away and had brought at least the churn and her two "greate butter pots" with her. By the time of her death in 1662, the family must have been well supplied not only with milk but also with farmer's cheese in season and with more than enough butter salted down to last from calving to calving. Mrs. Cole may even have been selling surplus butter to neighbors.[26]

The number of field hands Cole could use depended on how much land he had. By 1658, given the amount of his land already cropped, four to five hands were the maximum over the long run that good practice would allow for cultivating his best soils. Both tobacco and corn were very demanding of nutrients. Cole could plant tobacco on a parcel of land for only three years before yields decreased and became unprofitable. He could then grow corn on the same plot for another three years, since corn tapped a lower level of soil. But thereafter, the land had to lie fallow for twenty years before its fertility returned. To prevent overuse, a planter needed a minimum of twenty acres per hand.[27] Cole had perhaps ninety acres of first-rate land. The rest of the three hundred acres had poorly drained soils.[28] If Cole confined himself on the average to four hands, his good land would last until recycling could begin. With more labor he would have to move into his poorer soils.

Cole showed himself a careful man. In 1658 he upped his labor force to the equivalent of four adult men (counting himself and other males age sixteen as full hands) but thereafter never exceeded this number (see appendix 2). That year another freeman, Richard Sheppy, joined the household and married Mary Mills a few months later, but both remained with the Coles until Mary's term was up in 1660. Sheppy otherwise would have had to pay Cole for her remaining time. Although Seth Tinsley departed in the interim, with Sheppy on hand and Gates now age sixteen, Cole did not buy a replacement. In 1661, the Sheppys left the Coles, and Joseph Alvey finished his indenture. Cole replaced Alvey but not Sheppy. John Johnson was now full grown, keeping the adult male labor force at four. Rather than get another boy, Cole purchased two servant women to fill Mary Sheppy's shoes. Here he may have had bad luck. Sibelo Jackson may have died in her seasoning. She was gone from the household when Cole inventoried his servants in 1662. On hand at that time were Robert Gates, John Johnson, and the new servants, John Elton and Isabel Jones.[29]

Cole's field hands not only were expanding in number but also were becoming more productive. The number of tobacco plants a man could tend increased steadily through the 1650s. The increase in plants is an inference from increased weight produced per hand. Over the 1660s mean weight per hand was about 1,400 to 1,500 pounds, both on the Cole plantation and generally, where oronoco, the variety the Coles raised, was grown (see tables 2.1 and 2.2). This was a 70 percent rise over the mean

Table 2.1 Crop per Hand, Cole Plantation, 1662–1672

| | Working Hands for Tobacco Culture (N) | | | | | Crop per Hand (Pounds) | |
| | | | | | | | |
Year	Servants	Knott	Robt. Cole	Wm. Cole	Total Hands	Crop Pro-duced	Crop per Hand Produced
1662	3.00	0.5			3.50	6,336	1,810
1663	3.50	0.5			4.00	5,167	1,292
1664	3.75	0.5			4.25	6,950	1,635
1665	3.25	0.875	0.25		4.375	7,119	1,627
1666	2	1.0	0.25		3.25	3,854	1,186
1667	2.50	1.0	0.50		4.00	5,088	1,272
1668	2.25	1.0	0.875		4.125	8,275	2,006
1669	1.75	out	1.00	0.50	3.25	4,087	1,258
1670	2.50	out	1.00	0.50	4.00	4,206	1,052
1671	2.0	out	1.00	0.875	3.875	6,200	1,600
1672	2.5	out	1.00	1.00	4.50	6,200	1,378

Source: Cole Plantation Account, appendix 1.

Note: For hands, see appendix 2, tables 2.2 and 2.3. The assumptions under-lying the number of hands are laid out there. We have postulated that William Cole helped in the house in 1667 and 1668 but moved to field work in 1669, when he reached age twelve. Edward Cole is not listed as a field hand. Some-one had to cook, etc., and he was the youngest and hence the least able to do field work.

found in the region for the 1640s (see table 2.3). Gradually planters were learning to be more efficient. With this increase in productivity went an increase in the amount of land in production. By 1662, Cole and his ser-vants probably tended 9,000 plants each, planted on about three and three-tenths acres.[30] Four hands could tend about thirteen acres in to-bacco, as opposed to the six acres or so that three hands could manage in 1650. Since this number of hands required at least eight acres in corn, plus one for rent, Cole probably had in all approximately twenty-two acres in regular production when he left for England.

What allowed these increases in productivity is unclear. The main pro-cedures for tobacco culture were well established by the time Virginians made tobacco their staple crop. An account published in England in 1615

Table 2.2 Mean Crop per Hand, Cole Plantation and Maryland, 1662–1672

| | Cole Plantation | Maryland | |
| | | Observations[a] | Mean Crop |
Year	Crop per Hand	(N)	per Hand
1662	1,810		
1663	1,292	1	1,037
1664	1,635	1	1,621
1665	1,627	3	1,634
1666	1,186	1	2,520
1667	1,272	3	1,424
1668	2,006	1	1,142
1669	1,258		
1670	1,052		
1671	1,600	2	1,500
1672	1,378		

	Pounds of Tobacco
Mean crop per hand, Cole Plantation, 1662–72	1,465
Mean crop per hand, Maryland, without Cole, 1663–71	1,541
Mean crop per hand, Maryland, including Cole, 1662–72	1,500

Sources: See table 2.1; Russell R. Menard, "Economy and Society in Early Colonial Maryland" (Ph.D. diss., University of Iowa, 1975), table A-13. Crop per hand without the Cole observations can be calculated from Menard.

[a]The Cole Plantation crops are omitted from these observations.

had laid down most of the rules.[31] Yet increases in the number of plants and weight of leaf per hand had progressed steadily since the 1620s, when mean crop shares had been 400 pounds of tobacco, the result of 1,000 to 2,000 plants per hand. Possibly planters had not at first been willing to cut back the number of leaves per stalk to the degree necessary to maintain quality, but the adoption of this policy surely had not quadrupled the number of plants a man could tend or the weight of leaf he could produce.

Perhaps the change was the result both of increased experience—

Table 2.3 Productivity per Hand in Tobacco, 1640–1699

| Year | Crop per Hand, Maryland | |
	Observations (N)	Mean Crop per Hand[a]
1640–49	7[b]	911
1650–59	2[b]	1,296
1660–69	17	1,552
1670–79	12	1,527
1680–99	12	1,877

Percent Increase in Mean Crop per Hand	
1640s–1660s	70
1660s–1690s	21

Sources: Menard, "Economy and Society," table A-13; William Hand Browne et al., eds., *Archives of Maryland*, 72 vols. (Baltimore, 1883–1972), 23:89; Charles County Court and Land Record X#1:310, Maryland State Archives, Annapolis, Md.

Note: Observations from Virginia records taken by Walsh for the period after 1660 show somewhat lower figures for crop per hand for sweet-scented tobacco, but sweet-scented prices were higher. See also note 30.

[a]Includes Cole observations.

[b]Includes two observations from Virginia.

"learning by doing"—and of the secular fall of tobacco prices. Probably numerous improvements had proved cumulative. Planters had learned what fallow time was necessary. They had learned to plant their corn in old tobacco fields. They were discovering which soils could grow the more valuable sweet-scented strains of tobacco—confined, as it turned out, primarily to parts of Virginia—and which the common oronoco.[32] They had learned to cure the tobacco on its stalk rather than thread the leaves on strings to dry, to build tobacco houses that were properly weatherproof, and to mesh corn production with tobacco growing more efficiently.[33] Doubtless, falling tobacco prices gave planters incentives to discover and adopt such improved procedures. In addition, planters probably pushed themselves and their laborers to work harder. Together all these changes increased labor productivity that could maintain plantation income as prices fell. Whatever the reason, labor productivity was to continue to rise, but much more slowly, for another twenty years (see table 2.3).

This was part of a basic process in the expansion of the tobacco economy over most of the seventeenth century. Tobacco started as a high-priced luxury product with a small market. Prices fluctuated sharply, as with any staple crop, but the trend was down, steeply at first and then more gradually. Falling prices expanded the market, while improved productivity made it possible for planters to raise output and make a profit at lower prices. There were also significant improvements in packaging. Planters learned to pack tobacco in hogsheads, which preserved the leaf, and freight rates for hogsheads were keyed to volume of space, not weight. By packing the tobacco more tightly—improvements that continued until the mid-eighteenth century—planters steadily reduced freight charges and thus the costs of shipping. But rising output per hand was the most important source of increased productivity. As tobacco per hand leveled out in the 1680s, so too did the price and production of tobacco. The long seventeenth-century expansion of the tobacco industry ended, and a thirty-year stagnation followed. But during Cole and Gardiner's day, planter successes in improving efficiency enabled a growing population to take up land, acquire labor, and enter the tobacco industry.[34]

Plantation Production under Gardiner's Guardianship

Our most certain knowledge of the Cole family and the operation and productivity of its plantation comes from the will and inventory Robert Cole made before he left in 1662 and the account Luke Gardiner kept after Cole's death.[35] From these we know the composition of the family over the next eleven years, the number and terms of the servants, what was produced for sale on the plantation, and what was purchased to keep it functioning. The records end with a list of the property left to distribute among the children in 1673. The guardian account is not always clear. We must guess sometimes when children or servants entered or left the household, and toward the end of the account the data on sales and purchases are much less detailed than earlier. Nevertheless, the records allow us to reconstruct the workings of the household and follow the lives of its inhabitants over the years of the children's minority.

Robert Cole left two stepchildren and five children of his own. Two of the four children in his household at arrival had died by the time he wrote his will, but five more had been born to Rebecca in Maryland. His stepdaughter, Ann Knott, had just married and left the household in 1662. Quite possibly she was not yet sixteen. In this woman-short world, the pressure on young girls to marry very early was strong.[36] Her brother, Francis Knott, at age twelve was the oldest child left at home in a parentless household. Robert Cole was nine, and his brothers, William and Edward, were about seven and four, respectively. Their sister Mary was about eight and little Betty only about two. Gardiner sent Mary to her grandmother in England but allowed the rest of the children to live together on the plantation, and for a while he hired a housekeeper to run the household.[37]

Like Cole, Gardiner kept the equivalent of about four full-time male hands at work in the fields, and this labor force included Cole's sons (see appendix 2, tables A2.2, A2.3). Cole's will had specified that his children were not to be idle, although they were not "to bee kept as Common servants" and were to have some education. In 1662, Francis Knott was just beginning to learn planting skills and contributed about half the labor of an adult. By 1666, at age 16, he had the strength and skills of a full-time hand, and his half brother Robert was beginning a plantation apprenticeship. In 1669 Francis Knott probably left the household to set up on his own, but Robert was by then full grown.[38] Luke Gardiner and his wife, who lived a few miles away (see map 1.1), must have supervised servants and children, especially at first; but as Francis and Robert grew older the two boys undoubtedly took on increasing responsibilities. Robert Cole was to inherit the land, and by 1670, when he was age 18, he probably was running the plantation.

At first there were also women servants: Isabel Jones, under indenture, and a housekeeper who worked for wages. The women did not work in the fields. There were too many small children to tend, and in such a large household there was too much cooking and washing to do, not to mention milking, butter making, and the other chores that were ordinarily women's work.[39] But as the children grew older, Gardiner evidently thought the family could dispense with the women. When Isabel became free in 1665, he did not replace her, and in 1667 he dropped the housekeeper. That year he sent Betty Cole, age seven, to board where she could get further schooling. William and Edward, the youngest boys, must have done most of the housekeeping while she was gone; they were both still young for field work. On Betty's return in 1669, she and Edward, perhaps with help from William, probably ran the house together, but Betty died in 1670, and thereafter Edward probably did most of this work. He may never have had much time at the hoe, since he was slated to return to England in 1672 to finish his education. William started a local apprenticeship, of what kind is unknown, in 1673, and it is possible that he too did little field work. Their sister Mary must have returned at some point, but only to marry immediately; after 1663 she goes unmentioned in the account until 1673 and then appears only as the wife of Ignatius Warren. If she ever ran the house, it was very briefly. After both William and Edward left, Robert and his three servants had to shift for themselves until Robert married or bought a woman servant (see appendix 2, table A2.1).

Tobacco was the cash crop, which paid for all necessities not produced on the plantation. Even though the master and mistress were dead and Gardiner supervised from afar, production per hand was high, especially in the first years (see table 2.1). From 1666, when the accounts become less detailed, Gardiner may have paid less attention and left more to Knott and then to young Cole, with effects on general efficiency. Crop per hand fell somewhat during the next seven years.[40]

Apart from tobacco, plantation production was primarily for subsistence. Corn was the principal food crop. Gardiner planted only as much as he believed would be needed for the family. Some years the crop ran short. In others, there may have been extra to fatten hogs or help winter the cattle. One year he sold a small surplus. But he did not raise corn for regular sale. In this, as estate inventories tell us, he resembled other planters. Occasional surpluses could be sold to incoming new planters or to ships headed for the West Indies, but there was no developing export trade such as was to appear in the Chesapeake a century later.[41]

Cole's cattle and hogs produced ample milk, butter, and meat, and his orchard provided apples and cider. Gardiner probably grew beans and/or peas, and perhaps pumpkins Indian-style, in with the corn. (The account shows the purchase of beans in a year when corn was short.) At the end of his guardianship, if not before, the plantation was also growing a little barley, an unusual crop but one needed for making English ale. Although there is no mention of vegetables in Cole's inventory or the guardian account, this is not surprising. Perishables of this kind were not listed in any inventory or account of this period. But comments of observers and references in other seventeenth-century records to melons, cabbages, onions, cucumbers, various herbs, and root crops suggest what the Coles might have grown. All these farm products were grown primarily for home use, although Gardiner sold surpluses of animal products and fruit when available and when neighbors were in need.[42]

From the point of view of surpluses, livestock was the most important subsistence crop. How well cattle fared on open range depended on luck and on how much labor a planter devoted to their management. There are a handful of references to a "cow keep" in early Virginia and Maryland records, but taking a full-time hand from tobacco for this purpose was an extraordinary practice.[43] However, planters must have tried to keep track of their cows so that when they calved, the cows could be brought to a cowpen near the house for milking. There the bull calves could be gelded and all calves branded or their ears slit with the owner's mark, which, when registered in the records of the county court, would prevent anyone else from claiming the animals. If a cow and her calf were not found, the calf grew up in the "wild gang" of unmarked cattle and was useless to its owner.[44] In winter, planters supplemented forage on the range with corn husks and, when possible, with corn. (Although corn tops and blades made good fodder, there is no evidence that planters knew this yet.) In the spring, planters watched out for mirings. But without barns for shelter, little could be done to protect the stock from wolves.[45]

Such practices did not encourage increase, and what can be gleaned from the records does not paint a rosy picture. Virginia law required guardians of minor children to make an annual accounting to the county courts of cattle belonging to their charges; and although the law was not always observed, many such accountings survive.[46] Orphans' records tell a sad tale of calves killed by wolves and cows dead from miring or other causes. Cows were expected to produce a calf each year, but in orphans' estates cows were sometimes barren for a term, perhaps from malnutrition in the winter. If we suppose that over the long run, not quite half the calves were female (the usual ratio is 3.4 females to every 7 calves), the proportion of female calves surviving to maturity as shown in the Virginia accounts was only 32 to 48 percent, depending on assumptions made about missing data.[47] Cole's herd apparently did little better. Efforts to calculate female calf survival over the years of Gardiner's guardianship produce ranges from 31 to 53 percent, but the most reasonable schedules fall in the neighborhood of 40 percent (see appendix 3). Perhaps guardians did not manage the cattle of their charges as carefully as they did their own, and these estimates are therefore lower bounds. If so, the importance of care and winter feeding is underlined. On the other hand, Gardiner seems to have been a conscientious caretaker, and there was a limit to what he could do without abandoning the open range.[48]

Low calf survival limited the ability of a herd to grow. Heifers probably became pregnant in the third year and produced their first calves late in the third year or early in the fourth. Cow ages mentioned in Maryland and Virginia inventories indicate that few cows still bore beyond ages ten to eleven, a reproductive life of eight to nine years. Seven to nine years was the usual range for cows in medieval and early modern England.[49] If a cow lived a full reproductive life span and if nearly half her calves were female, given the survival rates for calves in York County or on the Cole plantation, she produced about one and one-third to two cows instead of about four. If the cow died young, she might even fail to replace herself.

Nevertheless, cattle did increase, and Chesapeake inhabitants saw no reason to mend their ways. Although European observers found the standard of cattle care atrocious,[50] how much better calf survival was in Europe at this time is unknown. However invidious the comparison, planters did not worry so long as herds provided a sufficiency of meat and milk for plantation use. Over eleven years, starting with thirty-four head, Gardiner supplied the family well, even selling off live animals and surplus beef and butter, and he distributed forty head to Cole's children. The judge of probate found this record satisfactory.

Hogs were far more prolific than cattle and doubtless survived more readily on the range. They were fierce animals, who suffered little from predators and did not mire down in mud.[51] Cole evidently had at least occasionally offered scraps or extra milk to his hogs, since in 1662 he had twenty-nine that "come home." In this way he could keep track of his stock and spay or geld pigs as necessary. He was planning to build a hog pen—he had nails for the purpose in his inventory—and Gardiner constructed it in 1663, but the pen was probably only for farrowing sows or for fattening animals intended for slaughter. It was certainly not for feeding the stock as a whole.

Gardiner did well with the hogs, much better than with the cattle. Twenty-nine plus four young pigs became fifty-odd (with some uncounted in the woods) by 1673, even though many were slaughtered for meat. Unfortunately, Cole did not itemize his sows, and there is little information available for the Chesapeake about litter sizes or the number of farrowings each year. English medieval farm accounts and sixteenth- and seventeenth-century manuals on husbandry suggest that about five to six pigs—at most eight—per litter could be counted on to survive to maturity and that two farrowings a year were usual. What little evidence there is for seventeenth-century Maryland indicates that five surviving pigs per litter was possible but three were much more likely and one far- rowing may have been the norm. Perhaps penning made a difference, but hogs were notorious for their ability to break out of pens. Sows, easily created by failing to spay a female piglet, were expected to produce pigs in their second year and to continue bearing for six.[52] Assuming three to six sows, one annual farrowing, and three surviving pigs per sow per year, Gardiner could have slaughtered 146 hogs over the twelve years and still have been left with at least forty-nine. One hundred forty-six hogs pro- vided ample food in most years and for the meat sales shown in the ac- count (see appendix 3). Pig survival may in fact have been higher or far- rowings more frequent. If so, Gardiner doubtless kept fewer sows.

Managing livestock for meat took foresight. There was no point in keeping a barren cow or male cattle that had already reached maximum size for beef. Such stock would use the meager winter food that could feed more productive animals. Cows were slaughtered once they were permanently barren, usually by age twelve. Except as needed for breed- ing, bulls were killed as calves or gelded and slaughtered for meat when older. Steers beefed at age five and were not usually kept beyond age six or seven, although those trained to the yoke might live much longer. Similarly, there was little point in allowing hogs to live beyond age two or at most three, at least so long as a breeding sow was regularly produc- ing more. Old hogs ate a lot and produced little additional usable meat. A planter could not simply let his stock increase with no attention and get the maximum benefit.[53]

Cole had managed his livestock with care, and Gardiner did so after him. Cole put instructions in his will that his thirty-five head of cattle be allowed to reach no more than fifty head. Evidently this was the maxi- mum that he believed the forage available could support without allowing the cattle to range too far afield, and perhaps fifty were as many as his labor force could effectively manage. Excess animals not needed for food or breeding he ordered sold "alive or dead," a practice he doubtless had been following already.[54] Gardiner followed these instructions. Through 1668 the account shows regular sales of cattle hides, beef, and pork. In addition, livestock was sold on the hoof—a steer in 1663 and "cattle" (probably pregnant cows) in 1668. Horses were also a valuable source of income. Cole had had none, but in 1663 Gardiner purchased a mare for the estate, with spectacular results. By 1673 there were more than thirty head to be divided, yet several mares had already been sold. After 1668, Gardiner must have cut back on selling cattle or hogs or slaughtering for more than family use. He needed animals sufficient to pay portions to the children as they reached age eighteen, another provision of Cole's will. Even so, income over the eleven years from all livestock sources was more than 20 percent of the total.[55]

Gardiner also kept the orchard tended and productive. Cole probably started his fruit trees from seeds, although grafting slips on to crab apple stocks was also early employed.[56] He likely started the seeds in a small nursery in his paled-in garden to keep animals from eating the seedlings.[57] When the trees were large enough, he transplanted them to the orchard. Six or seven years had passed before much fruit was available, but in 1662 the orchard was surely producing well.[58] By 1666 there was a small surplus of cider for sale. Cole showed in his will that he valued orchard produce. His son Robert was to inherit the orchard, but Robert's younger brothers were to have "halfe of all the benifitt . . . for the space of seaven yeares," presumably the seven years after Robert took possession. This provision gave his brothers time to set out orchards of their own, once they were of age to start their own plantations.

There was a market for livestock and other products because settlement in the area was expanding. When Cole took up his land there were only a handful of other plantations on the manor and only a few more across St. Clement's Bay. But by 1662 perhaps twenty-five families lived within the five or six miles that could be reached on foot within an hour or two, and by 1673 there were sixty such families.[59] Newcomers required livestock to start their herds and needed meat and perhaps butter or cider until their own produce was available. Horses, still in short supply, were especially in demand for transportation. Gardiner did not fail to take advantage of such opportunities. On the other hand, he probably did not plan to sell farm products regularly in a local market, with the likely exception of the horses. For one thing, the market was too unpredictable. When tobacco prices were low, neighbors were unable to buy and had to do without.[60] For another, Gardiner did not want to use the laboring hands in any way that would cut back on tobacco production. For example, raising more cattle for market would have required extra labor to improve animal survival, labor that Chesapeake planters regarded as not sufficiently productive.

Planters raised livestock for more than food and hides; animals were the growth stock of the seventeenth century and could provide an inheritance for offspring. At Cole's death, his cattle herd—thirty-five head—was exceptionally big, reflecting his economic position, and he was able to do very well by his children, even though his family was exceptionally large. Among herds inventoried on the lower Western Shore from 1658 through 1665, Cole's ranked sixth in size. Mean size was about thirteen head and the median less than nine. A man who had nine head of cattle and two to three children—a more usual family size—could leave only two to three head to each child. Cole had six children to endow, including his stepson. (His married stepdaughter had already received her portion.) He had cattle enough for nearly six head each.[61]

Gardiner, in fact, increased the number available for distribution, but he may have erred in selling some cows in 1668, the year after Knott received his one-eighth portion. The other children were supposed to get equal shares. However, after Robert and Mary had received their portions (eleven head each) in 1670 and 1672, only seven head—including two cows—were left; yet William was due his share in 1673 and Edward in 1676. Even supposing that all calves born after 1672 survived, an unlikely proposition, catching up would have been impossible. Gardiner must have planned on giving William and Edward their shares in horses, which brought high prices. The twenty-four hundred pounds of tobacco a mare had sold for in 1672 would buy at least three cows.[62] An extra horse or two each would buy the boys enough cattle to supplement the remaining stock.

Gardiner's success with horses is astonishing. A purchase of one horse in 1663 had produced more than thirty head ten years later. Supposing half the foals born were female, more than three-quarters of all horses born had to have survived to 1673—or until they were sold—to make this outcome possible, a great improvement over calf and cow survival (see appendix 3, table A3.12). One might speculate that Gardiner took special pains in fences and pasture for this valuable livestock were it not that the account describes the horses as "in the woods."[63] Possibly he had luck

Table 2.4 Selected Items in the Estates of St. Mary's County Decedent
Householders, 1658–1677

Item	N Estates with Item	% of All Estates
Carpenter's tools	24	14.5
Cooper's tools	6	3.6
Blacksmith's tools	0	0.0
Shoemaker's tools	2	1.2
Tailor's tools	1	0.6
Sheep	12	7.3
Hemp or flax	0	0.0
Spinning wheels	6	3.6
Looms	0	0.0
Hackle or break	0	0.0

Source: St. Mary's County Inventory File, St. Mary's City Commission, Maryland State Archives.
Note: Total N = 165.

and over these years more foals were born female than male.[64] Or perhaps horses were sufficiently more agile than cattle that they could outrun wolves or avoid getting mired down. Whatever the reason, Gardiner's success provided his charges with a valuable inheritance that their father had not anticipated.[65]

Cole's inventory and Gardiner's accounts tell us not only what Cole's sons and servants did but also what they did not do. Cole, compared with most of his neighbors, was well equipped with domestic and artisan tools. He had tools for carpentry, coopering, and shoemaking and also had tailor's shears. Nevertheless, there is little sign of activity in these crafts. Someone may have made repairs to buildings and mended shoes. But Gardiner paid a carpenter to build the new tobacco house and a cooper to make cask as needed. A tailor came each year to make and mend clothes for the children and servants, and Gardiner regularly purchased shoes. As elsewhere in the Chesapeake, few St. Mary's County planters tried to raise sheep—easy prey for wolves—or grew flax or hemp for fibers (see table 2.4). Hence no one in the Cole household spun yarn or wove cloth, nor was there equipment or materials for doing so. No one repaired tools or pots and pans, nor was anyone else paid for such work. Instead, Gardiner made frequent purchases of the hoes and axes necessary for plantation work and let other tools and household equipment wear out.

There is, furthermore, no sign that Gardiner purchased any manufactured products locally. Household inventories taken in St. Mary's County through 1677 show only 6 estates out of 165 with spinning wheels and none with looms. No one had tools for blacksmith's work. Indeed, over the first forty-odd years of the colony, there are only a handful of references in any records to forges or smiths. Two inventoried men of the 165 had shoemaker's tools, and among the living there may have been others, but not many country-made shoes were available (see table 2.4). Everything points to a household heavily dependent on imports. Clearly it was more cost-effective to put labor into raising tobacco to pay for imported goods than to spend time manufacturing goods locally.

European observers thought Chesapeake husbandry was careless and wasteful. Planters did not use manure or drain swampy land. New land had to be cleared nearly every year. Chesapeake planters did not house their livestock or feed animals properly in winter. They avoided European small grains, which required plowing, and planted Indian corn, which did not. Even their cleared fields, dotted with rotting stumps, suggested slovenly practice. In the 1680s the Reverend John Clayton blamed these practices on laziness and stubbornness, after planters paid no attention to his suggestions. It is certainly true, furthermore, that with the use of heavy manuring, planters could have grown tobacco on land for longer periods and on shorter rotations. In parts of Holland at the time, families grew tobacco on small plots, with short rotations to other crops, by using a combination of turf and animal manure. However, all agreed that animal dung produced an unpleasant taste and aroma for smoking the leaf, and there were also costs to consider—the time it would take to pen the animals for their manure, to raise fodder to feed them when penned, and to spread the manure on the soil. Seventeenth-century Chesapeake growers, with plenty of land available, preferred not to rely on such fertilizers.[66]

Indeed, given the abundance of land and the high cost of labor, there is little reason to believe that planters like Cole and Gardiner were wasteful farmers. So long as land was sufficient to allow long periods of fallow, the resource to husband was expensive labor. Land shortages that might lead to overcropping were not a threat in the seventeenth century.[67] Nevertheless, a planter had to watch the amount of labor he used on the land that he had. He could not allow more than one hand for every twenty acres of "plantable" soil, or he would clear too rapidly and run out of land before his old fields had finished their twenty-year rotation in fallow. Valuations of orphans' estates, required by Maryland law over the eighteenth century, show this concern. They usually stated the maximum acres of land that the guardian might clear and hence limited the number of hands that might work the orphans' land.[68] Cole and Gardiner were careful to follow the rules. If young Robert Cole did the same, his best tobacco soils were ready for reuse just at the point that he ran out of virgin land. Such planters were careful husbandmen, making creative adaptations in a New World.

3

. . . . .

The

Agricultural

Year

How did this Chesapeake system of husbandry affect the daily lives of the English settlers along the bay? We need to know the seasonality of tobacco and corn, the work routines that these crops generated, and the new skills required to ensure the planter's success. Were these new crops more demanding of time and strength than were English small grains? And how did other activities, within the house as well outside it, fit into the demands of this new husbandry?

Plantation Work

The rhythms of plantation work revolved around the needs of tobacco and corn. The tobacco year began in late January or in February, when the planter prepared and planted a small tobacco seedbed.[1] Since the seed was exceptionally fine, a bed of about fifty square yards produced enough plants for an acre.[2] On the Cole plantation about six hundred square yards, or a little more than a tenth of an acre, were needed. None of the contemporary accounts give details, except to say that land for a seedbed needed to be the best. Probably planters followed procedures similar to those observed by William Tatham and Richard Claiborne in the last quarter of the eighteenth century.[3] If so, Cole's sons and servants cleared a patch of land, took out what wood was needed for fencing, firewood, or other needs, burned the small branches and underbrush, and dug in the ashes for extra fertility. Burning not only facilitated clearing and provided ashes but also consumed insects and bacteria that might damage the plants. To guard against possible disaster, Gardiner may have had several beds planted in succession and in different locations so that if one failed, another might be available. Preparing and seeding the beds took four hands at least five days each.[4]

Once sowed, the beds required regular attention. References from the 1680s and after indicate that planters covered the beds with leaves and boughs as protection against the frost. Possibly the same was true in the 1660s. If so, on warm days planters had to uncover the beds for a while, and after the danger of frost had passed, they gradually had to remove such mulch entirely, although they might apply more brush to conserve moisture when the weather was exceptionally dry. In 1688 John Clayton commented on the dangers of the "fly," a small insect that "consumes the Plume of the Plant." This being the earliest reference, possibly these flies were not yet a threat in the 1660s. But if they were, flies could destroy a bed, especially during a drought. The only remedy then was to plant a new bed. The plants also needed watering twice a day when the weather was dry, as well as occasional weeding or thinning. When the leaves were the size of a shilling, they were ready for transplanting, usually sometime in May. They had to be ready by the end of June at the latest if the transplants were to mature before the first frost.[5]

Late March through May was the time for making hills, for corn as well as tobacco. The ground had to be unfrozen and not too miry, requirements that could delay beginning this task.[6] Like his neighbors, Cole had no plow. Since workers could only stir the ground with hoes, hills were needed to supply sufficient loose earth for root development. To make a hill, the laborer scraped the "earth around his foot until it form[ed] a heap round . . . [his] projected leg . . . like a mole hill, and nearly as high as the knee." He then pulled out his foot and flattened the top of the hill with his hoe. If Gardiner had the men put the tobacco hills four feet apart from hilltop to hilltop, he got just over 2,700 hills to an acre.[7]

The number of corn hills per acre depended on the variety of corn Gardiner grew. The kind most favored, later called gourdseed, had large ears with five hundred or more kernels to the ear, which grew on stalks ten to twelve feet high. Hills for these had to be about six feet apart, allowing about 1,210 hills to the acre. However, earlier-ripening varieties with smaller ears and stalks could be planted closer together. The yield per acre in kernels was nearly the same for all kinds, but the gourdseed took fewer hills and hence less labor.[8] This was probably the corn that Gardiner, and Cole before him, selected, although they may have allowed a few rows of short corn for early roasting ears.

How fast a worker could hill can be inferred from a seventeenth-century promotional tract that gave forty-eight hours as the time needed for a man to prepare ground and plant more than enough corn to feed himself for a year.[9] This would come to at least three barrels, which would require about an acre of land. Allowing ten hours for planting,[10] the hilling would take thirty-eight hours; hence at 1,210 hills to an acre, a worker would make about 320 hills in a ten-hour day, or one hill nearly every two minutes. (Landon Carter in the 1770s observed his slaves hilling at a similar rate.)[11] Gardiner needed 46,890 hills for his tobacco and corn (including his acre in rent corn). At 32 hills per hour, or 320 per day, workers in the Cole plantation fields required 146.5 man-days of labor. Four hands working full time would each have spent six and one-half fifty-five-hour weeks to complete the task.

Other necessary tasks undoubtedly spread out the time for hilling, although it had to be finished before the last tobacco seedlings were transplanted, usually by the end of June. Since February through April was miring time, one or more hands may have been partly diverted to check on the cattle or to rescue mired animals. If the planter had not yet built or repaired his fences, it would be essential to complete this work before the fields were planted. March was the time for planting a patch of barley in an old cornfield. In addition, the orchard trees would need pruning, and the vegetable garden would need spading. But the planter would cut back or neglect these last tasks should illness or other mischance severely reduce his available labor.[12]

About mid-April was also the time for planting corn.[13] There are no seventeenth-century descriptions of the procedure, but it is likely that practices of the eighteenth century differed little. Planters put three to four kernels about two inches deep in a hill in hopes that at least two would germinate and survive. Squirrels and birds stole many seeds, although such corn thieves were not yet the scourge that they became half a century later. A man could plant 780 to 1,333 hills in a day, depending on the lightness of the soil. Since Cole's was sandy loam, a total of 1,333 hills was likely.[14] Four hands could plant the whole year's crop in two days.

During April and May the corn continued to require attention. Once it had sprouted, the men checked the corn hills and transplanted young corn plants from the hills with extra plants to those hills that were bare. When the plants were about six inches high, the men weeded and rebuilt the hills with hoes, a task that took about 22 man-days. A second weeding was needed when the corn had grown another foot, sometime in late May or early June.[15] These tasks, added to hilling and tending the tobacco beds, made April and May the most hard-working months of the year, as can be seen from table 3.1.

Late May and June was the time for transplanting tobacco.[16] The seedlings had to be large enough, but not too large, and the weather had to be rainy. When a "season," as a rain was called, came on, all hands turned out to plant. They gently dug up seedlings and set them in the hills. Worms might attack the young leaves or roots, and if within a few days a plant died or looked peaked, it was replaced with a new plant. By one estimate, the average time for transplanting was about 200 to 220 plants per hour, or between 3 and 4 plants per minute. This speed was doubtless achieved by a division of labor. Some hands would dig the seedlings and carry them to the fields, others would drop the plants on the hills, and the rest would make holes for the roots and set the plants.[17] At this stage of tobacco cultivation, the Cole plantation had a scale advantage. A man working alone would take longer to plant his crop than he would if he worked in a group.

Four hands could plant Gardiner's 36,000 hills in four days, but since only rainy days were suitable, planting time might be spread out over several weeks. Everything else stopped for a "season." Court sessions might even be adjourned in anticipation of "plantable weather," lest later opportunities be insufficient.[18] All the tobacco had to be planted—the planter's term was "pitched"—by early July if it was to ripen before the frost.

On days not "plantable," Cole plantation laborers had other tasks. Even in June, hilling might still be continuing, and tobacco seedlings not dug needed weeding and watering. In addition, weeding and rehilling of early transplants began. The cornfield also required work. The second weeding and hilling might run into June, and a third was necessary by the end of the month or early in July. However, this was the last of the corn weeding. By then the corn was waist-high and could shade out other plants. In the language of the planter, the crop was "laid by."[19]

Once the corn was laid by, the months of July through September were

Table 3.1 Days per Hand, by Month of the Year, Required for Producing Crops on the Cole Plantation

Month	Work Days Available	Days Needed 9,000 Tobacco Hills		2722.5 Corn Hills		Days Left
		Days	Task	Days	Task	
January & February	45.5	5.0	Make beds	0		40.0
		0.5	Tend beds			
March	24.0	1.0	Tend beds	8.5	Hill	14.5
April	24.0	19.0	Hill	2.0	Plant	0.5
		2.5	Tend beds			
May	23.5	9.1	Hill	5.4	Weed (1)	0.1
		3.5	Tend beds	4.4	Weed (2)	
		1.0	Transplant			
June	24.0	1.5	Tend beds	1.0	Weed (2)	12.1
		3.0	Transplant	5.4	Weed (3)	
		1.0	Weed			
July & August	49.5	39.0	Weed, top, sucker & worm			10.5
September	24.0	4.0	Worm & sucker			9.0
		11.0	Cut & house			
October	24.5	5.0	Cut & house	5.5	Gather & house	9.0
		5.0	Strip			
November	23.0	15.0	Strip & pack			8.0
December	24.0					24.0
Total	286.0	126.1		32.2		127.7

Sources: See text.

Note: The number of days in the month assumes 5.5 working days per week (see text). If spring is late or very wet, all hilling probably has to wait until April, and corn planting is delayed. This will push tobacco hilling into June and corn weeding into July and use up most of the extra days through June and July. If the second weeding is omitted, there is time to hill and plant an additional acre or so of gourdseed corn, given some stretching out of hilling time for tobacco. Variations in the schedule are possible (see text). Cf. table 4 in Lois Green Carr and Russell R. Menard, "Land, Labor, and the Economies of Scale in Early Maryland: Some Limits to Growth in the Chesapeake Systems of Husbandry," *Journal of Economic History* 49 (1989): 414. Note that in this earlier table, rent corn is omitted and time is added for suckering corn because the time shown is the late seventeenth century.

3.1 Hoeing Tobacco Plants, Historic St. Mary's City. Note the worm fence in the background (see illustration 3.3). (Paul Leibe, Historic St. Mary's City)

devoted almost entirely to tobacco. In the years that barley was planted, a hand probably took a few hours late in June or in early July to cut the small amount grown and take it to the tobacco house, but otherwise everyone worked in the tobacco fields. Regular weeding was necessary from the time the plants were fully rooted until they were at least knee-high. At the same time, the laborer had to search each plant for hornworms, which could devour a whole crop in a few days. This was "a nauseous occupation" that required picking off the worms and crushing them underfoot. Six to eight weeks after transplanting, when the plants had grown to four feet or more, the laborer topped them to prevent blossoming and to stop upward growth. At the same time he "primed" them, that is, he cut off the bottom leaves, which were low in quality. Both procedures improved the size and weight of the leaves that remained. Topping encouraged suckers—new shoots from the roots or from the junction of the leaves and the stalk—which he had to remove for the same purpose. Topping and suckering required pinching the plant with the thumbnail. To facilitate the process, as William Tatham later reported, and "not for the use of *gouging* out people's eyes," many planters let that "nail grow long and harden[ed] it *in the candle*." To be done properly, all these tasks required experience and diligence, and some of the decline in output after the first few years of Gardiner's administration may be a sign that supervision was inadequate. Weeding, topping, priming, worming, and "succoring" were heavy work in the heat and humidity of the summer, the heat and moisture that was essential to the proper ripening of the crop.[20]

Planters had not always primed their plants or removed suckers that grew from the roots, but quality, nevertheless, had always been a general concern. From 1640 to 1642, a Maryland act of assembly had forbidden the shipment of damaged leaf, ground leaves, or second crops (grown from root suckers after the stalks had been cut). By the 1650s, references to tobacco in cask began to specify that it was free of ground leaves. In 1658 another act forbade ground leaves and second crops, and this remained in effect until 1671. Planters did not always conform, especially as to seconds, but from the 1650s the definition of "merchantable" tobacco seems to have at least excluded ground leaves. Possibly part of the improved production per hand over the second quarter of the seventeenth century reflected a greater willingness of planters to reduce the number of leaves on their plants.[21]

The tobacco began to ripen in late August or early September, and this was the time when the planter's skill could begin to make the difference between an excellent or a poor crop. Conscientious labor could get the crop seeded, pitched, primed, suckered, and wormed, but judgment determined when the tobacco was ready to be cut. The leaf had to have the right yellowish green color, be sufficiently thickened, and have "a certain mellow appearance and protrusion of the web." When bent in two, the ripened leaf snapped; unripened did not. If the tobacco was cut too green, it would not cure properly, and if it was left in the field too late, frost would ruin it.[22] Learning to make these decisions wisely was an essential part of apprenticeship for Cole's stepson and sons.

At harvesting time, Cole's sons and servants cut the tobacco stalks near the ground and let them wilt in the sun for a few hours on the hills. The next step was to drive pegs into the stalks, hang them by the pegs on poles, called tobacco sticks, and if weather permitted, begin the curing process by setting the sticks of tobacco stalks on fences or on temporary scaffolds set up in the fields. This allowed the tobacco leaves to wilt further, mak-

3.2 Reconstruction of a Seventeenth-Century Tobacco House, Historic St. Mary's City. Archaeological excavations and recorded contracts tell us that tobacco houses resembled other Chesapeake buildings of the seventeenth century. They were post-in-the-ground structures with siding and roofs of rived clapboard. (Paul Leibe, Historic St. Mary's City)

ing it possible to house the stalks more tightly. After a few days, the men then carried the tobacco to the tobacco house and hung it on permanent scaffolds in tiers that reached up into the peak of the structure. Here once again the Cole plantation had a scale advantage. The sticks of tobacco could be stacked faster and much higher in the house when two laborers were available to move a stick. Care was taken to see that there were several inches between tiers and that the plants were not crushed together on the sticks but were "so nigh each other" that they just touched— "much after the manner they hang Herrings in Yarmouth," in the words of a seventeenth-century account. By this means the air could circulate through the tobacco house and dry the leaf.[23]

The only seventeenth-century description of a tobacco house comes from John Banister, who lived in Virginia from 1678 to 1692. By his account, these houses were "usually built of clapboard about 20 or 25 foot wide; at every 5 foot there goes a range or rail quite across the house, the

Joists are ranges themselves, & there are usually three tire [tier] above, and one below." Further details come from snippets from the records and archaeological excavations. These indicate that tobacco houses were post-in-the-ground framed structures like others of the time and place. At first they may have been flimsy affairs, but by the 1660s, contracts in the records suggest more solid buildings. As Banister indicated, they had rived clapboard siding and roofs, although there are a few references to thatched roofs. Thatching, if well done, was better insurance than clap-boards against rain, but the materials, and perhaps the skills, were not as available in the Chesapeake as were wood and carpentry skills. Cole inventoried nails for the "raising" of a new tobacco house, and Gardiner paid a carpenter to build it. Nothing indicates thatch. Possibly the house had movable boards in its siding for better control of air and moisture. Dutch merchants active in the tobacco trade may have brought news of such construction, as seen in the tobacco houses of Holland. By a century later, movable boards were standard in the Chesapeake. However, no mention of such a feature appears in any seventeenth-century Maryland record.[24]

Cutting the tobacco, moving it to the tobacco house, and hanging it took four hands about sixteen days, or two and a half workweeks, which were probably spread out over a month. During this time all hands gave these tasks first priority. Dry weather was necessary for wilting, so if a weekday was rainy and a Sunday was sunny, the Cole plantation labor force doubtless cut on Sunday. The Act Concerning Religion of 1649 forbade Sunday work but excepted cases of "absolute necessity."[25]

Oronoco tobacco usually took five to six weeks to cure. If during this time too much damp weather caused the leaf to begin to mold, seventeenth-century planters probably rehung the plants more thinly, just as their eighteenth-century successors did. Perhaps they also resorted to small smoky fires to dry out the air, another eighteenth-century practice, but this was a risky expedient. It was easy to produce "firing"—a blight of hard brown spots—with a combination of heat and strong moisture, and "house burnt" leaf was not merchantable.[26] Careful attention and good judgment were necessary.

Judging how long the leaf should hang was another crucial decision. Tobacco leaves were ready for further processing when they were "in case," that is, when they were fully cured and when a spell of rainy weather had made them neither "so dry as to crumble, or so damp as to endanger a future rotting of the leaf." Given the need for dampness, "seasons" were the times for "striking down" the stalks and stripping off the leaves. But if wet weather lasted too long, the leaf might become too high "in case" and the process would have to stop until dry weather and a later "season" produced the proper state. After stripping, the leaves were made into small bundles and piled until the time was convenient for packing the casks. The planter had to inspect the pile regularly and, by moving bundles from the top to the bottom as their condition dictated, make sure that the leaf neither molded nor dried out too much. When the time came for packing, the leaves could not be stowed in the casks until they once again were "in case." There were multiple possibilities for error in all these stages of tobacco production, and error could spoil the crop.[27]

Clearly, young Francis Knott and the Cole sons had much to learn before they could successfully grow tobacco. Without good judgment, they could not benefit from sufficient labor or the best of weather. Boys needed to start work at an early age to acquire the necessary experience in judging the ripeness of the leaves and the stages of curing. Possibly the diminished crops per hand from 1666 reflected in part the transition of control from Gardiner to Knott and then to Robert Cole as they learned to grapple with these decisions.[28]

Packing in cask, called hogsheads, was usual, although some tobacco was shipped in bulk, either loose or in rolls. Ships from the outports were particularly likely to accept shipment in bulk. But the quality of tobacco suffered from being transported this way, and merchantable tobacco usually went into cask. In 1658, for the convenience of ship captains, both Maryland and Virginia passed laws to regulate the size of hogsheads, which for the rest of the century were forty-two to forty-three inches in length and twenty-six to twenty-seven inches "in the head." Since ship captains charged freight rates for space, not weight, planters gradually reduced their shipping charges by learning to pack more and more tobacco into the cask. In the 1620s, tobacco cask averaged less than 150 pounds of leaf; by Cole's day, mean weights were running close to 400 pounds. The savings produced were substantial. In the 1620s, planters often paid three pence per pound to ship tobacco to London; by the 1660s, freight could cost as little as a penny.[29] These improvements were achieved by packing a layer of bundles, pressing the leaves down, and continuing the procedure until the cask was filled. Just when the tobacco prize—an arrangement of levers and weights for pressing the layers down—was developed is unclear. However, a cask could be "foot-packt" to reach the weight of 400 pounds. Prizes were not essential. It was the 1,000-pound hogshead of the eighteenth century that required a prize for packing.[30]

Gardiner had a cooper make tobacco cask, doubtless finding it more efficient to buy cask than to expend labor making them and possibly bungling the job. The plantation laborers packed the leaf by placing boards on the layers and treading down. Once again judgment and care were critical for preventing both packing tobacco not "in case" and undue crushing and breaking of the leaves. Packing in frosty weather could also create damage. Stripping and packing a four-hand crop took about 80 man-days.[31] A crew of four working together would need 20 man-days, or three and a half weeks.

A minimum of six weeks elapsed from the time the first batch of tobacco was cut until it was ready for shipment. The first cask might be packed in mid-October, the last ones in November or December. If the cooper was late or the weather often unsuitable for putting tobacco "in case," the process could take longer. But the planter needed to finish, if possible, before hard frosts made packing difficult.

Indeed, delays in obtaining cask could be crucial. In 1653, Robert Brooke complained that his cooper was so late in preparing cask that the last two of the twenty-two promised hogsheads did not arrive until April. As a result—possibly because of a poorly constructed house—the tobacco "with long hanging [was] much wasted and a Greate part of it blown down & Spoiled, the latter End of the Winter for want of Caske." It was important, furthermore, to get the crop shipped out before hot weather returned. A ship generally arrived in late fall and left as soon as it was loaded, ordinarily early in spring. If a crop was not ready until after all the ships had left, it would spoil during the Chesapeake summer.[32] Robert Brooke was lucky if his last cask of tobacco did not miss the shipping and rot. Happily nothing suggests such disasters for the Cole plantation crops.

During the curing, stripping, and packing operations of October through December, the Cole plantation work force had time for other necessary tasks. The workers gathered the ears of corn and stored them, probably in the loft of the house. Shelling could wait. Since corn kept better in the ear than shelled, it was shelled only as needed. If no one had threshed the barley before the tobacco was stored, threshing was easily fitted in now. Two and a half bushels, the amount shown in Gardiner's account for 1672, took one hand little more than a day. This was also the season to make the last of the cider, to slaughter hogs and cattle, and to salt down and smoke the meat. If storms or invading livestock had damaged any fruit trees, transplanting new ones from the garden nursery was also a fall activity.[33]

January and February were the months for clearing and fencing new fields. Keeping twenty-two acres in production required a continuing program of clearance. Probably Gardiner had the workers clear between one and two acres per year per hand. The men undoubtedly girdled most of the trees but had to chop down some for fencing or firewood. Some kinds of timber had to be green when cut, since the tools available could not readily cut or rive dead white oak or hickory or locust. The men had to trim the cut trees of their small branches, which could be burned to help fertilize the field. The logs had to be hauled away. At the same time, the men must have burned over the fields already in use to rid them of fallen branches from trees girdled in earlier years. Time spent in clearance was probably two and one-half to five weeks.[34]

Riving fence rails and palings and making and repairing the fences that protected the crops doubtless took up the rest of the winter season. Until well into the eighteenth century, planters fenced in their crops, not their animals.[35] Men paled in their gardens, setting the palings well into the ground to prevent hogs from rooting under them. English gardening books of the period advised making palings six to seven feet high to keep out chickens, and the Chesapeake deer also required such a high barrier.[36] For orchards and for fields of tobacco and corn, planters usually used the "worm," "pannel," or "Virginia" fence. This they constructed of split rails from nine to fourteen feet long. Arranged as shown in illustration 3.3, seven to eight rails made a fence five to six feet high, considered sufficient to keep out horses as well as cattle. The zigzag foundation suggests why a drunken man was described as "laying out Virginia fences."[37] One advantage of a worm fence, which required no posts dug into the ground, was that the planter could move it to newly cleared land from fields he was leaving in fallow. But these fences blew down and took time to maintain.[38] Cole's twenty-two acres of field crops had about 3,900 feet of circumference, supposing they made up a single parcel. To fence this space required about 3,650 nine-foot rails. His orchard, assuming

3.3 A Worm Fence, Historic St. Mary's City. This variety is staked for stability, but such a fence could stand without stakes. The zigzag pattern of a worm fence can be seen in illustration 3.1. (Paul Leibe, Historic St. Mary's City)

one hundred trees planted at twenty-five feet, needed another 933 rails.[39] The Cole plantation workers had to inspect and replace as needed nearly 4,600 rails each year.

How long the rails lasted was variable. According to the Reverend John Clayton, a visitor in Virginia in 1687, rails rotted after about six or seven years, but Clayton may have exaggerated.[40] The longevity of rails depended on the wood. Wood from chestnut and locust trees endures a very long time; white oak, perhaps ten years; red oak, six or seven. There are no signs, as found elsewhere in the county, that chestnuts grew on Tomakokin Creek or that Indians had lived there, leaving old fields that would have provided locust trees. Both kinds of oak were probably available, but which kind was growing on the land used for crops probably varied from year to year. Nevertheless, by the end of every six to ten years, the Cole hands probably had to replace all 4,600 rails, at between 460 and 760 rails a year. In all, two to three weeks of a man's time may have been needed annually to inspect the fences, move them as necessary, and prepare and install new rails.[41]

Not all planters were careful about fencing. A Charles County cow, for example, regularly succeeded in using her horns to lift poorly secured rails from their places and caused great damage to the orchard of the planter who was taken to court for shooting her.[42] From 1663, Maryland law stated that a planter who had not built a sound fence, at least five feet high, around his cornfield could not collect damages from the owner of livestock that invaded the field. However, actions brought in the county courts suggest a trade-off for planters short on labor. Rather than put the required time into maintaining a fence, especially during busy periods, they risked the loss of crops.[43]

Although clearing and fencing were winter tasks for the Cole plantation hands, this was the easiest work period. Planters had not yet much developed the extra employments that could be deferred to this season, such as making shingles and barrel staves, products increasingly wanted in the West Indies. Two promotional works of the mid-century claimed that servants had little to do in winter except chop firewood and hunt. Of course, chopping firewood was no mean task. About thirty cords per year per cooking hearth were needed.[44] On the other hand, Cole's house, as we shall see, had only one hearth, and several laborers were available, making the work per hand much less than was required in households with fewer workers.

Did the planters and laborers who left England for the Chesapeake find themselves working harder than they had before? They probably did not in fall and winter but in spring and summer perhaps they did, and at tasks that were more monotonous and unpleasant than those required for raising small grains. Englishmen used animal power to till the land; Maryland workers did it all with hoes. Weeks of hilling, weeding, and rehilling were unremitting from late March or early April until at least mid-July, and the worming and suckering that followed were notably unpleasant occupations. Englishmen might weed their grain a little, but basically, once the field was plowed and seeded, there was little to do until the harvest. In England, the rest of the year was taken up with orchards and gardens and caring for the cattle and sheep that supplied manure for the fields and provided dairy, meat, and fiber products for the table or for sale. Such farming allowed a greater variety of activities over the whole year than did Chesapeake husbandry.[45] For those Chesapeake workers subject to gang labor under an overseer on large plantations, work for many months of the year must have been dreary indeed.

The seasonal demands of tobacco and corn, as seen in table 3.1, show labor constraints that help explain much about Chesapeake husbandry. The months of April and May were frantic. On the Cole plantation each hand had to make nearly 12,000 hills and had to plant and weed nearly 3,000 of these in corn. He had to keep the tobacco beds watered and weeded and begin transplanting tobacco seedlings as soon as they were ready. During these months he could do nothing else if these crops were to be planted in time to mature before the frost. In these circumstances it is no surprise that planters did not provide additional gourdseed corn for their livestock or produce much corn for sale. The hilling and weeding required could not be easily fitted into the months in which such work was best done.

If spring was not late, a planter determined to raise more feed for his stock could plant short corn in June and have some time to weed it in July and August. This variety ripened sooner than the gourdseed corn but took more hills for the same return, and therefore more labor time. Table 3.1 suggests that twelve days could be available in June for hilling, planting, and finishing part of a first weeding of this extra crop. Twelve days would allow the planter to make another 2,240 hills, which for this type of corn probably could be put on an acre, and an acre of old tobacco field would be available.[46] Hilling would take about seven days at 320 hills per day; planting would take nearly two days; and the first weeding at 500 hills per day would come to four and one-half days in late June and early July. Later weedings would take close to nine days later in July and in August, when extra time was available. The fifteen or so bushels of corn this would provide would not feed many animals for long, but it could provide an additional supplement for lactating cows or winter feed. However, the planter had to double the months of high-pressure labor. In years when spring was late he could not get the extra hills made, and the contemporary evidence suggests that even when he could, he did not. Two to three months was long enough to postpone all plantation business not connected with tobacco and corn.

Since an additional acre or so per laborer was the most a planter could add to his cornfield, it becomes clear why seventeenth-century planters did not make more than casual exports of corn.[47] Markets were opening up in the West Indies, but to grow more corn required giving up labor time needed for tobacco. Changes in husbandry practices were necessary if planters were to grow corn for export without cutting back on the primary staple.

In the eighteenth century, wealthy—and eventually middling—planters began to respond to the growing market for corn. They had slaves and worked them harder than seventeenth-century planters had worked white servants, requiring longer days and fewer days off. With virgin forest gone, planters also plowed their land, which hastened hilling and weeding and thus allowed still more labor time for this second crop.[48] Plowing required penning, feeding, and training draft animals, but part of the additional corn was available for feed, and manure from penned animals allowed more plants per acre. By the 1770s, the result was twofold: a doubling of the corn crop per hand for tobacco planters; but a tendency for some planters to shorten rotations and overwork their land, a disastrous outcome in the long run.[49]

Poor planters did not share in this rise in productivity. They were less likely to undertake the more complex management of livestock that plowing and manuring required, and they had too little land for additional corn hills unless they ruined it with shortened rotations. Insofar as they added corn, they had to give up land for tobacco, with uncertain improvement in income. Similar problems were to arise when wheat finally became a marketable product in the mid-eighteenth century. Plowing and the animal husbandry it entailed were necessary. Furthermore, although planters used old cornfields for wheat, the yields were very low on these worn-out lands—perhaps six bushels per acre—and other land was not likely to be available without cutting back on tobacco. In the predominantly tobacco regions of the Chesapeake, the husbandry of the seventeenth century remained the choice of most poor planters throughout the whole colonial period.[50]

Household Tasks

The seasons had less effect on work schedules inside the house, where the daily routines for tending children, cooking, and occasionally washing and cleaning were not as varied by time of year as those tied to work in the fields. The most time-consuming daily chore was grinding corn, which, in the absence of water mills, was a household task. The procedure was to soak the corn kernels for a few hours to soften them and then pound them with a pestle in a mortar. About four and one-half cups of corn per adult male per day was the standard ration. If we make allowance for women and children proportionate to their sex and age and suppose ten minutes to pound each cup, then in the Cole household, as much as five or six, even seven, hours of pounding were necessary each day (see appendix 2, tables A2.4 and A2.5). In almost any household, the planter's wife was likely to spend daily at least one and one-half to two hours at this task.[51]

How often planter families washed clothes is anyone's guess. Gardiner bought quantities of soap for the Cole household each year, so clearly washing was regularly done. Possibly Isabel Jones or the housekeeper boiled the linens in the copper, or perhaps they laundered everything in the creek. With care, woolens could be washed in cold water, but this was probably an infrequent practice. Brushing and airing, especially during winter, were doubtless the most usual treatments. Whether such measures kept vermin from pestering the household is debatable. "Pickeing" was among the services one planter described as needed by young twins he had cared for, and the Coles probably did not escape such problems.[52]

The list of household goods Cole made at his departure was unremarkable for the absence of cleaning equipment. He mentioned no brooms or scrub brushes, items also absent in the probate inventories of the period. Probably the Coles and their neighbors swept with brooms made of twigs that had no salable value and scrubbed with small versions of the same or with rags. To a modern eye, standards of cleanliness were undoubtedly low. A sixteenth-century English book on husbandry advised the housewife to sweep her house and set it in order each morning before milking her cows and then dressing her children. It seems unlikely that Maryland housekeepers of the seventeenth century did more.[53]

Apart from cooking (discussed in chapter 4), washing, and cleaning, the main household activities revolved around gathering and preserving food. If the Cole household had a vegetable garden, the women and boys planted herbs, cabbages, and root crops in spring and weeded, tended, and harvested them over the summer. These household workers gathered fruit as it ripened—probably wild strawberries and raspberries in May and June, peaches and early apples—if the Coles had them—in July and August, and later apples in September and October. Peaches and apples they may have sliced and dried; we know they made "mobby" and apple cider.[54] In the late fall, they salted down meat. When cows were calving, the women took charge of milking and butter making, but in what seasons is unclear. There was no control over breeding when animals ran in the woods. According to such references on seasonality that we do have, calving occurred in both spring and fall and dairying through October.[55]

The only cider-making equipment mentioned in Cole's inventory was a "Mobby tubb" and three "thight barrells for liquor," plus a ten-gallon "thight Ancor" and two cases of quart bottles. Possibly one of the three "Meale Sifters of haire" was also in use for cider making. The household had no cider press, an omission understandable when one finds a carpenter charging two thousand pounds of tobacco for making one.[56] English accounts of cider making say that the fruit either was ground or was beaten in a wooden trough and then put in the press in cider bags made of hair, which let the juices through. Doubtless the women or boys in the Cole household—and perhaps the men, once the tobacco crop was hung—pounded the fruit in a tub, then filled a hair sieve with the pulp and pressed out the juice into the mobby tub, presumably a kind of vat. The cider, or mobby, then sat for at least twenty-four hours, covered with a cloth or boards to allow some evaporation. A tap about four inches from the bottom of the vat was then used to decant the liquid into another container, leaving the lees behind. This process might have to be repeated several times to get rid of the lees. "The great thing to be taken care of in making of Cyder," J. Mortimer explained in 1708, "is only to let so much of the Spirit evaporate as may prevent its fermenting before the gross Lees are separated from it, and yet to keep Spirits enough to cause a Fermentation when you would have it; for if it ferment too much it will lose its Sweetness, and become harsh and small; and if it ferment not at all it will become dead and sowre."[57] When ready, the cider then was either bottled or "tunned," that is, put in cider casks. Cole had both kinds of equipment.

Cole had ample salt and a powdering tub for salting down pork and beef. The men surely did the slaughtering and butchering of cattle and hogs, but women and boys undoubtedly did the rest of the processing. The procedure probably differed little from that described two centuries later. They put the best pork in the tub, covered it with salt, and left it for a few weeks. They then washed off the salt and hung the pieces up in the chimney to smoke. (Cole's inventory gives no sign that he had a separate smokehouse.) The procedure produced excellent "bacon," as these smoked pieces were called. Beef and coarse pork pieces were pickled by packing in brine-filled barrels.[58] Most of the meat Gardiner sold was pickled.

The women servants continued Rebecca Cole's dairy, selling surplus butter in 1663 and 1666. The work of the dairy was time-consuming. For one thing, great care was necessary to keep utensils clean. The dairymaid had to scald all the equipment in use—milk pails, milk tubs, milk trays, cream pots, churn—each day in the eighteen-gallon copper pot. Any residue of old milk would help to sour what was fresh. Containers too big to go in the copper she had to scrub well with boiling water. Gervase Markham, writing early in the seventeenth century, advised that the dairying place be so clean "that a Princes Bedchamber must not exceed it."[59]

Milking in itself took time, and butter making took hours more. A good dairymaid could milk a cow in six to ten minutes, but if several cows were in milk at once, the process could take more than an hour a day. Chesapeake cows, furthermore, were probably rather wild and difficult, adding to the time required. After each milking the milk cooled in a tub for a while. The dairymaid then strained the milk through the straining dish, which was a wooden bowl with the bottom cut out and covered with a clean linen cloth. Once strained, the milk sat in milk trays. These were wooden or earthenware containers made broad and shallow to maximize cream and postpone souring. The dairymaid skimmed off the cream of the evening milk with a skimmer—a wooden paddle with holes for letting the milk fall away—into earthen cream pots in the morning and did the same with cream from the morning milk at the end of the day. Covered and kept in a cool place, the cream could keep from two to four days, depending on the weather, and be churned into butter at convenience. Churning could take several hours, depending on the weather. Cold retarded this process considerably. Once the dairymaid had made the butter, she squeezed out the buttermilk, which either humans or hogs could drink. She then put the butter in a pot, with salt in the bottom and on top. Butter from later churnings could be added with more salt until the pot was full.[60] In all, on butter-making days, as much as half of one woman's time must have been spent in dairying. It is no wonder that most households did not undertake to make butter, and especially not on any great scale.

In the Cole household, butter production depended on the number of cows in milk at any one time and on the time the women had for processing the milk. Milk yields were very unlike those of the present, perhaps as little as half a gallon per day. English authorities talked of a gallon or more per milking from some types of cows, but this yield appears to have required that the calves be weaned, a practice probably not followed for the range cattle of the Chesapeake. Scholars of early modern dairying have estimated that a yield of 120 to 150 gallons of milk per year per cow was usual unless feeding was superior.[61] In a large household like Cole's, the gallon or so per day produced by one or two cows may have been consumed at once, either as drink or as uncured cheese, which did not keep very long. But some or all of the milk from additional cows could be converted into butter. There probably were always at least eight cows in the Cole herd and usually ten or more. If the calvings were evenly spread throughout the year, the family could usually use all the milk produced. But if the calvings were bunched, as they more probably were, there were many months in which so many cows were producing milk that the only way to preserve it was as salted butter. The 129 pounds sold in 1663 was perhaps the product of three or four cows producing milk that the family could not use.[62]

Making uncured cheese was much simpler than butter making. The milk—or buttermilk left from butter making—could be poured into any shallow pan and set in the sun until curds formed. If necessary, a little boiling water could be added to hasten the process. The dairymaid then skimmed out the curds and drained them in a colander or squeezed the liquid whey out through a clean linen cloth. The Coles had a "cheese tubb" and a "Cullender," but neither was necessary to the process.[63] Doubtless, cheese making in this form was undertaken in any household where there were women to process milk, whether or not they also made butter.

Household work differed much less from that of England than field work differed from its counterpart. There were no innovations that we know of in procedures for dairying, meat preserving, cider making, or gardening. Differences in diet produced some differences in cookery, as we shall see, and the time needed to pound corn each day limited the time available for other tasks. Nevertheless, the housewife could rely on what knowledge she had brought with her. Chesapeake husbandry did not demand a new system of housewifery.

The Cole children grew up in southern Maryland at a time when the men and women who lived along the Chesapeake Bay were creating a new system of husbandry, an extensive agriculture that drew heavily on Indian practices and differed sharply from the more intensive farming styles then common in England. Chesapeake families learned to adapt their lives to the demands of cultivating tobacco and corn and raising livestock while pursuing work strategies that saved labor, always a relatively scarce and expensive commodity in the region during the seventeenth century. The gradual elaboration of a distinctive way of farming testifies to their willingness to experiment and their ability to invent in the face of new circumstances.

How well did this new system of husbandry serve the inhabitants of the bay colonies? Did small plantations supply more than a good subsistence? What life-style did these plantations permit the family? Was it possible to accumulate property, or was it all a family could do to hold its own? Again, close attention to the Coles will suggest some answers.

4

· · · · ·

Income, Growth,
and Living
Standards

Income and Accumulation

Robert Cole had done very well in his ten years as a Chesapeake tobacco
planter. He had used the opportunities available in tobacco production
and farm building to turn a modest capital of perhaps £54 into a substantial estate worth more than £200, sufficient to provide his family a comfortable life and to place him within reach of the local gentry. Luke
Gardiner continued this progress, but more slowly. In 1673, the estate
had grown to £360, despite the distribution of considerable property to
the heirs and without Robert Cole's hard work and careful attention to
detail.[1]

   Gardiner's account provides a detailed description of this progress over
its last eleven years. Table 4.1 reports the revenue earned from the sale
of plantation produce by year and in various categories from 1662 to
1672. Over the entire period, the estate earned an average annual gross
income of just under 8,700 pounds of tobacco. This works out to roughly
£38 in local currency, an apparently handsome return for a farm with a
market value of just over £200 in 1662. Revenues were fairly steady, falling between £30 and £40 in most years, but there were some sharp variations. Earnings were especially low in 1666—in the midst of a severe
depression when war disrupted trade and when extreme weather de-
stroyed crops throughout the region—and especially high in 1668, at the
beginning of a short but strong postwar recovery. The pattern suggests
the importance of foreign trade to a small plantation.[2]

Table 4.1 Income by Source, Cole Plantation, 1662–1672
(In Pounds Currency, Constant Value)

	Tobacco Crop	Livestock	Dairy	Grains	Orchard	Misc./ Unknown	Total Income
1662 Income	30.62					8.93	39.55
% Total Income	77.4					22.6	
1663 Income	27.77	17.29	3.47			6.84	55.37
% Total Income	50.2	31.2	6.3			12.3	
1664 Income	32.43	6.99				2.76	42.18
% Total Income	76.9	16.6				6.5	
1665 Income	31.24	4.94				.94	37.12
% Total Income	84.2	13.3				2.5	
1666 Income	13.97	.51	.32		1.09		15.89
% Total Income	87.9	3.2	2.0		6.9		
1667 Income	20.14	4.67				.78	25.59
% Total Income	78.7	18.2				3.0	
1668 Income	37.58	32.53			3.22	9.54	82.87
% Total Income	45.3	39.3			3.9	11.5	
1669 Income	17.37					14.82	32.19
% Total Income	54.0					46.0	
1670 Income	19.28	8.23					27.51
% Total Income	70.1	29.9					
1671 Income	23.77	6.51		1.09		1.15	32.52
% Total Income	73.1	20.0		3.3		3.5	
1672 Income	22.48	6.15		1.03		1.09	30.75
% Total Income	73.1	20.0		3.3		3.5	
Total Income	276.65	87.82	3.79	2.12	4.31	46.85	421.54
Annual average income	25.15	7.98	.34	.19	.39	4.26	38.32
Annual average % total income	65.6	20.8	0.9	0.5	1.0	11.1	

Source: Cole Plantation Account, appendix 1.

The table provides further evidence of the dominant role of the export sector. The tobacco crop was clearly the chief source of market income on the plantation. Tobacco production averaged about 5,800 pounds per year, worth roughly £25. There were short crops in 1666, 1669, and 1670 and an unusually large one in 1668—reflecting fluctuations in the work force, inconsistencies in climate, differences in judgment, and changes in luck—but output was fairly steady, in most years ranging between 5,000 and 7,000 pounds. Tobacco accounted for more than two-thirds of the total revenue earned on the market over the eleven years for which the accounts were kept, never less than 45 percent and in two years more than 80 percent.

Such a direct measure underestimates the importance of the staple. There was a strong relationship between total income earned in a year and the tobacco crop's share of all income produced. Tobacco's contribution to income grew (and income fell) with the approach of the severe depression in the export sector from 1665 to 1667, fell (while total income rose) with the sharp recovery of 1668, and then rose again as the economy slid into a minor slump in the early 1670s. Income from tobacco and income from other sources were directly related on the Cole plantation—and in the economy as a whole—as prosperity in the industry encouraged expansion and created markets for livestock and foodstuffs, whereas depressed markets for tobacco led to a general contraction in economic activity. Diversified agriculture as yet provided only the slightest hedge against the uncertainties of producing a staple crop for the international market.[3]

If the hedge was slight, the supplement was substantial. Livestock and livestock products—meat, tallow, hides, butter, and cheese—produced on average more than 20 percent of the farm's income, and a few shillings could be earned by the occasional sales of corn or cider. These figures may slight the contribution of livestock, grain, and the orchard because most items in the residual category were small bills paid by local residents for unspecified goods and services, doubtless often for agricultural products other than tobacco. All or nearly all plantation products except tobacco were sold locally, and the domestic market in the region grew rapidly in the third quarter of the seventeenth century as the demand for tobacco led to the creation of many new farms, which in turn provided opportunities for established planters. The local market was an important source of income for the Cole plantation and in many years proved the difference between profit and loss.

Not all the goods and services produced by the Cole plantation entered the market: a substantial proportion was consumed on the spot. The farm was nearly self-sufficient in food; all members of the household were provided shelter, fuel, washing, and other services; and the small children were supervised and nurtured. It is impossible to know the precise value

Table 4.2 Sources of Revenue, Cole Plantation, 1662–1672
(In Pounds Currency, Constant Value)

Year	Estimated Value of Subsistence Production	Export Earnings	Local Earnings	Revenue Total
1662	32.24	30.62	8.93	71.79
1663	40.76	27.77	27.60	96.13
1664	42.93	32.43	9.75	85.11
1665	40.30	31.24	5.88	77.42
1666	29.85	13.97	1.92	45.74
1667	29.19	20.14	5.45	54.78
1668	28.17	37.58	45.29	111.04
1669	27.70	17.37	14.82	59.89
1670	25.88	19.28	8.23	53.39
1671	25.12	23.77	8.75	57.64
1672	21.02	22.48	8.27	51.77
Mean	31.20 (44.9%)	25.15 (36.2%)	13.17 (18.9%)	69.52
Standard deviation	7.13	7.32	12.57	20.82
Coefficient of variability	.229	.291	.954	.299

Sources: See text and the Cole Plantation Account, appendix 1.

of such goods and services, but we can offer an estimate. There are occasional references in other records to the purchase of room, board, and washing by adult males in Maryland during the seventeenth century: these describe an average price of about £4.35 currency per year. If we assume that women and adolescents could purchase room and board for a proportionate part of the price charged, we can, given the composition of the Cole household, estimate the annual value of subsistence production on the plantation (see table 4.2).

The estimates suggest two points worth noting. Most important is the share of total income generated by self-sufficient activities. They accounted for 45 percent of the total, more than twice the share earned through local exchange and nearly 20 percent more than that gained by the sale of tobacco abroad. Second, the income earned through self-sufficient production was much less variable than that earned on the market. Although that stability reflects the method of estimation, it also approximates reality: the substantial degree of self-sufficiency achieved on tobacco plantations helped stabilize the standard of living against sharp fluctuations in the foreign sector and in opportunities for local exchange.[4]

Table 4.3 describes the annual expenditures of the Cole plantation in several categories; these are summarized and compared with market earnings in table 4.4. Expenditures were closely tied to income, and the data carry a clear suggestion of belt-tightening when earnings were low and of greater spending during good years. But the relationship was not perfect, and expenditures show less variation than income. Gardiner was able, either by drawing on earnings or by purchasing on credit, to run in the red for a year or two when necessary, to smooth out the effects of fluctuations in income, and to ride out bad years without greatly sacrificing standards of consumption. For planters who were less well off, less able to draw on the good years of the past or to borrow on the expectation of better years to come, the impact of depressed tobacco markets or of a poor crop must have been more immediate and painful.[5]

Perhaps the point about the pattern of expenditures on the Cole plantation that deserves the most emphasis is the large share, more than 55 percent, that went to imported goods and services. Cloth, clothing, shoes, and the like, virtually all of English manufacture, were by far the most important items, accounting for more than a third of the total and leading the list in all years but one. Indentured servants also commanded substantial outlays, on average nearly 15 percent of the total. Although the plantation was nearly self-sufficient in provisions, some items not made locally—chiefly spices, liquor, and soap—were purchased regularly. The work force required few tools: axes, hoes, and knives were sufficient for the Chesapeake system of husbandry. Gardiner purchased little in the way of household goods, cooking utensils, tableware, furniture, and the like, perhaps reflecting the peculiar situation of the Cole plantation. The absence of such purchases, doubtless an important item in the budgets of most households of similar wealth, makes the high share of income spent on imports even more striking. The spending pattern of the Cole plantation is clear evidence of the "colonial" structure of the Chesapeake economy and underscores the developmental problems faced by export-led plantation regions that watched much of their earnings flow to the metropolis to purchase essential goods and services.[6]

Table 4.3 Expenditures by Type, Cole Plantation, 1662–1672 (In Pounds Currency, Constant Value)

Year	Clothing	Tailor's Wages	Indentured Servants	Maid's Wages	Provisions	Tools	Cask
1662	13.41	1.89	9.67		1.79	1.03	
1663	13.82	1.44	10.21	3.33	.47	1.31	2.28
1664	12.58	1.69		4.67	.90	1.71	2.10
1665	16.75	.52		4.29	1.72	.13	2.68
1666	7.02	1.58	5.54	2.72	.95		.91
1667	9.99	3.12	7.27		2.42		1.38
1668	14.22	1.17	18.70		1.41		2.72
1669	10.97	.74	9.17		3.16		1.81
1670	16.14	1.54			4.66		.46
1671	12.38	1.21			3.36		.78
1672	11.71	1.14			3.18		.74
Mean	12.64	1.46	5.51	1.36	2.18	.38	1.44
Total	138.99	16.04	60.57	15.01	24.02[a]	4.18	15.86

Year	Rent	Taxes	Building Repairs	Medical & Education	Misc. Local Goods & Servs.	Misc. Import Goods & Servs.	Unidentified	Total
1662		.90		.05	2.75	3.34	11.20	46.03
1663	2.42	1.59	1.88	1.40	6.00	.39	4.30	50.84
1664		1.87		.93	12.17	.27		38.89
1665		2.00	4.94	5.19	.77	.24		39.23
1666		1.59		3.81	.16	.50		19.04
1667		1.41		6.18	4.57	.99		35.71
1668		3.86	1.82	4.54	5.33	.85	.11	43.19
1669	2.04	1.42			2.87	2.79		44.50
1670	2.06	.83	.55	1.83	7.50	2.12		46.86
1671	.64	1.21		.86	1.15	1.80	1.82	25.21
1672	.60	1.14		.82	1.09	1.70	1.72	23.84
Mean	.71	1.60	.84	2.33	4.03	1.36	3.83	57.58
Total	7.76	17.62[b]	9.19	25.61[c]	44.36[d]	14.99	19.15	413.34

Source: Cole Plantation Account, appendix 1.

[a] £8.01 in local provisions and £16.01 in imported provisions.

[b] £12.76 in taxes paid the government and £4.86 in donations to the church.

[c] £3.09 in medical expenses and £22.52 for education.

[d] Includes £16.84 in administration expenses.

Table 4.4 Summary of Income and Expenditure, Cole Plantation, 1662–1672
(In Pounds Currency, Constant Value)

Year	Income	Expenditures	Balance
1662	39.55	46.03	−6.48
1663	55.37	50.84	4.53
1664	42.18	38.89	3.29
1665	37.12	39.23	−2.11
1666	15.89	19.04	−3.15
1667	25.59	35.71	−10.12
1668	82.87	43.19	39.68
1669	32.19	44.50	−12.31
1670	27.51	46.86	−19.35
1671	32.52	25.21	7.31
1672	30.75	23.84	6.91
Mean	38.32	37.58	.74
Standard deviation	17.90	10.03	
Coefficient of variability	.467	.267	

Source: Cole Plantation Account, appendix 1.

Although the spending patterns of the Cole plantation support the traditional picture of the Chesapeake economy as one that laid out most of its income on imports, they also suggest that the domestic sector was more important than is usually allowed. Roughly 40 percent of the expenditures went to purchase locally produced goods and services. Wages—to the tailor for making and mending clothes, to the cooper for tobacco cask, to the maid for keeping house and caring for the younger children, to the carpenter for construction and repairs—were the principal expense, accounting for about 14 percent of the total and 35 percent of the portion spent locally. Gardiner paid a few medical bills and bought an occasional barrel of corn when the plantation's supply fell short. He also paid for the education and apprenticeship of the several children. This was an unusual expense for that time and place, but one consistent with Robert Cole's request that his sons be taught "to write and read and Cast accompt" and his daughters "to read and sewe with theire needle." Rent and taxes consumed little income: the Cole estate reminds one of Adam

Table 4.5 Net Income, Cole Plantation, 1662–1672
(In Pounds Currency, Constant Value)

Year	Market Income	Work Force and Plantation Expenses	Net Market Income	Net Subsistence	Total Net
1662	39.55	25.31	14.24	14.92	29.16
1663	55.37	37.42	17.95	15.92	33.87
1664	42.18	32.59	9.59	15.92	25.51
1665	37.12	25.98	11.14	15.16	26.30
1666	15.89	10.41	5.48	13.62	19.10
1667	25.59	18.36	7.23	12.88	20.11
1668	82.87	33.61	49.26	9.79	59.05
1669	32.19	38.76	−6.57	10.73	4.16
1670	27.51	31.87	−4.36	7.82	3.46
1671	32.52	18.26	14.26	4.89	19.15
1672	30.75	19.67	11.08	0.00	11.08
Mean	38.32	26.56	11.76	11.06	22.81

Source: Cole Plantation Account, appendix 1.

Note: Market Income is Export Earnings plus Local Earnings from table 4.2. Net Market Income is Market Income minus Work Force and Plantation Expenses. In most cases the account makes clear which expenditures are for other purposes, but some entries simply record purchases for food, cloth, or services without specifying for whom these items were needed. We allocated such expenditures to the work force according to the ratio of servants to total residents of the household as shown in appendix 2. Note that expenditures shown in tables 4.3 and 4.4 are for the whole household, hence the difference between total expenditures shown there and the expenses shown in this table. Net Subsistence is Estimated Value of Subsistence Production, shown in table 4.2, minus the estimated value of subsistence production for adults and servants age 12–15. Total Net is Net Market Income plus Net Subsistence.

Smith's colonial farmer who had "no rent, and scarce any taxes to pay," and therefore had "every motive to render as great as possible a produce which is thus to be almost entirely his own."[7]

The accounts are detailed enough to permit an estimate of the share of expenditures devoted to maintaining the work force and the plantation. These can be subtracted from gross earnings to yield a net figure for market income (see table 4.5). The Cole plantation showed an average an-

Table 4.6 Value of Cole Plantation, 1662 and 1673
(In Pounds Currency, Constant Value)

Category	1662	1673
Labor	27.14	15.70
Livestock	56.79	217.07
Other capital	6.50	.28
Consumer goods	63.48	11.71
Total movables	153.91	244.76
Home plantation	54.29	72.38
Other land		41.42
Total land	54.29	113.80
Total estate value	208.20	358.56

Source: Cole Plantation Account, appendix 1; see also chapter 1, note 76, and chapter 4, note 8.

nual net income from market transactions of £11.76 over the eleven years that the accounts were kept. Though this seems a meager return on an investment worth roughly £200, the figure does not include food, shelter, and fuel consumed by the children; if these are added, the total rises to £2.81. Nor does it include increases in the livestock herd or improvements to the plantation, gains that Gardiner chose to save rather than spend on current consumption. His prudence paid off, and the estate increased markedly in value over the period.

Just how substantially its value increased is revealed by the inventory of the plantation that Gardiner took in 1673 (see table 4.6). Movables on the estate were then worth £245, a gain of more than £90 since 1662. All the growth was accounted for by livestock, which had increased nearly fourfold, despite the distributions to Francis, Robert, and Mary; were those cattle and their offspring included, the gain would be closer to fivefold. Every other category of movables—labor, miscellaneous capital, and consumer goods—fell in value over the period. The value of the land and its improvements had also increased, from £54 to £72. And Gardiner had surveyed and patented 525 acres for the three Cole sons, using the land warrants left by their father. These lands, as yet unimproved, were worth about £43. All told, the Cole estate had grown to nearly £360 under Gardiner's management, up sharply from just under £210 in 1662. The annual rate of increase was nearly 5 percent, an impressive performance by any standard. If the livestock already distributed is included, with a reasonable allowance for its increase, the estate was worth more than £400, and the annual rate of growth was more than 6 percent.[8]

How representative was this handsome performance? Perhaps the earnings were somewhat below average. For one thing, the plantation was without the labor of its owner, which meant not only that management had to be paid for (Gardiner collected fees for administering the estate) but also that the person with the most powerful incentives for hard work, saving, and investment was absent. For another, administrators' incentives differed from those of owners. If Gardiner substantially increased the estate, he would reap only slight benefits; if he let its value diminish, he could pay dearly. Hence an administrator was more likely to avoid risk than would an owner; an administrator would sacrifice income and growth for security and stability. There is a suggestion of such behavior in Gardiner's choices: he invested in livestock rather than labor. The strategy paid off, but one wonders if the Cole estate would have done even better had Gardiner sold off some cattle or horses to purchase workers. Even though four hands were the maximum that could safely be used on Robert Cole's original plantation, additional hands could have been set to improving the land that Gardiner had purchased for Cole's sons. On the other hand, the plantation may have been fortunate, its returns higher than average. No servant died; the livestock, especially the horses, grew rapidly; the boys made growing contributions as they aged and gained strength; no new dependents were added to the household; and the family lived simply, perhaps more simply than would have been true had Robert and Rebecca not died. Perhaps these considerations balanced each other, and Gardiner's performance was typical.

There is evidence to suggest that this was the case, that many plantations did about as well as the Cole estate. Although there are assertions that this was an era of prolonged depression in the Chesapeake region,[9] several measures indicate that a rapid accumulation of wealth was a central characteristic of the southern Maryland economy during the third quarter of the seventeenth century. Real wealth per capita, for example, grew at roughly 2.7 percent per year from the 1650s to the 1680s on Maryland's lower Western Shore. Mean inventory values among probated decedents increased at even higher rates, and the average worth of decedent householders grew faster still. Further, there is evidence that this was not merely a local phenomenon, peculiar to southern Maryland. Rapid increases in wealth per capita in regions of recent settlement, with rates of growth that seem high even by modern standards and that are truly spectacular for preindustrial societies, were perhaps a regular feature of the colonial economy and of frontier societies generally.[10]

The Cole account sheds light on the sources of this rapid growth. Exports were not the dynamic force in the growth of the Cole plantation: income from tobacco actually fell slightly over the period 1662–73. Nor did the domestic market prove a source of growth: earnings from local exchange, like income from the export sector, did not increase during the years covered by the account. Our estimates of subsistence income per capita suggest a similar conclusion: the value of goods and services produced and consumed on the Cole estate did not grow after 1662. That, of course, is an artifact of our method, and the conclusion may require some qualification. Perhaps, for example, meat consumption increased with the growth of livestock herds. More generally, it is likely that subsistence production was a major source of growth early in the history of the region and early in the life of particular plantations. That is, there were real gains to the economy as a whole as the colony became self-sufficient in food and real gains to families as they became able to supply their needs internally. But there were limits to subsistence production as a source of growth, and those limits were quickly reached. Over the first decade or so of a farm's existence, a planter might see his real income grow as he cleared and fenced his land, cultivated an orchard, and raised herds of cattle, horses, and swine. But once those things were accomplished and the needs of the family met, the absence of lively markets for food meant that there would be little opportunity or incentive for further growth. We suspect that the Cole plantation had reached this stage by the time the account begins.

Why, then, did wealth increase? The Cole account suggests that most of the gains could be captured under the heading of "farm building" or "pioneering," which was "a process of capital making."[11] New settlements in British North America were initially characterized by low levels of wealth, but the process of constructing a working farm provided substantial opportunities for saving, investment, and accumulation. Consequently, wealth grew rapidly in the decades following settlement as planters cleared land, erected buildings and fences, built up livestock herds, planted orchards, began vegetable gardens, improved their homes, and the like. The Cole account suggests that this period was marked by a high ratio of savings and investment to income: we estimate that Gardiner saved 35 to 40 percent of the plantation's earnings.[12] Clearly, a substantial part of the income generated by the estate was reinvested, plowed back into the plantation, in large part in the form of unsold increase in live-stock and in the improvement and purchase of land. The rapid increase of wealth in the region indicates that other planters saved at similar rates.

Such high savings rates were not achieved primarily by limiting current consumption, although that was part of the process. A family might, for example, eat little meat until herds were large enough that harvesting could satisfy needs, or it might forego the purchase of furniture to acquire an additional servant. But an additional acre could be cleared, an orchard planted, a field fenced, or more animals tended without significant cash outlays. And the opportunity costs of such activities were low. Tobacco was a demanding, labor-intensive crop, but it left time for other activities without diminishing output and sacrificing export earnings. Farm building was not costless, but much of what was given up was leisure time. And insofar as this was a society of unfree labor, it was often someone else's time that the householder spent.[13]

The Cole account also suggests that this growth process could not continue indefinitely, for the income generated by the plantation did not keep pace with the growth in the value of the estate. The wealth-income ratio rose by roughly 80 percent over the period covered by the account: in the early 1660s, the estate generated £1 in income for each £2.4 in wealth; by the early 1670s, £4.3 of wealth produced £1 in annual income. The rising ratio of wealth to income defines the limits to growth in the early stages of settlement, limits the Cole plantation was fast approaching. In the absence of dependable markets for any crop but tobacco, diminishing returns quickly lowered the incentives to further farm-building activities. Once enough land had been cleared and fenced to meet the household's need for food, once livestock herds had become large enough to satisfy meat and dairy requirements, once the plantation had a fruit-bearing orchard and a comfortable house, there was little else most farmers could do to improve family welfare. We know little of the experience of the Cole plantation after 1672, but in St. Mary's County as a whole the early growth spurt ended in the 1670s. From then until the late 1740s, when world food shortages created new opportunities and the terms of

trade shifted in favor of primary producers, wealth levels, however measured, showed no tendency to rise.[14]

Why, we might ask, did Gardiner tolerate the rising wealth-to-income
ratio on the Cole plantation? Why did he not increase the work force, put
more land into production, and continue to capture the benefits of farm
building? Possibly, as we have suggested, it was his administrative role, a
position that encouraged caution and the conservation of the estate rather
than a more aggressive—and riskier—effort to grow. But the stagnation
of wealth levels in the region after the initial spurt of farm building suggests a more general constraint on plantation size and the expansion process. The characteristics of the new system of husbandry elaborated in
the Chesapeake colonies during the seventeenth century suggest some
such constraints; their interaction may have persuaded Gardiner that further growth was too risky for the potential gains.

The new system of husbandry offered few returns to scale. Most of the
operations required to produce tobacco and corn could be done by a few
workers as efficiently as by many. Small planters were not, therefore,
compelled to expand or else go under, and they could not expect their
rates of profit to grow if they added extra workers. Further, given the
substantial acreage per worker needed if planters were to maintain the
necessary rotations, adding labor required adding land. On this land often
distant from the home plantation, operations could not be closely supervised by the planter himself. In short, expansion much beyond the size
already reached by the Cole plantation when Gardiner took control required a plunge. The planter had to purchase several workers, hire an
overseer, and open a new farm, called a "quarter" in contemporary usage. Such an investment required capital reserves or a willingness to risk
all in a mortgage. Most lacked the resources or the nerve. Some men took
that plunge—in growing numbers as the colonial period progressed—
adding workers, developing quarters, building great estates, and contrib-
uting to a major transformation of Chesapeake society through their efforts. For most, however, the Cole plantation defined the limits of the
possible.[15]

The Standard of Life

So far we have approached the Cole account through the abstractions of
economics and bookkeeping. The documents also have a concrete social

dimension, one that enters the household and illuminates the material aspects of daily life. What standard of living did the Cole plantation support? What kind of house did the family occupy, and how well did household members eat? Did the Cole life-style resemble that of their neighbors of similar degree? Were there significant differences between them and those poorer or richer? And how did living conditions compare with those of similar social groups in England or in other English colonies?

Robert Cole's house was surely inferior to his childhood home in England. It was undoubtedly an impermanent framed structure, like those built everywhere in the seventeenth-century Chesapeake. Contracts in the records suggest that few dwellings were more than thirty to thirty-three feet by sixteen to twenty feet; most were smaller. Archaeological excavations in Maryland and Virginia show them to have been post-in-the-ground buildings, which decayed in fifteen to twenty years, requiring extensive repairs at the foundations if the dwellings were not abandoned. Nevertheless, there were advantages to this construction. It was fast and took less labor than did construction on brick or stone foundations. Recent excavations show that even Leonard Calvert, Maryland's first governor, chose this shortcut when he built his house at St. Mary's City. Such building practice was a live tradition in parts of seventeenth-century England, but more permanent construction was far more common. Neither in England nor in the Chesapeake do many such earthfast—or at one time earthfast—seventeenth-century structures survive today.[16]

Cole's house doubtless had other impermanent features. Seventeenth-century contracts tell of rived clapboard siding and roofs. Shingle roofs do not appear until late in the century and thatch not at all on dwelling houses, despite its waterproof qualities. These clapboard houses let in wind and rain, leading travelers to complain of the drafts and waterfalls they endured when they accepted hospitality in a poorly covered house. When roofs regularly leaked, rot started at the top of a house as soon as, or sooner than, at the bottom. Tar could seal clapboard, but the amount of tar required to truly seal a clapboard-roofed house created a major fire hazard.[17] Fire was an ever present danger and another cause of impermanence.

Cole's inventory indicates that the house was a two-room structure with lofts above. There was only one hearth, which must have been in what Cole termed the "hall." This was the main room of the house, the place for cooking, eating, and sitting and for sleeping, at least for some. The

4.1 Reconstruction of a Prosperous Planter's Dwelling House, Godiah Spray Plantation, Historic St. Mary's City. The prototype for this reconstruction is the earliest section of "Cedar Park," covered over by later additions but still standing in Anne Arundel County. When selected, "Cedar Park" was believed to date from the 1670s, but tree-ring analysis now places it about 1704. Note the clapboard siding and roofing, similar to that of the tobacco house in illustration 3.2; the glazed window at the far end of the house, which lights the "hall"; and the shuttered window at the near end, which lights the "kitchen." Mrs. Spray and her servant woman grind corn and heat water for washing in the work yard at the door. The paling fence beyond the shrubs surrounds the kitchen garden. (Paul Leibe, Historic St. Mary's City)

other room was the "kitchen," where dairying and most food preparation except cooking took place. There was no fire here. The chimney was probably between the two rooms, helping to create a partition. It may have had a brick base and firebox, but above, the chimney most probably was wattle and daub, another invitation to destruction by fire.

Westerners today would judge these to be crowded quarters for a large household. Before Robert and Rebecca died, they doubtless slept in the hall, probably with the three youngest children. The others slept in the loft over the hall. The servants must have had bedding in the other loft and on the kitchen floor. If he had lived, Cole likely soon would have added a room to his house. Room-by-room inventories of other planters at Cole's level of wealth sometimes show such additions, although there were usually still beds in every room.

Such impermanent and crowded multiple-purpose quarters were characteristic of all social groups. Poor planters often lived in one-room houses, although smaller families—with fewer children and fewer or no servants—meant that living spaces may have been less crowded than Cole's. The very rich sometimes expanded by building a new house, although one still impermanent and small. The old house then became a separate kitchen and/or housing for servants or slaves. With such arrangements, the separation of the planter family from the servants might be greater than in the Cole household, but the rooms still served several purposes. The hall or the parlor—as the second room was often called if it was not a kitchen—might be free of beds, but tools or bales of merchandise or other equipment shared space with furniture for sitting or dining. For example, the 1671 inventory of Cole's neighbor, the merchant Robert Slye, shows a parlor without furniture for sleeping in both his old and his "new" house, but stored in the old parlor were a variety of weapons, an axe, and cases of hats; stacked in the new one were the remains of a ship cargo. A room reserved solely for social intercourse, as seen in the more spacious house described in the inventory of Slye's son Gerard in 1704, does not appear.[18]

That poor planters would live in small impermanent dwellings need not surprise us, but why were men of wealth willing to do so? Even those who, like Slye, arrived with wealth had come in order to make fortunes in tobacco, and such fortunes were not made overnight. Men put their capital into the labor needed to raise the crop and to build the farm, not to construct a mansion. As late as the 1680s, William Fitzhugh, a prominent Virginia planter, warned an English correspondent heading for the colony not to count on building "a great English framed house, for labor is so intolerably dear . . . that the building of a good house to you there will seem insupportable."[19] Once the planter had gained the fortune, he could construct a better house, but by that time he was about to die. He did not have time to rebuild.

The contrast with New England is striking. There more than two hundred houses that were built in the seventeenth century still stand, whereas in Maryland, architectural historians have so far surely identified only one, and it was constructed in 1698![20] There are doubtless many reasons for this difference, but two are especially important. Immigrants to New England mostly came in family groups and started with more resources than did indentured servants in the Chesapeake. Equally significant, New Englanders occupied a healthier environment and hence well outlived inhabitants of Maryland and Virginia. In both regions, men built short-lived houses at first. But New Englanders had more time to build and enjoy permanent dwellings. In the Chesapeake, it fell to the native born, such as Gerard Slye, who began with a major inheritance and had a longer life span than had his immigrant father, to build bigger and better houses.

In the spaciousness and permanence of his shelter, Cole did not stand out, even though in accumulated wealth he was richer than most other planters. Nevertheless, there were ways in which his house may have been more comfortable than those of poorer men. The floor of his hall was probably planked and the walls plastered; perhaps he even had glass casements in the hall windows, allowing light when cold weather would otherwise have required closed shutters and darkness. Still the kitchen may have more resembled a room in a poor man's house, with dirt floors and shuttered windows and less protection from the wind that blew through the clapboards.

From all that travelers' accounts and room-by-room inventories tell us of seventeenth-century Chesapeake dwellings, their size and construction provided little clue to the status of their inhabitants. A Robert Slye might live in two houses, but both were basically two-room affairs with chambers above. A Robert Cole, well below Slye in wealth but better off than most others, had lofts, not finished rooms, over his hall and kitchen. A recent study of the vale of Berkeley, near Bristol in England, finds that houses there, even those of the poor, had more rooms than had most Chesapeake dwellings. In 1678, Charles Calvert, the third Lord Baltimore, described all houses on the St. Mary's Town Lands, including those of the colony's leaders, as being "very meane and Little and Genrally after the manner of the meanest farm houses in England."[21]

Shelter, then, in Maryland and Virginia was inferior to that available in England; but food was another matter. After the very earliest days in Virginia, food ceased to be a problem. There was no "starving time" in early Maryland, whereas famine in parts of England was still a threat until the middle of the seventeenth century.[22]

Food clearly was plentiful in the Cole household. Dried Indian corn, of course, was basic to the seventeenth-century diet. By the 1660s, there was little danger of serious shortages, although as late as the 1680s the proprietor or his governors issued proclamations to forbid temporarily any export of corn from the province when a poor crop meant the supply would be low. Corn was eaten as bread or was boiled to make hominy or porridge, and if mixed with peas or beans, it supplied adequate nutrition.[23]

Meat was also a basic element in the Cole household diet. Planters customarily used male cattle for meat, sometimes killing them young, sometimes waiting until they beefed. Cows were slaughtered once they were permanently barren, and hogs were killed when full-grown. There was no point in keeping animals beyond their period of usefulness, and in consequence there were regular slaughters. Nearly every year Cole's livestock could supply two hundred pounds of usable meat and soup bone for each adult male in the household, including servants, and proportionate amounts for women and children, even given the sales shown in the account.[24] This is an adequate meat allowance by any standard.

The household also had ample supplies of food from wild animals. In Maryland and Virginia trash pits, archaeologists have found the bones of deer, squirrels, rabbits, muskrats, turkeys, geese, ducks, and various sorts of fish such as drum and sheepshead. There is also evidence of turtles, oysters, and crabs. Before 1650, as much as 40 percent of the meat diet at several sites consisted of such wild fare. Thereafter, domestic animals began to dominate more heavily, but in the 1660s there was doubtless still considerable reliance on hunting and fishing.[25] Cole had several guns—including a fowling piece—lots of ammunition, and fishing lines and hooks in his inventory. When supplies of beef and bacon were low, William and Edward could be sent to fish, or Francis or Robert might shoot a deer or a goose. Gardiner once paid an Indian to hunt.

A variety of other foods supplemented corn and meat. Milk, uncured cheese, and some butter were available, although it is unlikely that so much time was given to dairying that cows were kept in milk year-round. That would have required carefully weaning the calves as early as possible—say, in two to three months—in order to milk the cows completely. In addition, a cow keeper would have been necessary to prevent the cows from straying far from the pen in search of food. Probably the milk and cheese were most available in spring and fall, the periods when cows were most likely to calve if breeding was not monitored. Poultry and eggs were also on hand (Francis Knott built a chicken house in 1670), and fruits and vegetables were on the table in season. In spring and early summer, wild strawberries and raspberries were to be had for the picking, and in later summer and fall, apples, peaches, and perhaps pears were available in the orchard. From spring through fall, wild purslanes and other greens could be picked for "sallets." Peas, beans, roasting ears of corn, and whatever cabbages, lettuce, cucumbers, squashes, melons, and root crops grew in the kitchen garden were also seasonally available. Cabbages and root crops, furthermore, could be stored for winter in a root cellar under the hearth. Sweet potatoes, indigenous to the New World, were especially nutritious. Nevertheless, by spring, the vegetable diet must have been much less varied. One can imagine the delight of the first fresh greens or wild strawberries or fresh green peas.[26]

The Coles probably resembled nearly all Maryland families in frequently eating essentially one-pot meals based on corn. Once the corn had been beaten, it was sifted to eliminate the shell and to separate the finer from the coarser grains. The coarse grains were boiled until they became a soft mush called hominy. The cook could add a variety of foods to this as it stewed—salt pork or beef (first soaked to desalt it), milk or cream, beans or peas. It took perhaps eight hours for the corn to soften enough to be edible, but it could then continue to simmer indefinitely in the pot, ready for hungry field hands. The finer cornmeal, mixed with water or milk, was baked in the coals to make corn bread. This bread could be dipped in the hominy or served with butter.[27]

Drink for the family, besides milk, was apple cider, peach "mobby," perhaps perry (from pears), a little beer, and spring water when all else failed.[28] How good the cider or mobby was and how long it could keep are questionable. English experts asserted that, properly bottled or casked and kept in a cool place, these fruit products could keep for at least a year. However, in 1672, the proprietor's son, Governor Charles Calvert, wrote to his father: "I am afraid itt will bee a very hard Matter to find such Casque here as shall preserve Syder good to England, for wee want good Coopers and such as are knoweinge in the Seasonings of Casque for such purposes. The Chancellors Cider is pretty good But I am of the opinion the best Syder in the Country will doe us noe Creditt in England." Cider, mobby, and perry evidently had to be consumed when ready.[29] Such drinks were probably available only from July through December, or perhaps January, given that cool weather enabled them to keep longer.

In the Cole household, servants and family probably ate the same fare unless there were temporary shortages of meat or fruits or vegetables. The house was small, and everyone must have eaten together. The family would not have wasted food, and the market for selling it was limited. When a beef was slaughtered, there was plenty for everyone, and the Coles' large livestock herds guaranteed regular supplies. Nor was cider left to spoil rather than passed to all. Perhaps under Gardiner's regime the Cole children were fed the best cuts of meat, and they surely were the last to be rationed when supplies were low, but in this household, food shortages cannot often have been a problem.

How typical was the diet of the Cole household? In most respects the very wealthy did not eat much differently, except that they consumed Malaga wines and other imported liquors in which Cole did not indulge, although he inventoried two and one-half gallons of rum. Some also grew a little wheat, which could give them wheat bread or a pie crust. On the other hand, servants in such households usually lived separately and were less likely than were Cole's servants to share the family's food. In households poorer than Cole's, the family (and servants when there were any) doubtless ate less varied fare. There was less labor available to put into raising food beyond corn and livestock, and livestock herds were smaller. Nevertheless, with any luck, the purchase of a sow would give a family the Cole's ration of meat within five years (see appendix 3 and tables A3.10 and A3.11). Furthermore, fish and small animal resources were available to all. The trash pits so far excavated indicate that colonists of all social levels quickly learned to fish and trap.

After the earliest days of settlement, most white Chesapeake colonists, whether free or servant, probably ate better than their counterparts did in England. Changes occurred in the colonists' diet as the seventeenth century progressed—wild foods became less and less important, and after 1700, domestic animals supplied nearly all the meat—but food supplies remained more than adequate for all the white population. By the time of the American Revolution, American soldiers were taller than were the British, French, or Germans. This is surely the result of a long-run improvement in the diet of the Europeans who settled in America.[30]

Social differences in the Chesapeake were not much evident in nutrition but were more visible in household furnishings and the daily routines the furnishings denote. Here Cole, at his death, stood out from his poorer neighbors, just as the very rich, in turn, stood well out from him. The inventory he himself took before he left for England allows us to compare him with others, both rich and poor, who died and left inventories at about the same time.

Inventories remain for forty-three people who died in St. Mary's County between 1658 and 1665.[31] Twenty-seven of these people owned land, and thirty-two were household heads. Two estates were those of rich men, representatives of an emerging "cosmopolitan gentry." John Bateman was a merchant worth about £950; Henry Sewell, a new immigrant, was Secretary of the Province and a member of His Lordship's Council and had an estate of about £700. Next in value was an estate worth nearly £400, followed by two valued at about £300 and one at about £210. All these planters exceeded Cole in wealth. The next three below Cole had estates that ranged from £150 to £190. These eight, including Cole, might be called prosperous planters, and four, among them the least wealthy, had offices or owned land enough to qualify as gentry. From George Mee, number 11 (with an estate valued at £125), we enter the ranks of the less well-to-do. Since Mee, a former burgess always addressed as "Mr.," was a member of the gentry, his wealth placement dramatizes the ill-defined character of this group. From Mee on down, the gaps between estates become much narrower, although there is necessarily another jump at the point where landholding ceases. Only two landowners were worth less than £50, and with one exception, no nonlandowner was worth more than £22. Of the very poorest decedents, the ten worth less than £10, only two had their own households.

A study of these inventories produced a surprise: the value of Cole's consumer goods. His household furnishings, cloth for clothing his family, and so on were valued at £63.48. Although seventh in overall value of estate, Cole was third in the value of consumer goods, with four and one-half times the mean of all estates (£14) and three and one-third times the mean of landowning householders (£19). However, table 4.7 shows that this overall picture is misleading.

The table compares Cole's wealth, in various categories, with that of eight others in the top ten[32] (the cosmopolitan gentry and the prosperous planters, the top 23 percent in the inventoried group) and with that of seven poorer planters who had consumer assets between £7.00 and £8.99.[33] The problem lies in the category "other" in Cole's estate, which

Table 4.7 Mean Values of Selected Household Furnishings Compared with
Other Components of Wealth: Robert Cole and Selected Contemporaries
(In Pounds Currency, Constant Value)

Group	Total Estate Mean Value[a]	Movables Mean Value	Sleep, Sit, Food Prep., & Dine Mean Value	Other Noncapital Mean Value	Total Noncapital Mean Value
Top 2	854.95	423.79	69.92	23.01	92.93
Next 3	314.15	193.71	18.90	9.39	28.29
Cole	208.20	153.91	18.39	45.09	63.48
Next 3	168.97	87.23	9.22	8.96	18.18
Modal 7	75.76	46.19	4.81	3.29	8.10

Sources: Cole Plantation Account, appendix 1; St. Mary's County inventories,
1658–65, scattered through Testamentary Proceedings, vols. 1–5, Maryland
State Archives, Annapolis, Md.; Career File of Seventeenth-Century St. Mary's
County Residents, St. Mary's City Commission, Maryland State Archives.
 [a]Includes value of land (see chapter 1, note 76).

shows £45.09. This includes many items that ordinarily do not appear in
inventories taken after death. Provisions are mostly missing from the
other estates, since the administrator was allowed to feed the family for a
year from what the farm could produce. Cole had £13.51 in such supplies; no one else had more than £1.00. Whether cloth would appear in
an inventory usually depended on how recently the crop had been sold to
a factor or shipmaster in return for imported goods. Once the cloth was
clothing, it would not be inventoried except for the decedent's apparel,
and often not then. Cole had £5.41 in cloth and £7.12 in his deceased
wife's clothing. In addition, goods he was taking to England—probably
apparel and a little bedding—he valued at £8.89. Cloth and clothing
came to £21.42, nearly twice the maximum value of such items in any
other estate in table 4.7 and more than ten times their value in all but
three. The reasons for these exceptional items are clear enough: Cole's
intention to leave his family equipped for eight months—the length of
time he expected to be absent—and his care to list all the supplies on
hand.[34]

When this difference is removed from consideration, Cole's inventory
shows that he lived much as did other men of his general wealth-level
and place in society. Table 4.8 compares the groups of table 4.7 as to

Table 4.8 Mean Values and Quantities of Selected Household Furnishings: Robert Cole and Selected Contemporaries (In Pounds Currency, Constant Value)

| | Household Size | | | All Accommodations | | Sleeping | | | |
	Family (N)	Servants (N)	All (N)	Value	(N)	Beds (N)	Bedsteads (N)	Accommodations per person (N)	Accommodations per person Value
Top 2	4.50	15.00	19.50	27.17	14.50	6.50	3.00	.74	1.39
Next 3	4.67	5.67	10.33	11.08	10.33	4.67	3.00	1.00	1.07
Cole	8.00	4.00	12.00	8.86	12.00	4.00	0.00	1.00	.74
Next 3	2.67	1.67	4.33	3.86	4.67	2.67	1.33	1.08	.89
Modal 7	3.57	.14	3.71	2.60	4.14	1.71	.86	1.12	.70

Sitting, Food Preparation, and Dining

Group	Household Size			Tables & Seats Value	Chairs (N)	All Seats (N)	Food Prep Value	Dining Value	Plate Value	Total Value	Per Family Member Value
	Family (N)	Servants (N)	All (N)								
Top 2	4.50	15.00	19.50	7.68	20.00	25.50	13.20	9.16	12.71	42.75	9.50
Next 3	4.67	5.67	10.33	.90	2.00	14.00	3.57	2.08	1.27	7.82	1.67
Cole	8.00	4.00	12.00	1.74	5.00	12.00	4.65	5.16	0.00	9.53	1.19
Next 3	2.67	1.67	4.33	.81	2.00	7.33	3.30	1.03	.22	5.36	2.00
Modal 7	3.57	.14	3.71	.55	2.29	5.29	1.05	.55	.06	2.21	.62

Source: See table 4.7.

Note: Sleeping accommodations include couches and hammocks, each assumed to sleep one, plus beds, each assumed to sleep two, unless the head of the house is unmarried, in which case one bed is counted as one. Blacks have not been counted in the household on the assumption that they did not share in the use of most house furnishings. If blacks are added in, the mean numbers of servants in the top group is 17.00, and in the second group 6.33, and mean totals are 21.50 and 11.00 respectively. Seats include couches (valued under beds only), assumed to seat three; forms, assumed to seat two; and chairs, assumed to seat one. All utensils for cooking, dairying, and curing meat are included under food preparation.

accommodations for sleeping, sitting, food preparation, and dining. Bate-man and Sewell outshine all others in furnishings for social intercourse: chairs, tables, and cooking and dining equipment, including silver plate in spoons, tankards, dram cups, and the like. There can be no question of Cole's inferior status compared with a truly great planter or merchant. He clearly fits into a category below the cosmopolitan gentry, represented by the prosperous planters. His investment in sitting and dining, although somewhat greater than others in his group, was smaller on a per-family-member basis, since his family was exceptionally large for the time. But the value of such furnishings per family member was twice as high for Cole as it was for those selected from the less well-to-do planters.

There was slightly less difference among social groups in accommodations for sleeping, in part because, as inventories tell us, a good bed was the first comfort a planter acquired as he moved up the economic ladder.[35] Here a puzzling aberration appears in the Cole household. A good bed was a ticking filled with feathers, raised off the ground on a bedstead and curtained for warmth and privacy. But Cole listed no bedsteads or curtains, and given the detail of his inventory, we can be certain that he had none. Robert and Rebecca slept on a feather mattress and were well supplied with sheets, pillows, and blankets, but the bed evidently had to be rolled into a corner or stacked away in a closet during the day. Doubtless the master and mistress slept in the hall, which was the only room in the house with a hearth but which in daytime was a place full of women and children. There was no room for a bedstead during the hours the hall was a place for work or family gathering. And if the head of the family had to do without, so could the rest of the family, regardless of where they slept.[36]

The Cole estate was the only one of the top nine in these tables to have no bedsteads, but such equipment was missing more often than not in poorer households. Three among the seven poorer planters had none, and in St. Mary's County such furniture was missing among 80 percent of the inventoried estates worth less than £50 in movables—the bottom half of the wealth structure in movables—throughout the seventeenth century. Houses in the Chesapeake were simply too small to make bedsteads convenient, although in England such a comfort was usual even among estates with movables worth less than £10. Surely Cole, had he lived, would soon have expanded his house.[37]

As table 4.8 suggests, chairs were a status item in the seventeenth century. They were single seats, and unlike stools, benches, or couches, they had backs and sometimes arms. Cole had five joined wooden chairs plus a chair table, an exceptional number for his category. These were probably valued relics of his life in England. The chair table (see illustration 4.2) surely functioned as a table during the day, there being otherwise none in the hall, but was folded to create the space-saving chair when the beds were brought out at night. However, Sewell had sixteen chairs and Bateman twenty-four. Indeed, some seventeenth-century inventories of rich men show incredible numbers, especially given the cramped spaces into which the chairs were evidently fitted. In 1679, Thomas Notley, who acted as governor for a few years while Charles Calvert was in England, had seventy-nine chairs stuffed into eight rooms and a passage.[38] By contrast, Forker Frissell, one of the poorer planters, had no seats at all.

Forker Frissell, indeed, represents the minimal household, although in many respects he had had considerable success. In 1659 he had been free long enough to claim the warrant for fifty acres that the proprietor owed him for his service to Robert Cager. That he did not sell the warrant but had accumulated enough to pay for a survey we know from his will. He died a landowner. However, a bed with sheets and blankets—but no bedstead—a hammock, a chest, a pot, a frying pan, and four wooden milk bowls were his only household possessions. There were not only no seats but also no table. The chest may have served as both. He doubtless pounded his corn in a hollowed stump with a stone or the head of his axe, prepared his meals on the ground before the fireplace, and ate from his pot or pan or bowl with shells or with his fingers. Or perhaps a wooden spoon went unnoticed in his estate appraisal or was considered too crude to be salable. He may have drunk from a gourd, since no drinking vessel is listed. The only luxury was his sheets, an item that poor planters usually did without. He had begun to upgrade his life-style with his bedding. Frissell had died unmarried, and the convenience of seats or a table surface did not take priority for a man without a family.[39]

Although few inventoried planters in St. Mary's County were as poorly equipped with furnishings as Forker Frissell, over the second half of the seventeenth century more than half of those with less than £50 of movables had no seats, and two-thirds had no tables. People sat on chests or other containers, dragged in logs, or squatted or sat on the floor. Perhaps they created makeshift work surfaces with logs and a few rived clapboards (sawn planks would surely have been inventoried), but often people must

4.2 A Chair Table in the Hall, Godiah Spray Plantation House, Historic St. Mary's City. The large round back of the chair folds down to make a table. When the back is turned up, there is space to lay out beds on the floor. (Paul Leibe, Historic St. Mary's City)

4.3 Preparations for Dinner in the Hall, Godiah Spray Plantation House, Historic St. Mary's City. The hall contains the only hearth. Note that, although the room is small, the floor of the hall is planked and the walls are plastered and whitewashed. The hearth and fireplace are brick, but above that level the chimney is wood and daub, as shown in illustration 4.1. The furnishings are based on those listed in Robert Cole's inventory (see appendix 1). Here the chair table is folded down to make a table. (Paul Leibe, Historic St. Mary's City)

simply have done without. As with bedsteads, the contrast with the homes they had left behind in England was striking; in the vale of Berkeley, at least, seats and tables were much more usual even among the very poor.[40]

Cole's inventory and Gardiner's account give many details that enable us to envision more explicitly the standard of amenities that the Cole family enjoyed. There were not only wooden and pewter utensils for dining but also a collection of "speckled" earthenware, doubtless saved for special occasions. Earthenware was breakable, and there was not much of it in seventeenth-century Maryland. On the other hand, the Coles had no silver tankards or spoons such as appear in the estates of Bateman and Sewell. Spoons, wooden and pewter, and fingers were the only utensils at Cole's for conveying food to the mouth. Forks to eat with were a new invention still infrequently found in England. Cole's pots for drinking

4.4 Interior (Reconstructed) of a Poor Planter's House, Historic St. Mary's City. This is a one-room house with a loft. Note the dirt floor, unplastered walls, and unglazed windows protected by shutters. The only furnishings beyond what is shown are a chest and a bedticking stuffed with flock. In winter the householder had to choose between shutting out the cold or admitting light through an open window. (Paul Leibe, Historic St. Mary's City)

were not enough to supply the whole household, especially if those of earthenware were not in daily use. The pewter pots passed from hand to hand, as drinking vessels must have in most households. However, the Coles' tablecloths and napkins helped keep house and person clean, a comfort not often shared by the poorer sort in England or in Maryland. Candlesticks and candlewick for interior lighting were another sign of Cole's affluence, although the wick probably burned in tallow. No mention is made of candles.[41]

Missing from Cole's inventory are any chamber pots or closestools. To a modern eye in the Western world such an omission seems extraordinary in the absence of any evidence for the existence of privies in this society. Nevertheless, chamber pots were uncommon at all levels of wealth, except the very richest, both in Maryland and in the vale of Berkeley in England. Among the cosmopolitan gentry and prosperous planters in table 4.7, only four were equipped with this elementary convenience, as were only two among the less well-to-do planters. People evidently went outdoors to relieve themselves, and archaeological evidence suggests that they did not go far. Excavations at St. Mary's City, Maryland, have revealed heavy concentrations of phosphates near the doors of seventeenth-century dwellings. People of the time did not understand the importance to their health of more sanitary behavior, and their noses must have become inured to the smells that were generated. Even when chamber pots were in use, they were emptied close to the door, creating stenches that must have permeated all rooms of the house.[42]

The Coles' clothing was serviceable. Clothes that had probably been Rebecca's included a shift (a long blouse that helped serve as underwear, which women did not wear until the nineteenth century), a penistone petticoat (i.e., a skirt), a pair of "bodies," a serge waistcoat, several aprons, worsted stockings, yarn stockings, three "cross cloths" (worn on the head), and several pairs of shoes. Two handkerchiefs were made of "fine Holland," a quality linen, but Cole's inventory describes nothing else as being of especially fine cloth. Gardiner's expenditures for the children indicate a similar standard: woolen and yarn stockings, "blue linen" for drawers for the boys and for an apron and "Frockes" for little Betty, holland for shirts and neckcloths, serge (a durable wool) for britches and coats. Kersey, canvas, lockram, penistone, osnaburg, and "cotten" were other materials purchased for clothing. The "cotten," which Gardiner described as for "the maide cloths," was not the cotton we know today but was a type of finish for coarse woolens. Kersey and penistone were coarse wools, lockram was a linen, and canvas and osnaburg were very coarse linens. These probably clothed the servants.[43]

Like their houses, planters' clothing did not necessarily give clues to their real social standing. Poor men and women would use the coarser materials in ill-fitting garments and doubtless wore their clothes for longer periods than did their betters. Robert Cole had a greatcoat, a garment poorer men could not afford. But in Robert Slye's store there were no imported silks and velvets or cavalier hats, although he had some silk cut out for a pair of britches. In ordering goods from England, merchants specified "coarse goods, useful for the country," and coarse goods were what appeared on the storekeepers' shelves. Even colony leaders did not always look their role. Complaints in the 1660s that justices of the provincial court could not always be distinguished from more ordinary men led to suggestions that the judges wear medals for identification! No man or woman in Maryland was a person of leisure, nor was there a court or a metropolis to visit and to provide occasions for elaborate dress.[44]

Overall, Cole salvaged more of the basic English standard of household amenities than did most other seventeenth-century immigrants to Maryland. His house was small, but his equipment for sitting, cooking, and dining was ample, despite sleeping arrangements more primitive than what most Englishmen would have tolerated. He had come as a freeman, with assets sufficient to become a landowning planter at once, and the best of his household furnishings he had probably brought with him or sent for later. By contrast, the great majority of seventeenth-century immigrants to Maryland arrived as indentured servants and brought nothing with them but their ability to labor.

Gardiner did not think it necessary to maintain the Cole household at the standard of comfort that Robert had achieved. As furnishings wore out, he did not replace them. When young Robert Cole came of age, the beds, the chair table, and the four chairs remained, but five of the stools, all the earthenware but one butter pot, and much of the pewter had disappeared. No drinking vessels remained, and there were only six spoons instead of eighteen, although these six were enough for the use of the household after Betty's death in 1670. Sufficient sheets for the beds and some table linen were also still on hand, but much of both was gone. So also was much cooking equipment, including the spit for roasting and some pudding pans, and all but one candlestick. The household was left with basic equipment; but once Mary received her father's legacy—the feather bed with sheets, the eighteen-gallon copper, one of the iron pots, and the spice mortar—the boys, who were to divide what was left, would begin with an incomplete supply of furnishings. Gardiner concentrated on livestock and servants that would maintain or improve the capital investment on the plantation. With a sound inheritance of capital, the boys could decide for themselves what standard of amenities each would pursue.

Gardiner also cut back on the household's comfort with the decision to eliminate the servant women after Betty was boarded out in 1667. Dairying, tending poultry, and raising vegetables and medicinal herbs were women's work, and the housekeeper and Isabel Jones had probably also ground the family corn. Once they had departed, it may have been that no one milked the cows, and not only milk but also vegetables, except peas and beans grown in with the corn, may have disappeared from the household diet. (Chicken and eggs evidently remained, since the hen-house was built after the women had gone.) The washing of clothing and linen doubtless was less frequent, and vermin must have been more abundant. Furthermore, Edward and William must have done some or all of the corn grinding, a tiresome and tiring task. Indeed, this job was so unpleasant that ex-servants making contracts to work as freemen sometimes specified that they should not be asked to do it.[45]

On Betty's return to the household in 1669, family life for a brief while became more comfortable. She was only nine, but even so young a girl could take on most household responsibilities, although she must have required help to empty the eighteen-gallon pot used for washing linens or utensils for the dairy. However, with Betty's death the next year, the house remained womanless for the rest of Gardiner's tenure as guardian. Women offered comforts and saved men time that could be spent doing other tasks on the farm, but the purchase of a woman servant or the payment of wages to a free woman clearly did not appear to Gardiner to be a justifiable expense, once there were no small children to tend.

How did servants fare in the Cole household? We can make some inferences from Cole's inventory and Gardiner's accounts, as well as from the information available about working conditions for servants in general. The servants obviously shared the family's food and shelter but slept in the less finished, colder sections of the house. Still, so also did some of the children. Gardiner regularly purchased suits, hats, and shoes to clothe

the servants, although the materials used were cheaper than those he purchased for the children. He also paid for medical care as necessary. When a servant's time was up, Gardiner provided him or her with the new clothes the law required, and nothing suggests that the departing servants did not also receive the year's supply of corn and (for men) the axe and hoe that were also part of freedom dues.

Work routines for family and servants must have been very similar, both before and after the deaths of Robert and Rebecca. The working day ran from sunrise to sunset, with a break for dinner in the early afternoon. On hot summer days the break could be longer. By custom, servants may have had Saturday afternoon off, a practice transferred from England. By law, no one did field work on Sundays, except in emergencies, although women must have carried on necessary household tasks and men or boys must have carried wood and water. Very wealthy planters like Bateman or Sewell had overseers—usually freed servants—to monitor their laborers, and these planters confined their participation in farm work to general supervision. But in the great majority of households, including Cole's, everyone shared the labor.[46]

If servants were ill-used—if their masters provided insufficient food, clothing, shelter, or medical care or beat them too severely—Maryland and Virginia law allowed servants to complain to the county court. The courts ordered masters to mend their ways if their treatment of servants violated customary standards. For example, if a servant showed signs of scurvy, the justices ordered his master to provide more meat; if a servant had clothing insufficient to protect him from cold weather, they insisted on warmer cladding. They even freed servants whose masters had been exceptionally brutal. In theory, at least, masters were forbidden to discipline their servants for petitioning, but the court itself might order a servant whipped for a frivolous complaint.[47]

Indentured servants, indeed, had given up some freedom possessed by servants in England. In England, servants in husbandry contracted for work by the year, and their labor was not usually bought or sold without their consent. But the Chesapeake servant owed for transportation across an ocean. His labor was the property of another for a four- or five-year term and was salable, like any other form of property. Furthermore, penalties for running away or for costing a master time by bearing a child were severe and could lead to months or years of additional service. There was probably also greater tolerance in the Chesapeake than in England for abuse of servants, especially those too sick or too unhappy to work diligently. Planter judges had heavy investments in their servants and could sympathize with masters whose bound laborers could not or would not work.[48]

The record suggests that Cole's servants were properly housed, clothed, and fed, and immoderate correction seems unlikely in those circumstances. However, two servants did run away, and Gardiner decided to sell one of them. Francis Knott on the first occasion and young Robert on the second may have been in charge, and the two lacked experience in disciplining the work force. Whether any of the servants petitioned the St. Mary's County Court we cannot know, since these records do not survive. If Gardiner did have to attend court to answer a complaint, the account would not show it. No court fees were charged to either servants or masters in such cases.[49]

On the whole, the Cole plantation shows the seventeenth-century Chesapeake labor system at its best, both in productivity and in working conditions. How exceptional the plantation may have been is another question. Certainly not every planter had servants who worked as successfully or who suffered—so far as we can tell—as little. Contemporary opinion was divided as to the humanity of indentured servitude. Some observers saw the system as a kind of slavery in which men exploited the helpless to their own advantage. Others argued that servants worked no harder than laborers did in England. What is clear is that during Cole's era, servants saw many men and women who themselves had begun as servants and who had found Maryland to be a place of opportunity.[50]

Several recent studies of living conditions in the seventeenth-century Chesapeake have demonstrated what the evidence here also indicates: differences in wealth and status were not reflected in living standards to the degree that they were in England or that they would be later along the tobacco coast. Contemporary observers commented on the absence of social distinction in housing, furnishings, and dress, at least between the middling planters and the great. There were distinctions, of course. A rich man's parlor free of beds gave him more social space than that enjoyed by Cole, and Cole's pewter, earthenware, and linens provided amenities that a Forker Frissell did without entirely. Nevertheless, once a family had acquired ample supplies of the basic furnishings for sleeping, sitting, cooking, and eating, there was no clearly defined assemblage of belongings that marked off the families at the top. Numerous chairs, wines, and quantities of silver plate were confined to the rich, but in combination were by no means universal. And signs of leisure-time activities—cards, dice, Jew's harps, violins—were no more common among the rich than in less affluent households. As late as 1715, a traveler described a leading Virginia planter, Robert Beverley, as a man who "lives well; but he has nothing in or about his house but just what is necessary, tho' rich. He hath good beds in his house but no curtains and instead of cane chairs he hath stools made of wood."[51]

Cole died calling himself a yeoman, and his household belongings reflected that fact with one exception—the lack of bedsteads his very small house demanded. His standard of amenities matched those of his St. Mary's County neighbors of similar wealth, the prosperous planters of tables 4.7 and 4.8. The numbers examined in these tables are small, and we cannot claim too much for them. But the difference between Cole's group and the very rich would undoubtedly survive a much larger collection of inventories, as would the differences between Cole and the poorer planters. Cole was not a great planter, and he did not live like one; but he had the necessaries for a careful husbandry, and his family had sufficiencies that were comfortable for the time and place.

Had Cole lived, he would surely have continued to improve his estate, as Gardiner did for the children. When Robert Cole, Jr., came of age, the family land had increased to 825 acres, and land and goods—worth, as we have seen, about £360—put his father's estate higher on the scale of decedent wealth for the surrounding years than it had been eleven years before. Among estates inventoried from 1672 through 1675 in St. Mary's County, Cole's was now fifth, instead of seventh, in total value, putting him in the top 10 percent of wealthholders. Those richer than the Coles held 33 percent of the decedent wealth instead of 56 percent, as in the earlier period. Consequently, the Cole estate was farther from the mean and median wealth both of all decedents and of all decedent landowners than it had been a decade before (see table 4.9). On the other hand, many others had also moved up. In the period 1658–65, St. Mary's County estates valued at more than £300 (five in number) were about 12 percent of the total; in the period 1672–75, the eleven estates above this value were 22 percent. Nevertheless, the very rich were still much richer than this increased group of the affluent. The top two had gross wealth of about £1,000 and £700, whereas the third had £425. Nor were the Coles or most of their peers likely to jump the divide and become great planters.

Table 4.9 Comparison of the Estate of Robert Cole in 1673 with the
Estates of All St. Mary's County Decedents, 1672–1675
(In Pounds Currency, Constant Value)

	Total Movables	Land Value[a]	Total Estate Value	Land Acres (N)
Robert Cole	244.76	113.81	358.57	825.00
All estates[b] (N = 50)				
Mean	107.47	47.89	155.36	376.62
Ratio, Cole to mean	2.28	2.38	2.31	2.19
Median	48.82	32.08	90.90	126.00
Ratio, Cole to median	5.01	3.55	3.94	6.55
Householders[b] (N = 38)				
Mean	136.09	59.27	195.36	442.92
Ratio, Cole to mean	1.80	1.92	1.84	1.86
Median	69.36	41.35	120.47	150.00
Ratio, Cole to median	3.53	2.75	2.98	5.50
Landowners[c] (N = 31)				
Mean	145.51	77.25	222.76	607.45
Ratio, Cole to mean	1.68	1.47	1.61	1.36
Median	80.80	47.90	141.47	150.00
Ratio, Cole to median	3.03	2.38	2.53	5.50
Gentry (N = 8)				
Mean	291.89	157.02	448.91	1554.88
Ratio, Cole to mean	.84	.72	.80	.53
Median	244.56	124.98	361.76	982.00
Ratio, Cole to median	1.00	.91	.99	.84

Sources: St. Mary's County Inventory File, St. Mary's City Commission; Cole
Plantation Account, appendix 1; Career File of Seventeenth-Century St. Mary's
County Residents, St. Mary's City Commission.
  [a]See chapter 1, note 76.
  [b]Includes two widows.
  [c]Includes two widows and three men without households.

As we have seen, they were approaching the limits of the prosperity that
farm building could bring without a major infusion of more capital.[52]

As Cole increased his wealth, and especially his land, he might have
served as a gentleman justice of the peace. He was ripe for such an appointment in a society where men born to hold such a position were few
and far between.[53] He would have expanded his house and raised his bed

off the floor. But if he was like others of his kind who came to Maryland, he would not have chosen a much more elaborate life-style. Instead, he would have continued to acquire land and improve his farm to increase his children's inheritance.

Comparisons

In Cole's day, and for some time thereafter, Englishmen evidently sacrificed comforts for opportunity in moving to the Chesapeake, and at the risk of a shortened life. Was the same true for immigrants to other colonies? We can offer only a partial answer. Systematic career studies that measure opportunity at the bottom are available only for Maryland, and information on rates of return, such as we have offered here, is not yet on hand for other areas. Nevertheless, some inferences are possible.

Until the last quarter of the seventeenth century, New England and the Caribbean were the main alternative choices and provided very different environments. New England's stony soils did not nurture a staple crop, like tobacco or sugar, that could ensure a profitable trade with Europe. Nevertheless, farm-building opportunities were available, although the returns were probably lower than in Maryland and Virginia, making a start from nothing more difficult. Furthermore, merchants and craftsmen in Boston and other towns did well; indeed, some Boston merchants were richer than any found in the Chesapeake. A major plus for New England was its health; the inhabitants had longer life expectancies than those of the Chesapeake or the Caribbean, or even of the mother country.[54] In contrast, the disease environment of the Caribbean was the worst, by far, of the three regions, at the same time that the profits to be made from sugar were spectacular. However, the opportunity to start from nothing was far less than in the Chesapeake, since sugar making required a large amount of capital. Still, even though migration out was a common choice for Caribbean ex-servants or other poor young men and women, many stayed to work for wages or at crafts and other services planters needed. The range from poor to rich was widest here, and social differences were greatest.[55]

The Chesapeake, then, was a middle ground for life expectancy and for the accumulation of riches, but possibly offered the best economic opportunities for the poor. What of other criteria for the standard of living? All three regions had a sufficiency of food, although small islands in the Caribbean had to import much of what they ate, and slaves, servants, and the very poor may have suffered in consequence.[56] Greater differences appear in shelter and household amenities.

In shelter, it seems that Chesapeake inhabitants were worse off not only than Englishmen of equivalent statuses but also than most people in New England and many in the Caribbean. We have already seen the striking contrast with housing in New England, where long-lived settlers, who had brought some capital with them, replaced their early cabins with permanent, well-sealed structures.[57] In the Caribbean, all early houses were probably as small and impermanent as those in the Chesapeake, and those of the rural poor may have continued to be so. But by the mid-seventeenth century, sugar planters in Barbados were building much larger houses and by the 1680s were using brick and tile. True, Englishmen in the islands at this time did not adapt their buildings well to the hot climate, the severe tropical storms, and the danger from earthquakes that characterized their environment. As in the Chesapeake, few seventeenth-century structures remain; but while they stood, many were more spacious and showed more signs of prosperity than houses of even the rich in Maryland and Virginia.[58] In the Caribbean the improvement lay not in family immigration or longer life, as in New England, but in greater wealth and in an early solution to labor shortages, a solution found by importing Africans.

When it comes to furnishings and other household amenities, most Chesapeake planters again fared less well than did inhabitants of New England. Recent work by Gloria Main and Jackson Turner Main allows some direct comparison. Carefully paralleling studies made for the Chesapeake, the Mains used the presence or absence, but not the number or value, of several kinds of nonessentials listed in estate inventories to show that through the 1680s in Connecticut and rural Massachusetts most people lived more comfortably than did Chesapeake settlers. This was especially true for farmers with movable estates valued at less than £225, the great majority in both regions. The reason for this difference is not far to seek. Once more, it lies in the immigration of New Englanders in family groups and the absence of large numbers of freed servants. New England families started with more equipment than did the ex-servants of Maryland and Virginia, who left service with only an axe, a hoe, and the clothes on their backs.[59]

Richard Dunn's study of seventeenth-century Caribbean life allows a less precise and more impressionistic comparison. Except among great planters, differences between householders of the Chesapeake and those of the Caribbean are hard to determine, partly because we have as yet no truly parallel definitions for identifying social or economic groups. Still, it seems likely that a small tobacco planter in Barbados in the 1630s may not have lived very differently from his Chesapeake counterpart three decades later. On the other hand, by the time such a man was raising sugar in the 1640s and 1650s, he had perhaps ten laborers—a large number by Chesapeake standards—and was enjoying a higher standard of amenities, including a much larger house. On a list of 1680, men of Barbados that Dunn describes as small planters—most too poor to make sugar profitably—were 40 percent of the property-holding population. But some of them were much wealthier than any ordinary or lower gentry-level Maryland planter. Although about 20 percent of the small planters in Barbados had no slaves, others had as many as nineteen slaves. At the same time, nearly half the men listed are not classified by Dunn as planters at all. They were freemen who owned less than ten acres of land—too little not only to grow sugar but also to qualify to vote, although nearly two-thirds owned at least one slave. How this translates into lifestyles is not very clear. Many small Caribbean planters, in Barbados and elsewhere, may have lived no better than small planters of the Chesapeake, despite large holdings in labor. Of the life-style of the freemen, or their equivalents on other islands, we know little, but it seems unlikely that many outdid the poorer small planters. We do know that the Caribbean sugar planters lived very well and that the richer ones lived far more luxuriously than did the richest Chesapeake or New England gentry.[60]

The early Caribbean, then, offered short lives to all and inferior prospects to the poor, but the sugar economy made large fortunes and luxurious lives possible for those who arrived with capital. New England offered the most longevity and, in its rural areas, the least opportunity to gain great wealth. Nevertheless, the life-style of ordinary inhabitants of this poorer region was more comfortable than what the Chesapeake could supply.

What if Robert Cole had chosen New England or the Caribbean? His career chances in the Chesapeake were probably better than in the islands, where his life might have been shorter and his fifty-four pounds too little to establish himself in sugar.[61] In New England he might have lived longer, and though he might have accumulated less wealth, his living standards might not have shown much difference. However, there is another aspect of his welfare to consider. In neither New England nor the Caribbean could Cole have openly practiced the Catholic religion or participated in public life. Maryland was the place to both improve his estate and raise his children in the religion of his choice.

5

. . . . .

Settlement Patterns, Community Development, and Family Life

Robert Cole found on St. Clement's Manor some elements of a world an English yeoman farmer could readily recognize. Although manorial organization was weakening at this time in the rapidly commercializing countryside surrounding London, manors, manor lords, and a community of leaseholders meeting in a manor court were still familiar. When Cole sailed for England in 1662, some of these elements of Old World society had taken root, albeit shallowly, in his new home in Maryland. The tobacco boom of the mid-1640s and the 1650s had lured enough migrants to the area to make manorial development a potentially paying proposition. However, the same boom offered newcomers a chance to become freeholders rather than tenants, and these greater opportunities were quickly undermining Old World modes of social and economic organization. A decade later, when Robert Cole, Jr., came of age in 1673, his local world looked very different. The varying experiences of father and son illuminate the rapid changes taking place in mid-seventeenth-century Maryland, as Old World transplantations gave way to New World forms.

Just as proprietary land policy affected settlement patterns and the pace of land acquisition in Maryland as a whole, so the policies of individual manor owners and other major colonial investors shaped the histories of particular localities.[1] Robert Cole's story is closely tied to that of Thomas Gerard, the lord of St. Clement's Manor. Gerard, the eldest son of a Lancashire landowner, first came to Maryland in 1638. He returned to England in 1640 in search of additional funds and was back in the colony the next year, ready to exploit New World opportunities. When Gerard began developing his estate on St. Clement's in 1641, he was in effect planting a tiny colony on the outer fringes of English settlement. Like Maryland's first settlers at St. Mary's City, Gerard started farming on or near lands previously cleared and seated by the Chaptico Indians. He selected for his manor farm a tract that he called "Mattapany," which took its name from and perhaps included the site "where the [Indian] Town of Mattapanient now standeth."[2] There he built a "manor house" and designated the farm demesne land.[3] Certainly Gerard chose well, for the tract contained some of the best tobacco lands on the manor.[4]

After the manner of contemporary English landlords, Gerard may have hoped to build a small empire based on dependent tenants, but in fact he began developing his estate with indentured servants, for there were few freemen in the colony willing to work as laborers or to rent farms. A listing of free adult male residents in Maryland in 1642 shows only twenty-three men living in the upper Potomac region where Gerard had settled. Most were small planters who had recently patented freehold tracts in the area north of Herring Creek and south of St. Clement's Manor.[5] Only three freemen had taken up leaseholds on Gerard's land. However, up to thirty indentured male servants were working in the area, perhaps twenty of them for Gerard. These laborers were first employed in clearing land, raising corn and tobacco, constructing buildings on the manor farm, planting orchards, and caring for growing herds of cattle and hogs. Subsequently they worked to set up quarters on outlying tracts on St. Clement's Manor and on Gerard's other manors of Basford and Westwood. By buying many servants, Gerard added to his landholdings while developing his estate. He was entitled to 1,000 acres in 1638, had acquired 6,000 acres more by 1642, and added an additional 7,200 acres by 1651, using headrights obtained from transporting his family and numerous servants as well as a few rights purchased from others.[6]

Just across St. Clement's Bay on Newtown Neck, William Brittaine, the clerk of the assembly and later of the council, also started building an estate in the early 1640s, on an 850-acre holding. He began letting land to tenants and selling surplus livestock to newcomers. Although Brittaine never achieved the economic leverage of Gerard, his home, like the Mattapany manor house, quickly became an important meeting place for area residents, especially for Roman Catholics living around St. Clement's and Bretton's bays. Many of them were related to Brittaine, and others were attracted by his efforts to organize a local Catholic church and school.

Becoming a successful estate developer in Maryland in the 1640s required many talents, and Thomas Gerard, more than most, tried to live up to expectations. First was an entrepreneurial role—raising capital, importing labor, starting farms, providing supplies for new settlers, attracting tenants, collecting rents, extending credit, and marketing the crops of small planters. At the same time, as one of the preeminent residents of the Upper Potomac, Gerard, like other large landowners, also provided political leadership. As the lord of a manor, he was entitled to hold a court leet to inquire into and punish minor offenses committed on the premises and a court baron to handle minor civil cases between manor residents.[7] In addition, as soon as Gerard began acquiring land in the St. Clement's area, Lord Baltimore commissioned him a "conservator of our peace" in St. Clement's Hundred, a jurisdiction that included freehold farms east and north of his manors. His powers were those of any two justices of the peace in England and included, in addition, the right to apprehend, fine, imprison, or sentence to corporal punishment those who violated the proprietor's rights; to arrest unlawful traders with the Indians; to protect the heron rookery on nearby Heron Island; and to require area residents to have sufficient arms for their own defense.[8]

Gerard's powers were not limited to the white settlers in the immediate area. In 1642 Gerard was granted extraordinary powers over local Indians after he complained that the natives were stealing livestock and corn from the white settlers. The government at far-off St. Mary's had had little success in dealing with these Indians, so Gerard, the man on the spot, was empowered to demand satisfaction for livestock killed and, if redress was not readily given, "to pillage them" within his "said lands." He could use force to expel natives who entered white farmers' lands and was authorized to kill any who resisted. If Gerard used this extravagant authority, he did so only briefly. By 1660 local Indian-white disputes were handled more conventionally, in the manor court.[9] Gerard became a provincial leader as well as a local one in 1643, when he was named to the colony's council in recognition of "his diligent endeavors for the advancemt & prosperity" of Lord Baltimore's domain.[10]

Given Thomas Gerard's many political offices, settlers in the St. Clement's area looked to the manor house at Mattapany for protection, advice, and legal services. In addition, during the initial years of settlement, ordinary planters depended heavily on large investors for credit, supplies, and marketing facilities. Usually only those with substantial resources could obtain corn from the Indians should the settlers not be able to grow enough to feed themselves. Even in good years, only those with many bound laborers, produced much surplus grain. The big men too owned most of the livestock in the colony, and ordinary settlers had to purchase animals from these landowners (usually on credit) to start herds of their own. Finally, until English traders became familiar with the new settlement, small planters depended on their larger neighbors, most of whom already had contacts with English merchants, to secure shipping for their tobacco or to provide introductions to ship captains.[11]

In the 1650s the growing flow of immigrants to the Maryland colony included a number of freemen of moderate means, some of whom, like Robert Cole, arrived with young families. The Roman Catholics among them may have been particularly attracted to the settlements on the Potomac because of the Jesuit mission just across St. Clement's Bay at Newtown, the presence of other Catholics already settled in the area, and the fact that Gerard himself was a Catholic. There was yet no church building, but missionary priests apparently conducted masses in the homes of various Catholic families.[12]

The arrival of these additional settlers offered Thomas Gerard new and welcome options for improving his estate. His early successes had been more political than economic. In 1652, a full ten years after seating his manor, Gerard had attracted only four tenant farmers. Most of his rich domain remained undeveloped, yielding no rents. He had had to bear the full cost of what improvements had been made through the purchase of servants, and he still owed £175 sterling borrowed from his brother-in-law in 1640. The manor "community" amounted to little more than Gerard's own household and servant quarters.[13]

In 1652 Gerard began a different development strategy, selling off parts of his manors as freeholds rather than retaining all for leasing, thus sacrificing future revenues for immediate profit. The lands offered were attractive enough that the purchasers were willing to pay Gerard annual rents (usually one barrel of corn or ten shillings sterling for every one hundred acres) higher than the quitrents due on freeholds held of the lord proprietor. On the other hand, those who purchased land from Gerard got some special benefits—such as the right to cut timber on any ungranted portions of the manor.[14] By 1661 Gerard had sold nine freeholds of three hundred to eight hundred acres each. Seven lay on the east side of St. Clement's Manor, farthest away from Gerard's own farm and in an area where he had established no quarters. Six went to Catholic families and one to a Protestant family sympathetic to Catholics. The other two freeholds were purchased by two of Gerard's former servants on largely undeveloped Basford Manor.[15]

By the late 1650s Gerard had had some success in attracting tenants; there were sixteen by 1661. Most of the men who took up leaseholds were his former servants or servants of other nearby landowners. They had not yet accumulated enough capital to purchase land and so had to begin by renting farms and housing. Gerard let them parcels of one hundred to three hundred acres on two peninsulas close to his Mattapany farm—on Thomas Donne's Neck and Foster's (now White's) Neck—and on outlying Basford Manor. By renting rather than selling land close to the manor farm, Gerard could keep a closer eye on his tenants, develop the property, and retain the options of expanding his own operations or of settling adjacent tracts on his children in the future.[16]

By this time Gerard's children—eight in all—were growing up, so accumulating portions for them figured more prominently in his plans. He began by reserving manor tracts around the Mattapany farm and lands farther up the Wicomico for the family. When his eldest daughter, Susannah, married Robert Slye in 1652, Gerard had little more than land to give the couple.[17] For the younger children he took greater pains, wishing to set them up with something more than undeveloped tracts of little immediate value. Thus he worked to have fully functioning plantations established on the parcels chosen for his younger sons and daughters by the time they came of age. He began by building up herds of livestock and flocks of poultry and used his own servants to clear land, build housing, plant orchards, and set up laborers' quarters. Thus, when his eldest son, Justinian, came of age in 1664, he deeded him not only the five-hundred-acre Bramley plantation but also a furnished dwelling house, tools, dairying equipment, six menservants, two horses, sixteen cattle, twenty-one hogs, six sheep, a flock of chickens, a canoe, corn and bedding for the servants for one year, and cask for the first season's tobacco crop.[18] The Gerard offspring would start off much better endowed than would the children of ordinary landowners, who had work enough to get their home farms well established.

Table 5.1 Status of St. Clement's Manor Residents, 1659–1672

Period	Freeholder		Leaseholder		Resiant		Total
	N	%	N	%	N	%	
1659–61	9	20.4	16	36.4	19	43.2	44
1670–72	21	25.0	7	8.3	56	66.7	84

Sources: St. Clement's Manor Court Records, in William Hand Browne, et al., eds., *Archives of Maryland*, 72 vols. (Baltimore, 1883–1972), 53:627–37; Career File of Seventeenth-Century St. Mary's County Residents, St. Mary's City Commission, Maryland State Archives, Annapolis, Md.

Surviving manor court records for 1659–61 allow us to reconstruct the St. Clement's Manor community as it existed about twenty years after initial settlement, and as Robert Cole knew it when he left Maryland (see table 5.1 and map 5.1). By 1661 there were at least 44 free adult men on the manor living in a minimum of 28 separate households. Nine householders (20% of the free adult male residents) owned freeholds, 16 (36%) held leaseholds, and an additional 19 men (43%) were listed as *resiants*, an archaic term for residents settled by arrangements other than ownership or leasing of land. This last group consisted of ex-servants and a few free immigrants who were working as laborers or sharecroppers and one adult son living at home.[19]

This small group of settlers lived on farms scattered along the sides of rivers and creeks. Each tract had convenient access to the water for shipping the crop, and each had patches of good tobacco and corn land. In 1660 there were still fewer than two households per square mile on the manor. However, even though the settlers did not live close to one another, informal neighborhood networks sprang up quickly. On the frontier, neighboring families had to rely heavily on each other for aid in time of sickness or in case of Indian alarms, for help with heavy work, for borrowing back and forth when supplies ran low or the proper tools were lacking, as well as simply for having someone to talk to and to share important personal and family events.[20]

If informal networks developed almost at once, more-structured institutions followed soon after. Since the settlers had arrived in no sort of organized migration, chance to a large degree determined who their

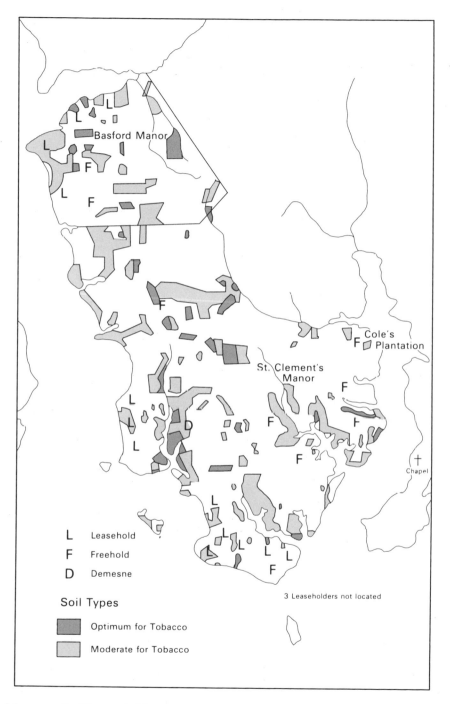

L   Leasehold

F   Freehold

D   Demesne

Soil Types

Optimum for Tobacco

Moderate for Tobacco

3 Leaseholders not located

Map 5.1. St. Clement's Manor c. 1660

neighbors might be. They were not content, however, for chance to define all their relationships.

It was probably in the early 1650s that the manor court was fully organized and regularly convened. For the first decade or so, Gerard could deal with his few tenants as individuals rather than in a formal meeting and had no need to hire a manor steward. But once more households were settled on the manor, problems of ill-defined boundaries, transfers of land, roving livestock, and occasional petty thefts and fights cropped up. In addition, most of the new farmsteads lay too far from Gerard's manor house for convenient access or constant personal supervision. Hence the residents began to meet in formal courts, and Gerard hired a steward to help with the management of the manor.[21]

The Roman Catholics living around St. Clement's and Bretton's bays also set about organizing a church, desiring to "repayre on Sundays and other Holy dayes appoynted & Comanded by holy Church to serve Almighty God & heare divine Service." In 1661 they "unanimously agreed amongst themselves" to build a chapel and prepare a graveyard. They selected a site on Newtown Neck as the most convenient for all, and William Brittaine deeded one and one-half acres to the area Catholics for this purpose. Among the organizers were Robert Cole and his friends and neighbors Luke Gardiner, William Evans, and James Thompson.[22] Families like the Coles supported the new church by paying voluntary taxes and by helping to build the chapel. Local Catholics also wanted parochial education for their children. A parishioner's bequest in 1653 for a schoolmaster's salary and support for poor scholars led the Jesuits to open a school on Newtown Neck. Nearby residents, including the Brittaines, helped by boarding students who, like Mary Cole, otherwise lived too far away to get to school regularly. Other residents cared for the cattle belonging to the school estate.[23]

Transplanted English social structure also gave form to the local community. Elements of the highly stratified society that Lord Baltimore had planned were visible on St. Clement's Manor in 1660. At the top was Thomas Gerard, the lord of the manor, who, one suspects, sought to exercise the social as well as the economic dimensions of his position. He enforced his prerogatives not only by collecting manorial rents and fines due on land transfers but also by demanding that manor freeholders swear fealty to him in a public ceremony and that leaseholders formally acknowledge their status by attorning tenants in the manor court. For

Gerard, the court was also a useful device for stopping leaseholders from renting to unauthorized undertenants and for collecting his half of the value of wild hogs killed.[24]

The nine manor freeholders also occupied a responsible and privileged niche in the manor community. Like Robert Cole, most of them were free immigrants and family men. William Barton, Cole's closest neighbor, had arrived with a teenaged son in 1654, soon purchased a freehold, and always styled himself "Gent." Luke Gardiner, Cole's next nearest neighbor, had immigrated at age fifteen with his family and, although he never developed it, had himself inherited a one-thousand-acre manor from his father. Next closest neighbors John Norman, Raphael Haywood, and Bartholomew Phillips had arrived with enough capital to acquire land quickly and had married by the early 1650s. Robert Slye, living farther away on Bushwood, had come as a wealthy merchant and soon won the hand of Gerard's eldest daughter. Only Christopher Carnall and John Goldsmith, both on freeholds on adjacent Basford Manor, had come as servants. As burgesses and justices of the peace, three of the freeholders—Barton, Slye, and Gardiner—commanded wide respect. Other manor residents and many settlers with no connection to the manor must have looked up to these men because of their wealth and political influence.

The freeholders' status and independence, moreover, set limits on how far Thomas Gerard might go in enforcing his privileges. When the manor court fined Robert Cole for killing a wild hog (which he believed his deed entitled him to do), Cole refused to pay Gerard anything and was willing to defend his position in the provincial court. Luke Gardiner too apparently viewed his manorial responsibilities lightly; he was fined repeatedly for neglecting to attend manor courts and once for failing to swear fealty to Gerard.[25]

The sixteen men who leased land on St. Clement's Manor stood lower in the social hierarchy. Most did not arrive with the status and resources of the freeholders, and they lacked the independence that landowning permitted. Of these sixteen leaseholders, only three were certainly free immigrants, whereas nine were certainly former servants. Although many eventually became landowners, they did not achieve the position of the early freeholders. Not one was ever called "mister" in extant court records, and none held important county office. So long as they leased land, there was an ever-present danger of eviction if they were unable to pay their rents. Gerard carefully scrutinized their activities, for example, closely regulating or entirely prohibiting any subleasing of rented tracts. Although the lord of the manor might have had to treat the freeholders with some respect, he did not hesitate to summon a leaseholder to the manor house and tell a bystander to "Give him a Kick on the Breech."[26] Resiants were lower yet on the social scale. Most were not even heads of households, and those who were worked as sharecroppers or as laborers for tenants and landowners. But some did sit on manor juries and participated in this way in community decisions.[27] Indentured servants were at the bottom of the social hierarchy. They had no say in local or manor government, and they were subject entirely to the control and discipline of the householders who had bought their terms.

When manor courts were convened, residents were concerned primarily with establishing boundaries, regularizing land transfers, and settling disputes among themselves. The concern with boundaries grew out of Thomas Gerard's haphazard method of making grants. A manor resident testified that Thomas "most Commonly sold and others bought land from him without Survey by Instruments bounding by guess from heads of Creeks to heads of Creeks or other parts as they agreed and Sometimes by Paths some times mentioning Courses & Distances and Sometimes not."[28] Consequently it fell to manor court juries to "regard the ascertaining and making the Bounds of their lands," which they did, at first with the assistance of Gerard and then on their own initiative. The communal control of boundaries apparently ceased after Thomas Gerard's death. From the mid-1670s on, manor residents began taking such disputes to the county and provincial courts for more formal adjudication. Thomas Gerard's haphazard legacy nonetheless persisted; the southeastern part of the manor, where boundaries and titles were inextricably jumbled, came to be known as Bedlam Neck.[29]

That the settlers' initial effort to structure local society in the New World should have included traditional English manorial institutions is hardly surprising. Familiar custom and proprietary vision gained reinforcement from uncertain frontier conditions that at first tended to magnify the role of the great landowner and to force most residents of a locality to cooperate closely to preserve order and provide aid and security for one another. St. Clement's Manor freeholders and leaseholders participated in the manor court so long as it provided needed services. However, the wide availability of land, the continued population growth, and a greater degree of social stability soon rendered Maryland manors obsolete, although the manor court of St. Clement's surely lasted longer than the others.

Manor court records for 1670–72 (when young Robert Cole was coming of age) provide our second and last complete profile of St. Clement's inhabitants in the seventeenth century. The records show a decline in such formal collective identity as had appeared ten years earlier. The composition of the manor's people was changing, and the manor itself had ceased to be an effective form of local economic or social organization.[30] Several circumstances contributed to this decline: diminishing leadership by the lord of the manor, the failure of manor courts to assume an essential role in local government, changes in the character of manor residents, decreased religious cohesion, high mortality, and geographic mobility.

Loss of leadership came first. Reverses in Thomas Gerard's political and economic fortunes were instrumental. For reasons that are not entirely clear, he ceased to support Lord Baltimore's government and instead became active in antiproprietary politics, "Aymeing at his owne Greatenes w[hi]ch in vnsettled times he might vphould," one critic later asserted.[31] In 1660 Gerard was temporarily banished from Maryland and his property confiscated for his support of the rebel governor, Josias Fendall. Although Gerard soon obtained a pardon, his political career was ended, since he was barred from holding office in the colony. Shortly after recovering his property from the proprietor, Gerard was sued for failing to repay money borrowed in the 1640s. Part of the manor was turned over to his creditor until his debt was repaid out of the profits of manor rents and crops raised on his Mattapany farm.[32] Gerard moved across the Potomac to Westmoreland County, Virginia, married a propertied local widow (his first wife having died), and turned to developing an estate there. By the time of his death in 1673, he had removed his younger children and almost all his servants and slaves to Virginia, a fact suggesting that he had lost interest in his Maryland properties.[33] Families who remained on St. Clement's had to turn elsewhere for legal and economic services.

Ample reason existed for Gerard's apparent disillusionment. Whereas rents constituted an important source of income for most English gentlemen of this period, Maryland manors did not pay as much as had generally been anticipated. In 1665 the annual value of St. Clement's Manor rents and dues was estimated at a respectable ninety-five pounds. By 1678 (when most of the land had been sold off as freeholds), the value of rents had dwindled to about thirty-one pounds per year, the equivalent of a tobacco crop produced by three to four hands. Even in 1665, when manor revenues were at their peak, the estimated *net* value of the annual crops of tobacco, corn, and cider produced on one farm, Gerard's Mattapany plantation, exceeded total manorial revenues by seven pounds.[34] Further, maximum revenues were seldom realized. According to a 1715 account, most freeholders had not paid any rents since the 1690s, and some had never paid any rents at all.[35] Clearly there were easier ways to make a fortune than finding and keeping reliable tenants, hounding recalcitrant freeholders who often failed to pay almost nominal rents, and collecting manorial rents in capons and corn rather than in currency or tobacco.[36]

By the late 1660s, Gerard apparently recognized this. He ceased renting manor land, except for the outlying Basford tract, to tenants, and he turned over as freehold tracts large portions of St. Clement's Manor to his eldest son, Justinian, and to his sons-in-law, Robert Slye, Nehemiah Blakiston, and Kenelm Cheseldyne. He allowed many former leaseholders to purchase their farms outright. And he sold off the remaining undeveloped but marketable waterfront properties to new purchasers. In addition, Gerard had begun purchasing slaves for his Virginia plantation during the 1660s and had acquired others through his second marriage. Slaves, he may have found, contributed more to a Chesapeake landed empire than did a reluctant and unstable Maryland peasantry.

The manor court ceased to be an effective entity soon after the departure of its original lord. In part this may have been a chance result of personality and character. Although Thomas Gerard's sons-in-law used a combination of political acumen and their wives' ample dowries to achieve prominence on the provincial level, the second lord of the manor, Justinian Gerard, never became anything more than an ordinary county justice of the peace, despite his early advantages. Even if Justinian had been more forceful, the outcome might not have been much different. The lord of the manor no longer had a monopoly on political power. Four of the twenty-one freeholders on St. Clement's in 1672 also held countywide powers and responsibilities, and three more would be named to such positions within a few years.

Moreover, St. Clement's residents were never a "community" unto themselves in the sense that they were isolated socially or economically from other county settlers. As common planters developed their own farms and forged their own ties with English ship captains, economic dependence on local magnates declined. In addition, St. Clement's residents had increasingly frequent dealings with nearby planters living off the manor and soon turned to agencies more comprehensive than the manor court to collect debts and to settle disputes. The county court had concurrent jurisdiction over land boundaries, petty suits, and breaches of the peace, as well as the right to settle more serious matters. The manor court met too infrequently and involved too few people to be an effective or essential institution. It soon proved an unnecessary adjunct to justices of the peace and to the county court that was evolving as an efficient agency for settling disputes among neighbors and for providing the rudimentary administrative machinery needed to keep a frontier community functioning.[37]

The decade between 1660 and 1670 marked as well an end to the close connection between manor and church. Many of the freeholders who had arrived during the 1660s were Protestants, as were most of the newly imported servants and resident ex-servants. Gerard's own children had been raised as Protestants, and he himself, as well as his three sons-in-law, became leaders of the antiproprietary (and hence pro-Protestant) faction. Certainly not all of the manor Catholics shared their lord's political views, and some felt decidedly uncomfortable in the increasingly anti-Catholic atmosphere that dominated gatherings in the home of Gerard's son-in-law Nehemiah Blakiston.[38] The remaining Catholic residents relied on the church at Newtown for spiritual comfort. Moreover, while they continued to turn to their closest neighbors—whatever their neighbors' religion—for some needs, for others they increasingly looked to coreligionists living farther away. Catholic residents on St. Clement's chose Catholics from other parts of the county as marriage partners, as godparents or guardians to their children, as estate administrators, and as witnesses to deeds, mortgages, and wills.[39]

At the same time, Thomas Gerard's policy of converting leaseholds to freeholds brought a marked change in the composition of the free adult male residents on the manor. By 1672 their number had increased to 84. However, leaseholders had dwindled to only 7 (8% of the adult males, compared with 36% ten years before), and they were of little importance in the manor hierarchy. Twenty-one freeholders (25%, nearly the same

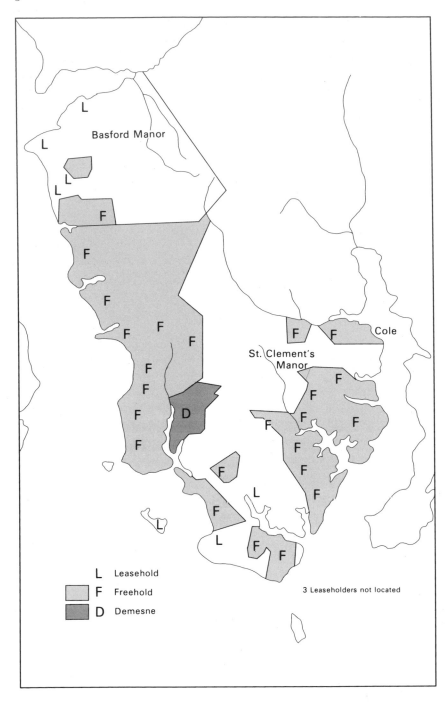

Map 5.2. St. Clement's Manor c. 1671

as before) now held most of the land, whereas 56 men (67%) were resiants. The decline of tenants, the most "manorial" of manor residents, removed a responsible but dependent group of male householders and left the manor, like the rest of the tobacco coast in the 1670s, largely a society of freeholders and of landless, often mobile freedmen (see table 5.1 and map 5.2).

By 1670 there was very little to distinguish manor freeholders from other county landowners who did not live on an organized manor. Theoretically manor freeholders paid slightly higher rents, but since these rents were less efficiently collected, the difference between manor and proprietary freeholders diminished. The freeholders in 1670 were also a more disparate group than in the 1660s, reflecting changes in immigration and opportunity. Some, like the merchant Robert Slye and the recent Barbadian immigrant Thomas Notley, had resources and connections enough to outdistance the Gerard family's wealth and political power. Others, like former leaseholders John Shankes and Richard Foster, represented the small planters who rose to landowning status from tenancy. Only about half of the landowners of 1670–72 were Roman Catholics, and some of the new Protestant freeholders were suspicious of the Catholic proprietary. These families got no benefit from the church and school organized by Catholic residents, and may have resented the failure of the government to help them establish similar facilities for their own children.[40]

Likewise the nonlandowners were little different from other unmarried men who had not yet established a niche for themselves on Maryland's lower Western Shore. Although a few were sons still at home (like Cole's son Robert), most were manor freeholders' ex-servants who had been transported in the late 1650s and early 1660s. William Felsteed, Humphrey Willy, and John Elton are typical. Felsteed finished his term on the Cole estate in about 1669, married a former servant, and remained as a sharecropper or casual laborer on the manor until his death about ten years later. Willy, a servant purchased by Robert Slye in 1669, was presented for keeping an unlicensed and disorderly tippling house on the manor in 1672 and apparently moved on shortly thereafter. Elton, another Cole servant, eventually rented a tract on Basford Manor after working some years for various local landowners.

Such men were bound by economic obligations to the freeholders for whom they worked or from whom they rented plots of ground. Often they were indebted to their former masters as well for help in starting out. Unlike men who had served Gerard or his family, former servants who had labored on the farms of others had few direct ties to the now absent lord of the manor. Most had not yet married and started families, and most were Protestants who had no organized local church. There was little to tie them to the neighborhood.

Some freedmen eventually married women who lived on or near the manor, but most did not find it easy to set up their own households. Falling tobacco prices made it ever harder for a poor man to get established. The proportion of such semidependent unmarried boarders rose on St. Clement's Manor, as it did in other places on the lower Western Shore, in the late 1660s and 1670s. In 1659–61 there was about one nonhouseholder for every two householders. Ten years later the proportion of boarders had nearly doubled. The presence of so many unattached males worked against a stable local population.[41]

Indeed the turnover among individuals was even more marked than the change in overall composition. Of the 44 adult males who lived on St. Clement's Manor in 1659–61 (see table 5.1), only 8 (18%) were still living there ten years later, in 1670–72. Family continuity was as slight as individual persistence. Only 10 of the 84 adult male residents of 1672 were sons or sons-in-law of residents of a decade earlier. The others had immigrated within the last ten years. High mortality was one reason for so much discontinuity. Of the 25 freeholders and leaseholders of 1659–61, eight (32%), including Robert Cole, had died within ten years. Early death struck parents and prospective heirs alike. However, geographic mobility was even more important. Of the surviving 17 property holders, only 5 (29% of those still alive and 20% of the original group) stayed put. What of the others? Three (including the lord of the manor) are known to have moved elsewhere; the other nine simply disappeared. The early nonhouseholders were even more footloose—only 2 of the original 19 remained on the manor ten years later. One was still landless and unmarried, one had acquired a leasehold, and a third, though now off the manor, had managed to purchase land nearby. Two of the remaining sixteen had died, and 14 had disappeared from the area, leaving few traces.[42]

A combination of push and pull was at work. A major push factor was that by 1672, the St. Clement's Manor and Basford Manor complex, for all its 12,500 acres, was filling up. The 1672 density of two to three households per square mile appears thin settlement indeed, but there was in fact not a lot of room for new households. By the early 1670s all the waterfront land well-suited to growing tobacco had been granted out. What remained were small, often land-bound parcels of fifty to one hundred acres that promised a barely adequate living for a family. So long as the landowners who had established themselves earlier were unwilling to sell part of their choice holdings, men who aspired to own enough land to endow their children, as well as to farm for their own use, had to move on (see map 5.2).

In the 1670s, pull strongly augmented push. Further up the Potomac, undeveloped waterfront land was still available. In adjacent Charles County, enough newly freed servants and unpropertied immigrants were advancing into the ranks of landowners to encourage those getting nowhere in the slightly older parts of St. Mary's County to head for what was then the frontier.[43] In addition, it clearly behooved any poor man who wanted to get married to move on. Women were still in short supply in Maryland in the 1670s. Some could be found who might let their hearts overrule their heads and would marry a man with few prospects. However, for the man more adept at farming than courting, the surest way of enhancing matrimonial prospects was to move to a place where he could more readily get land.

Clearly this does not mean that every man who was lured or pushed off St. Clement's Manor did better elsewhere. There is abundant evidence that many were not skillful or healthy or lucky enough. However, for most of these men, who had already left one life in England or Ireland or Scotland and had gambled an ocean passage and often a long stint of servitude in the bargain, this combination of push and pull proved irresistible.

Men who had already acquired land faced other imperatives in the early 1670s—and these too encouraged local, if not longer-distance, migration. In large families, prudent fathers like Robert Cole and Luke Gardiner took up additional land off the manor for most of the children and designated the manor tract for one child only. Good, undeveloped land in St. Mary's County remained a modest investment for anyone with a little spare capital or access to credit, and most landowners took up undeveloped tracts as an inheritance for their male and sometimes their female offspring. Given the region's high mortality, it was far from certain that the one child expected to inherit the manor farm would live to claim it, much less have children and thus continue the land in the family. Undoubtedly many fathers had some appreciation of this demographic lottery. However most, not too surprisingly, felt that title to fresh land elsewhere, rather than a right to some part of the home farm, would most benefit their posterity. Any close sense of identity between a family and a particular tract of land was clearly a thing of the future. In addition, since a man often gave the dwelling plantation to his widow for her life, the child who was to eventually inherit the home farm might marry and take up residence elsewhere before the mother died.[44]

The effect of inheritance strategies in dispersing families across the landscape is evident among early manor residents. Four of Thomas Gerard's eight children lived either in Westmoreland County, Virginia, or Charles County, Maryland. One of Luke Gardiner's sons also moved to an inheritance in Charles County, while two others lived on a tract above the manor in the interior of St. Mary's County. Three of Robert Slye's four children remained on the manor, but the other moved to Charles County. The surviving Cole children all moved on, and Robert Cole, Jr., choosing to remain on his wife's farm across St. Clement's Bay, eventually sold the home farm to a neighboring landowner.

The histories of St. Clement's Manor residents of the 1660s and 1670s indicate that a combination of push and pull continued to draw off most free immigrants and ex-servants who did not quickly acquire land in the area. Those who succeeded were more likely to remain in the county, but not necessarily to stay on the manor. However, the manor population continued to increase so long as landowners could readily get new servants to replace those whose time was finished. The freed servants in turn often stayed around a few years working as hired laborers before renting or purchasing a small farm or before moving on in search of greener pastures. Thus, although the population continued to rise, family continuity on the land remained low as early death, failure to have children, or better prospects elsewhere removed individuals from the immediate locality. So long as most of the St. Clement's area residents were immigrants, local ties remained weak. Economic success or failure was much more important than often nonexistent or tenuous family connections in determining whether an immigrant would stay or move on.[45]

Thus, formal, traditional forms of community organization proved short-lived. St. Clement's Manor was for a time a more organized neighborhood than most others in the early Chesapeake—economically, politically, and religiously. But Gerard's departure, competition from the county court, religious pluralism, and a rapid turnover of population undid the manor as an institution.

Informal Community Networks

Nevertheless, the decline of the manor court did not mean that informal community ties declined. Rather, these early settlers had forged other patterns of association so enduring that they continue to function today.[46]

Many obstacles hindered the creation of community networks. The physical landscape, sheer distance, and available means of transportation restricted the spatial scope of exchanges between families in the St. Clement's area, as elsewhere in the seventeenth-century Chesapeake. Scattered, low-density settlement limited the number of other households that one family could physically reach. The numerous rivers and creeks bisecting the region presented barriers of varying degrees of difficulty, whereas a scarcity of horses before the 1670s and a poorly developed road system tended to limit movement to foot traffic whenever boats could not be procured. Social barriers further restricted patterns of interaction. Maidservants, for example, could not readily wander off the plantation without their masters' or mistresses' consent, nor could they relate as equals to free women. Neither would common farmers ordinarily form close friendships with members of the provincial elite.[47]

The structure of the local economy too tended to limit the extent and density of networks. Since most mid-seventeenth-century planters tried to maximize tobacco production, other economic activities were more incidental. Sales of local products and especially of livestock did augment the income of most households, as we have seen in the Cole farm account. Nonetheless, tobacco was the chief source of farm income, and seasonal routines revolved around its production and annual exchange for manufactured goods. This exchange was often made directly between the planter and an English merchant, rather than through colonial middlemen. The tobacco trade required almost no local infrastructure. Economic transactions with other planters were too few, and exchanges of local products too irregular, to lead to the development of markets or marketing networks for other commodities.

In years of heavy immigration a number of new households were formed, all requiring corn and livestock to get started. In the absence of towns, there were no established local marketplaces where produce could readily be traded. Buyers usually found sellers through word of mouth, learning who had a cow or hogs or corn to spare through the neighborhood grapevine. Neither were there stable groups of local producers and consumers; buyers and sellers were seldom the same from one year to the next. New householders soon achieved self-sufficiency and no longer needed to purchase foodstuffs and livestock. Many established planters who could have produced commodities for the local market seem not to have done so intentionally. Rather they simply sold off accidental surpluses. The limits of the local market are clear in places where we can estimate population. In the area around St. Clement's in the 1660s, 1670s, and 1680s, there were probably no more than half a dozen new families who were buying provisions and livestock in quantity in a given year and perhaps no more than three or four within easy reach of most planters.[48]

Still, discernible patterns of association existed, even at this early stage of development. The lands of most St. Clement's householders of the 1650s, 1660s, and 1670s could be located on a tract map and their recorded contacts with other households plotted. Some regularities emerge. All the repeated and ordinary contacts of male residents involved other households lying within an approximate five-mile radius of the home, a journey of an hour or two. Since most communications and transactions were oral rather than written, a man's effective communication network seldom exceeded this five-mile area where face-to-face contacts were conveniently made. Families living on the periphery of one settler's network regularly gleaned news of those living up to five miles farther away; thus, the extent of the news network might in effect have doubled. However, because the first settler was probably unacquainted with many of the individuals known to the second, conversation was likely limited to news about mutual acquaintances living within effective reach of both.[49]

Moreover, the most frequent contacts involved even shorter distances— between two and three miles from the home. In Robert and Rebecca Cole's day, this meant a family's choices were limited indeed. In the St. Clement's area, the typical household of the early 1660s would find only about fifteen other families within two and one-half miles of the home farm and about twenty-five families within five miles. With contacts so restricted, it is not surprising to find that most families could not afford to erect much in the way of social fences against neighbors.

By the early 1670s the situation was changing. St. Clement's residents then had about twenty-five households within two and one-half miles of their homes and perhaps sixty within five miles. Greater density let individuals and families choose their friends. The difficult, dishonest, or ungenerous could be more easily avoided, and neighbors with like views in religion or politics could be more readily cultivated. This increased luxury of choice may have been one of the factors that contributed to the decline of cohesiveness on St. Clement's Manor.

For most married women, face-to-face contacts were probably confined to the fifteen to twenty-five households within about two and one-half miles of home. Since a planter's wife was soon burdened with nursing infants and caring for slightly older toddlers, she could not easily travel much farther from her own farm.[50] Evidence from depositions shows that women did travel greater distances. Such journeys, however, often entailed complicated arrangements for child care and were infrequent. Consequently, the planter's wife had to rely on her husband's somewhat wider contacts to glean news of what was going on in the larger neighborhood, and doubtless she learned as much as she could from passersby who stopped at the house on business or to seek refreshment or shelter.[51]

For men, the degree of geographic mobility was closely related to occupation and economic position. Freedmen, who had few livestock and few or no crops to tend and no encumbering families, often moved to where the work was. Tailors, coopers, carpenters, and ordinary laborers might live in the households of several widely scattered employers over the course of a year. Conversely, tenant farmers and small landowners were least likely to venture far from home. With little labor aside from their own and their wives', they could not leave crops and livestock unattended for long. More prosperous planters like Robert Cole were more likely to have wider connections between five and ten miles of their farms, as well as nearer by, and also had more occasion to travel to meetings of the county court or to the provincial capital at St. Mary's City. Such men were likelier to have surplus produce to sell locally and could leave their servants to tend to the farm on occasion.

A variety of activities—militia musters and expeditions, hunting forays, trips to the capital or county court, negotiations with ship captains, and in later years, visits to a local store—might bring adult male colonists together whatever their occupation. Such ventures did serve to draw men out of their usual neighborhoods to new areas and sometimes to centers of power. However, for ordinary planters these were infrequent occasions. As late as 1759 the *Maryland Gazette* eulogized the Anne Arundel County planter Robert Boone, "an honest and industrious Planter, who died on the same Plantation where he was Born in 1680, from which he never went 30 miles in his Life."[52] Once a planter was appointed to a county office, his local connections became more dense, and his travel within his own county (and to a lesser extent, neighboring counties) more frequent. Civic responsibilities also increased a man's access to information. A justice could learn much about local happenings without stirring far from home. Local constables often needed to consult with him, and dissatisfied servants and litigious neighbors kept him informed about local problems. Similarly, doctors and ministers also traveled widely and helped link neighborhoods.

Planter-merchants such as Robert Slye, of St. Clement's, or William Fitzhugh, of Stafford County, Virginia, across the Potomac, enjoyed the widest communication networks. Such men dealt regularly with merchants throughout England's Atlantic empire, linking the small communities along the bay to an international economy and a wider world. They also employed sailors and sloop captains to navigate surrounding rivers and creeks and to contact planters not only within the home county but in three or four adjacent counties as well. Unlike prosperous planters and ordinary county justices whose connections were usually confined to about a ten-mile radius of their homes, planter-merchants could maintain extensive contacts within a fifteen-mile compass and had some dealings within a twenty-five-mile radius of their home plantations. Although these connections were based on trade, they could be turned as well to political advantage on occasion.[53]

Early Maryland court records demonstrate that the function of such neighborhood networks was social in the broadest sense.[54] The touchstones of neighborhood were familiarity and frequent contact. Each family knew well, and was well known by, all the others. The economic and social position, reputation, and everyday affairs of each were familiar to all the rest; few pretenses were possible. The exchange of news and gossip, the main means of communication in a predominantly oral culture, continually supplied fresh information. In addition, informal neighborhood activities—mutual aid, bearing witness, watching and warding, and the neighborly mediation of disputes—contributed to the smooth functioning of community affairs. Land boundaries and economic agreements, for example, were preserved as much (or more) in the minds of the contracting parties and in the memories of the neighbors who bore witness to the transactions as they were by blazes on trees or by words on paper.[55]

Neighborhood consensus, more than formal statute, defined proper standards of behavior, and these were in turn enforced more often by informal sanction than by magisterial intervention. Local residence groups could exert considerable pressures for conformity. The penalties for flagrant and repeated violations of neighborhood norms were so severe that most heads of households were unwilling to risk the consequences. Informal sanctions, ranging from unfavorable talk to outright refusals of aid, could quickly become formal sanctions if neighbors made complaints to justices or grand juries or refused to stand as bondsmen. Free men and women who fell afoul of the law could escape corporal punishment and/or prison only if their neighbors were willing to act as securities for payment of fines or to post bond for the person's future good behavior. Even the most law-abiding needed securities when they wanted to borrow money locally, obtain credit from English merchants, administer an estate, or hold a public office that entailed fiscal responsibility.[56]

Neighborly contacts also involved a good measure of watching and warding. A community with no organized police had to rely heavily on the sharp eyes of private citizens to maintain order. For example, families who butchered a hog or cow were expected to retain the marked ears of the animal for inspection on demand. Any housewife with pork stewing in her pot was expected to account to her neighbors for its origin. Failure to do so constituted a tacit admission of poaching or at least being an accessory to poaching, a serious crime.[57] Neighborly watchfulness rendered thefts of less perishable possessions difficult indeed. Men and women knew every article of their nearer neighbors' property, and they would almost certainly notice if a missing pot, coat, or tablecloth appeared in someone else's house.[58] Neighborly intervention served as well to curb physical abuse, especially of dependent servants and orphans, and those living close by sometimes averted violence by reconciling differences between estranged husbands and wives or feuding landowners.[59]

On St. Clement's Manor, then, as elsewhere in the seventeenth-century

Chesapeake, informal neighborhood networks helped to bind individuals and separate households to the larger world, supplementing the more formal institutions of manor, church, county, and provincial government. This was crucial in a region that experienced so much flux due to migration, and high mortality that it remained largely a society of newcomers long after the land itself had been effectively settled. Immigrants continued to draw from many differing traditions—in religious practice, agriculture, landholding and estate management, building construction, customary contributions to community needs, and family arrangements. It was within the collective experience of small local residence groups such as this that a common and unique regional culture began to emerge from a variety of competing forms.

Family Life

The peculiarities of the region's demography helped to shape the character and functions of informal community networks. Here family life did not follow the same course as it did in other colonies, where migration patterns and environmental conditions differed. In what ways was the experience of the Cole family representative of the experiences of most other young families in the seventeenth-century Chesapeake?

From the outset the Coles had a better chance than most immigrants to establish a stable and comfortable family life. Unlike the majority of men and women who left England for the Chesapeake, Robert and Rebecca did not emigrate until after they had married, begun a family, and accumulated some property. More typical was the career of one of Cole's neighbors, John Shankes. At about thirteen years of age, Shankes arrived as a servant to Thomas Gerard in 1640. He served an eight-year term ending in 1648 and then remained in the St. Clement's area as a tenant. He did not marry until 1652, when he was about twenty-five and able to buy the remaining time of a maidservant, Abigail. He did not acquire his own farm until about 1670, over twenty years after he was freed. The region did offer poor Englishmen prospects they would seldom have achieved at home, but not always with the abundance and speed they had hoped for when they had first embarked for the New World.

Many did not survive to realize these advantages, for early death was the fate of most immigrants and their progeny in the seventeenth-century

Chesapeake. The life expectancy of a man who arrived at age twenty was only about another twenty-three years, and women may have had even shorter lives. Robert Cole was only about thirty-five when he died, and Rebecca was probably under forty. Native-born sons fared only slightly better than their immigrant fathers. A boy reaching majority in southern Maryland before 1720 had only about twenty-five more years to live. The Cole children illustrate the range of possibilities. Edward Cole lived to the relatively old age (for the region) of sixty, but Robert experienced a more typical life span, dying at about forty. William died early, sometime before his thirty-third birthday. Mary Cole lived at most to age forty-five, whereas Betty died when she was only ten. Two more children who had immigrated with Robert and Rebecca did not survive early childhood, dying sometime before 1662. This experience was typical of that of most seventeenth-century families.[60]

As we have seen, late age at marriage, early death, and sexual imbalance among immigrants to the Chesapeake long prevented the appearance of a population dominated by the native born. Many men never married, and those who did often died soon after. The Cole family was unusually large because Robert and Rebecca had already begun having children in England, but most couples had too few offspring to replace themselves in the adult population. As a consequence, in Cole's day and long after, the adult population had been born in Europe. Immigrant predominance is apparent in the St. Clement's Manor community. In the early 1670s, thirty years after initial settlement, only about 10 percent of the adult men living on the manor were native-born, whereas over 80 percent were immigrants who had arrived in the area within the past ten years.[61]

Furthermore, the majority of children in the region, like the Coles, were to lose one or both parents before they grew up. Many youngsters on the manor grew up in circumstances similar to that of the Coles. When Luke Gardiner died, only one of his children was of age; three others were under eighteen and still in school. Robert Slye left one son nearly eighteen, but the three other children were very young. Edward Clarke, who signed Robert Cole's will, died with only one surviving child, a "little son" not yet old enough to read. Robert Cole's former servant Joseph Alvey left at least two children too young to support themselves, and another servant, Robert Gates, died with sons and daughters aged twenty-two, twenty, seventeen, twelve, eight, and five.[62]

5.1 Aerial Photograph of Robert Cole's Land on Tomakokin Creek and St. Clement's Bay, 1988. The land is still farmed in corn and, until very recently, was still farmed in tobacco, as it was when the Cole children lived here. (United States Department of Agriculture, Agricultural Stabilization and Conservation Service)

The Cole children were unusual in that one of their parents did not live long enough to remarry. Since immigrant women were usually a few years younger than men at marriage (whether or not their life spans were shorter than men's), they tended to outlive their first husbands. A woman left alone on an isolated plantation with two or three young children, often with no laborers to tend the fields, may have found quick remarriage the only solution to her difficulties. Conversely, had the widower Robert Cole lived to return to Maryland, he would undoubtedly have tried to marry again in order to provide a mother for his five young offspring and one stepchild remaining at home.[63]

Cole's greater-than-average economic resources made it possible for the orphaned children to stay together on the home farm. Had he had no servants and thus insufficient income coming into the estate to hire a housekeeper, the county court would have bound the children out to other families. By Maryland law, only the income from a child's inheritance—and not the principal—could be used for the child's upbringing, and most estates were not large enough to permit this. For example, the widower William Watts, a former servant of Justinian Gerard's, died in 1678. He left three sons aged eight, six, and four. His will directed that the children should not be separated but should live together at home under the care of a tenant who was "used with my children; as also acquainted with my stock." However, the executor of the estate chose not to abide by this arrangement and instead put the boys to work on a quarter with some of his servants. Since the children's estate was small (£78), and included no menservants, the executor argued that their estate would not maintain them in the circumstances their father had wished.[64]

In England, a father was more likely to have the option of relying on kin to take in orphaned children, to aid his widow, and to help in managing his estate. In the Chesapeake, few had the luxury of choosing between kin or unrelated advisors. Since settlers to the region on the whole seldom arrived either in families or in organized groups, they had largely to rely on neighbors and on friendships formed after their coming to the region.

This is not to say that settlers failed to recognize even quite distant kin links when they were present. For example, Richard Sheppy left lower St. Mary's County indebted to the merchant Thomas Cornwallis. When Cornwallis learned that Sheppy was living with the Coles, he sent the county sheriff to see Robert about Sheppy's debt. Sheppy had just married Mary Mills, a kinswoman of the Coles'. Cornwallis believed that this relationship was sufficient to induce Robert to assume some responsibility for seeing that Sheppy repaid what he owed.[65] Similarly, Robert Cole was a cousin of the planter Benjamin Gill. When Gill fell ill, he was uncertain how best to dispose of his estate, for his only heir, a daughter, was then living in Europe and had not been heard from for several years; no one knew whether she and her husband were alive or dead. Thomas and Susannah Gerard advised Gill to leave a sizable part of his property to Robert Cole, his only kinsperson then alive in Maryland. Gill demurred, not because he considered the tie unimportant but because Robert had somehow deeply offended him. Gill did not live to draw up a proper will, although it seems fairly clear, from testimony offered by persons at his deathbed, that he did not intend Cole to be a major heir. Nonetheless, Cole sought to administer Gill's estate on the grounds that he was the only kinsman available.[66]

The plain fact was that few immigrants had any kin in the colony—
neither siblings, adult children or children-in-law, relatives by marriage,
or more distantly related blood kin. Given these circumstances, dying
husbands were understandably anxious about the welfare of their families. Most found similar solutions to their dilemma. The husband relied
heavily on the wife, trusting that even though the widow was likely to
remarry, she was the person most suitable to raise and educate his children. To ensure that the widow would have a maintenance that young
children could not supply, the man usually left his wife a substantial share
of the family property, more than the lifetime use of one-third of the
land, the dower that the law required. By the standards of the time, most
Chesapeake wives received highly favorable property settlements and
were accorded an influential role in managing the estate and in bringing
up the children. The absence of kin clearly served to enhance a wife's
status in the eyes of her husband.[67]

Some of these men were simply following traditional English solutions
to the problems of family maintenance. In some parts of England, surviving widows normally managed the family property and took on the burden of raising minor children. This may have been particularly true in
Catholic families, where the housewife would usually assume responsibility for seeing that the annual cycle of fasts, feasts, and seasonal devo-
tions was observed and that the children were suitably brought up in the
faith.[68] Elsewhere in England, however, older children, other kin, or unrelated outsiders more often managed the father's estate, whereas the
widow might not receive more than the obligatory dower, and that often
contingent on her remaining unmarried. With life, and especially family
life, so fragile in the Chesapeake, most men followed practices that favored their wives above children and other kin.[69]

When it came to their children, fathers were most concerned about
protecting them from abusive treatment by "unkind" stepfathers or ne-
glectful guardians. Most fathers who left wills made their wives the executor, and the Maryland probate court almost invariably appointed a
surviving widow the administratrix of an intestate's estate. Still, in the
1650s and 1660s, 60 percent of the men who left wills in St. Mary's and
Charles counties named male friends as overseers. Probably they believed this advisable because after the widow remarried she could not
take legal steps independent of her new husband to protect the interests

of the children. Almost always the overseers were charged to intervene not with the day-to-day administration of the estate but on the behalf of young children should a stepfather waste their inheritance or treat them badly.[70]

Widowers like Robert Cole had to depend entirely on such concerned friends for their children's welfare. The first hope was that the friends would act responsibly and tenderly in part from a realization that their own children might end up in similar circumstances. With no wife and no other kin in Maryland (other than the distantly related and not particularly well married Mary Mills Sheppy), Cole had few choices. He did name a London cousin, Henry Hanckes, to take care of his affairs in England. Hanckes, however, seems not to have acted; perhaps he too had died. At any rate, it was Cole's mother who inquired into his affairs, but she had no legal power over his estate.[71]

Cole left most of the burden of managing the plantation and caring for his children instead to his Maryland friends Luke Gardiner and William Evans. Again, the choice was typical. Both lived close enough by to look in at the farm at regular intervals. Even more significantly, both were county justices of the peace. In the 1650s, 1660s, and 1670s, many local officials showed a deep and personal concern about the welfare of local orphans. In selecting such men to administer his estate, Cole behaved like many other anxious fathers in naming officials who had real powers of protection should they trouble themselves to exercise these powers. Even so, Cole's anxiety about his family remained. Not satisfied with a "strict Charge" to his executors to attend to the children's spiritual training as well as to their physical well-being, he invoked divine wrath on Judgment Day should they fail to carry out his last wishes.[72]

Cole recognized as well that his older children might be most effectively protected by making them independent as soon as possible. Like many other Chesapeake parents in this period, he wanted his children to receive their property before they reached twenty-one, the legal age of majority. Thus, at age eighteen, his children were to receive their portions so that they might "know" their inheritance. It was under such an arrangement that young Robert began raising his own tobacco crop on the home farm in 1672. However, to prevent an inexperienced adolescent from making a foolish transaction, Cole's executors had to approve any bargain the children might make between the ages of eighteen and twenty-one. The only exception was his oldest daughter, Mary, who was to be granted absolute possession of her share at eighteen if she were then married to an "honest Catholique." [73]

Immigrant parents in early seventeenth-century Maryland were deeply concerned not only that their children should be provided for materially but also that the children's secular and religious education not be neglected in the harsh New World environment. Men and women who feared they would not live to guide their children through adolescence tried to ensure that their offspring would not be deprived of the cultural and spiritual values that had given meaning to their lives, and that the children would not be permitted, as Cole put it, to "forgett theire learning" before they came of age. [74]

Robert Cole's neighbors shared his concern that their children "have such Education in learning as to write and read." Like Cole, who was anxious that most of his precious books be preserved in a locked chest except for a half dozen left out for the children's present reading, Edward Clarke directed that his wife save his books for his young son and not "Lend or dispose of any of them for feare that any of them should be lost." He left the child to his wife's "tender care" but provided that should she marry a man who abused the boy, overseers of the will were to take custody and "to breede [him] up in the feare of god and with learning." Luke Gardiner wanted his three younger sons to "be kept at school & have Such Education as this Country & theyr Estates will afford them." Cole's ex-servant Robert Gates enjoined his wife and any subsequent husbands to "use their utmost Care & Indeavour in bringing up and Educateing all my Children in the Roman Catholic Faith I Now Live in and hopc to Die in." Robert Slye, a Protestant, expressed his hopes, similar to those of the Catholic fathers, that his wife would "take due Care that [his children] be brought up in the true fear of God and Instructed in such Literature as may tend to their improvem[en]t both for their present and future good." [75]

Like most other early Chesapeake settlers who were literate, the Coles taught their older children to read at home. After Robert sailed for England, the boys were apparently taught by a tutor who came to the farm, or else they went to a neighboring planter for lessons. The youngest daughter, Betty, spent two years away from home, probably attending the school operated by the Jesuits at Newtown. Her experience was unusual, for there were few organized schools in the area until the first decade of the eighteenth century. Each of the children received about four years of schooling, generous by the standards of the time. Most children who were schooled at all got only one or two years of instruction. Cole's care for his offspring's education reflects the desire of many early Chesapeake settlers to preserve aspects of an English culture that they deeply cherished.[76]

In apprenticing the middle son, William, to a trade, Luke Gardiner adopted an alternative means for seeing that a child was educated. Few parents in the region were willing to part with their children (or their labor) in this fashion, but courts and, to a much lesser extent, guardians might apprentice orphans to craftsmen to ensure an adequate supply of workers trained in the arts and mysteries of the woodworking and, to some degree, the tailoring and the leather-processing trades necessary to the local economy, as well as to provide for the education and maintenance of orphans in the home of a responsible householder and his wife. Had Cole lived, William would almost certainly have remained at home.[77]

Cole's provisions for his children's education also showed differing expectations—typical of the period—for sons and daughters. The boys were to learn to read and write and to cast accounts, whereas the girls were to learn only to read and to "sowe with theire needle." A boy was to be trained "to know how to gett his living," almost invariably by managing a plantation; it was assumed that a girl would need much less education in order to be a wife and mother.[78]

These different expectations were reinforced as well by inheritance strategies. Like many other Chesapeake fathers, Cole left all his land to be divided among his boys, although Robert as the eldest got a much larger share than did the younger sons. The opportunity to acquire enough property to set up all sons as landowners had of course drawn many to the region initially. In leaving his daughters only personal property, Cole also followed traditional practice. However, in this early stage of settlement, he could do so without hurting their prospects of a good marriage. With unmarried women so scarce in the region, girls like Mary and Betty, though endowed only with cattle, bedding, linens, and cooking equipment, were almost certain to marry a landowner.[79]

Having made provisions for his children once they came of age, Cole finally expressed two further concerns about their future: that they "bee kept from Idleness" but that they not "bee kept as Common servants." The second was a real danger. Only a few years after the Cole children came of age, for example, the acting guardian of William Watts's three orphan boys put them to hard adult labor in tobacco and corn on a manor quarter when they reached the age of nine or ten. Numerous complaints made to other county courts show that such abuses were not at all uncommon. Orphans who had no siblings of age or other nurturing kin all too easily fell victim to less scrupulous settlers. The Cole children were fortunate that one of the three executors their father chose lived to fully administer their estate.[80]

On the other hand, very few of the region's children seem to have been in much danger of growing up in idleness. The combination of early deaths of parents, early inheritance, duties to younger siblings, and early marriage meant that most youngsters soon took on adult roles and responsibilities. Here the Cole children were entirely typical. Francis Knott and young Robert Cole began working for themselves when they reached majority, if not somewhat before. William began serving an apprenticeship in his late teens. Mary married sometime before her twentieth birthday, and little Betty seems to have kept house for her older brothers once she finished her schooling at age nine. As soon as he turned twenty-one, Robert lost no time in joining with Mary's husband, Ignatius Warren, in demanding a final accounting and formal settlement of his father's estate.

The Coles provide an intimate example of the kinds of disruption that affected families in the process of transplanting Old World population and culture to the New World. In this immigrant society, family life was both fragile and brief, soon broken by the early death of one or both parents. In the absence of kin, the burden of supporting, supervising, and educating a good proportion of the first generation of children born in the region fell on friends, neighbors, and local officials. When these failed, the cost in human terms was appalling. On the other hand, the expressions of care and concern that continually surface in this one family's history show that, at the very least, some of the region's settlers had not abandoned traditional values and communal responsibilities in a mad scramble for riches.

6

. . . . .

Toward the
"Golden Age"

In Robert Cole's day, the Chesapeake region was indeed a "New World." Planters faced conditions different from those of their English or European counterparts—different prices for land, labor, and capital; different soils and climate; different marketing opportunities. The Chesapeake required a new husbandry: one that conserved labor, which was dear; one that exploited land, which was cheap, without destroying it; and one that centered on a crop able to command profits in distant markets. Chesapeake settlers found, in tobacco, a crop eagerly purchased in Europe and, in corn, an easily grown food crop. Neither crop required plowing, with its attendant equipment and animal power and its requirement for fully cleared land, difficult to achieve where virgin forest prevailed. Both crops required little capital per laborer and hence offered opportunities for poor men as well as rich, provided that new strains of disease did not kill them first.

By adapting Indian practices and devising experiments, planters developed a system of husbandry suited to their new needs. Since tobacco was labor-intensive, labor had to be conserved in other ways, ways unfamiliar to English eyes. English visitors severely criticized what seemed to them slovenly and wasteful practices: tree stumps left to rot in unplowed and unmanured fields; fields left in twenty-year fallow after short periods of use; cattle unpenned for their manure and left unhoused and little fed in winter. But these were inappropriate judgments, based on Old World conditions of cheap labor and expensive land. Hoe culture did not require the use of precious labor for clearing stumps from the land, an especially time-consuming process in virgin forest. Long fallows restored fertility to soils quickly exhausted by nutrient-hungry tobacco, and land was ample for this solution. Livestock ranging in the woods increased well enough to meet planters' needs for meat and hides without further care. Penned or housed animals could have supplied manure, which would have reduced fallow time, but penned livestock would have required food and attention, which seventeenth-century planters could not supply without cutting back on labor for the production of tobacco. All these practices were creative adaptations, not signs of laziness or stubbornness.

Farm building based on the new husbandry provided opportunities to Maryland settlers of all social origins over the middle decades of the seventeenth century; but the cultivation of tobacco also contained built-in limits to the growth of individual plantations. These limits were tied to economies of scale determined by travel time and supervision costs. When a planter expanded beyond the area his home farm could efficiently serve, he had to establish a quarter—that is, a new plantation—which was an expensive and risky enterprise that few but the rich tried to undertake. Hence tobacco culture lent itself to the creation of yeoman farms and a social landscape dominated by yeoman-headed households.

Yet this world was clearly on the wane by the 1680s. Although there was a tendency for this social structure to persist—more strictly, to be re-created—at the edge of Euro-American settlement, a quite different society, based on slavery, was taking shape in the older regions along Maryland's lower Western Shore. At the same time, even though the structural changes were striking, there were also significant continuities. Both are evident in the ever more dense web of community and kinship spun out by the descendants of Robert and Rebecca Cole and of their friends and neighbors. The complex pattern of transformation and persistence that marked Maryland's entry into its "golden age" can be traced through the careers of the people who lived on and around the Cole plantation in the 1660s and 1670s.

The Coles and Their Neighbors

Robert Cole, Jr., who inherited the home plantation, apparently lived there through the mid-1670s.[1] By 1677 he had married a widow, Ann Medley, thereby gaining control for the moment of the six-hundred-acre tract in Newtown Hundred and the substantial personal estate, valued at £157, left by her husband, John.[2] Presumably Robert then moved to his wife's lands: in 1678 he served on a jury of the neighborhood in New-town. He remained there for the rest of his life, remarrying when Ann died, raising a small family, buying and selling small tracts of land, grow-ing tobacco and corn, and participating in the life of the neighborhood as a juror, bondsman, and appraiser. Despite his substantial inheritance and promising first marriage, Robert did not prosper. He was dead by April 1693, at about age forty, leaving a personal estate worth only £68. Robert had not continued his father's progress but died a small planter in far less comfortable circumstances than his promising start might have led him to expect.

Most of the other children fared no better. Betty, of course, died young, when she was only ten. William also died young, although when is un-certain. We last hear of him in 1673, when at age eighteen he was bound out as an apprentice. He does not appear in the records as an adult, and he was surely dead by 1688, when Robert is described as his heir at law. Ann Knott's fate is also uncertain. She had married a "Harinton" by 1662, perhaps Jeremiah Harrington, of St. Michael's Hundred, whose wife, Ann, acknowledged a deed in 1669, but we cannot be sure. Ann Knott left few tracks for us to follow.

Mary Cole is only a bit less obscure. She had married Ignatius Warren, the son of a former servant and justice of the peace of Newtown Hundred, by 1673, when she was still not twenty years old. Mary then disappears from the record, although Ignatius lived on in Newtown for another twenty-five years, planting tobacco and, for a time, running an inn. In the early 1690s, Warren stood surety on bonds posted by two ship captains to guarantee their observance of the Navigation Acts. Their default ruined Warren, who was ordered to forfeit three thousand pounds to the Crown. His assets were clearly inadequate to cover the judgment: when he died in 1698, his personal estate was worth only twenty-six pounds. How long Mary lived or whether she had children is uncertain: neither wife nor children appear in the papers surrounding the settlement of Warren's affairs.

Francis Knott's life is more richly documented. He probably set up for himself in 1669, presumably on rented land. In late 1673 or early 1674, at about the time the Cole estate was settled, Francis, then twenty-four, married Elinor White, then perhaps sixteen. She was the daughter of Nicholas White (a servant to the Jesuit Thomas Copley), who had died in 1659, leaving two orphan children to be raised by Catholic families in the neighborhood. By the early 1680s the Knotts were living on a one-hundred-acre tract on St. Clement's Creek leased from William Shertcliffe for ninety-nine years, a secure tenure differing little from outright ownership. Among their closest neighbors were two of Luke Gardiner's sons, who lived on adjacent plantations; the record suggests that a close relationship, similar to that between the elder Cole and the elder Gardiner, developed among the Knotts and the younger Gardiners. Francis and Elinor had six sons and three daughters before Francis died in 1705 at age fifty-six. He left a modest estate worth only £62, most of it in livestock, after a long life as a small but respectable planter.

Edward, Robert Cole's third son, was the most successful of the children. In 1672 he went to England for further education, perhaps in the care of his father's London executor, Henry Hanckes. After his return, Edward remained on St. Clement's Manor until the early 1680s, apparently managing the Cole plantation after his brother Robert married and moved to his wife's land in Newtown Hundred. Edward had left the manor by 1688, probably settling on "St. Edward's," the land surveyed for him by Luke Gardiner and adjacent to Gardiner's holding at "St. John's." In that year Edward purchased, from Robert Cole, "St. William's" and "St. Robert's," the parcels taken out for his brothers by Gardiner. Edward remained in that area for some thirty years, raising seven children and participating actively in the affairs of his neighbors, who included the Knotts, Luke Gardiner's sons, members of the Brooke family, and numerous others whose lives had long been entwined with the Coles.

Edward Cole prospered after leaving the family farm. Sometime after moving to "St. Edward's," he set up a store and began selling goods to his neighbors, eventually becoming a factor for Captain John Hyde, one of the leading London tobacco merchants. He also continued to farm, operating a sizable, diversified plantation worked by seven slaves. We know little of Edward's first wife. He had married by 1683, probably to one Honor or Honory, and it is likely that she bore all of his children. Sometime after 1705, he married Robert Slye's daughter (and thus Thomas Gerard's granddaughter) Elizabeth, then the widow of Luke Gardiner, the son of Robert Cole's executor. Edward lived well, although in the "plain style" of his parents, choosing not to acquire many of the material symbols of gentility rapidly becoming common among successful Chesapeake planters. In 1717 he left a well-furnished, multiroom house, several hundred acres of land, and a personal estate worth £832 when he died at age sixty, firmly established as one of the leading Catholic gentlemen of St. Mary's County.

Luke Gardiner died in 1674, shortly after turning the Cole plantation over to young Robert. His career was marked by frequent conflict. In addition to the possible dispute over his management of the Cole estate, Gardiner got into trouble for talking disrespectfully to a councillor, attempting to raise a Protestant orphan as a Catholic, neglecting service in the St. Clement's Manor court, receiving stolen livestock, giving firearms to Indians, obtaining a patent by collusion, mistreating a servant, and trespassing on a neighbor's land. Nevertheless, by most measures he was successful. Despite his evident testiness, he was several times elected to the assembly and served as a county justice, sheriff, and militia captain. And he died a rich man by the standards of the day, leaving nearly seven thousand acres of land and personal property worth nearly five hundred seventy pounds, including ten servants and three slaves. Although Gardiner died just as the Cole children came of age and perhaps in a strained relationship with the heirs, the families remained intimate. Two of Luke's sons, John and Luke, settled just north of St. Clement's Manor, where they became close neighbors of their lifelong friends Francis Knott and Edward Cole.

The Cole plantation did not remain in the family. Robert sold it, probably in the late 1680s, to either William Rosewell or Joshua Guibert. Guibert owned it by 1691, and it remained in his family well into the eighteenth century. Guibert, a French Protestant born in Reims in 1645, came to Maryland as a servant in the 1660s. He had unusual success for a man with such a humble start so late in the century, gaining an advantage by marrying his master's daughter soon after becoming free in 1669. He served as justice of the peace for St. Mary's County from 1694 to 1701 and again in 1708, when he won election to the assembly as well. By this time he was married to his second wife, Elizabeth Gerard Blakiston Rymer, the daughter of Thomas Gerard and the widow of Councillor Nehemiah Blakiston. Guibert built a new house on the Cole plantation shortly before his death in 1713 at age sixty-eight. He left a personal estate worth £454 and several additional tracts of land, and he lived more elegantly than had the Coles, as his furnishings, silver plate, and "fine fashionable Coate" testify. By and large, however, as a productive unit, the Cole plantation had changed little since the days when Luke Gardi-

6.1 Plat of the Cole Plantation, c. 1724. This plat was made in connection with an action of ejectment brought after Joshua Guibert's death. The surveyor referred to the plat as "the Bounds of Land Called Coles," even though no Cole had owned the land for more than forty years. (Maryland State Archives)

ner ran it. Guibert grew flax, kept sheep, and spun yarn, but work rhythms on the farm were still dictated by cattle, swine, and horses, orchard and garden crops, corn and tobacco. Nevertheless, there was one momentous change. The Cole plantation was now worked by slaves, not servants. At his death Guibert owned eleven blacks.[3]

The Processes of Change

As the Cole children came of age and began families of their own they helped produce one of the primary transformations in late-seventeenth-century Chesapeake society: the rise of a native-born majority and the beginnings of reproductive population growth. In Maryland as a whole, natives became a majority among white adults around 1700, but in the older settled regions of the lower Western Shore the shift came earlier, in the 1670s. The process was slow and painful. Despite high rates of population increase, early Maryland suffered under a destructive demographic regime. High mortality, a shortage of women, and late marriages kept Maryland a society of immigrants long after the initial English invasion, ensured a surplus of deaths over births, and made for a fragile family system in which illegitimate births were frequent, brides often pregnant, marriages short, orphans common, and grandparents rare.[4]

Immigrants did have some children, however, and these children gradually transformed Maryland's demographic regime. Creoles (inhabitants of Old World descent born in the colonies) differed from immigrants in several important ways. For one thing, Creoles—at least the adult males among them—lived longer than their immigrant forebears. The gains were not large, however. It is also not clear that they extended to native-born women, and childhood mortality rates remained shocking by twentieth-century standards. Second, the sex ratio among those born in the colony was approximately equal, although as late as 1704—by which time there is firm evidence of reproductive population gain in the colony—men still outnumbered women by more than three to two. Finally, and perhaps most important, Creole women married at much younger ages than had their immigrant mothers. The vast majority of women born in Maryland during the seventeenth century were married before their twentieth birthday, and the average age at marriage may have been as low as sixteen years. Such youthful marriages meant that Creole women had enough children to ensure a growing population despite a continuing surplus of males and a persistent high mortality.[5]

The rise of a native-born majority and the beginnings of reproductive increase brought a dramatic shift in the composition of Maryland's population. There is no enumeration of Maryland's inhabitants for the early colonial period, but it is possible to construct rough estimates from tax lists and county court records. When the Cole family arrived in the 1650s, Maryland was a frontier society and a man's world. Men were about two-thirds of the population and outnumbered women by three or four to one. Only about a quarter of the inhabitants were children. In 1712, adult men were only 28 percent of the white population of St. Mary's County. They still outnumbered women, but only by a ratio of about eleven to nine. Children show the largest increase: in 1712, half the county's white inhabitants were under sixteen. At least by a demographic standard, St. Mary's County was no longer the Chesapeake frontier.[6]

The changes brought by the rise of a native-born majority went far beyond the composition of the population. Although it was hardly secure, Creole family life was more stable than that of immigrants. Native-born women seldom had illegitimate children, and with the telling exception of orphan girls who wed immigrants, they were rarely pregnant when they married. Greater parental control apparently returned levels of extramarital sex to the norm among the English yeomanry. Nearly all native-born men were able to find wives, and since natives married earlier and lived longer, marriages between them were more durable, lasting twice as long as marriages among immigrants. Their families were also larger: Creole women who married in Maryland during the seventeenth century typically had six children, two to three more than the average among immigrants. Creoles were still unlikely to live long enough to become grandparents, but they did so more often than had their immigrant forebears. Orphanhood too was less common, although it was hardly unusual, and children who lost their parents were more likely to have kin in their neighborhood to take them in. The gradual growth of a native-born majority brought more than biological population growth and a new demographic structure to early Maryland. It also brought a more durable and certain family life, a change with profound material and emotional consequences.[7]

The growth of a native-born population changed relationships along the bay in other ways. During Robert Cole's day, when most adult males were immigrants without parents, siblings, aunts, uncles, cousins, grand-parents, or in-laws living nearby, kin ties were confined to members of the same household. Kin rarely linked separate households to one another. As children born in the colony came of age and formed families of their own, households were bound together through increasingly dense kinship networks, bewilderingly complex to historians who try to unravel them but clear and tangible to those whose lives they structured.

It was more than a matter of kinship. By the early eighteenth century, the whites of St. Mary's County lived among people they knew intimately as a result of lifelong contact. In Robert and Rebecca's time, neighbor-hoods had been rudimentary associations born of necessity and conve-nience, rapidly shifting in composition with the steady arrival of newcom-ers. Now neighborhoods acquired new meaning and more familiar definition as they were built out of more elaborate kin ties and long-term friendships. Robert and Rebecca Cole had lived among relative strangers and had been forced to turn to Luke Gardiner and William Evans, men they had known for less than a decade, when faced with a severe family crisis. Francis Knott and Edward Cole, by contrast, lived in a much dif-ferent, more secure and familiar world, close to each other, surrounded by Brookes, Gardiners, and other old friends and relatives. Neighbor-hoods were becoming communities with a sense of cohesiveness and soli-darity, assuming responsibility for a wide range of common concerns from maintaining roads to regulating morality to caring for the unfortu-nate, changing in the process the whole fabric of life along the bay.[8]

Paradoxically, as neighborhoods gained cohesiveness, Maryland soci-ety lost the homogeneity that had characterized it in Robert and Rebec-ca's day. One major source of greater heterogeneity was a transformation in the labor force, a change personified by Edward Cole's seven slaves and by the eleven blacks who lived on the Cole plantation at Joshua Gui-bert's death. When Luke Gardiner had managed the Cole estate, the great majority of unfree workers in Maryland were indentured servants who were not sharply distinguished from the planters they served and who hoped to become masters in their own right. As the century pro-gressed, however, planters found it difficult to recruit enough English servants to work their crops. A declining population and higher wages in England improved prospects at home, while the opening up of Pennsyl-vania and the Carolinas joined with continued growth along the tobacco coast and in the sugar islands to produce greater colonial competition for workers. The result was a labor shortage along the bay and a change in the composition of the work force as planters purchased slaves to replace servants. In 1680, inventoried servants outnumbered inventoried slaves by almost four to one in Maryland, and blacks were only 5 percent of the living population. By 1710, there were roughly five inventoried slaves for each servant, and blacks were more than 15 percent of the living inhabitants; in some counties the proportion approached one-third.[9]

The process of farm building played a central role in the transition to a slave society, providing the capital base on which the structures of the "golden age" rested. In the middle decades of the seventeenth century, Marylanders simply lacked the resources for a large investment in slaves. "I have endeavoured to see if I could find as many responsible men that would engage to take a 100 or 200 neigros every yeare from the Royall Company," Charles Calvert explained to his father in 1664, "but I find wee are nott men of estates good enough to undertake such a businesse, but could wish wee were for wee are naturally inclin'd to love neigros if our purses would endure it."[10] By century's end, enough "responsible men" whose "purses would endure it" were available to sustain a large-scale slave trade, in part because they had built farms that generated sufficient income to pay for blacks or that stood as collateral for a loan from an English merchant to buy them. The transition to slavery was a complex process, more than a simple matter of building farms and buying blacks. Relative prices and shifting supplies proved critical, as did the elaboration of a legal system that safeguarded investments in slaves. But the accumulation of capital through farm making played an essential role by providing planters with the means to finance the Africanization of the Chesapeake work force.[11]

These new black workers faced a harsh environment. Their demographic circumstances were even more constraining than those encountered by immigrant whites. Blacks suffered not only from the volatile disease environment and a shortage of women that prevented reproductive growth but also from added burdens: a degrading slavery and abusive masters; isolation from other blacks on small plantations; and restrictions on their movement that prevented them from taking full advantage of the few opportunities left to form families.

Nevertheless, slaves experienced a transition remarkably similar to that among whites. Creole blacks, like their Euro-American counterparts, lived longer, "married" earlier, had more durable unions (despite their masters' frequent disregard of their family ties), and produced more children than had their African-born parents. By the 1720s there were enough native-born blacks in Maryland to create a naturally increasing slave population. Slavery remained harsh and oppressive, but demographic changes helped blacks to give structure, meaning, and dignity to their lives and to build ties of affection, family, and friendship that made their oppression more bearable and their condition less desperate. The growth of a native-born slave population also fostered the rise of a distinctive Afro-Chesapeake culture built out of common heritage and experience and articulated through kin networks. The addition of a distinct black culture ended the cultural homogeneity that had prevailed in Maryland during Robert Cole's age.[12]

The growth of slavery was only the most visible of the changes that worked to transform Maryland's labor system after 1670. There were also shifts in the distribution of labor, in the types of people who came as servants, in opportunities, and in master-worker relationships. When servants had dominated the work force, during Robert Cole's day, unfree workers had been widely distributed among Maryland households. Most small and middling planters owned servants, most laborers lived on small farms, and plantations manned by large gangs were rare, all of which promoted the integration of laborers into the families they served. However, the labor shortage drove servant prices up, and slaves required a capital outlay larger than what small men could manage. This drove many small planters out of the labor market and concentrated unfree workers on the estates of the wealthy. In the 1660s, half the householders worth thirty to fifty pounds owned servants, and the majority of bound workers labored for men worth less than two hundred pounds. Around the turn of the century, however, small planters, men like Robert Cole, Jr., and Francis Knott, rarely owned labor, and the majority of bound workers lived on the estates of richer men such as Edward Cole and Joshua Guibert. The rise of slavery accompanied the growth of large plantations while eliminating small planters from the ranks of labor owners, processes with far-reaching consequences for the structure of Chesapeake society.[13]

Indentured servitude did not disappear with the rise of slavery, but it did decline in importance, and it did change. Before 1680, a substantial proportion of the servants recruited to Maryland were drawn from England's middling families—young men in their late teens and early twenties who often arrived with job skills and work experience, men whose backgrounds resembled those of the planters they served. Such men continued to come after 1680, usually to work on large plantations as managers and artisans, but they were a much smaller share of the immigrants. Instead, servants were now drawn primarily from England's depressed and disadvantaged inhabitants. They were more often female, more frequently orphans or convicts, more often recruited from England's Celtic fringe, and more likely to be young, unskilled, inexperienced, and illiterate. The shift in composition widened the gap between master and servant, reinforcing the impact of the concentration of workers on large plantations.[14]

The change in the composition of servant immigrants was accompanied with a sharp decline in prospects. Tenancy, sharecropping, and wage labor, once steps up an agricultural ladder leading to ownership of a plantation, became the lifelong fate of a growing proportion of former servants. In St. Mary's County in 1660, about 10 percent of householders were tenants; in 1704, the figure was about 33 percent, and rising land prices were making it much harder than before to move from a lease to a freehold.[15] The change is evident in the lives of the servants on the Cole plantation. The most successful of them, Joseph Alvey and Robert Gates, arrived early, in the 1650s, and gained their freedom while St. Mary's was still a good poor-man's country. No servants purchased under Luke Gardiner's guardianship did as well; most simply disappeared after a few years as hired hands or after brief stints as tenant farmers, apparently either dying early or moving on in search of brighter prospects elsewhere. Late in the seventeenth century, Maryland exchanged the existing labor system, one that promised men who started at the bottom an eventual integration into the society they served, for one that enslaved the majority of its laborers and offered its servants and other whites who started with nothing a choice between poverty and migration.[16]

Although the transformation of the labor system represents a profound watershed in the history of the Chesapeake colonies, it would be an error to exaggerate the differences between the organization of work in Robert Cole's world and during the "golden age" of the great tidewater planters. For one thing, the change occurred in most areas without a major shift in the agricultural base. Farming did become everywhere somewhat more diverse, as Joshua Guibert's sheep and flax crop suggest, and there were subtle changes in the Chesapeake system of husbandry as some planters, with no virgin forest and with farms well established, began to plow and fertilize their fields and to pen and feed their livestock. But the work routines of Guibert's slaves still turned on tobacco and corn, cattle and hogs, much as had the routines of Robert Cole's servants. For another, although the scale of operations increased noticeably, plantations remained small by the standards of the sugar islands or the Carolina low country: as late as the 1750s in St. Mary's County, half the slaves still lived and worked on plantations with no more than ten blacks.[17] Further, even though a larger proportion of planters escaped manual labor altogether and more men found positions as overseers or opportunities in skilled crafts, slavery did not change work routines for the great majority of whites. Most men and boys remained in the fields; women and girls still worked at or supervised household tasks.[18]

Continuity in work regimes did not signal an economic steady state. Perhaps the most important change was in the *pace* of change. Robert and Rebecca Cole had arrived in Maryland in the midst of a great expansive phase of Chesapeake economic history, a period marked by substantial gains in wealth and income, by an enormous rise in settled area and in the number of farms, and by an impressive creativity in agriculture as planters established the Chesapeake system of husbandry. By the 1670s, when the Cole children reached maturity, this expansive phase was winding down in most areas of early settlement, which may explain why all but one of the Coles were unable to match their parents' accomplishments. The tobacco industry entered a long period of stagnation stretching from the 1680s to the 1710s, an era in which exports did not increase, in which population, settled area, and the number of farms grew slowly, and in which productivity gains achieved through an innovative, experimental agriculture were no longer evident.[19] In the 1730s and 1740s, the Chesapeake colonies entered a new growth era, one driven by a revitalized export sector and characterized everywhere by greater economic diversity. Marked regional differentiation began to appear as opening overseas markets for wheat and corn began to encourage planters with inferior tobacco soils to cut back on the "sot-weed" or abandon it for grains. This new expansionary phase provided an essential prop for the "golden age," supported a more cosmopolitan culture, and made many families comfortable and some rich. However, it lacked the dynamism of

Robert and Rebecca's day, when planters built farms and created a new style of agriculture appropriate to Chesapeake conditions. Economic growth was faster before 1675 than it was to be again in colonial times.[20]

The passing of Robert Cole's world—the end of the age of the yeoman planter—is also evident at the top of Maryland society, in the rise of a clearly defined Chesapeake gentry.[21] In the middle decades of the seventeenth century, short life expectancies, late marriages, and an immigrant majority worked to keep early Maryland society fairly open and fluid. Men in the process of accumulating fortunes were, like Robert Cole, cut down before they acquired great wealth and before their sons were old enough to take their place. An absence of dense kin networks, the steady arrival of men from England with capital and connections, and the frequent success of those who began without such advantages but who exploited opportunities in farm building forestalled the development of solidarity and group consciousness among those at the top.

The character of Maryland leaders began to shift around the turn of the century. The growth of a Creole majority meant longer lives, earlier and more durable marriages, dense and elaborate kin networks. In turn, these developments had a profound impact on wealth distribution and inheritance, on group consciousness among the great planters, and on public life in the colony. Longer lives gave some men more opportunity to accumulate fortunes and were an element in increasing inequality. Moreover, older men were more likely to have adult sons when they died, and thus those in high position were better able to pass on their political power and their social status intact.[22] In consequence, over the first half of the eighteenth century, the rise of a class-conscious, native-born gentry transformed public life as a small group of "First Families" assumed the responsibility (and captured the benefit) of government at both the local and the provincial levels.

This Chesapeake-wide process of class formation was slowed in southern Maryland by religious division, a conflict resolved in a way that must have been painful for the Cole family, especially for Edward, the most successful of Robert and Rebecca's children. Anti-Catholic and antiproprietary sentiments had simmered in Maryland after 1660, occasionally bubbling up but not posing a serious threat to public order and Calvert rule until the late 1680s, when they boiled over in rebellion. The occasion for rebellion was the Glorious Revolution in England, which deposed the Catholic James II in favor of his Protestant daughter Mary and her husband, William of Orange. Taking advantage of rumors of a French-Indian invasion and of the failure of Lord Baltimore's government to proclaim William and Mary, a small group of malcontents moved against the proprietor. They convinced the militia of the southern Maryland counties that Catholics were conspiring with the French and Indians. Late in July 1689, the militia marched on St. Mary's City and forced the government to surrender. In 1692, after several years of uncertainty, the Crown ended Calvert rule and sent a royal governor to Maryland. Until 1715, when a Protestant Lord Baltimore regained governing powers, Maryland was a royal colony, and for the rest of the colonial period it remained under exclusively Protestant rule.[23]

Although achieved with a minimum of disorder or disruption of daily life and productive of little basic, structural change, Maryland's "Revolution of Government" necessarily had momentous consequences for local Catholics. In the privacy of their homes, they were allowed to continue their religious observances, their estates were not attached, and there was no overt, government-sanctioned harassment. However, the Church of England was established in Maryland, which meant that Catholics had to pay taxes in support of a Protestant faith. More important, all officials, and eventually all voters, were required to take oaths that repudiated papal authority and denied transubstantiation. By this means Catholics were excluded from public office, including jury duty, and from the vote.

In St. Mary's County, where perhaps one-third of the population was Catholic, the impact of their exclusion was the most pronounced, although it was felt everywhere on the lower Western Shore. Juries proved difficult to impanel, minor offices were hard to fill, and successful Catholic gentlemen such as Edward Cole had to sit by and watch lesser men gain positions of power and responsibility, positions that in Robert Cole's day Catholics could have claimed. Some prominent Catholics had informal methods of exerting the influence of their wealth and social position through business partnerships, marriages, and friendships with leading Protestant families. Nevertheless, religious differences constituted a serious breach in the development of solidarity and class consciousness among the region's great planters.[24]

Robert and Rebecca Cole had come to Maryland to practice freedom of religion; their grandchildren lived in a land as restricted as the one the grandparents had left. Insofar as we can trace them, Cole's descendants maintained their Catholic faith, but to practice it openly before the

American Revolution, they had to recross the ocean. In the 1740s and 1750s, three of the Coles' great-grandchildren, grandsons of Edward Cole, left Maryland for France and Spain to become Jesuit priests and may never have returned to the land of their birth.[25]

By the time Cole's son Edward died in 1717, Maryland was a much different place from what it had been in his parents' day. For many, life was more secure and more comfortable. Mortality rates had declined, kin networks had flowered, neighborhoods had become more cohesive, public life had lost its rough-and-tumble quality. Many planters were modifying the system of husbandry that had enabled seventeenth-century planters to exploit a virgin forest but that had built-in limits to growth. Those who could adapt their ways were soon to enjoy a new wave of prosperity in a more diversified economy that provided buffers against the uncertainties of international markets. But security and comfort brought a high price. The fluid society of the yeoman planter's age had disappeared, and Maryland's experiment with religious pluralism had come to an abrupt end. In its place had emerged a society in which wealth and high position were more often inherited than achieved, in which Roman Catholics were excluded from public life, and in which men on the bottom found few opportunities. Maryland now had a social structure marked by clear (though not unbridgeable) class distinctions and harsh caste barriers. This was no longer Robert and Rebecca Cole's world, but for good or for ill, their farm-building enterprise, and others like it, had helped to lay the foundations for what Maryland had become.

Appendixes

Appendix 1

· · · · ·

Transcripts of
Robert Cole's Will
and the Cole
Plantation Account

Robert Cole's will and the Cole Plantation Account are recorded in the Testamentary Proceedings of the Maryland Prerogative Court, located in the Maryland State Archives, Annapolis, Maryland. The original documents do not survive. In 1663 the will was recorded in Testamentary Proceedings 1(D): 118–22. In 1725 it was copied into Wills 1:182–86, with slightly different spelling, punctuation, and capitalization. We have printed here the earlier recordation. The Cole Plantation Account, really a guardian account, was recorded on Tuesday, March 3, 1673, in Testamentary Proceedings 6:118–47. Since the clerk used old-style dating, in which the new year began on March 25, the year in our terms was 1674. Throughout the will and account, dates between January 1 and March 25 are old-style.

We have followed the original spelling and capitalization with the following adaptations: (1) we have written *th* instead of *y* for the thorn (for instance, *the* instead of *ye*), and (2) given that *u* and *v*, and *j* and *i*, were interchangeable letters in the seventeenth century, we have followed modern usage in spelling words that contain them. Most abbreviations are expanded. However, we retained the ampersand, the abbreviation *lb.*, and abbreviations of titles, such as *Mr.* Where words were crossed out in the original record, we have printed the word with a line through it. A handful of words are illegible. To indicate these, we have printed [*illegible*]. Page numbers from the documents are in brackets and are inserted in the text where pages changed.

Robert Cole's Will, 1662

[118]
In the name of God amen the Second day of Aprill in the yeare of Our
Lord 1662 I Robert Cole of St Clements Bay in the Province of Maryland
Yeaman being in Good health and perfect memory praise bee Given to
God for the Same and being desirous to settle thinges doe make this my
last will & testament in manner and forme following.

That is to say, first and principally I comend my Soule to Almighty God
my Creator and my Body to the Earth from whence it was taken and
touching such worldly Estate as the lord in mercy hath lent my will and
meaning is the same shall be imployed and bestowed as hereafter by this
my will is Expressed, and first I doe revoke renounce frustrate and make
voyd all wills by mee formerly made and declare & appointe this my Last
will and Testament after my death Certainly knowne.

1. Item I give and bequeath to my honored friend Mr Francis Fitzherbert
or his Successor the best hogshead of tobaccoe of my Crop and the best
Steere of my Stock in Testimony that I dye a Roman Cathelicke and desire the prayers of the holy Church.

2. Item I give and bequeath unto my Loving Sonn in Law Francis Knott
the eighth part of all my Cattle when hee doth attaine the age of eighteen
yeares but in Case he should dye before that time then my will is that his
Sister Ann Harinton shall have one halfe of the Eighth part and my owne
Children the other halfe but in Case Ann Harinton be dead before Francis come to that age and Leave no issue that then my Children shall have
the whole gift equally amongst them.

[119]
3. Item I give and bequeath unto my sonn Robert Cole my Daughter
Mary Cole my sonn William Cole my sonn Edward my daughter Elizabeth Cole all the rest of my Cattle to bee equally shared amongst them as
each of them to the age of Eighteene yeares that is to say when my Sonn
Robert comes to that age hee shall the fift part of my Cattle taken from
the rest and knowne to bee his and so forth till the two youngest com to
the same age as aforesaid.

4. Item I give and bequeath to my Daughter Mary Cole One Feather bed Boulster pillowes Blanckitt Red rugg and One paire of my best sheets, and my Spice mortar and pessell, and one Iron pott and my Copper kitle and One smoothing Iron.

5. Item I give and bequeath Elizabeth Cole my best Flock bed and Bolster greene rugg one blanckitt. One pair of sheets one Iron pott Six napkins one diaper table Cloath & one Smoothing Iron.

6. Item I give and bequeath unto my sonn Robert Cole to him & his heires for ever my plantation I now live on and all the land and howses belonging to it with the Orchard, hee the said Robert paying unto his Brother William and his Brother Edward the halfe of all the benifitt of the Orchard for the space of Seaven yeares as aforesaid.

7. Item my will is that my foresaid Children have such Education in learning as to write and read and Cast accompt I meane my three sonns my two daughters to learne to read and sowe with theire needle, and all of them to bee kept from Idleness but not to bee kept as Common servants and that the learning soe bestowed on my Children bee out of my whole Estate before they doe Come to the age aforesaid and after such learning so bestowed that such Care bee taken of my Children that they may not forgett theire learning before they doe Come to the age as aforesaid.

8. Item my will is that my servants may bee imployed for the most benifitt and good of my Children, and when or as they bee Free such or soe many others may bee put in theire roomes to serve my Children Joyntly.

9. Item my will is that my Executors hereafter named have such power by this present writinge of this my will as to sell or dispose of any part of my Estate for the good of my Children in Generall.

[120]
And my will is that my Stock of Cattle never exceed the number of fifty, One whole yeare together but they may bee sold either alive or dead for the use of my Children as aforesaid, but not soe sold as to Scant Either my Children or servants of necessary and holsom provisione for their health & strength.

10. Item I give and bequeath to my sonn in law Francis Knott the rights of 50 acres of land as they doe stand upon the Record whereas I had a

warrant to survey fower hundred acres and I did Survey but 350, the which survey I did assigne to John Wheeler.

11. Item I give & bequeath unto my three sonns, Robert William & Edward Cole the rights of 600 acres of Land equally amongst them whereof I have a warrant of 450 acres amongst my papers, since that warrant was granted I have rights for John Elton, Sibelo Jackson, & Isabella Joanes for theire transportations.

12. Item I give and bequeath all the Estate whatsoever bee it Land howses or mony that doth any wayes belong to mee in England or of right should belong to mee unto my Children in Generall after the death of my Loving mother Mrs Jone Cole of heston in the County of Middlesex but in Case my Mother should bee necessitated & empoverished then my will is that my Mother have sent to her a Competent yearely and every yeare a reasonable Sustenance out of my Estate during her naturall life. My will is allso that if any of my Children doth dye before the age aforesaid or under the age of twenty one yeares without issue that then such a part as did belong to such an one shall bee equally divided amongst them that are living. My will is allso that if any of my Children dye without issue that then it shall not bee in ther powers to give to any other then their Brothers or sisters more then one fowrth part of such goods or Chattles given by mee to them as they shall be possessed of at the day of theire death.

13. Item I give all the rest of my Estate as hoggs beding pewter potts kittles spoones tubbs payles trayes bottles Juggs rundletts tables Chaires Stooles Linnin and woollen pottry and all other Goods that doth belong to mee or may hereafter belong to mee unto my 3 sonns Robert William and Edward

[121]
Together with my Gunns powder and shott reserving onely two sowes and a Barrow of two yeares old for my son in Law Francis Knott if hee doth live to the age aforesaid if hee should dye before that age then all to my three sonns aforesaid or to those that do survive the rest that are departed this life.

14. Item My will is and I doe by these presents Constitute and appointe my loving friendes Collonell William Evans and Captain Luke Gardner

both of St. Clements Bay, and my loving Couzin Mr. Henry hanckes of holborne in the Citty of london to bee my Executors and or overseers or any two of them in this Country and in England any one of them to Execute this my last will giveing them power and Authority over all my Children and theire Estates tell they doe attaine the age of twenty and One yeares as allso power over all the premises aforesaid, as allso power and authority to make and appointe one or more Overseers after theire death for the fullfilling of this my will, giving to them all a strict Charge that my Children bee brought and taught in the Roman Catholique Religion, as they shall the Contrary att the dreadfull day of Judgment. In testimony that is my last will and Testament I doe hereunto sett my hand and seale the day and yeare above written with five enterlines which bee these, Brother, my, will, wright, or sisters.   Robert Cole

                                                            Locus Sigille

Witnessed by us and signed
and sealed before us
Justice & Coram
Thomas Brooke
James Thompson Clarke
Edward Clarke

The power that is given to my Executors is Joyntly and after the death of any one of them then my will is that the other may Act by himselfe or Chose one to him to assist himme if the departed hath not appointed one in his steed before his death but my Couzin Hanckes is to act in England by himselfe or with advice as wittnes my hand

                                                            Robert Cole

[122]
My sonn Robert Cole was borne 15th October 1652. My Daughter Mary Cole was borne the 26th January 1653. My son william Cole was borne the 23d June 1655. My son Edward Cole was borne 9th November 1657. My daughter Elizabeth Cole was borne 2d March 1659. Francis Knott is 3 yeares older then my sonn Robert Cole is, as wittnes my hand this 25th of Aprill 1662 Robert Cole

My meaning is that my Children shall know theire porcons att 18 yeares old but not have absolute possession till they bee 21 yeares of age unless my Daughter bee marryed to an honest Catholique then att 18 yeares.

                                                            Robert Cole

September 8th 1663
James Thompson Gentn sayth uppon Oathe that being att Newtowne Robert Cole requested hime to sett his hand to this paper telling hime withall that it was his will (hee the said Cole being then bound for England) and it was signed and sealed in this deponants presence by the said Robert Cole and hee knoweth of no other will that ever Robert Cole made

James Thompsone

Sworn before me
Wm Bretton
September 16th 1663
Thomas Brooke Gentn sayth uppon Oath that hee signed this will as a wittness and that it was Robert Coles Act and deed and that hee knoweth of no other will made by the said Robert Cole

Thomas Brooke

Sworne before mee
Henry Sewall Secretary

The Cole Plantation Account:
Luke Gardiner's Guardian Account
for the Cole Estate, 1662–1673

[118]
Die Martis Martij 3: <u>1673.</u>
Whereas Luke Gardner the sole Surviveing Executor of Robert Cole late of St. Clements Bay in the County of St. Maries deceased, att the request of Robert Cole Sonn and heire of the Said Deceased,[1] & Ignatious Warren[2] who married Mary the daughter of the Said Deceased was Cited to this Court to Render an Account of his Executorshipp, whereuppon the Said Luke 17: Octobris 1673 appeared and in presence of the Said Cole and Warren[3] delivered in his account of and concerning the Execution of the Said Last will and Testament in writeing Signed with his hand of which account the Said Robert Cole the heire & the Said Ignatious Warren prayed Coppies and time till the tenth of November then next Following to make theire Exceptions to the said account which was then Accordingly granted, att which Said tenth day of November appeared as

well the Said Luke Gardner the Executor as the Said Robert Cole and Ignatious Warren and the said Robert Cole the heire to the deceased Delivered in his Exceptions in writing to the account of the Said Executor: (vizt) in thirteene Articles in particular; to which the Executor Imediatly made answeres which were taken in writeing by the Judge or Comissary general for Testamentary causes;[4] which being read and considered by the Said Robert Cole and nothing further objected in particular materiall to hinder the passing the Said accounts, the Said Judge would further Advise himselfe uppon the Said account in Regard of the last Exception

[119]
Exception in General to the Said account made by the Said Robert (vizt) the Executors account (of which hee prayes Allowance), being Soe Imperfect in many the particulars, there being noe Express time of the Delivery or to whome or for what account whereby itt is Impossible for the Said Robert to make his Just Exceptions to severall particulars, therefore Recommends the Said Account to the Judgement of the Judge in Testamentary busines to Rectify the same as to his Honor Seemes meete & Agreeable to Equity; and thereuppon the Said Judge did take into his hands the account of the said Luke and after mature Consideration thereof & the Exceptions to the Same made caused the same to bee Rectifyed in many particulars not mentioned in the Exceptions of the Said Robert & uppon the 14th: of February 1673 called the Said Executor to make oath to the particulars of his owne account that Stood allowed by the Said Judge, which the Said Executor not being able to doe in Common forme butt onely in the speciall manner as att the foote of the account is annexed, The Said Judge declared that in Regard the Said Luke Gardner never tooke out Letters Testamentary uppon probate of the will of the Said Robert Cole Deceased, never tooke the oath of Executor to make a true Account, nor never made Inventory or appraisement of the goods, chattells Rights and creditts of the Said Deceased nor hath kept such an Account of his Administration of the goods chattells Rights and creditts of the said Robert deceased as hee dares Absolutely Sweare to as an Executor ought to doe, the said Luke hath lost all benefitt or advantage of an Executor and is punishable att the Discretion of the Judge here; butt for asmuch as itt appeares hee hath Improved the Stock of Cattle & hoggs to a greater number then Robert Cole left att his Depar-

ture for England; and Raised a Stocke of Horses for the Orphans where
the testator left none; The Said Judge doth order that the Orphans of
Robert Cole deceased Shall Receive the househould goods in the Condition they are in, the Cattle & hogs as they are Shared to them, and the
horses to bee devided Amongst them after the Said Luke Gardiner hath
chosen one Mare & foale by her Side, which the Judge testamentary doth
hereby order him as the onely Reward of his paines and care taken in
maneageing the Said estate,[5] and doth further order him to Detaine out
of the cropp of tobacco now made[6] the ballance of the account as itt
Stands Rectified and allowed by the Said Judge (vizt) Eleaven hundred
Eighty three pounds of tobacco together with 2553: £ tobacco for Itinerat
Charges in twelve years time Expended by the said Executor.[7]

[120]
The account of Luke Gardner gent the Sole Surviveing Executor of the
last will & Testament of Robert Cole late of St. Clements Hundred in the
County of St. Maries as itt Stands allowed by the Judge for probate of
wills & graunting Administrations after Exceptions made by Robert Cole
Sonne & heire of the Testator & Ignatious Warren who married Mary the
Daughter of the Testator.

Imprimis The accountant Stands charged with all & Singular the goods
& chattells of the Said Deceased according to an Inventory of them made
by the Said Robert Cole the Testator & left in the hands of the Account-
ants by the Said Testator att his Departure for England, which is as
followeth:
March 9th 1661.
An Inventory of the cattle belonging to mee Robert Cole and the markes
of them att this time.

Imprimis Twelve Cowes young and old five Steeres young & old[8] four heifers two yeares old;[9] Eleaven yeare old calves; one two yeare old heifer of my Sonn Roberts given by John Thimbleby; one bull att brambley[10] or thereabouts; one black steare about Bassfoord Mannor[11]   In all thirty & three cattle att home & two from home which makes 35

The markes[12] of these Cattle are severall. My owne marke is underkeeled
on the Right Eare & overkeeled on the left eare, the Cattle I doe in-

tend for my children hath a Slitt in the left Eare on the underside of the eare.

The marke of my Sonn Roberts heifer is underkeeled on the Right Eare and a slitte and the left Eare is overkeeled & Slitt.

Some of my cattle are branded in the Horne thus R:$\overset{\text{R:}}{\underset{\text{C:}}{}}$

The number of my hoggs is uncertaine butt of them that come home I thinke there is twenty nine of them and four young piggs they bee all underkeeled on the Right Eare and Overkeeled on the left eare & noe other marke.

My Desire is that all my cattle bee branded in the horne as above & that all the Calves bee this yeare onely under & overkeeled & noe Slitt att all.

God bless my Stock and send itt to thrive for the good of my poore children.

April 29th 1662. The cattle are all Liveing butt onely my Sonn Roberts heifer is Supposed to bee dead as Witness my hand.

Ro: Cole

[121]
I doe ow unto one of mr. Slyes[13] Servants two Cowes & Calves to bee paid in June next. I hope my wife will not pay the best for itt is butt Cowes & Calves that I must pay.

Signed Ro: Cole

The accountant Standeth further charged by goods Contained in an Inventory all writt in the hand of Robert Cole & left in the hands of the Said accountant which is as Followeth:

	£ Tobacco
Imprimis Four Servants: John Elton Robert Gates John Johnson Isbell Jones	
Two tobacco hogsheads full of Salt 28 bushells	
Six bushells more of Salt five Iron potts two pair of potthookes two small Iron Kettles[14] two Skelletts[15] one Copper Kettle 18 gallons	350
Two Fryeing panns[16] two pair of bellowes one pair of fire tongs & Shovell	
One spitt mortar & pestle bell mettle[17]	65
One Iron pestle one Iron chaine for the Chimney three	

Small hookes[18] fiveteene Milktrayes[19] five Cedar tubbs for
the Dary one Cedar cheese tubb, one oaken Milke tubb
one Coule & Coule Staffe,[20] one powdring tubb[21] one
great Round bowle five payles

One Mobby[22] tubb two dozen of trenchers[23] one dozen &
halfe of Spoones one Cullender of tinn; three tinn dripping panns;[24] one tinn Funnell; five tinn Candlesticks;
two Wyar candlesticks; one pewter bottle; one pepper box
of tinn; one pepper grinder; on Straineing Dish

One chafeing dish[25] one tinn Scummer[26] two wooden platters two Sifting trayes one grid Iron,[27] one Iron Ladle, five
pewter platters, one pewter bason four pewter porrengers;[28] two small pewter Dishes; five wooden Spoones;
three wooden Ladles; two pewter pint potts one pewter
quart pott one tinn quart pott one tobacco knife, one
charne to charne butter

One Salt box two greate butter potts; five Smaller earthen;
one Earthen fryeing pann one three Legged creame pott
earthen one Corne barrell; three thight barrells for liquor
one thight Ancor tenn Gallons[29] four good small Rundletts[30] three Meale Sifters of haire one homany Sifter[31]

Three [*illegible*] Tobacco Hogsheads   75

[122]

Four other casque in the Lofts five Joynt Stooles;[32] five Joy-
ner chaires the arme of one is broken, one chaire table,[33]
one table and Dresser[34] in the Kitchen; three three Legged Stooles

One Canow none of the best although Shee bee new   80

One warming pann Six pictures[35] in the Hall three Lardge
Stone Juggs

One Small pair of Stilliards[36]   60

One Iron bound case with Six bottles pewter Screwes;[37] one
earthen pitcher, one earthen Jugg, two gallons of Sweete
oyle

One butter tubb   25

Two case of quart bottles; five Specled Dutch potts to drink in[38] nine other like peeces; butt they bee butter potts dishes & porringers

Four paire of Sheetes, one od Sheete, one towell four pillow beares[39] one dyaper[40] tablecloth, two tablecloths Six new napkins, two napkins from my mother[41] two white woomans aprons; one greene Say[42] appron

One white woomans shift	40
One Counterpaine[43] att	80
A parcell of child bed Linnen	
Two woomans fine Holland[44] Handkecheifes	50
Three Cross cloths[45]	28
Three fine dressings	60
Two handkecheifes	30
One Holland neckcloth	30
One holland appron	50
One pair of thred[46] gloves one pair of Cotten gloves	
One Stometcher[47]	20

One pair of Sheetes for use Left; thirty one yards of Canvas, one pound of Candleweeke, one pound more for use left

One pair of woomans bodies[48]	50

Four pair of woomans Shooes; two pair of old woomans Shooes one pair of buckskinn gloves; one pair of woomens new Shooes one pair of woomens woosted[49] Stockins; one pair of woomens yarne Stockins

Three old child's blanketts	30
One Red broad cloth[50] suite	300
One pennistone[51] petticoate	60

[123]

One serge[52] wastcoate	60

Four pair of Irish Stockins;[53] one canvas Jackett, Eleaven pair of childrens Stockins; one & 1/2 yards of Flannell for the child, two & 1/2 yards of Red Shagcloth[54] four & 1/2 yards of penistone; Six & 1/2 yards of penistone: three yards & 3/4 blew linnen[55] four & 1/2 yards of course Holland

Eleaven ells[56] of Lockrome,[57] four yards of Red Serge, 1/2

pound of pepper, one ounce & 1/2 Saffron, Some nutt-
megs cloves & Cynamon two Raysors one pound of Ginger 1/2 pound of Starch use one pound more in the chest
nine Shoomakers lasts Joseph[58] hath one of these four
Shoomakers Alls a parcell of Greene galume[59] & other
laces of two Sorts

A parcell of Linnen in a bundle & one Silver bodkin[60]
& one Silver whistle a Curvell[61] 1/2 pound of whited
browne thred, four severall sorts of fair thred 3/4 lb. Red
thred, four ounces of Silke,[62] one Silke lace Three par-
cells of Ribbon 2000 of pinns Some tape[63] & Filleten[64]
bindeing[65] points;[66] Cotten Ribbon; nine pair of Sissers;
pinns & thred needles Sope Soft & hard; Ginger nutt-
megg cloves Some, biskett delivered for this years use to
Mary[67] with Sugar

One branding Iron R:C: two Ivory Combes for the children
one fetherbed boulsters two Pillowes with blanketts two
pillowes with blanketts red Rugg[68] two Flock beds[69] with
boulsters pillowes two blanketts two greene Rugs one
greene Rugg more in the chest [illegible] the Red one
before Spoke of

My Servants bedding is Sufficient besides the have two
white blanketts coverled and Small greene old Rugg

One pair of Cart Wheeles   200

One barrell of Tarr aboute some 18 gallons one grindstone,
bramble tooth Saw three Iron Wedges, one pair of small
hoopes or Rings for a Mall,[70] two handsawes one tennent
Saw[71] one pair of brass compasses;[72] two hammers, three
Axes, five weeding hoes,[73] five hilling hoes[74]

Four Fishing Lines and hookes of all sorts two peeces of
new Line reserved one new fishing line reserved

One new strong rope to hould Cattle   60

A parcell of nailes to build a hoghouse[75] & lift the tobacco
houses[76] in all by gess 2000 one Coopers Howell[77] & one
Spade new a parcell of Coopers timber heading to make
twenty hogsheads, Staves for Eight hogsheads one pair
of Taylors Sheeres

[124]

Three guns lardge & good, or Fowling peeces two Rundletts of Shott in wayght 112 lbs. thirty pound of other
Shott for use 12 lbs. powder in a Roundlett that is full

Ten pound of powder in a Rundlett & some in a bottle left
for use 2 lbs. two Round bottles of glass, one Carpenters
Ads,[78] one broad chissell five other chissells 10 quarts
of Rumm in bottles for use 8 lbs. of sugar for my childrens use

Goods I carry with mee is in Tobacco[79]   1900

One gunn to be fixed, one chest ~~one small chest~~ one small
bed boulster blankett two pair of Stockins two pair of
britches two wastcoates one Lardge Coate, one short
Coate four Shirts

The Goods above mentioned I doe Vallue them att the
price of   18987

    My cattle att the price of   9900
                                                               28887

One looking glass two tinn pudding panns Several small
goods nott here putt Downe.

One trunk & one greate chest one new chest with Linnen
in itt in which chest there is 1/2 one pound of asneck or
Ratts bane,[80] one old chest 3 small chests

I doe Suppose I have left my children Indifferent well Furnished with cloaths till Christmas onely they will want
Shooes the which I desire may bee bought for them as
soone as they may be gott

               = Signed Rob't Cole.

I doe suppose I have left in the house twelve barrells of
corne att least and aboute & just 18 Middle peeces of
bacon[81] for this years provision.

Most part of these goods before mentioned are about the
house & what is nott is in the two biggest chests which
are Locked and the Keys are given to Coll Evans[82] or to
Capt Gardner.[83]

Two Table cloths & five napkins for the use of my house
left with Mary Sheppey. Seaven bookes in a chest, Six
other bookes left out for the children to Read in in the
biggest of the bookes in the chest you may find the birth
Dayes of my children in particular Francis Knott is three
yeares older than my Sonn Robert Cole is. Severall small
goods not here sett downe.

 This Inventory is taken by mee Robert Cole on the
25th Day of Aprill 1662 as Witness my hand. Rob:ᵗ Cole.

[125]

The Accountant Standeth further charged with Diverse summes of Tobacco by him received Due to the Said estate in Anno <u>1662</u> (vizt)

 £ Tobacco

To tobacco received of Richard Sheppy due uppon account for goods sent in to him by Robert Cole	445
To tobacco Received of Richard Bennitt due to the estate	355
To tobacco Received of Colonel Evans due to the said estate	385
To tobacco received of Joseph Allvy	200
To tobacco received of Mathew Rowse	463
To the cropp of tobacco made uppon the plantation in Anno <u>1662</u>	6336
<u>1663</u>	
To tobacco received of Richard Sheppy due to the estate	385
To the cropp of tobacco made in Anno 1663	5167
To tobacco received of Doctor Lumbrozio[84]	100
To tobacco received for a pair of Small Cart wheeles	200
To tobacco received for two gallon & 1/2 of tarr	30
To tobacco received of John Shankes	60
To tobacco received of Mr. Rouse itt being the Remainer of a bill Due by the said Rowse unto the Estate	82
<u>1428</u>	
To tobacco received for a Steare sould out of the estate	557
To 1967 lbs. porke sould out of the estate for one pound 3/4 per pound[85]	2458
To Tobacco received of Peter Mills	415
To Tobacco received for hydes Sould	157

To Tobacco received for one hyde more	45
To Tobacco received for 129 lbs. of butter sould at 5 lbs.	
per pound	645
To tobacco received of Mr. Brittaine[86]	48

1664

To the cropp of tobacco made in Anno 1664	6950
To tobacco received of woodbury for six hydes	540
To tobacco received of warren for meate Sould	836
To tobacco received for a gun Stock that was broaken in	
the march[87]	60
To tobacco received for building of the chappell[88]	532
To tobacco received for 61 lbs. of hyde Sould	122

1665

To the crop of tobacco made in Anno 1665[89]	7119
To tobacco received for meate Sould mr. Foxhould[90]	1036
To one peece of a hogshead cout	161
To tobacco received for 57 lbs. of hyde att 2 lbs. per pound	114
To more tobacco received for building the chappell	57

1666

To the cropp of tobacco made in Anno 1666	3854
To tobacco received for the Cyder Sould out of the produce	
of the orchard	300

[126]

To tobacco for two hydes Sould	100
To tobacco received for 10 lbs. of tallo Sould	40
To tobacco received for 20 lbs. of butter Sould	88

1667

To the cropp of tobacco made in Anno 1667	5088
To tobacco received for 84 lbs. of bacon Sould att 3 lbs. per	
pound	252
To tobacco received for one tunn of casque[91] Sould	100
To tobacco received itt being the Remaineing part of a bill	97
To tobacco received for one hyde	37
To tobacco received for porke Sould	891

£ Tobacco

47007:

To the Cropps of tobacco made in Anno
  1662:63:64:65:66 & 67 as also for severall

summes of tobacco due to the estate for the
which this account standeth charged for on the   £ tobacco:
other side Amounting unto   47007

1668

To the cropp of tobacco made in Anno 1668	8275
To tobacco received for a servant that was prest to goe out the march[92]	430
To tobacco received for pork delivered to William Felsteed	200
To tobacco received for a horse that was Sould	2000
To tobacco received for a Servant Sould	1600
To tobacco received for cattle Sould	2700
To tobacco received for an Iron pott Sould	70
To tobacco received for hydes Sould	160
To tobacco received for Cyder Sould	710
To tobacco received for porke & bacon Sould	2102

1669

To the cropp of tobacco made in Anno 1669	4087

1670

To the cropp of tobacco made in Anno 1670	4206
To tobacco received uppon the balance of Accounts betweene the estate & mee 1669	3486
To tobacco received for mares Sould out of the estate	1795

1671

To the cropps tobacco made in Anno 1671 & 1672 togethcr with some other goods which hee had out of the estate amounting to the summe of	12400
To goods to the Vallue of tenn pounds Sterling Some od money the which is uncertain sent out of England by Robert Cole in the yeare 1662	
Idem two bushells & 1/2 of barley taken from the plantation presently	118
To 18 lbs. of tallos Sould Mr Salley[93]	90
To tobacco received of John Prentice being tobacco lent him	400
Idem to tobacco received of Richard Sheppy for betty Coles[94] cloaths	200

Idem to tobacco received for 3 barrells of Corne Sould	450	
Idem by Severall bills lyeing in the hands of this Accountant itt being due for mares Sould out of the Estate	3305	
by 9 lbs. of tobacco overcharged in this account in the year 1664	9	
The summe total of the charge	£ tobacco[95]	95800

[127]

The Accountant Stands Discharged by severall summes Goods and chattells Cattle horses & hoggs partly delivered to the children of the Said Robert & the rest ready to bee Delivered unto whome they shall appertaine which are as Followeth:

Imprimis: By cattle delivered unto Ignatious Warren in Right of his wife Mary the daughter of Robert Cole deceased vizt five Cowes	05:	
One two yeare old heifer	01:	
One yeare old heifer	01:	11:
Two Steares one five the other 3 yeares old	02:	
Two yeareling Bulls	02:	

Idem by goods Delivered to the Said Ignatious.

One feather bed boulster pillow & Rugge	Due to her
One Copper Kettle of 18 gallons	by her
One pair of Sheets	father's
One Iron pott	will.
One bell mettle Morter & pestle	

Idem: By cattle delivered to Robert Cole as his childs part.

Seaven Cowes & heifers the heifers 3 yeares old & one yeareling heifer	08:	
Two Steares one five the other 3 years old & one yeareling bull	03:	12:
one fatt Calfe Killed abroad	01:	

By Cattle and hoggs Delivered unto Francis Knott as his Eighth part due by the will of the testator

Idem by two Cowes	02:	
Two heifers one three the other one yeare old	02:	05:

One steare four years old   01
Two hoggs
Payd by order of mr. Cole deceased as appears
    by the Inventory: to a man of mr. Slyes (vizt)
Idem by two Cowes & Calves   04
    Paid unto mr. Francis Fitzherbert as Legacy
    given by the Testator as appeares by his will.   05:
Idem by one Steare   01
    By Cattle Delivered in the hands of the Execu-
    tor for the use of William Cole & Edward Cole
    Sonns of the Said Testator they being as yett un-
    der age (vizt)

[128]
Idem: By one Cow and Calfe two heifers two years
    old apeece   04
    One Cow of Six yeares old   01   07.
    Two Steares one four yeares old and the other
        three yeares old & the Advantage[96]   <u>02</u>

                          In all: 40: head of Cattle

Soe that itt appeares that the Accountant hath mainteined the Children
& Servants in provisions and hath Encreased the number of Cattle five
head

The Accountant Further Standeth Discharged By 3 servants
    Samuell Hewson five years to serve
    Daniel Pritcherd 3 years to serve
    Timothy Maham three mounths to serve
    Two Flock beds two boulsters & two Ruggs
    Three chests
    four Iron potts
    Two Iron Kettles one broak
    One pair of potthookes
    One pair of pott Rackes
    Two Iron hookes & one pair of fire tongues
    Two Fryeing pannes
    One Iron pestle & one brass warming pann:
    One pair of Small Stilliards
    Six spoones & one Candlestick

Seaven pewter dishes & one brand Iron: R: C:

Two Iron Wedges and two Iron hoopes for a berdle: [97]

Two handsawes one hammer one ax one chissell

Three lardge gunns one small one

Six Milke trayes one milke tubb; two Cowles

Three pailes one pepper grinder

One Strayneing dish one Sifting tray

Two churnes one earthen pott

One Corne barrell & thight barrell

One small Rundlett & one homeny Sifter

Four Joint chaires & one chaire table

One three Legged Stoole

By one Iron bound case five bottles in itt with pewter
  topps

[129]

The Discharge By two pairs of sheets & four napkins

  By one dyaper table Cloth & three other

  By one holland apron & one Counterpaine

  By a parcell of child bed Linnen

  By one Pair of Cotten gloves & one Stometcher

  By one Grindstone

  By horses mares & Colts in the woods the number uncer-
    taine butt as is supposed 30 od

  Alsoe by hoggs now to bee Delivered the number of them
    uncertaine butt as is supposed 50 od

    By which itt appears that the Accountant hath En-
    creased the Stocke of hoggs 20 head more than he re-
    ceived & Emproved the Estate 30 head of horses of
    which sort of chattells hee received nott one

The Accountant Standeth Further discharged by goods worne out and
Consumed in the house by the children & servants which goods were part
of those goods contained in the Inventory left under the hand of the
Testator

(vizt)

  Imprimis By two pairs of belloes

  One fire shovell

  One Iron chaine for the chimney

nine milk trayes broken
five milk tubbs
One Mobby tubb
Two dozen of trenchers
One dozen of spoones
One tinn Cullender
Three tinn drippin pannes
One tinn Funnell
Four tinn Candlestickes
One pepper box

[130]
One chafeing dish
One tinn Scummer
Two wooden platters
One grindstone & one Iron Ladle
One pewter bason
Four pewter porrengers
Two small pewter dishes
Five wooden spoones & 3 wooden Ladles
Two pewter pint potts & one quart pott
One tinn quart pott
One tobacco Knife
One greate butter pott
Five Small butter potts
One Earthen Fryeing pann
One Earthen 3 Legged creame pott
Two thight barrells
Four Small Rundletts
Three meale Sifters of Haire
Five Joynt Stooles
Two three Legged Stooles
One Canow
Six picktures in the hall
Three Lardge Stone Juggs
One Earthen pitcher & one Jugg
Two gallons of Sweet oyle
Two cases of quart bottles

Three pairs of Sheets
Two table Cloths
Eight napkins
Two white aprons
One woomans shift
Two Holland Handchecherfes
Three Cross cloths
Three fine dressings
Two Handkecherfs

[131]

Two Holland neckcloths
One Holland apron
One pair of Sheets
Thirty one yards of Canvas
Two pound of Candleweeke
Four pair of childrens Shooes
Two pair of woomens Shooes old
One pair of buck Skinns gloves
Three old childs blanketts
One Red broad cloth suite
One pennistone petticoate
Four pair of Irish Stockins
One Canvas Jackett
Eleaven pair of childrens Stockins
One 1/2 yards of Flannell
Two & 1/2 yards of Red Cloth
four yards of pennistone
Three yards 3/4 of Linnen blew
Six & 1/2 yards of pennistone
Four & 1/2 yards of Course Holland
Eleaven Ells of Lockrome
five yards of Red Cloth Searge
halfe a pound of pepper
One 1/2 pound of Starch
A parcell of Ginger
Nine thred laces
Four Shoomakers Alls

a parcell of Greene Galume & some other lace
Half a pound of whited browne thred
Some other fine thread
1/4 pound of red thred
Four ounces of silke
Two thousand of pinns

[132]
Tape Filleting bindeing & points & cotten Ribben
Nine pairs of Sissers
Soape soft and hard
Two Ivory Combes
Eighteen gallons of lard Some spent the rest Leaked out
One grinding Stone
Three Axes five weeding hoes & hilling hoes
Fishing Lines & hookes
One Strong Rope to hold Cattle
Two thousand of nailes greate & Small
One new spade
One pair of Taylors Sheeres
One hundred & twelve pound of Shott
Thirty pound more of Shott
Twenty four pound of powder
Two Round glass bottles
One Carpenters Adds
One broad Chissell & five other chissells
Two & 1/2 gallons of Rumme & eight pound of Sugar

The Testator haveing nott particularly apprized all the goods in the Inventory nor the Executor after his Death; the Judge testamentary cann make noe Estimate or ballance of the Said Inventory & account as to the Value butt must have itt uppon the oath of the Accountant as to the particulars.

1662:	£ Tobacco
Imprimis By tobacco for Sallery[98] for receiving 1848 lbs. of tobacco	185
By tobacco payd mr. Fitzherbert given to him by Robert Cole in his will	495
by tobacco payd the Sheriff for Fees	384

by tobacco payd mr. Barton[99] due by bill	285
by tobacco payd to Captain Cooke[100] for Mary Coles passage four pound Sterling which in to-bacco att 3 1/2 pence per lb. amounts unto	640
by tobacco due to my selfe uppon Account	537
by Tobacco payd Captain Martin for a man servant[101]	2000

1663

by Sallery for receiveing 857: lbs. tobacco	88

	£ Tobacco	
By Severall summes of tobacco payd by this Ac-countant out of the estate as alsoe tobacco for Sallery for receiveing of tobacco due to the Said Estate the particulars whereof on the other side maketh mention amounting unto	4614	
By Sallery for receiveing 4325 lbs. tobacco in Anno 1662 & 63		432

[133]
1662

By payd the Sheriff for 3 Leavies[102]	186
by tobacco payd Joseph Allvy for Six barrells of Corne	371
by tobacco payd ~~Josep~~ Richard Sheppy due by condition[103]	1000
by tobacco payd Walter Beane due to him for two bookes	50
by two pair of Irish Stockins for John Ellton & Robert Gates two of the servants att 12 lbs. per pair	24
by two pairs of woolen Stockins for Fran. Cole[104] & Francis Knott att 18 per pair	36
by one pair of fine Wollen hose for William Cole	24
by one pair of woollen Stockins for Johnson a Servant	21
by one pair of Shooes for William Cole	20
by two pair of Shoes for Mary Cole att 25 lbs. per pair	50

by two pair of Shoes for John Elton and John Rey Servants	50
by one pair of Shooes due to Mary[105] att Bartons[106] which mr. Cole owed in his life time	25
by two Monumouth Caps[107] for the Servants	40
by two hatts for Robert Cole and Francis Knot	120
by Six broad hoes[108] att 20 per hoe	120
by four Narrow hoes[109] att 14 per hoe	56
by 15 yards and 1/2 blew Linnen att 11: lbs. per yard to make drawers Lyneings and Aprons for the children	171
by Six yards blew Linnen for Elizabeth Cole three aprons two Frockes at 11 lbs. per yard	66
by Six ells of Holland to make the children dressings and neckcloths att 32	192
by 34 Ells & one yard of Lockrome att 11: lbs. per ell	374
by Eight ells of Lockrome att 11: lbs. per ell	88
by 4 Ells & 1/4 of Canvas for drawers & pocketts	43
by 7 yards & 1/4 of Searge att 32 per yard	232

By Severall summes of tobacco payd by this Accountant as also tobacco for Sallery and diverse goods bought for the use of the family the particulars whereof make the mention on the other Side Amounting unto	£ Tobacco 8385:	

by Seaventeen yards of Kersey[110] for cloths att 34 per yard.	578
by 4 yards & 1/4 of Penistone att 24 lbs. per yard.	102
by 2 yards of tradeing cloth att 35: per yard	70
by one pair of Shooes & Stockins for John Elton	43
by one pair of Stockins for John Rey	12
by two yards of Ozen briggs[111] for cheese clouts[112]	20
by one Rugg for Mary Cole for Sea	70
by 2000 of pinns	20

[134]

By Two pound of whited browne thred & two bundles of twine	38
by two falling axes & 1/2 pound of ~~whited~~ [*illegible*] black thred	53
by one bottle of Drames [113] one pair of Shooes for Robert Gates	35
by tanned Leather to mend shoes	15
by Taylor worke for making of Robert Cole and Francis Knott each one suite of Cloaths	110
by makeing William Cole a suite	20
by makeing Edward Cole a suite	20
by makeing Mary Cole a suite	50
by makeing two Frockes for Elizabeth Cole	16
by makeing a wastecoate and mending a petticoate	30
by makeing a pair of Drawers	20
by makeing John Elton a suite	45
by makeing Robert Gates a suite	45
by makeing John Johnson a suite	35
by a pound of thred to make them	30
by buttons & Silk for these cloaths	120

By severall summes of tobacco payd by this Accountant and diverse goods bought for the use of the family as alsoe sallary for receiving of the particulars whereof maketh mention on the other side	£ tobacco 9982.

Anno 1663

by a Taylor seaven daies to make & mend att 24 per diem	168
by 14 dozen of buttons for wastecoats	40
by one yard & 1/2 cotten	24
by one Cake of Sope	9
by four pair of yarne Stockins	48
by one pair of Shoes for John Rey	25
by a Vomitt [114] for Robert Gates	30
by pills for Robert Cole	30

by cureing an Impostume[115] in the mades[116] mouth	30
by paid mr. Brittaine for Mary Coles Dyett	400
by a pair of Shoes for William Cole	20
by 100 of double tenns & one of Single tenns[117]	8
by 1100 6 penny nailes	40
by building a 30 foote hogg penn	350
by a pair of Shooes and Stockins for John Rey	30

[135]

By 12 dozen of buttons to mend theire cloaths	36
by a taffity[118] hood for Elizabeth Cole	30
by a bunch of tape	8
by four Neckcloths & a pair of Stockins for Elizabeth Cole	46
by cloth for Robert Cole and Francis Cole[119] each a suite	270
by makeing with buttons & thred	100
by each of them a pair of Linnen Drawers	30
by each of them a pair of woosted Stockins & gloves	54
by bottles of drames	45

By severall sumes of tobacco payd by this Accountant and Diverse goods bought for the use of the family as alsoe Sallery for receiveing of tobacco due to the estate the particulars whereof maketh mention on the other Side	£ tobacco 11853	
by tobacco payd to Cloise mr. Slyes Negro for Cureing Ann Knott of the Spleene		125
by one pound of thred		25
by tobacco payd Ann Thornton for a year's Service		600
by four weekes more		20
by Six Knives & one Comb		28
by 15 pound of Sope		68
by a pair of Shoes for the Maide[120]		18
by one pair of Shoes for Felsteed		18
by one pair of Shoes for John Johnson		18

by a pair of Stockins for the Maide	12
by a pair of Stockins for Francis Knott	12
by a pair of Stockins for Robert Cole	12
by 3 Suites of Cloths of Kersey for the servants	420
by a pair of Stockins for William Felsteed	8
by a hatt for Robert Cole and Francis Knott	90
by 5 yards of Cotten [121] to make the maide cloths	65
by one Capp for William Felsteed	20
by one pair of Stockins for John Rey	8
by one pair of Shoes for William Cole	15
by a man Servant 11 pounds sterling in tobacco next yeare [122]	1900

[136]

By Seaventeene hogsheads to putt their Cropp in	425
by 21 Ells of Lockrome att 8: lbs. per ell	168
by 22 yards of Ozenbrig att 5 lbs. per yard	110
by tobacco payd Mr. Piles [123] for 2 hogsheads Mr. Cole carried for England and sent noe Retourne	800

By severall summes of tobacco payd by this Accountant and Diverse goods bought for the use of the family the particulars whereof made mention in folios 16: 18: 20: 22: and 23: Amounting unto	£ tobacco 16838	
by four weeding hoes & four hilling hoes		120
by a pair of Shoes for John Rey		20
by a pair of Shoes & Stockins for John Hilton [124]		32
by two pair of Shoes for Robert Cole and Francis Knott		40
by a pair of Shoes & Stockins & Six ells of Linnen for Shirts		92
by 2 hoes & one Ax and a Capp		96
by one suite of Cloth for one of the servants Freedom cloths [125]		140
by 19 Ells & 1/2 of Canvas att 9: lbs. per ell		171 [126]
by 1/2 pound of thred		13
by 1000 pinns & 25 needles		12

by 11 yards of blew Linnen   66

by 15 fathoms of Fishing line and four drumm[127]
    hookes   13

by one bottle of Sallett Oyle   10

by a petticoate for Elizabeth Cole   20

by a corne bagge & Linnen for cheese clouts   20

by 3 porringers   12

by one pair of Stockins for John Hillton   20

by three falling Axes[128]   48

by three barrells of Corne for Rent to Mr.
    Gerard[129]   450

by four Leavies   246

by tobacco payd to the Church   ·   50

by a Certificate under the Seale of the office to
    send into England to Mrs. Cole to sattisfy her
    how many children Mr. Cole had Liveing in this
    Country & Recording the same[130]   100

by tobacco payd for two depositions [*illegible*] the
    certificate[131]   56

by tobacco paid for Recording Mr. Coles will   40

by one bunch of twine   8

by one tanned hyde to mend their Shoes   100

by 10 Ells of Barbiers Linnen   90

£ Tobacco
    18918

[137]

By severall summes of tobacco payd by this Ac-
    countant & Diverse goods bought as alsoe sal-
    lery for receiving tobacco due unto the Estate
    the particulars whereof is mentioned on the
    other Side Amounting   18918

1664

By Sallery for receiving of 2090: lbs. tobacco att 10
    per cent is   209

by 16 pair of Shoes for the Children & servants   348

by 17 pair of Stockins for the Children & servants   204

by 22 yards 3/4 blew linnen   123

by 44 Ells 3/4 of canvas	396
by 16 Ells & 1/4 of Sheeting [132]	192
by 22 yards & 1/4 of white Linnen	289
by 5 Ells & 1/4 of Holland	88
by severall sorts of Iron Ware as Nayles axes & hoes	366
by one Stock Lock and Staple one gimblitt [133] & two thimbles	22
by two Match coates [134] for a Canow & Hunting	120
by whale bone thred & buttons & facing [135]	54
by one casque of beare	110
by a suite of Cloaths for William Felsteed	140
by one dozen of Spoones	26
by makeing five Wastcoates	100
by makeing two suites of Cloaths for William & Edward Cole	60
by makeing a Jumpp [136] and wastecoate for Elizabeth Cole & for hookes & eyes	58
by tobacco payd to the Church	120
by 18 empty casques	450
by one packe of Cards needles & pinns	13
by 8 Dozen of buttons & Startch	24
by 5 yards & 1/4 Cotten	75
by Tobacco payd Vincent Mansfeild for Killing a Bull gott into the wild Gange	100
by a purge for John Rey	30
by tobacco payd Richard Foster for his Attendance att the Court about bussines betweene Mr. Gerard & Mr. Cole [137]	100
by a mare which I bought of woodbury	2200

£:24935:

By severall summes of tobacco payd by this Accountant and Diverse goods bought as alsoe Sallery for Receiving tobacco due unto the said estate the particulars whereof is mentioned on the other Side Amounting unto	24935

by one suite of Cloaths for John Johnson	140
by 2 yards of Kersey & a pair of bodies	100
by thred & silke	79
by two yards 3/4 of tammy [138]	55
by tape and three Kinnes	16
by 16 pound of Sope	80
by John Hilltons Freedome Cloaths and hatts	225
by five Leavies	280
by payd Ann Thornton for wages	1000
by a Vomitt for John Johnson	30
by cureing John Reys Sore Legg	100
by 1/4 pound of pepper	3
by a Taylor Six dayes	144
by 1/2 pound of browne thred	15
by a purge for the three children	40
by one pound of powder	10

1665

by Sallery for Receiveing 1368 pound of tobacco	137
by one pair of Shooes to William Felsteed	24
by one pair of Shooes for betty Cole	18
by one pair of Shooes for Johnson	24
by a Vomitt and purge for Johnson	30
by a purge for the French man [139]	30
by a purge to Betty Cole	20
by Isabells Freedome Shoes	40
by a pair of Lined bretches for William	150
by four pound of Sugar	16
	£:27741:

[138]

By severall sumes of tobacco payd by this Accountant and Diverse goods bought as alsoe Sallery for receiving of tobacco due unto the Estate the particulars whereof on the other side maketh mention	27741:
by a tray	9
by two pair of Shoes for William & Edward Cole	80
by Isbell for part of her Freedome Cloaths	250

by Ann Thorneton for a year Service	1000
by tobacco payd to Thomas Bennitt for building of a house	950
by 20 lbs. of Sugar	100
by two pair of Shoes for the Servants	90
by 15: Ells & 1/2 of Canvas att 25: lbs. per ell	389
by 2 pair of Shoes for the biggest children	90
by one pound of thred	46
by Six tunn & 1/4 of Casque	625
by one Cake & 1/2 of Sope	21
by two holland Shifts for Betty	100
by a wastecoate	100
by 3 Leavies to the church	150
by 4 Leavies	316
by 2 boyes Schooleing 5: mounths & 1/2	350
by Schooleing for William Cole	150
by Edward & Betties Schooleing for one yeare	600
by four daies work of the Taylor	100
by makeing one Petticoate & Silke and bindeing	21
by two barrells of Corne	220
by two pound of Sope	24
by nailes to mend the tobacco house	48
by two Laces	5
by canvas 3 Ells 3/4 one naile	112
by thred	10
£:Tobacco	33695

[139]

By Severall summes of tobacco payd by this Accountant & Diverse goods bought as alsoe Sallery for receiveing of tobacco due unto the estate the particulars whereof on the other Side maketh mention amounting unto	33695	
By a purge for Betty Cole		30
by a broad hoe of Mr. Foxwell [140]		30
by one pair of Shoes for Johnson		40
by 2 pound of Sope		22
by 3 Fishookes and 4 Scanes of thred		10

by one pair of Shooes for Francis Knott	60
by two pair of Shoes for William & Noel [141]	120
by one pair of Shooes for William Cole	60
by one pair of Shoes for Robert Cole	60
by five Ells & 1/4 of Canvas	157
by 8 yards & 1/4 of Kersey	650
by 3 yards & 1/2: 1/2:quarter of white Cotten	63
by 13 Skinns [142]	390
by 3 Scanes of browne thred	5
by one Ell of canvas	30
by 3 yards & 1/2: 1/2:quarter galume	13
by one pound of blacke thred	75
by 1/2 pound of whited browne thred	40
by 3 Scanes of colloured thred	5
by one pair of childrens Stockins	15
by one pair of Shoes for Johnson	60
by two pair of Stockins for the servants	50
by two yards & 1/2 of Cotten	67
by one pair of Shoes and two pair of Stockins for the children	100
by two yards of blew Linnen for Betty	40
	£:tobacco 35787

[140]

	£ Tobacco
By severall summes of tobacco payd by this Accountant and diverse goods bought as alsoe Sallery for receiveing of tobacco due unto the estate the particulars whereof on the other Side maketh mention Amounting unto	35787
By the Carpenter for mending of the tobacco house	200
by 5 leavies	285
by Recording the Account of Mr. Coles estate	48
by one peece of Fustian [143] & a Dozen of buttons	188
by a petticoate for Betty	77 1/2
1666	
by Sallery for receiveing of 528 pound of tobacco	43
by Iron Ware	89

by Stockins for the family	204
by pepper & Ginger	6
by Shooes	264
by one barrell of Mackrill[144]	200
by tobacco paid to Dorothy Sittwell for wages	750
by a Ladle	5
by thred pinns needles & tape	88
by Linnen Cloth	907
by Taylors worke	436
by Sope	56
by casque 250 and two church Leavies 100; in all	350
by a Hatt 28 & a pale 30; in all	58
by powder & Shott	44
by woollen cloth	300
by four childrens Schooleing	1050
by a Taffity hood	56
by a Second hand bed:tickin	60
£tob	£ tobacco 41551
41551	

[141]

By Severall summes of tobacco payd by this Accountant and Diverse goods bought as alsoe
Sallery for receiving of tobacco due unto the estate the particulars whereof the other Side   £ Tobacco
Relateth   41551

1667

By Sallery for receiving of 1377 pounds of tobacco	137
by Linnen	441
by thred	105
by Laces & tape	37
by hatts	125
by mistake in the last yeares account	28
by Iron ware	166
by powder	24
by Sope	24
by Shoes	473
by Skinns	21

by Knives	61
by woollen	1273
by 2 dozen of pills	60
by Salt 200 by Sugar 12	212
by boarding and Schooling Elizabeth	1000
by casque	350
by Country Leavies	246
by the chappell Lengthening 60 by church Leavy 50	110
by Taylors worke	788
by a Comb and Candleweeke	9
by Mallasses	36
by 3 boyes Schooleing	500
by Silke and Galume 50 by the Surveyor 550 [145]	600
by the Secretary [146]	348
by 3 barrells of Corne	330
by a Canow	120
by a Servant [147]	1400
£ tobacco	50575

[142]

By Severall summes of tobacco payd by this Accountant & diverse goods bought for the use of the Family as alsoe Sallery for receiveing of tobacco due to the estate the particulars whereof maketh mention amounting unto   £ tobacco 50575

1668

By Sallery for receiveing 9972 lbs. of tobacco	997
by Linnen	1100
by woollen	885
by Shoes	426
by Stockins	288
by Leavies	849
by a Servant [148]	1600
by Schooling & boarding Betty	1000
by the Chancellor	123
by Hatts	135
by Salt	245
by Carpenters worke	400

by Coopers worke	600
by Taylors worke	258
by Iron ware	121
by Sope 65: & bodies 30	95
by buttons & Silke 68: galume & tape 35	103
by Needles & pinns 18: by knives and Combes 17	35
by drames 10: by a bridle 16: by Sifters 20	46
by payles 30: by Linnen makeing 120	150
by tobacco Lent to Fillen Hegoes[149]	53

1669

By Sallery for receiveing of tobacco itt being 5281 lbs.	528
by tobacco payd for Country Leavy	184
by church Leavies	150
by a man Servant[150]	2400
	£:Tobacco 64343

[143]

By severall summes of tobacco payd by this Accountant & Diverse goods bought for the use of the family as alsoe Sallery for Receiveing of tobacco due to the estate the particulars whereof on the other side maketh mention amounting unto

	£ Tobacco	
	64343	
by a man servant[151]		2000
by one barrell of Mackrell		150
by 12 Armes Length of Roancoake[152]		60
by Ribbening tape and bindeing		56
by thight & dry casque		425
by Combes & 3 barrells of Corne for Rent to Gerard		480
by wooden ware and one Fishing Line		46
by Rent for Edward Coles land 33: & Clerkes Fees		88
by a Saddle & bridle		230
by powder		40
by Boddice Laces pinns & paper		85
by buttons and thred		74
by Taylors worke		175
by Sope washing and Iron ware		325

by Linnen	1274
by Shoes & Stockins	600
by woollen	492
by Salt	190
by Knives	15
by Strong drinke	334
by Sugar	69
<u>1670</u>	
by woollen	1324
by Linnen	1355
by Shoes and Stockins	729
by Rumm	<u>368</u>
£: Tobacco	75307

[144]

	£: Tobacco	
By severall summes of tobacco as on the other Side	75307	
By Sugar		96
by hatts		115
by Salt		103
by pepper & for one butter pott and a Jugg		27
by Iron ware & wooden ware		211
by Taylors worke		335
by Sope and Combes		35
by Coopers worke for Heughing Staves & Heading		100
by Tobacco for bringing John Prentice from Virginia [153]		300
by Francis Knott for building of a Henn house		120
by Edward Coles Schooleing		400
by buttons thread & tape		159
by Knives		31
by a windeing Sheete [154] and a Coffin to Betty		110
by makeing of her grave		100
by her buriall in the Chappell		400
by Expenses for her funerall		700
by 3 barrells of corne		450

by 3 barrells of Corne for Rent to Mr. Gerard	450
by Country Leavies	81
by Church Leavies	100
by Rent payd for the Lands of Edward Cole	27
by woollen Cloth	1929
1671 & 1672	
by Linnen	1676
by Shoes and Stockins	2189
by buttons Silke and thred	240
by Sope	208
by Salt	405
by hatts	120
£: Tobacco	86524

[145]

	£ tobacco	
By severall summes of Tobacco as on the other Side	£86524	
by Combes		28
by tape		15
by Taylors worke		150
by Seamsters worke		480
by pinns & needles		21
by Iron Ware		199
by Knives		53
by nailes		18
by Stronge Liquor		584
by powder & shott		144
by casque and paper		408
by mustard Seed		15
by Irish Cloath		220
by Capt Mathew Paine for Edward Coles Passage to England		500
by John Standley for takeing upp of a Runn away Servant belonging to the Estate and bringing him out of Virginia		600
by Edward Coles Schooleing		350
by William Coles Schooleing		100

by 2 pound of Sugar	10
by corne	478
by Rent of land	334
by Church Leavies	400
by Country Leavies	232
by pipes	24
by beanes	36
by gloves	24
by Candleweeke	20
by two hogsheads of tobacco Robert Cole had out of the last yeares Crop	<u>948</u>

£: Tobacco 92909

[146]

By severall summes of tobacco as on the other
  Side amounting unto £92909

<u>1673</u>

By one hatt for William Cole	50
By one Knife	8
by 8 bushells of Corne att 40 per bushell	320
by tobacco Expended on William Cole when he was bound an apprentice	400
by payd to Mr. Sly for goods taken upp by Francis Knott	185
to the Cooper this yeare	380
by my charges Comeing last to St. Maries to make upp this account	311
by a mare which Robert Cole Sould for	2400
by two Munmouth Capps ommitted in this account in the year <u>1662</u>	40

By goods Sent in by Robert Cole out of England
  amounting unto 10 pounds Sterling Some od
  moneys the which this accountant Expended in
  the use of the family & charged for the same
  among other things in this account

The sume totall of the Discharges £ 96983
lbs.Tobacco
The sume totall of the charge £ 95800

From which sume deducting the whole charge there
Remains Due unto the Executor

1183

£ Tobacco 96983 [155]

Soe that the Executor is Creditor to the estate 1183 pound
of Tobacco & for Itinerent charges for 12: yeares 2553:
pounds of tobacco

I Luke Gardner one of the Executors of the last will and Testament of
Robert Cole deceased doe sweare that the Cattle in my Account Said to
be Delivered to Ignatious Warren were by mee delivered to him as alsoe
all the goods the pestle onely Excepted; and that the Cattle Said to bee
delivered to Robert Cole in the Said Account were according to his fathers will Shared out to him as Soone as hee did gett them upp after the
Said Robert Arrived to Eighteene yeares of Age; that the Cattle were delivered to Francis Knott and Porke by Agreement in Lieu of the hoggs;
that hee payd the Cowes & Calves to Mr. Slye's man and the Steare to
Mr. Fitzherbert; that hee kept in his hands for Edward and William Cole
the Cattle in the account mentioned; That the goods in his account mentioned were either worne out in the Service of the family or sume shared
or Still ready to bee Shared Amongst the Orphans; that there is betweene
forty Eight and fifty hoggs (as in the account) already Shared besides
others yett in the woods unshared and that as to the goods mentioned in
the Said Account & the Disposall of tobaccoes and Delivery of Goods
Knoweth of nothing false in the Said Account but will not possitively
Sweare to particulars some of which by his wife [156] and others in his absence (Sometimes within Sometimes out of the Province) and he further
Sweareth

[147]
Sweareth that whensoever any of the goods in the Account Specified were
bought with the Tobaccoes properly belonging to the estate of the Said
Cole they were allwayes Rated att the prices hee bought them att to the
best of his Remembrance and understanding

Luke Gardner:

Juravitt 14 February

1673

Appendix 2

· · · · ·

People Living at
the Cole Plantation,
1662–1673

Determining who was in the household when and what their ages were is complicated. We know the following: the birthdays of the children from Cole's will; the years that the servants were acquired, either from head-rights or from the account or both; when servants became free, from the account and other biographical information; and the number of taxables in the household through 1665. We also know that Gardiner paid for passage to England for Mary Cole in 1662 and for Edward Cole in 1671 or 1672 and had paid for an apprenticeship for William Cole by 1673. We have inferred from the fact that ships usually arrived in the Chesa-peake in the fall to pick up tobacco that servants were most likely to have been purchased then. Servants' terms changed over the twelve years of the account. For this data, see chapter 2 note 24. From these facts and inferences we have made a list of the members of the household from 1662 through 1673. Since boys age twelve to fifteen were considered half hands, we have indicated when boys in the household entered or left this age category.

Some decisions are arbitrary. Five payments for levies (i.e., poll taxes) are shown in 1664, but only four taxables (white males born in the colony age sixteen or over and white immigrant male servants age ten and over were taxed) appear in the account.[1] An additional male, probably a free-man, must have been in the household, working part time for his keep (the account shows no wage payments to him or payments for board from him). He may have been the "French man" for whom Gardiner pur-chased medical care in 1665. Problems also arise for 1665 and 1666. In 1665 the account shows two payments for levies, one for four taxables and one for five, but there is no mention of levy payments for 1666. If the second levy shown for 1665 was in fact the levy for 1666, there were five males age sixteen or more in the household that year, but only three show in the account. We have accepted the account as correct. The second levy of 1665, for five taxables, reflects Francis Knott's arrival at age sixteen in the second half of the year. We have also assumed that Edward went to England with the spring shipping of 1672 and that William did not depart from the household until the beginning of 1673. Finally, we have assumed that Francis Knott set up on his own in 1669.

Any of these assumptions can be changed. Perhaps there were five taxables in the household in 1666; perhaps Francis Knott left late in 1667, when he turned eighteen and received his inheritance, or perhaps he stayed until he married in 1673 or 1674 (see appendix 4). Perhaps Edward went to England at the end of 1672. Such changed assumptions change the figures that are based on household or labor force size but not enough to change the outcome of any arguments.

It was customary in the 1660s to use old-style dating, in which the new year began on March 25. In all the tables that follow, the year is assumed to begin on that date.

Table A2.1 The Cole Household, 1662–1673

Year	Levies	Servants	Family
1662	3	Isabel Jones	Robert Cole, Sr. (gone in late
		John Elton	April)
		Robert Gates	Francis Knott (age 12 1/2–13 1/2)
		John Johnson	Robert Cole (age 9 1/2–10 1/2)
		John Rey (1/4 yr.)[a]	William Cole (age 6 3/4–7 3/4)
			Edward Cole (age 4 1/2–5 1/2)
			Betty Cole (age 2–3)
1663	4	Ann Thornton (hired)	Francis Knott
		Isabel Jones	Robert Cole
		John Elton	William Cole
		Robert Gates	Edward Cole
		John Johnson	Betty Cole
		John Rey	
		William Felsteed (1/4 yr.)[a]	
1664	5	Ann Thornton	Francis Knott
		Isabel Jones	Robert Cole (age 11 1/2–12 1/2)
		John Elton (3/4 yr.)	William Cole
		John Johnson	Edward Cole
		John Rey	Betty Cole
		William Felsteed	
		Frenchman	
1665	4, 5	Ann Thornton	Francis Knott (age 15 1/2–16 1/2)
		Isabel Jones (3/4 yr.)	Robert Cole
		John Johnson	William Cole
		John Rey	Edward Cole
		William Felsteed	Betty Cole
		Frenchman	
1666		Dorothy Sittwell (hired)	Francis Knott
		John Rey	Robert Cole
		William Felsteed	William Cole
			Edward Cole
			Betty Cole
1667		John Rey (3/4 yr.)	Francis Knott
		William Felsteed	Robert Cole
		John Prentice[b]	William Cole (age 11 3/4–12 3/4)
			Edward Cole
1668		William Felsteed (3/4 yr.)	Francis Knott
		John Prentice	Robert Cole (age 15 1/2–16 1/2)
		Servant (1/2 yr.)[c]	William Cole

Table A2.1 (*continued*)

Year	Levies	Servants	Family
		Timothy Maham (1/4 yr.)	Edward Cole
		Samuel Hewson (1/4 yr.) (age ca. 12)*d*	
1669		John Prentice	Robert Cole
		Timothy Maham	William Cole
		Samuel Hewson	Edward Cole (age 11 1/2–12 1/2)
			Betty Cole
1670		John Prentice	Robert Cole
		Timothy Maham	William Cole
		Samuel Hewson	Edward Cole
		Daniel Pritchard (1/4 yr.)*e*	
1671		Timothy Maham	Robert Cole
		Samuel Hewson	William Cole (age 15 3/4–16 3/4)
		Daniel Pritchard	Edward Cole
1672		Timothy Maham	Robert Cole
		Samuel Hewson	William Cole
		Daniel Pritchard	
1673		Timothy Maham (3/4 yr.)	Robert Cole
		Samuel Hewson (age 16)	
		Daniel Pritchard	

Source: Cole Plantation Account, appendix 1.

*a*Since this servant would have made an additional levy, we have assumed that he was purchased after the crop had been sold, probably in November or December.

*b*Prentice was purchased in the country, and therefore we have assumed that he started about when hilling began in March or April.

*c*A servant was purchased, ran away, and was sold.

*d*Hewson had five years left to serve in 1673, hence his estimated age in 1668.

*e*Pritchard had three years left to serve in 1673 and his purchase goes entirely unmentioned in the account, hence the assumption that he was purchased late in 1670 and that he was at least sixteen years old.

Table A2.2 Summary of Cole Household, 1662–1673

Year	Male Servants Age 16+	Family Males Age 16+	Adult Women	Boys 12–15	Children Under 12	Total
1662	3.25	0.00	1.00	1.00	4.00	9.25
1663	4.25	0.00	2.00	1.00	4.00	11.25
1664	4.75	0.00	2.00	1.50	3.50	11.75
1665	4.00	0.50	1.75	1.50	3.00	10.75
1666	2.00	1.00	1.00	1.00	3.00	8.00
1667	2.75	1.00		1.75	1.25	6.75
1668	2.50	1.50		1.75	1.00	6.75
1669	2.00	1.00		2.50	1.50	7.00
1670	2.25	1.00		3.00		6.25
1671	2.00	1.75		2.25		6.00
1672	2.00	2.00		1.00		5.00
1673	2.75	1.00				3.75

Source: Cole Plantation Account, appendix 1.

Note: Fractions indicate changes from one age group to another or an arrival or departure from the household that created a presence for a fraction of a year. For example, Isabel Jones, a servant woman, was present for only three-quarters of the year in 1665. In 1664 Robert Cole is counted for half a year as under twelve and for half a year as age twelve.

Table A2.3 Working Hands for Deciding Tobacco Acreage to Plant, Cole Plantation, 1653–1673

Year	Working Hands	Total N
1653	Cole, Goodrich, Carpenter	3.00
1654	Cole, Goodrich, Carpenter	3.00
1655	Cole, Goodrich, Carpenter	3.00
1656	Cole, Goodrich, Carpenter, Gates (.25)	3.25
1657	Cole, Gates (.50), Johnson (.25), Alvey (.50), Tinsley (.50)	2.75
1658	Cole, Gates (.50), Johnson (.50), Alvey, Tinsley, Sheppy[a]	5.00
1659	Cole, Gates, Johnson (.50), Alvey, Sheppy, Rosewell (0)	4.50

Table A2.3 (*continued*)

Year	Working Hands	Total N
1660	Cole, Gates, Johnson (.50), Alvey, Sheppy	4.50
1661	Cole, Gates, Johnson, Elton (.50)	3.50
1662	Gates, Johnson, Elton, Knott (.50), Rey (purchased end of yr., 0)	3.50
1663	Gates, Johnson, Elton, Knott (.50), Rey (.50), Felsteed (purchased late in yr., 0)	4.00
1664	Johnson, Elton, Knott (.50), Rey, Felsteed (.50), Frenchman (.25, no wages)	4.25
1665	Johnson, Knott (.875), Rey, Felsteed, Frenchman (.25, no wages), R. Cole (.25)	4.375
1666	Knott, Rey, Felsteed, R. Cole (.25)	3.25
1667	Knott, Rey, Felsteed, R. Cole (.50), Prentice (.50), W. Cole (helps in house, 0)	4.00[b]
1668	Knott, Felsteed, R. Cole (.875), Prentice, new servant (runaway, sold, counts .50 for land, .25 for culture), Maham (purchased end of yr., 0), W. Cole (helps in house, 0)	4.375, land 4.125, culture[c]
1669	R. Cole, Prentice, Maham (.50), W. Cole (.50), Hewson (.25), E. Cole (helps in house, 0)	3.25[d]
1670	R. Cole, Prentice, Maham, W. Cole (.50), Hewson (.50), E. Cole (helps in house, 0)	4.00[e]
1671	R. Cole, Maham, W. Cole (.875), Hewson (.50), Pritchard (.50), E. Cole (helps in house, 0)	3.875[f]
1672	R. Cole, Maham, W. Cole, Hewson (.50), Pritchard, E. Cole (to England, 0)	4.50
1673	R. Cole, Maham, Hewson, Pritchard	4.00

Sources: Tables A2.1, A2.2; see also chapter 2 at notes 22–24, 29.

Note: Fractions indicate changes in age or arrival or departure during the year. In their first year, new hands are counted as only half hands for tobacco culture and hence land acreage because of their "seasoning" illness. In 1668 a runaway servant receives a half ration of land but is assumed to have worked as only a quarter hand because of his runaway time and his ultimate sale.

[a] Sheppy here in 1656, already seasoned.
[b] If W. Cole in fields, total N is 4.50.
[c] If W. Cole in fields, total N is 4.625.
[d] If E. Cole in fields, total N is 3.75.
[e] If E. Cole in fields, total N is 4.50.
[f] If E. Cole in fields, total N is 4.375.

Table A2.4 Daily Corn Requirements, Cole Household, 1662–1673

Year	Men 16+		Women		Boys 10–15		Boys 5–9		Girls 5–9		Under 5		Total
	N	Cups Corn	N	Cups Corn	N	Cups Corn	N	Cups Corn	N	Cups Corn	N	Cups Corn	Cups Corn
1662	3.25	14.85	1.00	3.35	1.50	6.16	2.00	6.48			1.50	3.00	33.84
1663	4.25	19.42	2.00	6.70	2.00	8.22	2.00	6.48			1.00	2.00	42.82
1664	4.75	21.70	2.00	6.70	2.00	8.22	2.00	6.48			1.00	2.00	45.10
1665	4.50	20.56	1.75	5.86	1.75	7.19	1.75	5.67	1.00	3.05			42.33
1666	3.00	13.71	1.00	3.35	1.75	7.19	1.25	4.05	1.00	3.05			31.35
1667	3.75	17.14			2.50	10.28	.50	1.62					29.04
1668	4.00	18.28			2.75	11.31							29.59
1669	3.00	13.71			3.00	12.33			1.00	3.05			29.09
1670	3.25	14.85			3.00	12.33							27.18
1671	3.75	17.14			2.25	9.25							26.39
1672	4.00	18.28			1.00	4.11							22.39
1673	3.75	17.14											17.14

Sources: Table A2.1; chapter 3, note 51.

Note: Corn rations for women and for children under sixteen are calculated as a proportion of the corn ration for men sixteen and over, using the proportions provided by the Food and Agricultural Organization of the World Health Organization shown in Robert William Fogel, "Biomedical Approaches to the Estimation and Interpretation of Secular Trends in Equity, Morbidity, Mortality, and Labor Productivity in Europe, 1750–1980" (Unpublished paper, Center for Population Economics, University of Chicago, 1987), table 2. The male ration is 4.57 cups. Women are allowed 73 percent; boys 10–15, 90 percent; boys 5–9, 71 percent; girls 5–9, 67 percent; and children under 5, 44 percent.

Table A2.5 Time Required Daily to Pound Corn, Cole Plantation, 1662–1673

Year	Cups Required Daily	Hours to Pound[a]
1662	33.84	5.64
1663	42.82	7.14
1664	45.10	7.52
1665	42.33	7.05
1666	30.54	5.09
1667	29.04	4.84
1668	29.59	4.93
1669	29.09	4.85
1670	27.18	4.53
1671	26.39	4.40
1672	22.39	3.73
1673	17.14	2.86

Source: Table A2.4.

[a]Time is estimated at ten minutes per cup (see chapter 3, note 51).

Appendix 3

. . . . .

Livestock
Survival and Meat
Consumption

Meat was important to the diet in the seventeenth-century Chesapeake, more so than in England, because maize has nutritional deficiencies absent in English grains. There is little evidence that the deficiencies were understood, but the value of meat was recognized. County courts even ordered masters to supply servants with the meat essential to their health.

How much meat could the Cole herds supply the family? The answer depends not only on the information about livestock offered in the Cole Plantation Account but also on the fertility and mortality of the animals. It is possible to dovetail livestock schedules, sales of meat and hides, and human food consumption on the Cole plantation, 1662–73, in such a way as to estimate likely ranges of animal survival and quantities of meat available to the household over the twelve years of the account. These calculations are elaborated in Lois Green Carr, "Livestock Increase and Its Implications for Diet in the Seventeenth-Century Chesapeake," *St. Mary's City Research Series* (St. Mary's City, forthcoming). A brief summary is included here, with a few tables by way of illustration. We end with a demonstration that if a man and wife (with children born at two-year intervals) purchased a pregnant cow and a pregnant sow when they formed their household and if livestock survival resembled that on the Cole plantation, they could establish within five years the level of meat consumption that may have been enjoyed by the Coles.

We begin with an estimate of the meat required to feed the family, an estimate based on a number of references in seventeenth-century Maryland records that show a maximum of 200 pounds per year per adult man. We have used this maximum figure to see if the Coles could reach it. In estimating the needs of women and children, we have provided 73 percent of the adult male ration for adult females; 90 percent for boys age ten through fifteen; 71 percent for boys age five through nine; 67 percent for girls age five through nine; and 44 percent for children under five. These proportions are based on those calculated by the World Health Organization for estimating nutritional needs. However, the meaning of these rations has some ambiguity. The records on which our 200-pound estimate is based may have referred to dressed carcass, plus such organs as were edible, rather than cuts of meat. Practically all of a hog except its hide was edible, but a larger proportion of a beef was not. In the calculations that follow, we have assumed that the meat ration for an adult male was 200 pounds of edible meat, not carcass, but that this included edible organs and bone marrow.[1]

Could the Cole livestock provide the necessary quantity of meat? The first step in answering this question is to estimate what cattle were available for slaughter from year to year, given the size of the Cole herd in 1662, the sales and gifts made over the twelve years of the account, and the stock remaining in 1673. A by-product of the calculation is a survival rate for calves. We know the following:

1. The herd in 1662 consisted of twelve cows "young and old," six steers "young and old," eleven yearlings, four two-year heifers, and one bull.

2. Gardiner paid away two cows and calves in June 1662.

3. In 1663 Gardiner paid a legacy of one steer to Father Francis Fitzherbert.

4. Over the years 1663–68, hides and meat were sold off the plantation. Table A3.1 shows estimates of the cattle that these sales represent.

5. In 1667, when age eighteen, Francis Knott received his legacy of one-eighth of Cole's cattle and hogs, which Gardiner delivered in the form of two cows, one three-year heifer, one yearling heifer, one steer, and two hogs. Knott received at least another hog in the form of pork.

6. In 1668, Gardiner sold "cattle" for twenty-seven hundred pounds of tobacco.

7. In 1670, when Robert Cole reached age eighteen, he received cows and three-year heifers to the number of seven, one yearling heifer, one five-year steer, one three-year steer, and one yearling bull. One calf, surely a male, was "killed abroad" for him, presumably to celebrate his reaching the age at which his father had specified that all his children should receive their cattle.

8. In 1672, Ignatius Warren, the husband of Mary Cole, received five cows, one two-year heifer, one yearling heifer, one five-year steer, one three-year steer, and two yearling bulls.

9. Left for William and Edward were one six-year cow, one cow and a calf, two two-year heifers, one four-year steer, and one three-year steer.

A number of assumptions supplement the above information.

1. Cows bore their first calves between ages three and four. Heifers are capable of becoming pregnant at twenty-four months but probably did not if as poorly fed as seventeenth-century cattle were.

2. The sex ratio of calves was 3.4 females for every 7 calves, the present-day ratio, which is genetically determined.[2]

3. Male calves, if born in the fall, had lower survival rates than females because males had less fat for surviving the winter.[3]

4. Steers were slaughtered at age five or six.

5. Cows became barren by age twelve and were slaughtered then. They had the opportunity to produce nine calves over their calf-bearing years. Of the nine, 4.36 would be female. Maryland inventories rarely show cows more than age ten, but ages are usually omitted. Early modern authorities thought ten to twelve years was the useful life for a cow.[4]

6. The possibility of twins is ignored.

7. Finally, it is assumed that all cows lived to age twelve. If we relax this assumption, which is certainly unrealistic, calf survival necessarily has to rise on the Cole plantation in order to supply enough cattle to meet the distributions recorded in the account, but the overall effect on herd size and availability of meat remains the same.

A further set of assumptions fills out the information missing from the account.

1. The cows paid away in 1662 were not young. Cole's instructions to his wife, still living when he made his inventory, were that she "not pay the best for itt is butt Cowes & Calves that I must pay."

2. The "cattle" sold in 1668 were five pregnant cows worth 540 pounds of tobacco each, based on the fact that the mean price in 1668, taken from St. Mary's County inventories, of cows with calves was 557 pounds of tobacco; of cows alone, 527 pounds of tobacco.

3. The age distribution of the seven cows and three-year heifers listed as given to Robert Cole, Jr., is assumed to be five cows over three years old and two three-year heifers.

Evidence of animal slaughter appears in the guardian account in the

Table A3.1 Signs of Slaughter of Cattle and Hogs, Cole Plantation, 1663–1668

Year	Signs of Slaughter	Meat Sold	Hides
1663	Pork sold came to 1,967 lbs. @ 1.25 lbs. tob. per lb. (hereafter noted as lbt.).[a] 1 hide sold for 45 lbt. (@ 2 lbt. per lb. = 22 lbs.). (2) hides sold for 157 lbt. (@ 2 lbt. per lb. = 78 lbs. or 39 lbs. each).	21 hogs	1 2-yr steer 1 cow 1 steer
1664	6 hides sold for 540 lbt. @ 2 lbt. per lb. = (270 lbs. or 45 lbs. each). 61 lbs. of hides sold for 122 lbt (@ 2 lbt. per lb. = 2 hides, 30.5 lbs. each). Meat[b] sold = 836 lbt. (@ 1.2 lbt. per lb. = 697 lbs.).	1 steer 2 3-yr steers	3 cows 2 3-yr steers 3 steers
1665	Meat (pork)[c] sold for 1,036 lbt. (@ 1.25 lbt. per lb. = 829 lbs.). 3 hides sold for 115 lbt. (@ 2 lbt. per lb. = 57 lbs. or 19 lbs. each).	9 hogs	3 2-yr steers
1666	2 hides sold for 100 lbt. (@ 2 lbt. per lb. = 50 lbs., 1 = 20 lbs., 1 = 30 lbs.).		1 2-yr steer 1 3-yr steer
1667	Bacon sold for 252 lbt. (@ 3 lbt. per lb. = 84 lbs.). Pork sold for 891 lbt. (@ 1.25 lbt. per lb. = 713 lbs.). 1 hide sold for 37 lbt. (@ 2 lbt per lb. = 18.5 lbs.).	9 hogs	1 2-yr steer
1668	Pork sold for 200 lbt. (@ 1.25 lbt. per lb. = 160 lbs.).	18 hogs	2 steers or cows

form of hides and meat sold in particular years (see table A3.1), and this data has to be included in our calculations. Since nothing is said of what animals were killed—sometimes we do not even know the kind of animal—Carr had to make some further assumptions. She used the most restrictive possible, since one of the purposes was to determine the avail-

Table A3.1 (*continued*)

Year	Signs of Slaughter	Meat Sold	Hides
	Pork and bacon sold for 2,102 lbt. (30 lbs. bacon @ 3 lbt. per lb. = 90 lbt.; 1,609 lbs. pork @ 1.25 lbt. per lb. = 2,011 lbt.)[d] Hides sold for 160 lbt. (@ 2 lbt. per lb. = 80 lbs. or 2 hides, 40 lbs. each).	18 hogs	2 steers or cows

Source: Cole Plantation Account, appendix 1.

Assumptions: See text.

Note: Carr used the observations in the guardian account that show the price of meat per pound or weight and price per pound of hides to reconstruct the number and sizes of animals slaughtered. Inferences are in parentheses. The price of beef does not appear in the account and has been established from the ratio of pork to beef prices found in St. Mary's and Charles counties in the 1660s. Steers cannot be substituted for cows in 1663 and 1664 because the number of steers is insufficient (see table A3.3). For weights of usable meat, see appendix 3 text and note 1. We have assumed that animal organs were sold fresh.

[a]The account says 1,967 pounds sold at 1.75 pounds of tobacco per pound but puts the value at 2,458 pounds of tobacco. The error appears to be in the value, which should be 1.25 pounds of tobacco per pound. Doubtless the clerk misread the figure in transcribing the account.

[b]Meat is assumed to be beef, given strong evidence of beef supplies from hides.

[c]Here we have supposed that all the meat was pork. If beef was sold instead of eaten, fewer hogs would be needed for sale.

[d]The proportion of pork to bacon sold is unknown. We have confined the bacon sold to what was left of the two hogs killed to create the 160 pounds of pork in the first entry for 1668. This maximizes the number of hogs needed and contributes to a worst case scenario.

ability of meat under the most adverse conditions. Hence she assumed that over the years that hide sales were recorded (1663–68), the hides sold represented all the cattle that were slaughtered. (She assumed that no effort was made to preserve hog hides because scraping off the bristles is so time-consuming). During these years we cannot provide the family with meat from cattle that do not show up in the account as hides. Other cattle may have died but in circumstances that prevented the rescue of meat or skins. She also assumed that all cattle slaughtered were males or were barren cows. Such animals needed to be killed regularly, both to supply meat and to keep them from eating feed that could otherwise go to reproducing cows. Presumably no one slaughtered a cow capable of bearing a calf, hence cows represented by hides are assumed to be age twelve. Of course, a younger animal could have become barren, died of illness, or been mired and its hide later recovered, and tables that suppose a range of deceased cow ages (not shown here) make this assumption. It should be noted that in the year 1663 at least one slaughter represented by a heavy hide, and in 1664 at least three such slaughters, had to have been of twelve-year-old cows because the number of full-grown, or nearly full-grown, steers is insufficient.

To show calf survival and hence the ability of a cow to reproduce herself, Carr included among dead calves those not conceived because a cow was temporarily barren. We have no way of knowing how often this occurred in Cole's herd, but orphans' court accounts recorded in Virginia indicate that this was a frequent occurrence. For convenience, calves that did not reach maturity are assumed to have died before age one. Necessary exceptions are (1) the female yearlings and two-year-olds listed in Cole's inventory of 1662 that died before reaching maturity and (2) the young male cattle that died in 1663–64, as indicated by hides.[5]

Given that we have as hard facts the number and kinds of cattle on the Cole plantation in 1662 and 1673, the age structure of the cow herd in 1662 determines the survival rate of calves. Carr found that female calf survival rates as high as 50 percent could be obtained if all the cows were at least ten years old, allowing cows to reproduce themselves more than twice (2.18 times); but this is an unusual age structure. The very lowest rate she calculated, 31 percent, also required a very odd age structure—no cows age four to nine. The most evenly distributed ages produced a survival rate in the neighborhood of 40 percent. Table A3.2 illustrates this middle range, supposing that all cows lived a full reproductive life span, based on the following age structure for 1662:

Age	N Cows
12	0
11	1

10	3
9	1 paid away
8	1
7	1 paid away
6	1
5	1
4	2
3	1

The result is a survival rate for female calves of 40 percent, and a cow over her lifetime reproduces herself 1.74 times. If the young cattle represented by the hides of table A3.1 had been female instead of male, the survival rate to maturity would not be different, since at least this number of young females disappeared from the herd in any case.

More evenly distributed age structures for 1662 are possible if we assume that cows died before age twelve. Then there need not be three cows age ten as required by the hides sold in 1664. If we suppose that cow deaths are distributed fairly evenly across ages (3–5, 30 percent; 6–9, 30 percent; 10–12, 40 percent), female calf survival is 48 percent and a cow produces 2.09 future cows. If half are age twelve at death, and half under six, the survival rate climbs to 53 percent and cows produce 2.33 future cows. This was the highest female calf survival rate that Carr could devise. Many other combinations of age structures are possible, but calf survival appears to range between 30 and 55 percent and cow increase from 1.3 to 2.4 future cows per cow.

In table A3.3 we take the male calves shown as born in table A3.2 and make calculations for male survival in the herd that table A3.2 represents. The age structure assumed for steers in 1662 is as follows: one seven-year steer (the bull), one six-year, one five-year, two four-year, one three-year, and one two-year steer. The result is a bull calf survival rate of 38 percent, slightly lower than that of the cow calves in the same population.

These calculations fit the ranges of other estimates. Carr in her livestock report has used livestock records from accounts of orphans' estates to estimate calf survival in York County from 1658 through 1662 and found that 32 percent of female calves (including calves not conceived because cows were barren) survived to age three. Among calves actually recorded as born, 48 percent survived that long. Sam B. Hilliard has sug-

Table A3.2 Survival of Female Calves to Cowhood, Cole Plantation, 1662–1673

| Year | Cows in Herd | Calves | | | Cows Gone | | |
| | | Females | Male | Heifers | Sold Alive | Died (Killed/ Eaten) | Legacies |
		born	live					
1662	12 − 2 = 10	4	2	6	6 − 4 = 2 1-yr 4 − 1 = 3 2-yr	2 cows with calves		
1663	10 + 3 − 1 = 12	6	1	6	2 1-yr 2 2-yr		1 12-yr[a]	
1664	12 + 2 − 3 = 11	5	3	6	1 1-yr 2 2-yr		3 12-yr[a]	
1665	11 + 2 = 13	5	3	8	3 1-yr 1 2-yr			
1666	13 + 1 − 1 = 13	7	1	6	3 1-yr 3 2-yr		1 12-yr	
1667	13 + 3 − 3 = 13	6	4	7	1 − 1 = 0 1-yr 3 2-yr			2 7-yr 1 3-yr 1 1-yr
1668	13 + 3 − 6 = 10	6	1	4	4 1-yr 0 2-yr	1 11-yr 2 10-yr 1 9-yr 1 7-yr	1 12-yr	

Year	Herd				Age detail	Ages retained
1669	10 = 10	4	2	6	1 1-yr 4 2-yr	2 8-yr 1 7-yr 2 6-yr 2 3-yr 1 1-yr
1670	10 + 4 − 7 = 7	3	1	4	2 − 1 = 1 1-yr 1 2-yr	4 7-yr 1 4-yr 1 2-yr 1 1-yr
1671	7 + 1 = 8	4	3	4	1 1-yr 1 2-yr	
1672	8 + 1 − 6 = 3	3	0	0	3 − 1 = 2 1-yr 1 − 1 = 0 2-yr	1 12-yr
1673	3 − 1 = 2	1	1	1	0 1-yr 2 2-yr	1 12-yr 1 6-yr[b] 1 4-yr[b] 2 2-yr[b] 1 calf[b]
Total		54	22	58		

Calf survival = 41%   Calf production = 1.76% future cows per cow

Sources: Cole Plantation Account, appendix 1; table A3.1.

Assumptions: See text.

[a] From hides sold.

[b] Remain for Edward and William.

Table A3.3 Survival of Steers to Age of Beefing, Cole Plantation, 1662–1673

Year	Steers, Age 5+	Male Calves Born	Male Calves Live	Steers Age 1–4	Steers Eaten	Steers Sold	Steers Sold Live	Steers Legacies
1662	1 7-yr + 1 6-yr + 1 5-yr − 1 6-yr = 2	6	1	5 1-yr 1 2-yr 1 3-yr 2 4-yr				1 6-yr
1663	1 8-yr + 1 6-yr + 2 5-yr − 1 6-yr − 1 5-yr = 2	6	4	1 1-yr 5−1=4 2-yr 1 3-yr 1 4-yr	1 5-yr[a] 1 2-yr[a]		1 6-yr	
1664	1 9-yr + 1 6-yr + 1 5-yr − 1 9-yr − 1 6-yr − 1 5-yr = 0	6	2	4 1-yr 1 2-yr 4−2=2 3-yr 1 4-yr	1 5-yr[a] 1 6-yr[a]	1 9-yr[a] 2 5-yr[a]		
1665	1 5-yr = 1	8	3	2 1-yr 4−3=1 2-yr 1 3-yr 2 4-yr	3 2-yr[a]			
1666	1 6-yr + 2 5-yr = 3	6	2	3 1-yr 2−1=1 2-yr 1−1=0 3-yr 1 4-yr	1 3-yr[a] 1 2-yr[a]			
1667	1 7-yr + 2 6-yr +	7	4	2 1-yr 3−1=2 2-yr 1 ?	1 2-yr[a]			1 5-yr

Year	Age breakdown	No.	Herd A	Herd B	No.	Reconciliation
	2 5-yr 1 4-yr		1 ?-yr	1 ?-yr		
1669	1 1-yr 4 2-yr 2 5-yr 2 4-yr	6	1 8-yr 1 5-yr	1 8-yr 1 5-yr	3	1 8-yr − 1 7-yr = 1 1 8-yr + 1 5-yr − 1 5-yr − 1 8-yr = 0
1670	3−1=2 1-yr 1 2-yr 4−1=3 5-yr 2 4-yr	4	1 5-yr 1 calf[b]	1 5-yr 1 5-yr 1 1-yr	1	2 5-yr − 2 5-yr = 0
1671	1 1-yr 2 2-yr 1 3-yr 3 4-yr	4	2 5-yr		2	2 5-yr − 2 5-yr = 0
1672	2−2=0 1-yr 1 2-yr 2−1=1 3-yr 1 4-yr	0	2 5-yr	1 5-yr 1 3-yr 2 1-yr	0	3 5-yr − 3 5-yr = 0
1673	0 1-yr 0 2-yr 1 3-yr 1 4-yr	1	1 5-yr	1 5-yr[c] 1 4-yr[c]	0	1 5-yr − 1 5-yr = 0
Total		58			23	

Calf survival = 40%

Sources: Cole Plantation Account, appendix 1; tables A3.1 and A3.2.
Assumptions: See text.
[a]Inferred from hides.
[b]Specifically mentioned.
[c]Remain for William and Edward.

gested a 50 percent survival of calves in a population that probably was to some degree similar—range cattle in the South in the mid-nineteenth century.[6]

On the basis of tables A3.2 and A3.3, we argue that supplies of beef were available for the Coles to eat. Cattle needed to be slaughtered to regulate herd size, and it is unlikely that the Coles would have thrown away the meat. The next question is how many hogs would have to have been supplied to bring meat consumption to the level we have set. We must start with Cole's twenty-nine hogs and four little pigs, allow for the pork and bacon sales shown in the account (see table A3.1), and end with about fifty hogs. Evidence from hides will not be used because none were sold.

We begin by asking at what age sows started bearing, how often they farrowed, at what age they failed and were slaughtered, and what was the usual litter size. Studies of medieval farm accounts and contemporary English handbooks indicate that sows were expected to produce pigs for six years, beginning in their second year. These sources also suggest two farrowings a year with five to six surviving pigs per litter.[7] However, table A3.4 suggests that sows ranging in the Maryland woods did not fare as well. A litter size of five to six pigs is suggested from records that show pigs per sow, but the number of observations is very small. Mean litter sizes taken from inventories that show more than one sow indicate that three pigs per sow is a more reasonable figure. Most of the inventories suggest only one farrowing a year, but here the evidence is more ambiguous. However, Sam Hilliard estimated that one farrowing and three surviving pigs per sow were the norms for range sows of the mid-nineteenth century.[8]

Table A3.5 shows possible pig production and availability of pork and bacon for food on the Cole plantation. On the basis of table A3.4, the table assumes that annually each sow farrows once and produces three pigs that reach slaughter age. It dovetails (1) information about meat sales shown in table A3.1, (2) speculations about slaughters of cattle shown in tables A3.2 and A3.3, and (3) estimates for total meat needed for the family, shown in tables A3.6 and A3.7. In table A3.5, we calculate how many sows were necessary to produce the number of hogs needed to supply what was sold and eaten and have fifty-odd hogs on hand in 1673. The schedule offered is not the only one possible. For simplicity's sake, we have assumed that the sows on hand in 1662 were all in their second

Table A3.4 Pigs per Litter in Seventeenth-Century Maryland Inventories

Pigs per Sow	Estates with 1 Sow	Estates with 2 Sows or More	All Estates
1	0	0	0
2	0	1	1
3	3	16	19
4	1	7	8
5	2	4	6
6	4	3	7
7	0	0	0
8	0	1	1
9	0	0	0
10	0	1	1
Total	10	33	43

Sources: Testamentary Proceedings, 1(D):95–96, 1(F):42–44, 2:64–69, and Inventories and Accounts, 1:445–46, 689–90, 2:62, 144–45, 179–86, 196, 4:140–43, 152–53, 170–71, 251–53, Maryland State Archives; William Hand Browne et al., eds., *Archives of Maryland*, 72 vols. (Baltimore, 1883–1972), 4:83, 54:93.

Note: When figuring pigs per litter, we usually used mean calculations when there were two or more sows, but sometimes the records indicated that particular pigs were associated with a litter.

year and that all were slaughtered six years later. However, the age structure of the sows is of no importance, since sow replacement was a simple matter. Any female pig could be left unspayed and become a sow after its first year.

Tables A3.6 and A3.7 show the meat requirements for the household year by year and the animals available to meet them, based on tables A3.1 through A3.5. Besides those already outlined, the assumptions here are that edible food from a hog came to 95 pounds; from a full-grown steer, to 300 pounds; from a cow, to 225 pounds; from a three-year-old steer, to 220 pounds; from a two-year-old, to 185 pounds; from a yearling, to 110 pounds; and from a calf, to 25 pounds.[9] Given the schedules for cattle and hogs in tables A3.2 through A3.5, the beef and pork the Cole herds could supply reaches, or overreaches, the proposed allowance of 200 pounds of usable meat per adult male annually, except in 1662 and 1663. Not enough pork can be supplied in those years because of the pork

Table A3.5 Hog Production, Cole Plantation, 1662–1673

Year	Total Hogs	Sows	Pigs	1-yr	2-yr	3-yr +	Killed		
							Eaten	Sold	All
1662	33 + 15 − 2 = 46	5	19	12	12 − 2 = 10	0	2	0	2
1663	46 + 18 − 21 = 43	5 + 1 = 6	18	19	12 − 12^a = 0	10 − 10 = 0	0	21	21
1664	43 + 18 − 8 = 53	6	18	18	19 − 8 = 11	0	8	0	8
1665	53 + 18 − 22 = 49	6	18	18	18 − 11 = 7	11 − 11 = 0	13	9	22
1666	49 + 18 − 11 = 56	6	18	18	18 − 4 = 14	7 − 7 = 0	11	0	11
1667	56 + 18 − 21 = 53	6	18	18	18 − 7 = 11	14 − 14 = 0	12	9	21
1668	53 + 9 − 26 = 36	6 − 6 + 3 = 3	9	18	18 − 12^b = 6	11 − 11 = 0	7	19	26
1669	36 + 9 − 8 = 37	3	9	9	18 − 2 = 16	6 − 6 = 0	8	0	8
1670	37 + 9 − 11 = 35	3	9	9	9 − 0 = 9	16 − 11 = 5	9	2^c	11
1671	35 + 9 − 6 = 38	3	9	9	9 − 0 = 9	14 − 6 = 8	6	0	6
1672	38 + 9 − 5 = 42	3	9	9	9 − 0 = 9	17 − 5 = 12	5	0	5
1673	42 + 12 − 5 = 49	3 + 1 = 4	12	9	9 − 1^d = 8	21 − 5 = 16	5	0	5

Sources: Cole Plantation Account, appendix 1; tables A3.1, A3.6, A3.7.

Assumptions: See text. On these assumptions there were 4 sows farrowing in 1660 and 1661. Otherwise there would have been more than 29 hogs in 1662.

  Note: Cole listed 29 hogs and 4 pigs in his inventory. The 4 pigs are included in both the starting number (33) and the pig column for 1662.

  ^{a} 1 is moved to sow column.
  ^{b} 3 are moved to sow column.
  ^{c} 2 are given to Francis Knott as part of his inheritance.
  ^{d} 1 is moved to sow column.

Table A3.6 Estimated Meat Requirement, Cole Plantation, 1662–1673

Year	Men 16+		Women		Boys 10–15		Boys 5–9		Girls 5–9		Under 5		Total Meat
	N	Lbs. Meat Req.	N	Lbs. Meat Req.	N	Lbs. Meat Req.	N	Lbs. Meat Req.	N	Lbs. Meat Req.	N	Lbs. Meat Req.	
1662[a]	3.25	596	1.00	134	1.50	248	2.00	260			1.50	121	1359
1663	4.25	850	2.00	292	2.00	360	2.00	284			1.00	88	1874
1664	4.75	950	2.00	292	2.00	360	2.00	284			1.00	88	1974
1665	4.50	900	1.75	255.5	1.75	315	1.75	248.5	1.00	134			1853
1666	3.00	600	1.00	146	1.75	315	1.25	178	1.00	134			1373
1667	3.75	750			2.50	450	.50	71					1271
1668	4.00	800			2.75	494							1295
1669	3.00	600			3.00	540			1.00	134			1274
1670	3.25	650			3.00	540							1190
1671	3.75	750			2.25	405							1155
1672	4.00	800			1.00	180							980
1673	3.75	750											750

Sources: See text and appendix 2; table 2.1.

Note: The ration is 200 pounds of edible meat, including organs and bone marrow, per adult male. Women are allowed 73 percent of this ration; boys 10–15, 90 percent; girls 10–15, 80 percent; boys 5–9, 71 percent; girls 5–9, 67 percent; and children under 5, 44 percent.

[a]Eleven months.

Table A3.7 Estimated Meat Consumption, Cole Plantation, 1662–1673

Year	Lbs. Meat Required	Cattle Kind & Size	Usable Meat	N	Hogs Lbs. Meat	Total Lbs. Meat	% Re- quire- ment
1662	1359[a]			2	190 450[b]	640	47
1663	1874	1 2-yr steer	185	0		710	38
		1 cow	225				
		1 steer	300				
1664	1974	3 cows	675	8	760	2035	103
		2 steers	600				
1665	1853	3 2-yr steers	555	13	1235	1790	97
1666	1373	1 2-yr steer	185	11	1045	1450	106
		1 3-yr steer	220				
1667	1271	1 2-yr steer	185	12	1140	1325	104
1668	1295	2 steers	600	7	665	1265	98
1669	1274	2 steers	600	8	760	1360	107
1670	1190	1 steer	300	9	855	1180	99
		1 calf	25				
1671	1155	2 steers	600	6	570	1170	101
1672	980	2 steers	600	5	475	1075	110
1673	750	1 steer	300	5	475	775	103

Sources: Tables A3.1 through A3.6.

[a] Eleven months' ration.

[b] Eighteen middle pieces of bacon that Cole noted as on hand on April 25.

sold in 1663. Why so much was sold that year instead of eaten is something of a mystery. The problem may be an artifact of our restriction that no cattle can be used for meat before 1669 unless the hides appear in the guardian account. Perhaps, in fact, in 1662 and 1663, cows were slaughtered and eaten, but their hides were used on the plantation and hence do not appear in the account. Then there would have been plenty of meat without the pork that was sold. Given the meat available thereafter, it seems in fact implausible that Gardiner limited the family to the amounts calculated here for those first two years.

These schedules should not be taken too seriously. They are too inflexible, and all have problems. For example, table A3.3 shows full-grown steers available in 1665 through 1667, but they cannot be shown as slaughtered for meat because their hides do not appear. We must presume that the animals went unkilled until 1668 and 1669 because they had joined the wild gang and had to be hunted. (The account shows a payment to Vincent Mansfield for killing a steer that had got into the wild gang.) Lifting the hide restriction would make available additional beef not only from steers but also from old cows. Table A3.5 suffers from a superfluity of old hogs. Various adjustments in the number of sows or in pig survival would eliminate this problem. We do not know what actually happened, only the initial and the final size of the herd. The intention here is to show the possibilities that livestock culture offered and the certainty that plenty of meat could have been available. Two hundred pounds of meat per year offered a man more than half a pound of meat per day. Given the available supplements from wild animals, birds, and fish,[10] this was surely an ample supply.

How long would it take a new planter to reach the point that he could supply his family with as much meat per person as the Coles could have been eating in the 1660s? Let us suppose a family with a child born every two years, starting in the second year. Tables A3.8 through A3.10 show that one sow farrowing once a year with three surviving pigs from each farrowing would provide plenty of meat for a family after five years. The first two years would be meatless. But thereafter it would be easy to obtain pork, and as cattle herds grew, beef would become more and more available. Overall, the Coles, with a large household but well-established stocks of animals, had at least 41 percent of their diet in beef (see table A3.7) and in fact may have had much more. The hypothetical family shown in table A3.11 has 10 percent in beef, once slaughtering starts, but the proportion will rise as their cattle herd grows.

The presence of considerable beef is a finding that archaeological excavations support. Henry Miller, in examining sites of poor as well as rich households, found that 58 percent of the meat from domestic animals was beef and that poor families did not confine themselves to inferior cuts.[11] Good management of cattle herds required slaughtering cattle, and Chesapeake inhabitants were unlikely to have wasted the meat.

Tables A3.12 and A3.13 show (1) how Gardiner's investment in a pregnant mare in 1663 could become thirty horses ten years later, and (2) what the increase from the children's legacies of female cattle would be, based on the survival rates and sex ratios of calves in tables A3.2 and A3.3.

Table A3.8 Estimated Need for Meat, Seventeenth-Century Chesapeake Family over Twelve Years

	Men 16+		Women		Children 1–4		Children 5–9		Children 10–15		
Year	N	Meat Ration	N	Meat Ration	N	Meat Ration	N	Meat Ration	N	Meat Ration	Total Meat
1	1	200	1	146	0						346
2	1	200	1	146	1						346
3	1	200	1	146	1	88					434
4	1	200	1	146	2	88					434
5	1	200	1	146	2	176					522
6	1	200	1	146	3	176					522
7	1	200	1	146	2	176	1	138			660
8	1	200	1	146	3	176	1	138			660
9	1	200	1	146	2	176	2	276			798
10	1	200	1	146	3	176	2	276			798
11	1	200	1	146	2	176	3	414			936
12	1	200	1	146	3	176	2	276	1	170	968

Assumptions: See text.

Note: Children are born into the first age group and then leave it for the second age group, hence the variations in size. Children are not given a meat ration until their second year. Children in the age group 5–9 are given 69 percent of the adult male ration, a mean of the rations for boys and girls. The child age 10 in year 12 is given 85 percent, the mean for boys and girls age 10 to 15.

Table A3.9 Cattle Slaughters, Seventeenth-Century Chesapeake Family over Twelve Years

Year	Cows	Calves Female Bn	Live	Male Bn	Live	Heifers	Bulls & Steers	Slaughters	Lbs. Meat
1	1 4-yr	1	1	0	0				
2	1 5-yr	0	0	1	1	1 1-yr			
3	1 6-yr	0	0	1	0	1 2-yr	1 1-yr[a]		
4	1 7-yr	1	0	1	0		1 2-yr[a]		
	1 3-yr								
5	1 8-yr	1	1	1	1		1 3-yr[a]		
	1 4-yr								
6	1 9-yr	1	0	1	0	1 1-yr	1 4-yr[a]		
	1 5-yr						1 1-yr[a]		
7	1 10-yr	1	1	1	1	1 2-yr	1 5-yr[a]		
	1 6-yr						1 2-yr[a]		
8	1 11-yr	1	0	2	1	1 1-yr	1 6-yr[a]		
	1 7-yr						1 3-yr		
	1 3-yr						1 1-yr		
9	1 8-yr	1	1	1	0	1 2-yr	1 7-yr[a]	1 12-yr cow	225
	1 4-yr						1 4-yr		
							1 2-yr		
							1 1-yr		
10	1 9-yr	1	0	2	1	1 1-yr	1 8-yr[a]	1 5-yr steer	300
	1 5-yr						1 3-yr		
	1 3-yr						1 2-yr		
11	1 10-yr	2	1	1	0	1 2-yr	1 9-yr[a]		
	1 6-yr						1 4-yr		
	1 4-yr						1 3-yr		
							1 1-yr		
12	1 11-yr	2	0	2	0	1 1-yr	1 10-yr[a]	1 5-yr steer	300
	1 7-yr						1 4-yr		
	1 5-yr						1 2-yr		
	1 3-yr								
Total		12	5	14	5				

Assumptions: See text.

Note: Until the first male reached the age to impregnate a cow, the cow was serviced by other bulls.

[a] A bull.

Table A3.10 Hog Slaughters, Seventeenth-Century Chesapeake Family over Twelve Years

Year	Sows	Pigs	1-yr	2-yr	3-yr+	Kill	Meat
1	1	3				0	0
2	1	3	3			0	0
3	$1+1=2$	6	3	$3-3^a=0$		2	190
4	$2+1=3$	9	6	$3-3^a=0$		2	190
5	3	9	9	$6-6=0$		6	570
6	$3+1=4$	12	9	$9-9^a=0$		8	760
7	$4-1+1=4$	12	12	$9-9^a=0$		9	855
8	4	12	12	$12-10=2$		10	950
9	$4-1+1=4$	12	12	$12-8^a=4$	$2-2=0$	10	950
10	4	12	12	$12-6=6$	$4-4=0$	10	950
11	4	12	12	$12-5=7$	$6-6=0$	11	1045
12	$4-1+1=4$	12	12	$12-3^a=9$	$7-7=0$	10	950

Assumptions: See text.

^{a}1 moved to sow column.

Table A3.11 Meat Provided for Seventeenth-Century Chesapeake Family over Twelve Years

Year	Beef	Pork	All	Requirement	% Require-ment
1	0	0	0	346	0
2	0	0	0	346	0
3	0	190	190	434	44
4	0	190	190	434	44
5	0	570	570	522	109
6	0	760	760	522	146
7	0	855	855	660	130
8	0	950	950	660	144
9	225	950	1175	798	147
10	300	950	1250	798	157
11	0	1045	1045	936	112
12	300	950	1250	968	129

Sources: Tables A3.8, A3.9, A3.10.

Table A3.12 Production of Horses, Cole Plantation, 1663–1673

Year	Horses	Mares	Foals F	Foals M	1-yr F	1-yr M	2-yr F	2-yr M	Sold	N Head
1663	1	1	1							2
1664	1	1	1		1					3
1665	1			1	1	1				4
1666	2	1	1	1−1=0	1	1				5
1667	3	2	1	1	1			1		8
1668	1−1=0	3	1	2−1=1	2	1	1		1 horse	9
1669		4	2−1=1	2	1	1	2	1		12
1670	1	6	3	3−1=2	1	2	1	1		17
1671	2	7	3−3=0	4−1=3	3	2	1−1=0	2	1 2-yr mare	19
1672	4	7	4−1=3	3−1=2		3	3−1=2	2	1 2-yr mare	23
1673	6	9−1=8	4	4	3	2		3	1 mare	30
Total			22−5	21−5						

Survival of foals = 77%; of female foals, 77%. Mares are producing 4.24 future mares.

Source: Cole Plantation Account, appendix 1.

Note: Cole had no horses when he made his inventory in 1662. Gardiner purchased one for the orphans in 1663. There were thirty horses in 1673. In 1668, one horse was sold for 2,000 pounds of tobacco; in 1671–72, 3,305 pounds of tobacco was due for "mares" sold. The mares could not have been sold before 1671 if the estate ended up with thirty head in 1673. Their price suggests youth, since a mare was sold in 1673 for 2,400 pounds of tobacco. No more than two can be sold without unreasonably lowering mortality. In addition, deaths must concentrate toward the end of the schedule to reach the number of horses on hand in 1673.

Assumptions necessary for this table are:

1. The mare was pregnant at purchase and produced her foal soon afterward
2. The mare was age 3 at purchase
3. Two mares were sold at age 2, 1 in 1671 and 1 in 1672
4. One half the foals born were female
5. Mares bore their first foals during their fourth year (before age 4)
6. All foals that survived to age 3 survived over the rest of the period
7. Gardiner allowed the original mare to run with his own horses for a while, until a stallion was available from the orphans' increase
8. The original mare produced foals over the whole period

Table A3.13 Increase of Cattle Given to Children, Cole Plantation, 1667–1673

Year	Cows	Female Calves Surviving	Male Calves Surviving	Heifers	Steers
			Knott		
1667	3	0.60	0.62	1 1-yr	1 4-yr
1668	3	0.60	0.62	0.60 1-yr	0.62 1-yr
				1 2-yr	1 5-yr
1669	4	0.79	0.83	0.60 1-yr	0.62 1-yr
				0.60 2-yr	0.62 2-yr
					1 6-yr
1670	4.60	0.91	0.95	0.79 1-yr	0.83 1-yr
				0.60 2-yr	0.62 2-yr
					0.62 3-yr
					1 7-yr
1671	5.20	1.03	1.07	0.91 1-yr	0.95 1-yr
				0.79 2-yr	0.83 2-yr
					0.62 3-yr
					0.62 4-yr
					1 8-yr
1672	5.99	1.19	1.24	1.03 1-yr	1.07 1-yr
				0.91 2-yr	0.95 2-yr
					0.83 3-yr
					0.62 4-yr
					0.62 5-yr
					1 9-yr
1673	6.90	1.37	1.42	1.19 1-yr	1.24 1-yr
				1.03 2-yr	1.07 2-yr
					0.95 3-yr
					0.83 4-yr
					0.62 5-yr
					0.62 6-yr
					1 10-yr

Table A3.13 (*continued*)

Year	Cows	Female Calves Surviving	Male Calves Surviving	Heifers	Steers
			Cole		
1670	7	1.39	1.44	1 1-yr	1 1-yr
1671	7	1.39	1.44	1.39 1-yr	1.44 1-yr
				1 2-yr	1 2-yr
1672	8	1.59	1.65	1.39 1-yr	1.44 1-yr
				1.39 2-yr	1.44 2-yr
					1 3-yr
1673	9.39	1.86	1.94	1.59 1-yr	1.65 1-yr
				1.39 2-yr	1.44 2-yr
					1.44 3-yr
					1 4-yr
			Warren		
1672	5	0.99	1.03	1 1-yr	1 1-yr
				1 2-yr	1 2-yr
1673	6	1.19	1.24	0.99 1-yr	1.03 1-yr
				1 2-yr	1 2-yr
					1 3-yr

Total Herd, 1673		Total Herd, 1662
Knott	18.24	
Cole	21.70	
Warren	13.45	
Orphans	7.00	
	60.39	34.00

Increase of 5.36% per year

Sources: Cole Plantation Account, appendix 1; tables A3.1 through A3.3.

Assumption: Survival rate of female calves is 41%, as in table A3.2. Survival rate of male calves is 40%, as in table A3.3. The proportion of female calves was 48.4%.

Appendix 4

• • • •

Biographies of
the Cole Family,
Their Servants, and
Persons Mentioned
in Robert Cole's
Account and Will

The biographies are compiled from files prepared by Historic St. Mary's City: prosopographical files of all St. Mary's County residents appearing through 1705 and files of inventoried decedents through 1775. We have adopted, with gracious permission, the format of Edward C. Papenfuse, Alan F. Day, David W. Jordan, and Gregory Stiverson, eds., *A Biographical Dictionary of Maryland Legislature, 1635–1789* (Baltimore, 1979), and have drawn on the *Biographical Dictionary* for the careers of legislators. In the few instances where our materials differ from what appears in the *Biographical Dictionary*, we found additional information, mainly in collections of private papers, not available when the *Biographical Dictionary* was compiled. Italicized names indicate individuals whose biographies appear elsewhere in this appendix. Estate values are not deflated to constant value.

ALVEY (ALLVY), JOSEPH (?–1679). BORN: in England. IMMI-GRATED: in 1657 as a servant to *Robert Cole*. RESIDED: "Cole's," St. Clement's Manor, through 1661; later, in Newtown Hundred above the manor on "Knotting" or "Rome." **FAMILY BACKGROUND.**

BROTHER: Pope (?–1679), of Bretton's Bay, who immigrated in the early 1660s. **MARRIED** by 1667 Elizabeth, a former servant. **CHILDREN.** SONS: Arthur (?–1701); Joseph (?–1729). **PRIVATE CAREER.** EDUCATION: literate. OCCUPATIONAL PROFILE: servant, free by 1661; planter. **WEALTH DURING LIFETIME.** LAND: patented total of 200 acres in 1668 and 1671. **WEALTH AT DEATH.** PERSONAL PROPERTY: TEV £58, including two servants. LAND: 300 acres.

BARTON, WILLIAM (c. 1605–early 1680s). BORN: in England. IMMIGRATED: by 1654 as a free adult with two children. RESIDED: "Barton Hall," St. Clement's Manor; may have moved to Charles County by 1672. **CHILDREN.** SON: William (?–1717), a justice of Charles County from 1672 to 1696 and from 1704 to 1709, who married Margaret, the widow of William Hungerford and daughter of William Smoote. DAUGHTER: Margaret. **PRIVATE CAREER.** EDUCATION: literate. RELIGIOUS AFFILIATION: Protestant. SOCIAL STATUS: no title on arrival; "Gent." by the late 1650s. OCCUPATIONAL PROFILE: mariner; planter. ADDITIONAL COMMENTS: Mary, probably a former servant to *Robert Cole*, was living at Barton's in 1662. **PUBLIC CAREER.** PROVINCIAL OFFICES: lower house, St. Mary's County, 1659/60 (election voided), 1661; COUNTY OFFICES: justice, St. Mary's County and Potomac, 1655–probably 1658; justice, St. Mary's County, 1658–68. MINOR OFFICES: manor court juror and bailiff. STANDS ON PUBLIC ISSUES: rewarded by Lord Baltimore in 1656 for his loyalty, probably for his services in the Battle of the Severn. **WEALTH DURING LIFETIME.** LAND: leaseholder, St. Clement's Manor, 1654; 300 acres on St. Clement's Manor, 1657; 500 acres in 1661. **WEALTH AT DEATH.** LAND: at least 600 acres.

BEANE (BEAN, BAYNE), WALTER (?–1670). BORN: in England. IMMIGRATED: in 1641 as a free adult from Virginia. RESIDED: St. George's Hundred, 1643; probably later in Newtown Hundred; Charles County after c. 1654. ADDITIONAL COMMENTS: immigrated to Virginia in the mid-1630s, probably as a servant; came to Maryland, with a manservant, to join his brother, probably on completion of his own indenture. **FAMILY BACKGROUND.** BROTHER: Ralph (?–1655), who was transported by Leonard Calvert as an indentured servant in 1634 and who owned 1,500 acres by the time of his death. **MARRIED** Elinor (Helene) (?–1701). **CHILDREN.** SONS: John (c. 1662–1701), a Charles

County burgess, sheriff, and justice, who married by 1687 Ann (?–1702/03), the widow of Thomas Gerard, Jr.; Thomas; Walter. DAUGHTERS: Edith (1660–before 1670); Judith, who married Matthew Hill; Elinor, who married first, John Stone, second, Hugh Tears, and third, John Beale; Elizabeth, who married ? Dutton; Ann. **PRIVATE CAREER.** EDUCATION: illiterate. RELIGIOUS AFFILIATION: Protestant. SOCIAL STATUS: "Gent." by the mid-1650s. OCCUPATIONAL PROFILE: probably a servant, 1630s; planter, by 1643; merchant. ADDITIONAL COMMENTS: *Luke Gardiner* bought two books from him for the *Cole* children in 1662. **PUBLIC CAREER.** PROVINCIAL OFFICES: assembly, present 1641/42, St. Mary's County, 1650–1650/51. COUNTY OFFICES: justice, St. Mary's County, 1655–58, Charles County, 1660–67. MINOR OFFICES: provincial court juror. STANDS ON PUBLIC ISSUES: probably a supporter of Lord Baltimore against Fendall's Rebellion in 1660. **WEALTH DURING LIFETIME.** LAND: c. 700 acres in 1650. **WEALTH AT DEATH.** PERSONAL PROPERTY: TEV £373, including three slaves and six servants. LAND: 2,800 acres.

BENNET (BENNITT), THOMAS (?–?). BORN: probably in England. IMMIGRATED: either as an indentured servant in late 1640s or as a freeman in 1651. RESIDED: "Poplar Neck," from 1663. **PRIVATE CAREER.** OCCUPATIONAL PROFILE: possibly servant; later, carpenter. **WEALTH DURING LIFETIME.** LAND: 50 acres on Bretton's Bay, 1663, sold next year; 100 acres in Newtown Hundred, 1666. ADDITIONAL COMMENTS: built a house for the *Robert Cole* estate in 1665; indicted for hog stealing in 1666; posted bond for good behavior in 1668. Presence of at least three Thomas Bennets in the area in the 1660s makes identification tentative.

BENNITT (BENNETT), RICHARD (c. 1614–c. 1667). BORN: probably in England. IMMIGRATED: probably by the early 1640s; transported wife and five children in 1646. RESIDED: "Tenny Hill," Poplar Hill Hundred, from 1651. **FAMILY BACKGROUND.** MOTHER: Sarah, the wife of John Taylor by 1651. **MARRIED** Elizabeth by 1646. **CHILDREN.** SONS: Thomas; Richard. DAUGHTERS: Sarah; Mary. **PRIVATE CAREER.** EDUCATION: illiterate. OCCUPATIONAL PROFILE: planter. ADDITIONAL COMMENTS: supplied provisions for and accompanied Leonard Calvert's party from Virginia when Calvert returned after Ingle's Rebellion; owed *Robert Cole* a debt that he repaid in 1662. **PUBLIC CA-**

REER. MINOR OFFICES: county juror. **WEALTH DURING LIFE-TIME.** LAND: possible leaseholder, 1651, St. Clement's Manor; 200-acre freehold in Poplar Hill, 1651; 100 acres on Bretton's Bay, 1663; patented and subsequently sold 350 acres in Charles County.

BRITTAINE (BRETTON, BRITTON), WILLIAM (?–c. 1672). BORN: probably in England. IMMIGRATED: in 1638 as a free adult with his wife, child, and three servants. RESIDED: first, St. George's Hundred; from 1640, on "Little Bretton," Newtown Hundred. **FAMILY BACK-GROUND.** KINSMEN: Thomas Turner (?–1662), of St. Clement's Hundred; Edward Parker (?–1669), of St. Inigoe's Hundred, both Roman Catholics. **MARRIED** first, Mary, the daughter of Thomas Nabbs; second, Temperance Jay, of Surry County, Virginia, in 1651. **CHILDREN.** SON: William (c. 1633–?). DAUGHTER or STEPDAUGHTER: Mary, who married William Thompson (?–1660). **PRIVATE CAREER.** EDU-CATION: literate; extensive clerical skills. RELIGIOUS AFFILIATION: Roman Catholic. SOCIAL STATUS: "Gent." on arrival; brought three servants with him; clerical skills led to quick and profitable patronage in a series of clerkships. OCCUPATIONAL PROFILE: placeman; planter. ADDITIONAL COMMENTS: paid *Robert Cole*'s estate 48 lbs. tobacco in 1663 and boarded *Mary Cole* in 1663. **PUBLIC CAREER.** PROVIN-CIAL OFFICES: clerk, assembly, 1637/38–50; clerk, council, by 1638–47; clerk, lower house, 1650–51, 1661–66; assembly, present 1637/38, present 1641/42, special writ 1642A, present 1647/48; burgess, St. Mary's County, 1649. COUNTY OFFICES: justice, St. Mary's County, 1658–68; coroner, 1669–70. MINOR LOCAL OFFICES: provincial juror. **WEALTH DURING LIFETIME.** LAND: acquired "Little Bretton," 750 acres, in 1640 and another 100 acres in 1649; sold both tracts in 1668.

BROOKE, THOMAS (1632–1676). BORN: in England; second son. IMMIGRATED: in 1650 as a minor with father and siblings. RESIDED: "Delabrooke Manor," Resurrection Hundred, Calvert County. **FAMILY BACKGROUND.** FATHER: Robert Brooke (1602–55), a councillor and county justice. MOTHER: Mary (?–1635), the daughter of Thomas Baker, Esq., barrister, and granddaughter of Sir Thomas Engham, of Goodneston, Kent, England. BROTHER: Baker Brooke (1628–78/79); HALF BROTHERS: Charles (1636–71); Roger (1637–1700); Robert (1639–67); John (1640–77); Basil (?–1651), who died in infancy; Henry (1655–72). SISTERS: Mary (1630–by 1650); Barbara (1639–by 1650).

HALF SISTERS: Mary (1642–?); Ann (1645–?); Elizabeth (1655–?), who married Richard Smith (?–1714). **MARRIED** Elinor (1642–1725), the daughter of Richard and Margaret Hatton. She subsequently married Henry Darnall (c. 1645–1711). Her brothers were William (?–1712) and Richard. Her sisters were Mary, who married Zachary Wade (c. 1627–78); Elizabeth, who married first, *Luke Gardiner* (1622–74), and second, Clement Hill (?–1708); and Barbara, who married James Johnson. **CHILDREN.** SONS: Thomas (c. 1659–1731), who married first, Ann, and second, Barbara (1676–1754), the daughter of Thomas Dent (c. 1630–76); Robert (1663–1714), a Jesuit priest; Ignatius (1670–1751), a Jesuit priest; Matthew (1672–1703), a Jesuit priest; and Clement (1676–1737), who married Jane, the daughter of Nicholas Sewall (1665–1737). DAUGHTERS: Elinor, who married first, Philip Darnall (1671–1705), the son of Henry Darnall, and second, William Digges, the son of William Digges; Mary, who married first, James Bowling (?–by 1693), second, Benjamin Hall (1667–1721), and third, Henry Witham. **PRIVATE CAREER.** EDUCATION: literate; probably had considerable schooling. RELIGIOUS AFFILIATION: raised as a Protestant but converted to Roman Catholicism. SOCIAL STATUS: second-generation provincial officeholder; father and brother served on the council, and another brother was a burgess. OCCUPATIONAL PROFILE: planter. ADDITIONAL COMMENTS: witnessed *Robert Cole*'s will. **PUBLIC CAREER.** PROVINCIAL OFFICES: lower house, Calvert County, 1663–64, 1666, 1671–74/75, 1676. COUNTY OFFICES: justice, Calvert County, 1661–66, 1667–68, 1669/70–74, 1675/76–76; sheriff, Calvert County, 1666–67, 1668–69. MILITARY SERVICE: captain, 1658; major, 1660/61. **WEALTH DURING LIFETIME.** LAND: inherited 2,000 acres from his father; 3,000 acres by 1663. **WEALTH AT DEATH.** PERSONAL PROPERTY: TEV £575, including ten slaves and ten servants. LAND: 8,401 acres.

CARPENTER (CARPINTER), THOMAS (?–c. 1659). BORN: in England. IMMIGRATED: as a servant to *Robert Cole* in 1652. RESIDED: "Cole's," St. Clement's Manor through 1657. **PRIVATE CAREER.** OCCUPATIONAL PROFILE: servant, probably free in 1657; then probably laborer.

CLARKE, EDWARD (?–1676). BORN: probably in England. IMMIGRATED: as a freeman in 1653. RESIDED: "Clarke's Rest," Newtown

Hundred. **MARRIED** Anne, the daughter of John Shertcliffe, between 1663 and 1668; she married second, John Dabridgecourt, by 1679. BROTHERS-IN-LAW: John and William Shertcliffe. **CHILDREN. SONS:** Edward (?–before 1676); Edward (?–1714). **PRIVATE CAREER. EDUCATION:** literate; possibly educated at a Benedictine seminary in Douai or Paris, France, institutions that were residuary legates of his will. RELIGIOUS AFFILIATION: Roman Catholic. SOCIAL STATUS: "Mr." by 1670; "Gent." by 1674. OCCUPATIONAL PROFILE: planter. ADDITIONAL COMMENTS: witnessed *Robert Cole*'s will. **PUBLIC CAREER.** COUNTY OFFICES: clerk, St. Mary's County, 1674–76. MINOR OFFICES: provincial court juror. **WEALTH DURING LIFETIME.** LAND: surveyed 100 acres in 1667, 350 acres in 1673, and 300 acres in 1674; acquired additional land through his marriage. **WEALTH AT DEATH.** PERSONAL ESTATE: TEV £76, including one servant. LAND: 550 acres.

CLOISE (CLANSE) (?–?). BORN: probably in Africa. IMMIGRATED: prior to 1661 as a slave. RESIDED: "Bushwood," St. Clement's Manor. **PRIVATE CAREER.** OCCUPATIONAL PROFILE: quarter foreman; doctor; possibly cooper. ADDITIONAL COMMENTS: one of 12 slaves listed in *Robert Slye*'s inventory in 1671 and apparently foreman of one of three all-black quarters that included a slave cooper; paid by *Robert Cole*'s estate in 1663 for curing *Ann Knott Harinton* of "the Spleene."

COLE, EDWARD (1657–1717). BORN: November 9, 1657, on St. Clement's Manor. NATIVE: first generation, third son. RESIDED: "Cole's," St. Clement's Manor, until c. 1688; then "St. Edward's," above the manor. **FAMILY BACKGROUND.** FATHER: *Robert Cole* (c. 1628–c. 1662). MOTHER: *Rebecca* (?–1662), the widow of ? Knott, probably of Middlesex, England; married Robert Cole by 1652. BROTHERS: *Robert* (1652–93); *William Maria* (1655–by 1688). SISTERS: *Mary* (1653–?); *Elizabeth* (1659–70). STEPBROTHER: *Francis Knott* (c. 1649–1705). STEPSISTER: *Ann Knott Harinton*. GRANDFATHER: probably William Cole (?–1633 or 1634) of Heston, Middlesex. GRANDMOTHER: *Joan Cole* of Heston, Middlesex. **MARRIED** possibly first, Honor (Honory) by 1683, and second, Elizabeth Slye (c. 1668–1734), the daughter of *Robert Slye* (c. 1628–1671), who married first, Luke Gardiner (?–1705), the son of *Luke Gardiner* (1622–74). **CHILDREN.** SONS: Edward (?–1763); Robert (?–c. 1720). DAUGHTERS: Elizabeth, who married William Heard (?–1733) by 1717; Honor, who married Thomas Spalding by 1717; Ruth, who married Thomas Mattingly by 1717; Susanna, who married George or Edward Jenkins by 1717; Mary, who married George or Edward Jenkins by 1717. **PRIVATE CAREER.** EDUCATION: five years of schooling in Maryland, possibly more in England. RELIGIOUS AFFILIATION: Roman Catholic. SOCIAL STATUS: "Mr." by death. OCCUPATIONAL PROFILE: planter; merchant; at death, factor for the London merchant John Hyde. ADDITIONAL COMMENTS: went to England in 1672, possibly for further schooling; returned in 1679. **PUBLIC CAREER.** MINOR OFFICES: county land juror; provincial court juror. **WEALTH DURING LIFETIME.** LAND: inherited rights to 200 acres; patented 150 acres in 1682; purchased 210 acres from his brothers in 1688; surveyed 150 acres in 1682 and an additional 100 acres before 1707. **WEALTH AT DEATH.** PERSONAL PROPERTY: TEV £778, including seven slaves. LAND: c. 575 acres.

COLE, ELIZABETH (BETTY) (1659–1670). BORN: March 2, 1659, on St. Clement's Manor. NATIVE: first generation, youngest daughter. RESIDED: "Cole's," St. Clement's Manor; boarded in Newtown Hundred in 1688. **FAMILY BACKGROUND.** FATHER: *Robert Cole* (c. 1628–c. 1662). MOTHER: *Rebecca* (?–1662). BROTHERS: *Robert* (1652–93); *William Maria* (1655–by 1688); *Edward* (1657–1717). SISTER: *Mary* (1653–?). STEPBROTHER: *Francis Knott* (c. 1649–1705). STEPSISTER: *Ann Knott Harinton*. GRANDFATHER: probably William Cole (?–1633 or 1634) of Heston, Middlesex. GRANDMOTHER: *Joan Cole* of Heston, Middlesex. **PRIVATE CAREER.** EDUCATION: four years of schooling in Maryland. RELIGIOUS AFFILIATION: Roman Catholic. OCCUPATIONAL PROFILE: kept house for her brothers in 1669.

COLE, JOAN (JONE) (?–?). BORN: in England. RESIDED: Heston, Middlesex, England. **MARRIED** probably William Cole (?–1633 or 1634). **CHILDREN.** SON: *Robert* (c. 1628–c. 1662). **PRIVATE CAREER.** RELIGIOUS AFFILIATION: Roman Catholic; charged as a recusant in the 1630s. SOCIAL STATUS: referred to as "Mrs." ADDITIONAL COMMENTS: helped to settle Robert's estate in England. **WEALTH DURING LIFETIME.** One of the two Joan Coles, widows, assessed for three and four hearths in the Heston Hearth Tax records of 1664; she may have had dower rights in a manor lease.

COLE, MARY (1653–?). BORN: January 26, 1653, on St. Clement's Manor. NATIVE: first generation, first daughter. RESIDED: "Cole's," St. Clement's Manor; visited England in 1662; boarded at "Little Bretton," Newtown Hundred, in 1663; after marriage, on "Newtown," Medley's Neck, Newtown Hundred. **FAMILY BACKGROUND.** FATHER: *Robert Cole* (c. 1628–c. 1662). MOTHER: *Rebecca* (?–1662). BROTHERS: *Robert* (1652–93); *William Maria* (1655–by 1688); *Edward* (1657–1717). SISTER: *Elizabeth* (1659–70). STEPBROTHER: *Francis Knott* (c. 1649–1705). STEPSISTER: *Ann Knott Harinton*. GRANDFATHER: probably William Cole (?–1633 or 1634) of Heston, Middlesex. GRANDMOTHER: *Joan Cole* of Heston, Middlesex. **MARRIED** *Ignatius Warren* (late 1640s–1698), the son of John Warren, a former servant and eventually county justice, by 1673. **PRIVATE CAREER.** EDUCATION: schooling in Maryland. RELIGIOUS AFFILIATION: Roman Catholic. OCCUPATIONAL PROFILE: planter's wife. **WEALTH DURING LIFETIME.** Inherited 11 cattle, a bed, and kitchenware at age 18.

COLE, REBECCA (?–1662). BORN: in England. IMMIGRATED: in 1652 from Heston, Middlesex, with her husband, four children, and two servants. RESIDED: "Cole's," St. Clement's Manor. **FAMILY BACKGROUND.** KINSWOMAN: *Mary Mills Sheppy*. **MARRIED** first, ? Knott, and second, *Robert Cole* (c. 1628–c. 1662) between 1649 and 1652. **CHILDREN.** SONS: *Francis Knott* (c. 1649–1705), who married Elinor White in 1673 or 1674; *Robert Cole* (1652–93), who married first, Ann, the widow of John Medley by 1677, and second, Rebecca by 1687; *William Maria Cole* (1655–by 1688); *Edward Cole* (1657–1717), who married possibly first, Honor (Honory) by 1683, and second, Elizabeth Slye. DAUGHTERS: *Ann Knott Harinton*; *Mary Cole* (1653–?), who married *Ignatius Warren* (late 1640s–1698); *Elizabeth Cole* (1659–70). **PRIVATE CAREER.** RELIGIOUS AFFILIATION: Roman Catholic. OCCUPATIONAL PROFILE: planter's wife.

COLE, ROBERT (c. 1628–c. 1662). BORN: in England. IMMIGRATED: in 1652 from Heston, Middlesex, with his wife, four children, and two servants. RESIDED: "Cole's," St. Clement's Manor. **FAMILY BACKGROUND.** FATHER: probably William Cole (?–1633 or 1634). MOTHER: *Joan Cole* of Heston, Middlesex. KINSMAN: Benjamin Gill (?–1657), of Wollaston Manor, St. Mary's County. **MARRIED** *Rebecca* (?–1662), the widow of ? Knott, between 1649 and 1652. **CHILDREN.**

SONS: *Robert* (1652–93), who married first, Ann, the widow of John Medley, by 1677, and second, Rebecca by 1687; *William Maria* (1655–by 1688); *Edward* (1657–1717), who married possibly first, Honor (Honory) by 1683, and second, Elizabeth Slye. DAUGHTERS: *Mary* (1653–?), who married *Ignatius Warren* (late 1640s–1698); *Elizabeth* (1659–70). STEPSON: *Francis Knott* (c. 1649–1705), who married Elinor White in 1673 or 1674. STEPDAUGHTER: *Ann Knott Harinton*. **PRIVATE CAREER.** EDUCATION: literate. RELIGIOUS AFFILIATION: Roman Catholic. OCCUPATIONAL PROFILE: planter. SOCIAL STATUS. Occasionally "Mr." from 1658. **PUBLIC CAREER.** MINOR OFFICES: provincial court juror; manor court juror. MILITARY SERVICE: ensign by 1662. **WEALTH DURING LIFETIME.** LAND: purchased 300-acre freehold, "Cole's," on St. Clement's Manor; surveyed 350 acres in Charles County in 1654, which he later sold. **WEALTH AT DEATH.** PERSONAL PROPERTY: TEV £212, including four servants. LAND: 300 acres plus warrants for additional 1,100 acres.

COLE, ROBERT, JR. (1652–1693). BORN: October 15, 1652, on St. Clement's Manor. NATIVE: first generation, oldest son. RESIDED: "Cole's," St. Clement's Manor, through about 1676; from 1677, "Medley House Plantation," Newtown Hundred. **FAMILY BACKGROUND. FATHER:** *Robert Cole* (c. 1628–c. 1662). MOTHER: *Rebecca* (?–1662). BROTHERS: *William Maria* (1655–by 1688); *Edward* (1657–1717). SISTERS: *Mary* (1653–?); *Elizabeth* (1659–70). STEPBROTHER: *Francis Knott* (c. 1649–1705). STEPSISTER: *Ann Knott Harinton*. GRANDFATHER: probably William Cole (?–1633 or 1634) of Heston, Middlesex. GRANDMOTHER: *Joan Cole* of Heston, Middlesex. **MARRIED** first, Ann (?–by 1687), the widow of John Medley, (?–1676) by 1677, and second, Rebecca by 1687; Rebecca subsequently married Thomas Warren (?–1698) by 1693. **CHILDREN.** DAUGHTER: Sarah. Possibly other children, unnamed. **PRIVATE CAREER.** EDUCATION: schooling, probably for four years, in Maryland. RELIGIOUS AFFILIATION: Roman Catholic. OCCUPATIONAL PROFILE: planter. **PUBLIC CAREER.** MINOR OFFICES: provincial court juror; county juror. **WEALTH DURING LIFETIME.** PERSONAL PROPERTY: inherited 11 cattle and household goods, 1670. LAND: inherited 500 acres including "Cole's," 1673; had the use of 600 acres in 1677 through marriage; subsequently inherited 200 acres and purchased 200 more, but sold 700 acres. **WEALTH AT DEATH.** PERSONAL PROPERTY: TEV £68. LAND: at least 200 acres.

COLE, WILLIAM MARIA (1655–by 1688). BORN: June 23, 1655, on St. Clement's Manor. NATIVE: first generation, second son. RESIDED: "Cole's," St. Clement's Manor. **FAMILY BACKGROUND.** FATHER: *Robert* (c. 1628–c. 1662). MOTHER: *Rebecca* (?–1662). BROTHERS: *Robert* (1652–93); *Edward* (1657–1717). SISTERS: *Mary* (1653–?); *Elizabeth* (1659–70). STEPBROTHER: *Francis Knott* (c. 1649–1705). STEPSISTER: *Ann Knott Harinton.* GRANDFATHER: probably William Cole (?–1633 or 1634) of Heston, Middlesex. GRANDMOTHER: *Joan Cole* of Heston, Middlesex. **PRIVATE CAREER.** EDUCATION: five years' schooling in Maryland. RELIGIOUS AFFILIATION: Roman Catholic. OCCUPATIONAL PROFILE: bound out as an apprentice in 1673. ADDITIONAL COMMENTS: does not appear in records as an adult. **WEALTH DURING LIFETIME.** Was to inherit cattle, household goods, and 200 acres from father.

COOKE, CAPTAIN [MILES] (?–1676). BORN: in England. RESIDED: London; his wife and children lived in Surrey County, England, in 1676. **FAMILY BACKGROUND.** KINSMAN: James Sedgewick of Talbot County. **MARRIED** in England before 1676. **PRIVATE CAREER.** EDUCATION: literate. OCCUPATIONAL PROFILE: mariner, active in Maryland in the tobacco and servant trades between 1650 and 1676; began as a ship's mate, 1650, and was a ship captain by 1658. ADDITIONAL COMMENTS: made voyages to Maryland in the *Hopeful Adventure*, 1652, and as captain of the *Baltimore*, 1659, of the *Maryland Merchant*, 1663, of unnamed ships in 1671 and 1673, and of the *John*, 1676, bringing servants and merchandise; transported *Mary Cole* to England c. 1662. **PUBLIC CAREER.** PROVINCIAL OFFICES: rear admiral of Maryland, 1659–76. ADDITIONAL COMMENTS: was favored by the Calverts and was in close communication with them; Cooke's refusal to pay Maryland port duties because of his office of admiral angered colonial officials. **WEALTH DURING LIFETIME.** LAND: 1,000 acres, the Manor of Cookes Hope in Talbot County, due for importing servants, 1659; sold additional headrights due.

ELTON (ELLTON, HILTON, HILLTON), JOHN (c. 1643–1705). BORN: in England. IMMIGRATED: in 1661 as a servant to *Robert Cole.*

RESIDED: "Cole's," St. Clement's Manor, through 1664; on Basford Manor from 1676. **MARRIED** Jane, the widow of ? Flower, by 1697. **CHILDREN.** SONS: Francis (1687–?); John. STEPSON: William Flower. **PRIVATE CAREER.** EDUCATION: illiterate. OCCUPATIONAL PROFILE: servant, freed in 1664; laborer; tenant farmer. **PUBLIC CAREER.** MINOR OFFICES: county juror. **WEALTH DURING LIFETIME.** LAND: leasehold on Basford Manor. **WEALTH AT DEATH.** PERSONAL PROPERTY: TEV £18.

EVANS, WILLIAM (?–1669). BORN: probably in England. IMMIGRATED: in 1646 as a free adult. RESIDED: in Newtown Hundred. **MARRIED** first, by 1650, Ann, the widow of William Thompson, and second, Elizabeth, who subsequently married John Jordaine (?–1678) in 1669 and Cuthbert Scott in 1678. **CHILDREN.** Died without progeny. **PRIVATE CAREER.** EDUCATION: literate. RELIGIOUS AFFILIATION: Roman Catholic. SOCIAL STATUS: low status on arrival; rose through years of faithful service. OCCUPATIONAL PROFILE: planter. ADDITIONAL COMMENTS: executor of *Robert Cole*'s will. **PUBLIC CAREER.** PROVINCIAL OFFICES: lower house, St. Mary's County, 1658, 1659/60 (election voided, but was reelected), 1661, 1662; upper house, 1664, 1666; muster-master general, 1661–68/69; council, 1664–68/69; justice, provincial court, 1664–68/69. COUNTY OFFICES: justice, St. Mary's County, 1658–63; sheriff, St. Mary's County, 1663–64. MILITARY SERVICE: lieutenant, 1646–58; captain, 1658–60; colonel, 1660–68/69. STANDS ON PUBLIC ISSUES: strong supporter of the proprietary interests against Ingle's Rebellion and the Parliamentary Commissioners. **WEALTH DURING LIFETIME.** LAND: c. 200 acres, 1658; over 650 acres by 1665. **WEALTH AT DEATH.** LAND: 900 acres.

FELSTEED (FELSTEAD), WILLIAM (?–c. 1679). BORN: in England. IMMIGRATED: by 1663 as a servant to the *Robert Cole* estate. RESIDED: "Cole's," St. Clement's Manor. **MARRIED** before 1679 Elizabeth, a former servant who immigrated in 1666. **PRIVATE CAREER.** OCCUPATIONAL PROFILE: servant, freed in 1668 or 1669; then, laborer or tenant farmer. ADDITIONAL COMMENTS: present at St. Clement's Manor courts in 1670 and 1672.

FITZHERBERT [alias DARBY], FRANCIS (1611–?). BORN: in England. IMMIGRATED: in 1653 as a freeman. RESIDED: St. Mary's County through 1662. **PRIVATE CAREER.** EDUCATION: extensive, probably in a seminary. RELIGIOUS AFFILIATION: Roman Catholic. OCCUPATIONAL PROFILE: Jesuit priest. ADDITIONAL COMMENTS: had served in Ghent and Madeira before coming to Maryland and had taught theology at Liège, Spanish Netherlands. Recalled to England in 1662, possibly for his abrasive manner. Got in trouble with the Maryland authorities in 1658 for admonishing *Robert Slye* for allegedly harassing his Protestant servants, for threatening to excommunicate *Thomas Gerard* if he would not bring up his children as Catholics, and for trying to convert people at militia musters. Fitzherbert argued successfully that the Toleration Act allowed such preaching and teaching. *Robert Cole* bequeathed him a hogshead of tobacco and a steer as a gift to the church.

FOSTER, RICHARD (c. 1621–c. 1675). BORN: probably in England. IMMIGRATED: from Lynnhaven, Lower Norfolk County, Virginia, in 1652 with his wife, three children, and two servants. RESIDED: "Foster's Neck," St. Clement's Manor. **MARRIED** first, before 1652, Ann, the sister of Thomas Jackson (?–1660), and second, Sarah (?–c. 1675), the widow of ? Greene. **CHILDREN.** SON: Richard (?–before 1675). DAUGHTERS: Jane (?–before 1675) and Ann (?–before 1675), one of whom married *Vincent Mansfield*. STEPSON: John Greene. **PRIVATE CAREER.** EDUCATION: illiterate. OCCUPATIONAL PROFILE: planter. ADDITIONAL COMMENTS: had long-standing dispute with the St. Clement's manor lord, *Thomas Gerard*, over his leasehold. Testified in a suit Gerard brought against *Robert Cole* in the St. Mary's County court. **PUBLIC CAREER.** MINOR OFFICES: county juror; afferer and constable of St. Clement's Manor. **WEALTH DURING LIFETIME.** LAND: leased manor tract, then purchased 500 acres in 1667; part later sold or leased. **WEALTH AT DEATH.** PERSONAL PROPERTY: TEV £63, including three servants. LAND: 400 acres.

FOXHALL (FOXHOULD), JOHN (?–?). BORN: in England. IMMIGRATED: in 1664 from Bristol with his family and seven others. RESIDED: on a leasehold on Thomas Donne's Neck, St. Clement's Manor, between 1665 and 1667; then moved to Westmoreland County, Virginia. **FAMILY BACKGROUND.** KINSMAN: Abraham Foxhall of Burningham, County Warwick, England, with whom he joined in selling a cargo of goods shipped to Maryland in the *Jacob* of Bristol in 1664. **MARRIED** Mary before 1664. **CHILDREN.** DAUGHTER: Mary. **PRIVATE CAREER.** EDUCATION: literate. SOCIAL STATUS: referred to as "Mr." OCCUPATIONAL PROFILE: merchant in Bristol, later in Maryland and Virginia; planter. ADDITIONAL COMMENTS: in 1666 convicted of trading illegally with *Col. William Evan*'s servants, and assessed 5,000 lbs. in damages in a suit brought by *Thomas Gerard*. Purchased meat from the *Robert Cole* estate in 1665. **PUBLIC CAREER.** MINOR OFFICES: provincial grand and petit juror. **WEALTH DURING LIFETIME.** Transported 13 people into Maryland and had some mercantile capital but never acquired land in the colony.

FOXWELL, GEORGE (?–1673). RESIDED: Boston, Massachusetts. **PRIVATE CAREER.** OCCUPATIONAL PROFILE: merchant, trading to Maryland and Virginia between 1664 and 1670, most active in the Patuxent River area. Died in Virginia.

GARDINER (GARDNER), LUKE (1622–1674). BORN: probably in England; second son. IMMIGRATED: in 1637 as a minor with parents from Virginia. RESIDED: "Saccawakitt," Resurrection Hundred, in 1644; returned briefly to Virginia during Ingle's Rebellion; on Herring Creek in St. George's Hundred in 1651; from 1652, on "Canoe Neck," St. Clement's Manor. **FAMILY BACKGROUND.** FATHER: Richard Gardiner (?–c. 1651), who served in three unelected assemblies but was not a man of great wealth. MOTHER: Elizabeth. BROTHERS: Richard (1616–?); John (1633–?). SISTER: Elizabeth (1618–?), who married Richard Lusthead (?–1642). **MARRIED** by 1654 Elizabeth, the daughter of Richard Hatton and niece of Thomas Hatton (?–1655). She subsequently married Clement Hill (?–1708). Her brothers were William (?–1712) and Richard. Her sisters were Mary, who married Zachary Wade (c. 1627–78); Elinor (1642–1725), who married first, *Thomas Brooke* (1632–76), and second, Henry Darnall (c. 1645–1711); and Barbara, who married James Johnson. **CHILDREN.** SONS: Richard (?–1687), who married Elizabeth, the daughter of Maj. John Ware, of Rappahannock, Virginia; John, who married Mary, the daughter of William Boreman (c. 1630–1709); Luke (?–1705), who married first, Monica, and second, Elizabeth Slye (c. 1668–1734), the daughter of *Robert Slye*; Thomas. **PRIVATE CAREER.** EDUCATION: literate. RELIGIOUS AFFILIATION: Roman Catholic. SOCIAL STATUS: servant or apprentice to Thomas Copley in 1637; designated "Gent." or by a military title after 1660. OCCUPATIONAL PROFILE: servant or apprentice, 1637; planter. ADDITIONAL COMMENTS: executor of *Robert Cole*'s will. **PUBLIC CAREER.** PROVINCIAL OFFICES: lower house, St. Mary's County, 1659/60 (elected to fill vacancy), 1661, 1662, 1671 (resigned after the second session to become sheriff). COUNTY OFFICES: justice, St. Mary's County, 1661–66, 1668–72; sheriff, St. Mary's County, 1672–74. MINOR OFFICES: county juror. MILITARY SERVICE: lieutenant by 1660/61; captain by 1664, still serving in 1670. ADDITIONAL COMMENTS: during the 1650s, Gardiner got into trouble for talking disrespectfully to a councillor, for attempting to raise a Protestant orphan as a Catholic, for neglecting service in the St. Clement's Manor court, for receiving stolen livestock, for giving firearms to Indians, for obtaining a patent by collusion, for mistreating a servant, and for trespassing on a neighbor's land. **WEALTH DURING LIFETIME.** LAND: 4,280 acres by 1662. **WEALTH AT DEATH.** PERSONAL PROPERTY: TEV £633, including three slaves and ten servants. LAND: nearly 7,000 acres.

GATES, ROBERT (c. 1643–1698). BORN: in England. IMMIGRATED: in 1655 as a servant to *Robert Cole*. RESIDED: "Cole's," St. Clement's Manor, to 1664; then in Benedict Hundred, Charles County. **MARRIED** before 1676 Dorothy (?–after 1698). **CHILDREN.** SONS: John (1681–after 1733); Robert (1686–1734); Joseph (1693–after 1733). DAUGHTERS: Katherine (1676–?), who married ? Popleton by 1695; Susannah (1678–?); Anne (1690–?). **PRIVATE CAREER.** EDUCATION: literate. RELIGIOUS AFFILIATION: Roman Catholic. SOCIAL STATUS: designated as "Mr." at death; styled self "Gent." in 1668. OCCUPATIONAL PROFILE: servant to 1664; planter; carpenter. **PUBLIC CAREER.** MINOR OFFICES: overseer of highways, Charles County. **WEALTH DURING LIFETIME.** LAND: patented 375 acres, 1668; purchased additional land throughout his lifetime. **WEALTH AT DEATH.** PERSONAL PROPERTY: TEV £112. LAND: 1,567 acres including two lots in Newport.

GERARD (GERRARD), THOMAS (1608–1673). BORN: New Hall, Lancashire, England; oldest son. IMMIGRATED: in 1638 as a free adult; returned to England in 1640; settled in 1642 on "Mattapany," St. Clement's Manor; moved to Mathoticks, Westmoreland County, Vir-

ginia, in 1664. **FAMILY BACKGROUND.** FATHER: John Gerard, of
New Hall, England, the son of Thomas and Jane Gerard of Garswood,
England. MOTHER: Isabell. BROTHERS: Marmaduke; William; Fran-
cis; Richard. **MARRIED** first, Susannah, the daughter of John Snowe, of
Brookehouse, Chedulton, England. Her brothers were Abel, Justinian,
and Marmaduke. **MARRIED** second, Rose (?–1712), the widow of John
Tucker (?–1671), of Westmoreland County, Virginia. She subsequently
married John Newton, of Westmoreland County, Virginia, in 1677.
CHILDREN. SONS: Justinian (?–1688), of "Bramley," St. Clement's
Manor, a justice of Westmoreland County, Virginia, in 1672, and of St.
Mary's County, Maryland, from 1676 to 1677, who married Sarah; Thomas (?–1686), of "Westwood Manor," Newport Hundred, a justice of St.
Mary's County from 1676 to 1679, who married Ann (?–1702/03); John
(?–1678), of Westmoreland County, Virginia, who married Elizabeth.
DAUGHTERS: Susannah (?–by 1685), who married first, *Robert Slye* (c.
1628–71), and second, John Coode (c. 1648–1709); Frances, who married first, Thomas Speke, second, Valentine Peyton, third, John Appleton,
fourth, John Washington, and fifth, William Hardwick; Temperance,
who married first, Daniel Hutt, second, John Crabbe, and third, Benjamin Blanchflower; Elizabeth (?–1716), who married first, Nehemiah
Blakiston (?–1693), second, Ralph Rymer, and third, Joshua Guibert
(?–1713); Mary, who married Kenelm Cheseldyne (1640–1708). STEP-
SONS: John and Gerrard Tucker. STEPDAUGHTERS: Sarah Tucker
(1633–after 1701), who married William Fitzhugh (1651–1701), of Stafford County, Virginia, in 1674; Rose Tucker, who probably married Ebenezer Blakiston (1650–1709), of Cecil County, Maryland. **PRIVATE
CAREER.** EDUCATION: literate, probably well-educated. RELIGIOUS
AFFILIATION: Roman Catholic, but his wife and children were Protestants. SOCIAL STATUS: "Gent." with high status on arrival in the
colony; brought five servants with him and by 1648 had imported over 40
servants; became manor lord of St. Clement's in 1639; sold his English
holdings and brought his family to Maryland in 1650, in which year he
also claimed land in Northumberland County, Virginia, using the same
headrights; involved in a celebrated legal action against his brothers-in-
law over control of extensive lands in Maryland. OCCUPATIONAL
PROFILE: physician; planter; landlord. ADDITIONAL COMMENTS:
sold *Robert Cole* a farm on St. Clement's Manor for which he collected
rents from the estate. **PUBLIC CAREER.** PROVINCIAL OFFICES: as-

sembly, St. Mary's County, 1638/39, special writ 1641; special writ 1641/ 42, special writ 1642A; upper house, 1658, 1659/60; council, 1643–49, 1651–60 (suspended from October 1658 to October 1659 for maligning other councillors); justice, provincial court, 1643–49, 1650/51–60. COUNTY OFFICES: conservator of the peace, St. Clement's Hundred, 1639/40. STANDS ON PUBLIC ISSUES: a very controversial figure in provincial politics and frequently at odds with the proprietor's spokesmen; supported Fendall's Rebellion in 1659/60, for which he was permanently barred from voting or holding office in the colony. **WEALTH DURING LIFETIME.** PERSONAL PROPERTY: valued at £300 in 1664. LAND: 1,030 acres in 1639; 11,000 acres by 1642; 14,000 acres by 1651, plus at least 3,500 acres in Virginia; claimed 2,100 acres in Virginia in 1664 for transporting 42 persons, including 15 blacks. **WEALTH AT DEATH.** LAND: c. 16,000 acres, including St. Clement's and Basford Manors in St. Mary's County, and four plantations in Virginia.

GOODRICH (GOODRICK), ROBERT (?–?). BORN: in England. IMMIGRATED: in 1652 or 1653 as a servant to *Robert Cole*. **PRIVATE CAREER.** OCCUPATIONAL PROFILE: servant; does not appear in records as a freedman.

HANCKES (HANKS), HENRY (?–?). BORN: in England. RESIDED: Holborne, London. **FAMILY BACKGROUND.** COUSIN: *Robert Cole*. **PRIVATE CAREER.** ADDITIONAL COMMENTS: executor of Cole in England.

HARINTON (HARRINGTON), ANN KNOTT (KNOT) (?–?). BORN: in England. IMMIGRATED: from Heston, Middlesex, in 1652 with *Robert* and *Rebecca Cole*. **FAMILY BACKGROUND.** MOTHER: *Rebecca Knott Cole* (?–1662). STEPFATHER: *Robert Cole* (c. 1628–c. 1662). BROTHER: *Francis Knott* (c. 1649–1705). STEPBROTHERS: *Robert Cole* (1652–93); *William Maria Cole* (1655–by 1688); *Edward Cole* (1657–1717). STEPSISTERS: *Mary Cole* (1653–?); *Elizabeth Cole* (1659–70). **MARRIED** by 1662 possibly to Jeremiah Harrington, of St. Michael's Hundred. **PRIVATE CAREER.** RELIGIOUS AFFILIATION: Roman Catholic.

HEWSON (KEWSON, LAWSON), SAMUEL(L) (c. 1657–?). BORN: in England. IMMIGRATED: by 1669 as a servant to the *Robert Cole* estate. RESIDED: "Cole's," St. Clement's Manor. **PRIVATE CAREER.** OC-

CUPATIONAL PROFILE: servant. ADDITIONAL COMMENTS: in 1673 he had five years left to serve. He does not appear in the records as a freedman and may have either died or migrated.

JACKSON, SIBELO (?–?). BORN: in England. IMMIGRATED: in 1661 as a servant to *Robert Cole*. **PRIVATE CAREER.** OCCUPATIONAL PROFILE: servant. ADDITIONAL COMMENTS: did not appear in Cole's inventory of 1662, so her term of service had been sold to someone else or she had died.

JOHNSON, JOHN (c. 1644–?). BORN: in England. IMMIGRATED: in 1657 as a servant to *Robert Cole*. RESIDED: "Cole's," St. Clement's Manor, through 1665. **PRIVATE CAREER.** OCCUPATIONAL PROFILE: servant through 1665. ADDITIONAL COMMENTS: may have been the John Johnson, a cooper, who died in Chaptico Hundred, St. Mary's County in 1687, leaving a wife and four minor children, 100 acres of land, and a personal estate of £113.

JONES (JOANES), ISABEL (ISBELL, ISABELL) (?–?). BORN: in England. IMMIGRATED: in 1661 as a servant to *Robert Cole*. **PRIVATE CAREER.** OCCUPATIONAL PROFILE: servant, freed in 1665.

KNOTT (KNOT), FRANCIS (c. 1649–1705). BORN: in England, probably in Middlesex. IMMIGRATED: in 1652 with his mother and stepfather. RESIDED: "Cole's," St. Clement's Manor, to at least 1669; from 1673 on "Shertcliffe," Newtown Hundred. **FAMILY BACKGROUND.** MOTHER: *Rebecca Knott Cole* (?–1662). STEPFATHER: *Robert Cole* (c. 1628–c. 1662). SISTER: *Ann Knott Harinton.* STEPBROTHERS: *Robert Cole* (1652–93); *William Maria Cole* (1655–by 1688); *Edward Cole* (1657–1717). STEPSISTERS: *Mary Cole* (1653–?); *Elizabeth Cole* (1659–70). **MARRIED** in 1673 or 1674 Elinor White, the daughter of Nicholas White (?–1659), of St. Inigoe's Manor, and ward of Captain William Boreman. **CHILDREN.** SONS: Francis (?–1724), who married Jane; William (?–1738), who married Ann; Edward (?–1734); John (?–c. 1753); James (?–1734), who married Mary; Charles (1700–?). DAUGHTERS: Rebecca; Elinor; Ann. **PRIVATE CAREER.** EDUCATION: educated at home by his stepfather, later by a tutor. RELIGIOUS AFFILIATION: Roman Catholic. OCCUPATIONAL PROFILE: laborer; then planter from 1674. **WEALTH DURING LIFETIME.** Inherited livestock and rights to land from his stepfather. LAND: held 100-acre tract on 99-year lease from 1683. **WEALTH AT DEATH.** PERSONAL PROPERTY: TEV £62, no bound labor. LAND: 100-acre long-term lease.

LUMBROZIO (LUMBROZO), JOHN (JACOB) (?–1666). BORN: in Portugal. IMMIGRATED: as a freeman in 1656 from Lisbon, Portugal; naturalized in 1663. RESIDED: first, Newtown Hundred; by 1662 on Nanjemoy Creek, Charles County. **FAMILY BACKGROUND.** SISTER: Priscilla, in Holland. **MARRIED** in 1663 Elizabeth Wild, his maid-servant. **CHILDREN.** SON: John (1666–1666). **PRIVATE CAREER.** EDUCATION: literate, highly educated with a knowledge of English religious and secular literature. RELIGIOUS AFFILIATION: Jewish. OCCUPATIONAL PROFILE: physician; planter; merchant; innkeeper. ADDITIONAL COMMENTS: a controversial character, charged at various times with defamation, receiving stolen goods, blasphemy, adultery, attempted rape, and abortion. Acted frequently as a lay attorney. Paid the *Robert Cole* estate 100 lbs. in 1663. **PUBLIC CAREER.** MINOR OFFICES: provincial court juror. **WEALTH DURING LIFETIME.** LAND: purchased 200 acres in 1660. **WEALTH AT DEATH.** PERSONAL ESTATE: TEV £21. LAND: 50 acres.

MAHAM (MAUGHAN), TIMOTHY (?–?). BORN: probably in England. IMMIGRATED: in 1668 as a servant to the *Robert Cole* estate. RESIDED: "Cole's," St. Clement's Manor, through 1675. **PRIVATE CAREER.** OCCUPATIONAL PROFILE: servant, free in 1673; laborer, 1675. ADDITIONAL COMMENTS: may be the same Timothy Mahony (Mahonie) who died in Resurrection Hundred in 1710, leaving a widow, Elizabeth, 100 acres, and a personal estate of £37. This man died indebted to four St. Clement's manor residents and to *Edward Cole*.

MANSFIELD (MANSFEILD, MANSELL), VINCENT (?–1687). BORN: probably on St. Clement's Manor; of age by 1664. RESIDED: St. Clement's Manor. **FAMILY BACKGROUND.** FATHER: probably John Mansfield (?–1660), a manor leaseholder. **MARRIED** first, by 1672, Jane or Ann Foster (?–before 1675), the daughter of *Richard Foster*, of "Foster's Neck," St. Clement's Manor, and second, Jane Tennison (?–1687), the daughter of Justinian Tennison (?–1699), of St. Clement's Manor. **CHILDREN.** SON: Edward. DAUGHTER: Sarah, by first wife, and others unnamed, by Jane. **PRIVATE CAREER.** EDUCATION: illiterate. OCCUPATIONAL PROFILE: laborer; planter. ADDITIONAL COMMENTS: was paid for killing an escaped bull by the *Robert Cole* estate in 1664. **PUBLIC CAREER.** PROVINCIAL OFFICES: Indian interpreter for the council from 1676 to at least 1681. MINOR OFFICES: county and manor court juror. MILITARY SERVICE: served in expedition to the Susquehanna Fort, 1676, where he lost a horse. **WEALTH DURING LIFETIME.** LAND: had the use of 400 acres through first marriage; patented 300 acres in St. Clement's Hundred in 1687. **WEALTH AT DEATH.** TEV £18, no bound labor.

MARTIN, CAPTAIN [JAMES] (?–1669). BORN: probably in England. IMMIGRATED: as a freeman by 1661. RESIDED: "Cole's Park," St. Clement's Hundred. **MARRIED** Anne before 1669. **CHILDREN.** SONS: James; John. **PRIVATE CAREER.** EDUCATION: literate. OCCUPATIONAL PROFILE: planter; merchant. ADDITIONAL COMMENTS: sold a servant to the *Robert Cole* estate in 1662. **PUBLIC CAREER.** COUNTY OFFICES: justice, St. Mary's County, 1668. MINOR OFFICES: county juror. **WEALTH DURING LIFETIME.** LAND: surveyed 350 acres in 1665. **WEALTH AT DEATH.** PERSONAL PROPERTY: TEV £127, including three servants. LAND: 350 acres.

MILLS (MILES), PETER (c. 1635–1685). BORN: in Holland. IMMIGRATED: in 1652 with his father and brother. RESIDED: "Mill's Birch," Newtown Hundred. **FAMILY BACKGROUND.** FATHER: Nicholas (?–c. 1656). BROTHER: John (?–1658). **MARRIED** by 1667 Mary, the eldest daughter of John Shertcliffe (?–1663), a planter of Newtown Hundred. **CHILDREN.** SONS: Nicholas; Peter (?–by 1762), who married Frances, the daughter of *Robert Slye*. DAUGHTER: Elizabeth. **PRIVATE CAREER.** EDUCATION: illiterate. OCCUPATIONAL PROFILE: planter; carpenter; smith. ADDITIONAL COMMENTS: owed 415 lbs. tobacco to the *Robert Cole* estate. **PUBLIC CAREER.** MINOR OFFICES: county juror. **WEALTH DURING LIFETIME.** LAND: inherited 150 acres; obtained 100 acres by marriage. **WEALTH AT DEATH.** PERSONAL PROPERTY: TEV £61, including one servant. LAND: 374 acres.

PAINE, CAPTAIN MATTHEW (MATHEW) (?–?). BORN: in England. RESIDED: Stepney Parish, London, England. **PRIVATE CAREER.** EDUCATION: literate. OCCUPATIONAL PROFILE: mariner involved in the servant trade between London and Maryland from 1664 to 1678; in 1671 and 1676 he was captain of the *Joseph and Benjamin*. ADDITIONAL COMMENTS: transported *Edward Cole* to England in 1671 or 1672.

PILES (PILE), JOHN (?–1676). BORN: in England. IMMIGRATED: in 1643, planning a partnership with Benjamin Gill whereby all lands due for transporting their families were to be granted in a single block. RESIDED: Newtown Hundred to 1658; by 1664 on "Sarum," Newport Hundred. **MARRIED** on arrival to ?; by 1648 to Sarah (?–after 1676), the daughter of Thomas Matthews, a prominent Maryland Catholic. **CHILDREN.** SON: Joseph (?–1692), who married Mary, the daughter of Thomas Turner (?–c. 1663) and the stepdaughter of *William Rosewell*. DAUGHTERS: Anne (?–by 1676); Mary (?–by 1676). **PRIVATE CAREER.** EDUCATION: literate, probably highly educated. RELIGIOUS AFFILIATION: Roman Catholic. SOCIAL STATUS: acquainted with Lord Baltimore in England; called "Mr." on first appearance in Maryland; "Gent." in 1648. OCCUPATIONAL PROFILE: placeman; planter; merchant. ADDITIONAL COMMENTS: *Robert Cole* took two hogsheads of tobacco to England for him in 1662. **PUBLIC CAREER.** PROVINCIAL OFFICES: assembly, special writ 1649; upper house, 1650–50/51 (did not attend); council, 1648–52; justice, provincial court, 1648–52; perhaps private secretary to the proprietor through 1648. **WEALTH DURING LIFETIME.** Purchased livestock in Accomac County, Virginia, on arrival. LAND: acquired a plantation in Newtown Hundred, which he sold along with all his personal property in 1651; granted 1,000 acres by Lord Baltimore in 1658 and 1662 "for good and acceptable services performed" and as encouragement for "his constant fidelity."[1] **WEALTH AT DEATH.** PERSONAL PROPERTY: TEV £756, including nine servants and four slaves. LAND: over 2,050 acres.

PRENTICE, JOHN (?–?). BORN: in England. IMMIGRATED: in 1663 as a servant to *Col. William Evans*; by 1667 to the *Robert Cole* estate. RESIDED: "Cole's," St. Clement's Manor. **PRIVATE CAREER.** OCCUPATIONAL PROFILE: servant, free by 1671; then probably laborer. ADDITIONAL COMMENTS: ran away in 1670 to Virginia, where he was recovered; probably left the area soon after 1671.

PRITCHARD (PRITCHERD), DANIEL (c. 1655–?). BORN: in England. IMMIGRATED: in 1670 as a servant to the *Robert Cole* estate. RESIDED: "Cole's," St. Clement's Manor. **PRIVATE CAREER.** OCCUPATIONAL PROFILE: servant. ADDITIONAL COMMENTS: had three years remaining to serve in 1673; does not appear in local records as a freedman, so may have either died or migrated.

REY (RAY, WRAY), JOHN (?–c. 1671). BORN: probably in England. IMMIGRATED: in 1662 as a servant to *Robert Cole*. RESIDED: St. Clement's Manor. **PRIVATE CAREER.** OCCUPATIONAL PROFILE: servant, 1662 to 1668; then laborer.

ROSEWELL, WILLIAM (c. 1637–1695). BORN: probably in England. IMMIGRATED: by 1659 as a freeman. RESIDED: "Cole's," St. Clement's Manor, in 1659 and 1660; by 1664 on "St. Winifred's," St. Clement's Hundred. **MARRIED** in 1664 Emma (1630–after 1695), the widow of Thomas Turner (?–c. 1663). **CHILDREN.** DAUGHTER: Elizabeth (1667–after 1733), who married Anthony Neale (1659–1723). STEP-DAUGHTER: Mary Turner, who married Joseph Pile (?–1692), the son of *John Piles*. **PRIVATE CAREER.** EDUCATION: literate. RELIGIOUS AFFILIATION: Roman Catholic. SOCIAL STATUS: a free immigrant, but did not acquire land until after his marriage. OCCUPATIONAL PROFILE: planter; merchant; innkeeper. ADDITIONAL COMMENTS: lived first with *Robert Cole* in 1659 and 1660, then owned a farm adjacent to the Coles. May have purchased "Cole's" from *Robert Cole, Jr.* **PUBLIC CAREER.** COUNTY OFFICES: justice, St. Mary's County, 1664–78. MINOR OFFICES: county juror. **WEALTH DURING LIFETIME.** Began importing servants and patenting land after his marriage. **WEALTH AT DEATH.** PERSONAL PROPERTY: TEV £1,290. LAND: 1,165 acres.

ROWSE (ROUSE), MATTHEW (MATHEW) (?–1671). BORN: in England. IMMIGRATED: in 1661. RESIDED: "Bushwood," St. Clement's Manor. **PRIVATE CAREER.** SOCIAL STATUS: his transportation costs were paid by the merchant *Robert Slye*, whom he may have assisted in some way. He was a freeman designated as "Mr." in 1662. ADDITIONAL COMMENTS: owed *Robert Cole*'s estate a debt that he repaid in 1662 and 1663.

SALLEY (SOLLEY), BENJAMIN (?–1674). BORN: in England. IMMIGRATED: from Bristol in 1670 with his wife and nine servants. RE-

SIDED: "Barton Hall," St. Clement's Manor. **MARRIED** before 1670 Lidia, who after administering her husband's estate, returned to England. **CHILDREN.** Several, unnamed. **PRIVATE CAREER.** EDUCATION: literate. SOCIAL STATUS: "Mr." on arrival. OCCUPATIONAL PROFILE: merchant; innkeeper. ADDITIONAL COMMENTS: administered *Robert Slye*'s estate and took over many of Slye's business customers. Purchased tallow from the *Robert Cole* estate in 1671. **PUBLIC CAREER.** COUNTY OFFICES: justice, St. Mary's County, 1670–74. **WEALTH AT DEATH.** PERSONAL PROPERTY: TEV £871, including four servants. LAND: c. 1,200 acres.

SHANKES (SHANKE, SHANKS), JOHN (c. 1627–1685). BORN: in England. IMMIGRATED: in 1640 as a servant to *Thomas Gerard*. RESIDED: St. Clement's Manor as a servant; near Shank's Hollow above the manor in the early 1650s; on "Little Hackley," St. Clement's Manor, by 1659. **MARRIED** in 1652 Abigail (?–after 1685), a servant to Robert Brooke. She subsequently married ? Simons. **CHILDREN.** SON: John (?–1717). DAUGHTERS: Emma (Amey) (?–c. 1678), who married William Watts (?–c. 1682); Mary; Elizabeth. **PRIVATE CAREER.** EDUCATION: illiterate, but proficient in the Indian language. RELIGIOUS AFFILIATION: Anglican. OCCUPATIONAL PROFILE: servant, free in 1648; planter. ADDITIONAL COMMENTS: owed the *Robert Cole* estate a debt that he paid in 1663. **PUBLIC CAREER** PROVINCIAL OFFICES: Indian interpreter for the council, 1652–81; chief interpreter in negotiations between Maryland and Virginia troops and the Indians at the Susquehanna Fort in 1676. MINOR OFFICES: provincial court juror; county juror; manor court juror and bailiff. **WEALTH DURING LIFETIME.** LAND: surveyed 200 acres in 1652 and sold in 1654; leased 300 acres on St. Clement's manor, 1659, which he purchased as a freehold by 1670. **WEALTH AT DEATH.** PERSONAL PROPERTY: TEV £93, including three slaves and an Indian servant. LAND: 300 acres.

SHEPPY (SHEPPEY), MARY MILLS (?–?). BORN: in England. IMMIGRATED: in 1657 as a servant to *Robert Cole*. RESIDED: "Cole's," St. Clement's Manor, to c. 1661; then in Newtown Hundred. **FAMILY BACKGROUND.** KINSWOMAN: *Rebecca Cole* (?–1662). **MARRIED** by 1659 *Richard Sheppy*. **PRIVATE CAREER.** OCCUPATIONAL PROFILE: servant; then planter's wife.

SHEPPY (SHEPPEY), RICHARD (?–?). BORN: in England. IMMI-GRATED: before 1656. RESIDED: St. Michael's Hundred, 1656; on "Cole's," St. Clement's Manor, between 1658 and 1661; in Newtown Hundred through 1684. **MARRIED** by 1659 *Mary Mills*, servant to *Robert Cole*. **PRIVATE CAREER.** OCCUPATIONAL PROFILE: cooper to 1666; then planter. **WEALTH DURING LIFETIME.** LAND: patented 100 acres in 1666 and 100 acres in 1684. ADDITIONAL COMMENTS: left St. Michael's Hundred in debt; Robert Cole may have assisted him with repayment. Indicted for, but acquitted of, hog stealing in 1672. Disappeared from records after 1684.

SITTWELL, DOROTHY (?–?). **PRIVATE CAREER.** OCCUPATIONAL PROFILE: paid wages by the *Robert Cole* estate in 1666.

SLYE (SLY), ROBERT (c. 1628–1671). BORN: in England. IMMI-GRATED: in 1654 as a free adult. RESIDED: "Bushwood," St. Clement's Manor. **FAMILY BACKGROUND.** SISTER: Elizabeth Russell of London, England. NEPHEWS: Timothy and Thomas Cooper of Springfield, Massachusetts. COUSIN: Samuel Smith of Charles County. KINSMAN: Strangeways Mudd of London, England. **MARRIED** in 1652 Susannah (?–by 1683), the eldest daughter of *Thomas Gerard*. She subsequently married John Coode (c. 1648–1709). **CHILDREN.** SONS: Gerard (1654–by 1703), justice of St. Mary's County, 1675/76–77, 1679–81, sheriff of St. Mary's County, 1677–79, and a merchant, who returned to England for a while in 1681 and who married Jane; Robert (?–1695), who married Priscilla. DAUGHTERS: Elizabeth (c. 1668–1734), who married first, Luke Gardiner (?–1705), the son of *Luke Gardiner* (1622–74), and second, *Edward Cole* (1657–1717); Frances, who married Peter Mills (?–by 1762), the son of *Peter Mills*. Other children predeceased their father. **PRIVATE CAREER.** EDUCATION: literate, probably some higher education. RELIGIOUS AFFILIATION: Protestant. SOCIAL STATUS: transported 12 others on arrival; was a prominent colonist, one of the wealthiest men in Maryland, and also one of the most important legislators during the assembly's first 50 years. OCCUPATIONAL PROFILE: planter; merchant. **PUBLIC CAREER.** PROVINCIAL OFFICES: Parliamentary Commission, 1655–57/58; assembly, Potomac (St. Mary's County), 1657; lower house, St. Mary's County, 1659/60, 1663–64, 1666, 1669; justice, provincial court, 1655–

57/58; council, 1660. COUNTY OFFICES: justice, St. Mary's County, probably 1658–60, 1663–70/71. MILITARY SERVICE: captain, by 1655. STANDS ON PUBLIC ISSUES: supported Fendall's Rebellion in 1659/60 and temporarily lost his offices on the restoration of the proprietary government. **WEALTH DURING LIFETIME.** LAND: at least 1,000 acres through marriage in 1655. **WEALTH AT DEATH.** PERSONAL PROPERTY: inventory unvalued, but clearly among the richest men of the period in Maryland; property included 11 servants and 14 slaves. LAND: c. 2,500 acres.

STANDLEY (STANLEY, STANTLEY), JOHN (?–?). BORN: in England. IMMIGRATED: c. 1662 as a servant to Captain William Boreman. RESIDED: Chaptico Hundred, 1662–c. 1670; on a leasehold on St. Clement's Manor, 1670–76; in Virginia from 1677. **PRIVATE CAREER.** EDUCATION: literate. OCCUPATIONAL PROFILE: servant, freed in 1666; planter. ADDITIONAL COMMENTS: took up a runaway servant in Virginia belonging to the *Robert Cole* estate in 1671 or 1672. **PUBLIC CAREER.** MINOR OFFICES: county juror; manor court juror. **WEALTH DURING LIFETIME.** LAND: rented a farm on St. Clement's Manor c. 1670–75; patented 50 acres, "Stanley's Dream," St. Clement's Hundred, in 1676.

THIMBLEBY, JOHN (?–1659). BORN: in England. IMMIGRATED: between 1633 and 1641 as a servant. RESIDED: "Thimbleby," Newtown Hundred. **FAMILY BACKGROUND.** Died unmarried and without progeny. GODFATHER: to *Robert Cole, Jr.*, and Mary Browne. **PRIVATE CAREER.** EDUCATION: literate. RELIGIOUS AFFILIATION: Roman Catholic. OCCUPATIONAL PROFILE: servant, freed by 1647; planter. **PUBLIC CAREER.** MINOR OFFICES: provincial court juror. **WEALTH DURING LIFETIME.** LAND: took up 150 acres in partnership with ex-servant William Brown in 1648. **WEALTH AT DEATH.** LAND: 150 acres.

THOMPSON (THOMPSONE), JAMES (?–after 1687). BORN: in England. IMMIGRATED: by 1661 as a freeman. RESIDED: Calvert County; moved to Baltimore County by 1687. **FAMILY BACKGROUND.** SISTER: Anne, sent to Maryland as an indentured servant "by reason of the late troubles in England,"[2] was—according to Thompson—abused by her second master, *Luke Gardiner*. **MARRIED** by 1687 to a relative of

? Tasker. **PRIVATE CAREER.** EDUCATION: literate, probably some higher education. RELIGIOUS AFFILIATION: Roman Catholic. SOCIAL STATUS: styled self "Gent." by 1664; was acquainted with the Calverts and visited Lord Baltimore in England in 1687. OCCUPATIONAL PROFILE: placeman; planter. ADDITIONAL COMMENTS: witnessed *Robert Cole*'s will. **PUBLIC CAREER.** COUNTY OFFICES: clerk, Calvert County, 1661–65; deputy surveyor, Calvert County, 1666; clerk, St. Mary's County, 1671. MINOR OFFICES: surveyor of proprietary manors by 1675; provincial court juror. **WEALTH DURING LIFETIME.** LAND: patented land in Calvert, St. Mary's, and Baltimore counties between 1663 and 1687; owned c. 1,300 acres in 1687.

THORNTON (THORNETON), ANN (AN) (?–?). RESIDED: area of St. Clement's Manor. **PRIVATE CAREER.** OCCUPATIONAL PROFILE: worked for annual wages for the *Robert Cole* estate between 1663 and 1665.

TINSLEY, SETH (?–?). BORN: in England. IMMIGRATED: in 1656, presumably as a freeman. RESIDED: "Cole's," St. Clement's Manor, through at least 1659; in 1669–70, in Charles County. **PRIVATE CAREER.** OCCUPATIONAL PROFILE: laborer. ADDITIONAL COMMENTS: both he and *Robert Cole* claimed headrights for his transportation. He was probably a free immigrant who worked for Cole as a laborer. He then moved to Charles County and disappears from the records after 1670. **PUBLIC CAREER.** MINOR OFFICES: manor court juror.

WARREN, ————. Purchased meat from the *Robert Cole* estate in 1664. Probably was either (1) John Warren, the father of *Ignatius Warren*, a former servant who had acquired a plantation on Medley's Neck and was a county justice; (2) Henry Warren, a Jesuit missionary who took control of Roman Catholic landholdings, including those on Bretton's Bay, in 1662; or (3) Humphrey Warren, a London merchant then living at Hatton's Point on the Wicomico River in Charles County.

WARREN, IGNATIUS (IGNATIOUS) (late 1640s–1698). BORN: on Medley's Neck, Newtown Hundred. NATIVE: first generation, eldest son. RESIDED: "Newtown," Medley's Neck, Newtown Hundred. **FAMILY BACKGROUND.** FATHER: John Warren (?–1692), a former servant who became a justice of St. Mary's County in 1668. BROTHER: Augustine (?–1685). **MARRIED** by 1673 *Mary Cole* (1653–?), the eldest daughter of *Robert Cole*. **PRIVATE CAREER.** EDUCATION: literate. RELIGIOUS AFFILIATION: Roman Catholic. OCCUPATIONAL PROFILE: planter; innkeeper. **WEALTH DURING LIFETIME.** PERSONAL PROPERTY: inherited cattle and household goods through his marriage. LAND: inherited 450 acres. ADDITIONAL COMMENTS: stood security on two bonds posted by ships' captains to observe the Navigation Acts in 1691 and 1692. When they defaulted, the provincial court levied a £3,000 sterling fine against Warren in 1696. His estate was insufficient to satisfy the debt. **WEALTH AT DEATH.** PERSONAL PROPERTY: TEV £26. LAND: 450 acres.

WHEELER, JOHN (c. 1632–c. 1694). BORN: in Sweden or Holland. IMMIGRATED: by 1642; naturalized in 1661. RESIDED: Charles County. **MARRIED** Mary (?–after 1694) by 1654. **CHILDREN.** SONS: John (1654–before 1691); James (1656–by 1685), who married first, Elizabeth Theobalds Corker, the daughter of Clement and Marie, and second, Katherine; Thomas (1661–1736); Ignatius (1665–99), who married Frances Gardiner (?–after 1699); Francis (?–?), who married Winifred (1672–after 1712), the daughter of Leonard and Anne Greene. DAUGHTERS: Mary (1659–?), who married Robert Middleton; Winifred (1664–?), who married John Speake. **PRIVATE CAREER.** EDUCATION: illiterate. RELIGIOUS AFFILIATION: possibly Roman Catholic. OCCUPATIONAL PROFILE: planter; land speculator. ADDITIONAL COMMENTS: purchased a land warrant from *Robert Cole*. **PUBLIC CAREER.** COUNTY OFFICES: justice, Charles County, 1685–89. MINOR OFFICES: provincial court juror; county juror. MILITARY CAREER: ensign by 1660; captain by 1676; major by 1681; did not serve after 1689. **WEALTH DURING LIFETIME.** LAND: acquired first land in 1654; traded extensively in land in Charles and Prince Georges counties. **WEALTH AT DEATH.** LAND: 1,500 acres.

WOODBURY (WOODBERIE, WOODBERRY), [HUGH] (?–1677). BORN: in Salem, Massachusetts. NATIVE: first generation. RESIDED: usually in Beverly, Massachusetts, but in Charles County, Maryland, between Maryland Point and Nanjemoy Creek, from 1662 to 1671. **FAMILY BACKGROUND.** FATHER: William Woodbury (Woodberry), an early settler of Salem. BROTHER: Andrew (?–1685), a Salem merchant trading in the Patuxent area and in Baltimore County. KINSMAN: Isaac Woodberry, Jr., of Massachusetts, also active in the Maryland trade.

PRIVATE CAREER. EDUCATION: literate. OCCUPATIONAL PRO-FILE: merchant, active in trade between New England, Barbados, and the Chesapeake between 1661 and 1671; kept a store in Charles County. Probably the man who purchased hides from and sold a mare to *Robert Cole*'s administrator, *Luke Gardiner*.

Notes

. . . . .

Preface

1. The literature on the early Chesapeake is reviewed in Thad W. Tate, "The Seventeenth-Century Chesapeake and Its Modern Historians," in *The Chesapeake in the Seventeenth Century: Essays on Anglo-American Society*, ed. Thad W. Tate and David L. Ammerman (Chapel Hill, 1979), 3–50; Ian K. Steele, "Another Early America: Getting and Begetting in the Chesapeake," *Canadian Review of American Studies* 12 (1981): 313–22; Allan Kulikoff, "The Colonial Chesapeake: Seedbed of Ante-bellum Southern Culture?" *Journal of Southern History* 45 (1979): 513–40; John J. McCusker and Russell R. Menard, *The Economy of British America, 1607–1789* (Chapel Hill, 1985), 117–43; Anita H. Rutman, "Still Planting the Seeds of Hope: The Recent Literature of the Early Chesapeake Region," *Virginia Magazine of History and Biography* 95 (1987): 3–24; and Introduction to *Colonial Chesapeake Society*, ed. Lois Green Carr, Philip D. Morgan, and Jean B. Russo (Chapel Hill, 1988), 1–46.

2. The phrase is from Robert Beverley, *The History and Present State of Virginia*, ed. Louis B. Wright (Chapel Hill, 1947), 291. Beverley's book was originally published in 1705. For other contemporary critiques, see, for example, Hugh Jones, *The Present State of Virginia* (1724; reprint, Chapel Hill, 1956), 77, and Harry J. Carman, ed., *American Husbandry* (1775; reprint, New York, 1939), 154–97. For a more recent view, see Aubrey C. Land, "The Tobacco Staple and the Planter's Problems: Technology, Labor, and Crops," *Agricultural History* 43 (1969): 69–81. The literature on early American agriculture is reviewed in McCusker and Menard, *Economy of British America*, 295–308.

3. George Washington to Arthur Young, December 5, 1791, in *The Writings of George Washington from the Original Manuscript Sources, 1745–1799*, ed. John C. Fitzpatrick, 39 vols. (Washington, D.C., 1931–44), 31:440.

Chapter 1

1. Unless otherwise noted, biographical information is drawn from the Career File of Seventeenth-Century St. Mary's County Residents, which belongs to the St. Mary's City Commission and is housed at the Maryland State Archives, Annapolis, Maryland. Cole did not die on the voyage over. The account of 1671–72

mentions money he sent out of England. The Heston Parish Register, St. Leonards, Greater London Record Office (hereafter GLRO) DRO.26 A1/1 shows the burial of a Robert Cole, son of ——— Cole, on August 16, 1662. This could, but need not, be our Robert Cole. We thank James P. P. Horn for this information. Cole inventoried his animals on March 9, and on April 29 he noted that all but one were still alive. After this notation appears an instruction to his wife about the cattle. One might infer that on April 29 she was still alive. However, his wife went unmentioned in his will, dated April 2, which consigned the care of his children to guardians. She was surely dead by then. Cole must have inserted the final comment on his cattle after his wife's death.

2. Quotations from Testamentary Proceedings 6:119, Maryland State Archives, printed below, appendix 1. Unless otherwise indicated, all manuscripts cited are at the Maryland State Archives.

3. Ibid.

4. William Hand Browne et al., eds., *Archives of Maryland* (hereafter *Archives*), 72 vols. (Baltimore, 1883–1972), 41:169–73; Patents AB&H:27.

5. James P. P. Horn and Thomas Purvis examined for us the remaining parish records for Heston in the Greater London Record Office and found no baptism for a Robert Cole, 1600–1640; no marriage for a Robert Cole and Rebecca Knott, 1645–52; and no marriage for any Cole to a Joan, Jone, or Jane, 1600–1630. According to John Bossy, *The English Catholic Community, 1570–1850* (London, 1976), 133–36, Catholics at this time did not feel the need to register their marriages, but they often did register baptisms to avoid inheritance problems that could arise from lack of proof that a child was legitimate. Horn informs us that probate records for Heston do not survive before 1660 and that there are only fourteen for the rest of the seventeenth century. Cole's parentage is inferred from the Middlesex County recusancy records, which show Joan Cole, the wife of William Cole, a yeoman, indicted in 1632 and indicted again as a widow in 1634. John Cordy Jeaffreson, ed., *Middlesex County Records* (London, 1974), 3:130, 136. However, Horn found two Joan Coles, both widows, on the Hearth Tax of 1664 but no way to distinguish which one had been married to William or which was Robert's mother. GLRO (Middlesex Records) MR/TH 6.

6. We thank Thomas Purvis for this information.

7. Manor Court Rolls show the land sale. GLRO Acc. 1379/30. We thank Thomas Purvis for this information. Cole must have paid his mother for her dower rights. If Cole's father died with manor copyhold—a form of lease—his widow probably had the use of it for her life or her widowhood (custom varied from manor to manor). In that case, Cole had rights to the land at her death. On English inheritance practices, see Carole Shammas, Marylynn Salmon, and Michel Dahlin, *Inheritance in America from Colonial Times to the Present* (New Brunswick, N.J., 1987), 23–30; Margaret Spufford, *Contrasting Communities: English Villages in the Sixteenth and Seventeenth Centuries* (Cambridge, 1974), 85–90, 111–18, 161–64; Barbara J. Todd, "'In Her Free Widowhood': Succession to Property and Remarriage in Rural England, 1540–1800" (Paper presented at the

Fourth Berkshire Conference on the History of Women, June 1976); Cicely Howell, "Peasant Inheritance Customs in the Midlands, 1280–1700," in *Family and Inheritance: Rural Society in Western Europe, 1200–1800,* ed. Jack Goody, Joan Thirsk, and E. P. Thompson (Cambridge, 1976), 141–43; and James P. P. Horn, "Social and Economic Aspects of Local Society in England and the Chesapeake: A Comparative Study of the Vale of Berkeley, Gloucestershire, and the Lower Western Shore of Maryland, c. 1660–1700" (Ph.D. diss., University of Sussex, 1982), chap. 5.

Of the two widowed Joan Coles on the Hearth Tax of 1664 for Heston, one had 3 hearths and one had 4. Out of 177 households, 61 had 3 or more hearths (26 had 5 to 20, and 1 had 50), and 102 were too poor to be charged. GLRO (Middlesex Records) MR/TH 6. We thank James P. P. Horn for this data.

8. The name may have been Hawkins. Thomas Purvis, in looking unsuccessfully for a Henry Hanckes, found in the Edward Dwelly Index at the Society of Genealogists in Holborn a Henry Hawkins identified as a cousin of Cole's who immigrated to Maryland in 1666. Since we have only recorded versions of Cole's will, it is possible that the name became Hanckes in the process of transcription. In any case, if the Dwelly Index is correct (so far we have not identified the source given in the index and therefore can not check it), a Cole cousin came to Maryland in 1666 and became a major figure in Charles County. However, the Maryland records show no connections between this Hawkins, who was a rabid Protestant, and any Cole. Unpublished research of Lorena S. Walsh.

9. For Cole's will, see appendix 1. James P. P. Horn found the baptismal record for William Cole, son of William and Joane Cole, December 12, 1632. If Robert was the child of this couple, he had a younger brother for a while. Heston Parish Register, St. Leonards, GLRO (Middlesex Records) DRO.26 A1/1. For young Robert's baptism, see Testamentary Proceedings 5:348. Recusancy indictments are printed in Jeaffreson, *Middlesex County Records* (London, 1972, 1974), 1:242, 2:21, 130, 146, 216, 232, 3:20, 26, 86, 129, 130 (Joan Cole, wife of William), 131, 133, 134, 136 (Joan Cole, widow), 139, 153. Twenty people from Heston appear in these records between 1595 and 1642, some many times.

10. Cole gave his age as thirty-four in a deposition early in 1662. *Archives* 41:565. We assume that he did not marry before age twenty-one. This would be an early, but possible, age for a man with some property. On age at marriage in England, see E. A. Wrigley and R. A. Schofield, *The Population History of England, 1541–1871: A Reconstruction* (Cambridge, Mass., 1981), table 7.26. The legacy that Cole willed his stepson, Francis Knott, and that Gardiner gave him in 1668 we valued at 1668 prices and converted to constant value (see n. 55). It came to about £14. Francis's older sister, Ann, had married, and Cole evidently had already given her her portion of her father's estate, which presumably had the same value. Rebecca must have received a third of the movable property, unless her first husband had made a will making other arrangements. If he had not, his estate must have come to about £42. We have assumed that he had no equity in land, since Cole did not feel obliged to supply Francis Knott with land, devising

to him only a warrant for fifty acres, the value of his own headright. A headright was a right to a fifty-acre warrant granted in return for transportation of a settler. These rights were not worth a lot, since the expenses of surveying and patenting the land were not included.

11. On Catholicism in England, see Edward Ingram Watkins, *Roman Catholicism in England from the Reformation to 1950* (London, 1957), 67–72, 84, 91–94; Martin Havran, *The Catholics in Caroline England* (Palo Alto, Calif., 1962); and Bossy, *The English Catholic Community*, 1–60, 278–81. The quotations are from Bossy's essay "Reluctant Colonists: The English Catholics Confront the Atlantic," in *Early Maryland in a Wider World*, ed. David B. Quinn (Detroit, 1982), 149.

12. Estimates of the number of Catholics are for 1603 and 1641 and are from Bossy, *The English Catholic Community*, 188, 193. Estimates for the general population for 1600 and 1640 (4,066,132 and 5,054,987 respectively) are from Wrigley and Schofield, *The Population History of England*, table A3.3. The percentage of Catholics remained at about 1 percent.

13. See references to Middlesex County records in n. 9. Of the seventeen women, twelve were Coles or wives of Coles, and most appeared several times. None of the three men were Coles.

14. See chap. 2, text near n. 4, and annotations; chap. 5.

15. John Kilty, *The Landholder's Assistant, and Land Office Guide* . . . (Baltimore, 1908), has a good discussion of this charter provision (27–28) and reprints the "Conditions of Plantation" for 1636 (30–33). The "conditions" for 1633 and 1634 are printed in two promotional pamphlets: *A Declaration of the Lord Baltemore's Plantation in Mary-land* (London, 1633), 2; and [John Lewger and Jerome Hawley], *A Relation of Maryland* . . . (London, 1635), in *Narratives of Early Maryland*, ed. Clayton Colman Hall (New York, 1910), 91–92. On earlier colonization plans that included manors, see Russell R. Menard, "Economy and Society in Early Colonial Mayland" (Ph.D. diss., University of Iowa, 1975), 15–16.

16. On Gerard, see Edward C. Papenfuse et al., eds., *A Biographical Dictionary of the Maryland Legislature, 1635–1789* (Baltimore, 1979), 1:348–49, and below, chap. 5, text near nn. 1–33. Throughout this book, the sign refers to pounds in Maryland currency unless sterling is specified. There is no information for this period on the exchange between the two currencies.

17. William Page, ed., *The Victoria History of the County of Middlesex*, 8 vols. (London, 1911–85), 2:206–7 (quote), 3:88, 109, 116–17.

18. Only eight of the forty-four adult males who lived on the manor between 1659 and 1661 were still there in 1670. See chap. 5, text near n. 42, and *Archives* 53:627–37. The issues discussed in this paragraph are treated more fully below, in chap. 5, text near nn. 24–30, 37–42.

19. George Alsop, *A Character of the Province of Maryland* . . . (London, 1666), in *Narratives of Early Maryland*, ed. Hall, 363. Recent literature on the Chesapeake economy is reviewed in John J. McCusker and Russell R. Menard, *The Economy of British America, 1607–1789* (Chapel Hill, 1985), 117–43. On to-

bacco, see Russell R. Menard, "The Tobacco Industry in the Chesapeake Colonies, 1617–1730: An Interpretation," *Research in Economic History* 5 (1980): 109–77. On the "culture of tobacco," see T. H. Breen, *Tobacco Culture: The Mentality of the Great Planters on the Eve of Revolution* (Princeton, N.J., 1985), chap. 2.

20. The discussion of early Maryland that follows draws on Menard, "Early Colonial Maryland"; Russell R. Menard and Lois Green Carr, "The Lords Baltimore and the Colonization of Maryland," in *Early Maryland in a Wider World*, ed. Quinn, 167–215; and Garry Wheeler Stone, "Manorial Maryland," *Maryland Historical Magazine* (hereafter *MHM*) 82 (1987): 3–36.

21. Cecilius Calvert to Thomas Wentworth, January 10, 1634, in William Knowler, ed., *The Earl of Strafforde's Letters and Dispatches*, 2 vols. (London, 1739), 1:178–79.

22. The quotations are from [Lewger and Hawley], *A Relation of Maryland . . .* , in *Narratives of Early Maryland*, ed. Hall, 70.

23. For biographies of the gentleman adventurers, see Harry Wright Newman, *The Flowering of the Maryland Palatinate* (Washington, D.C., 1961), 165–336. All the passengers probably came on the larger vessel, the *Ark*.

24. Biographies of servants who can be identified are in ibid. See also Lois Green Carr, "The First Expedition to Maryland," in *A Relation of the Successefull Beginnings of the Lord Baltemore's Plantation in Mary-land*, Maryland Hall of Records 350th Anniversary Documents Series, no. 3 (Annapolis, Md., 1984), xxv–xxx. For more on servants, see below, chap. 2 n. 24, and chap. 4, text near nn. 46–50. The institution is described in Abbot E. Smith, *Colonists in Bondage: White Servitude and Convict Labor in America, 1607–1776* (Chapel Hill, 1947), esp. chaps. 1 and 12, and in David W. Galenson, *White Servitude in Colonial America: An Economic Analysis* (Cambridge, 1981), 3–51 and passim.

25. Cornwallis to Cecilius Lord Baltimore, April 16, 1638, in *The Calvert Papers, Number One*, Maryland Historical Society, Fund Publication no. 28 (Baltimore, 1889), 174–76.

26. On politics in early Maryland, see Lois Green Carr, "Sources of Political Stability and Upheaval in Seventeenth-Century Maryland," *MHM* 79 (1984): 44–70, esp. 52–64, and Russell R. Menard, "Maryland's 'Time of Troubles': Sources of Political Disorder in Early St. Mary's," *MHM* 76 (1981): 124–40. J. Frederick Fausz, "Merging and Emerging Worlds: Anglo-Indian Interest Groups and the Development of the Seventeenth-Century Chesapeake" in *Colonial Chesapeake Society*, ed. Lois Green Carr, Philip D. Morgan, and Jean B. Russo (Chapel Hill, 1988), 47–98, is an especially valuable discussion of the role of Virginians and the Susequehannock Indians in early Maryland history.

27. *Archives* 3:165.

28. John Lewger in Chancery 24/690/14:509, Public Record Office, London.

29. For references to the "time of troubles" and "the plundering time," see *Archives* 4:357, 362, 395, 396, 421, 422, 423, 427, 429. Recent excavations at St. Mary's City have discovered the fortifications of Leonard Calvert's house.

Henry M. Miller, *Discovering Maryland's First City: A Summary Report on the 1981–1984 Archaeological Excavations in St. Mary's City, Maryland,* St. Mary's City Archaeology Series, no. 2 (St. Mary's City, Md., 1986), 47–64.

30. The quotation is from Cornwallis to Cecilius Lord Baltimore, April 16, 1638, in *Calvert Papers, Number One,* 176.

31. The estimate is from A. Gray and V. J. Wycoff, "The International Tobacco Trade in the Seventeenth Century," *Southern Economic Journal* 7 (1940): 1026. For tobacco production per head and tobacco prices and exports, see Menard, "Tobacco Industry," 145, 157–61. The term *sot-weed* is taken from Ebenezer Cooke, *The Sot-Weed Factor* (London, 1708), a satirical poem reprinted in *Early Maryland Poetry . . . ,* ed. Bernard C. Steiner, Maryland Historical Society, Fund Publication no. 36 (Baltimore, 1900), 11–32.

32. E. H. Clarendon, *The History of the Rebellion and Civil Wars in England Begun in the Year 1641* (Oxford, 1888), 5:263.

33. Details on prices, exports, population growth, and the spread of settlement in Maryland and Virginia during the mid-century boom are provided in Menard, "Tobacco Industry," 132–34.

34. This characterization of Maryland society in the decades after 1650 is developed more fully in Menard, "Early Colonial Maryland," 213–77, and in Lorena S. Walsh, "Charles County, Maryland, 1658–1705: A Study of Chesapeake Social and Political Structure" (Ph.D. diss., Michigan State University, 1977), 182–91, 215–16, 325–64. Using (1) proprietary rent rolls for 1659, which list every landowner and the land he owned, and (2) estimates for the number of householders in that year, Menard and Walsh have found that only 10 percent in St. Mary's County and 7 percent in Charles County did not own land. Rent Roll 0. See also Allan Kulikoff, *Tobacco and Slaves: The Development of Southern Cultures in the Chesapeake, 1680–1800* (Chapel Hill, 1986), 30–37. On rent rolls, see below, n. 58. For an example of the term *ordinary planter,* see *Archives* 53:194, 208–10.

Under the term *yeoman,* we include very poor planters who might have been termed *husbandmen* in England, except that they owned their land. On English yeomen, see Mildred Campbell, *The English Yeoman in the Tudor and Early Stuart Age* (1942; reprint, New York, 1968), chap. 2, and Peter Laslett, *The World We Have Lost* (London, 1968), 43–44. For an excellent discussion of the term *yeoman* and its use in later American society, see Allan Kulikoff, "The Transition to Capitalism in Rural America," *William and Mary Quarterly* (hereafter *WMQ*), 3d ser., 46 (1989): 140–44.

35. On migration patterns, see Russell R. Menard, "British Migration to the Chesapeake Colonies," in *Colonial Chesapeake Society,* ed. Carr, Morgan, and Russo, 99–132, esp. 120–21, and idem, "Early Colonial Maryland," table V-2. For Lloyd, Slye, and Stevens, see Papenfuse et al., *Biographical Dictionary of the Maryland Legislature,* 1:534, 739, 776–77, and below, appendix 4 (Slye).

36. For example, 41 percent of the 190 free adults identified as living in Charles County in 1660 had come as free immigrants, a much higher percentage

than appeared from 1670 to 1700. Lorena S. Walsh, "Staying Put or Getting Out: Findings for Charles County, Maryland, 1650–1720," *WMQ*, 3d ser., 44 (1987): table 1. See also the biographies of the early migrants to Somerset County, first settled in the early 1660s, in Clayton C. Torrence, *Old Somerset on the Eastern Shore of Maryland: A Study in Foundations and Founders* (Richmond, Va., 1935), esp. 275–334.

37. Exceptions to this generalization regarding scale economies are discussed in chaps. 2 and 3, which also provide a detailed description of the techniques of tobacco cultivation and the process of farm building.

38. For example, of 158 servants who arrived in Maryland before 1643 and survived to be freedmen, 94 still lived in the colony ten years after freedom, and of these, 79 to 81 owned land by that time. Eventually, 75 to 76 of the 94 participated in local government as jurors or officeholders, and 22 achieved positions of authority. Servants who appeared in the Charles County area between 1648 and 1674 and remained there show somewhat less progress but still did well. Close to three-fifths became landowners, and two-thirds were jurors or officers. Russell R. Menard, "From Servant to Freeholder: Status Mobility and Property Accumulation in Seventeenth-Century Maryland," *WMQ*, 3d ser., 30 (1973): 37–64 (esp. 40–43); Walsh, "Charles County, Maryland," tables 21 and 22. See also Lois Green Carr and Russell R. Menard, "Immigration and Opportunity: The Freedman in Early Colonial Maryland," in *The Chesapeake in the Seventeenth Century: Essays on Anglo-American Society and Politics*, ed. Thad W. Tate and David L. Ammerman (Chapel Hill, 1979), 206–42.

39. See appendix 4. John Elton, the fourth servant, married but was still a tenant at his death in 1705.

40. See chap. 6, near nn. 2–3, 13–16.

41. Lorena S. Walsh and Russell R. Menard, "Death in the Chesapeake: Two Life Tables for Men in Early Colonial Maryland," *MHM* 69 (1974): 211–27.

42. Carr and Menard, "Immigration and Opportunity," in *The Chesapeake in the Seventeenth Century*, ed. Tate and Ammerman, 211; Lorena S. Walsh, "'Till Death Us Do Part': Marriage and Family in Seventeenth-Century Maryland," in ibid., 127.

43. Walsh and Menard, "Death in the Chesapeake," 221–22; Lois Green Carr and Lorena S. Walsh, "The Planter's Wife: The Experience of White Women in Seventeenth-Century Maryland," *WMQ*, 3d ser., 34 (1977): 552–53; Russell R. Menard, "Immigrants and Their Increase: The Process of Population Growth in Early Colonial Maryland," in *Law, Society, and Politics in Early Maryland*, ed. Aubrey C. Land, Lois Green Carr, and Edward C. Papenfuse (Baltimore, 1977), 88–110.

44. Walsh, "'Till Death Us Do Part,'" in *The Chesapeake in the Seventeenth Century*, ed. Tate and Ammerman, 151–52; Carr and Walsh, "The Planter's Wife," 558–59; Lois Green Carr, "The Development of the Maryland Orphans' Court, 1654–1715," in *Law, Society, and Politics*, ed. Land, Carr, and Papenfuse, 41–52. Darrett B. Rutman and Anita H. Rutman found that for 239 children born

in Middlesex County, Virginia, between 1655 and 1724, more than half had lost one or both parents by age eleven. "'Now-Wives and Sons-in-Law': Parental Death in a Seventeenth-Century Virginia County," in *The Chesapeake in the Seventeenth Century*, ed. Tate and Ammerman, 158–60.

45. Carr, "Sources of Political Stability," 55–58, provides a more detailed description of Maryland politics in the aftermath of Ingle's Rebellion, as do Aubrey C. Land, *Colonial Maryland: A History* (Millwood, N.Y., 1981), 33–56, and David W. Jordan, *Foundations of Representative Government in Maryland, 1632–1715* (New York, 1987), 34–59.

46. On Fendall's Rebellion, see Land, *Colonial Maryland*, 54–56, which is the source of the quotations, and Jordan, *Foundations of Representative Government*, 57–59.

47. Alsop, *Province of Maryland*, in *Narratives of Early Maryland*, ed. Hall, 381.

48. This estimate is based on the ratio of population to taxables for Charles County in 1660 (unpublished research of Lorena S. Walsh), plus estimates for taxables in that year for St. Mary's and Calvert counties, estimates produced by interpolations from figures for 1657 and 1667. These appear in Menard, "Early Colonial Maryland," 457, 459.

49. Kevin P. Kelly, "'In dispers'd Country Plantations': Settlement Patterns in Seventeenth-Century Surry County, Virginia," in *The Chesapeake in the Seventeenth Century*, ed. Tate and Ammerman, 183–205, esp. maps on 186–89.

50. *Archives* 5:265–66. On St. Mary's City, see Lois Green Carr, "'The Metropolis of Maryland': A Comment on Town Development along the Tobacco Coast," *MHM* 69 (1974): 124–45, esp. 124 (quotes), 129–31.

51. The figure for the number of households is derived from the estimate of household size. Walsh has estimated only three people per household in Charles County, but this is clearly too small a figure for the whole region. Darrett B. Rutman and Anita H. Rutman found about eleven people per household in Middlesex County, Virginia, in 1668. *A Place in Time: Middlesex County, Virginia, 1650–1750* (New York, 1984), 62. We have split the difference for a region that includes large areas of new settlement.

52. Here we have borrowed a term from ibid., 156–57.

53. On Charles Calvert, see Papenfuse et al., *Biographical Dictionary of the Maryland Legislature*, 1:187–88. Charles Calvert was governor from 1661 until he became the second proprietor in 1676.

54. For England, see C. W. Chalklin, *Seventeenth-Century Kent: A Social and Economic History* (London, 1965), 197; Keith Wrightson and David Levine, *Poverty and Piety in an English Village: Terling, 1525–1700* (New York, 1979), 34–35 (quotation); Paul Slack, *Poverty and Policy in Tudor and Stuart England* (London, 1988), 40–43, 50–55; James P. P. Horn, "Adapting to a New World: A Comparative Study of Local Society in England and Maryland, 1650–1700," in *Colonial Chesapeake Society*, ed. Carr, Morgan, and Russo, 142–43; idem, "Adapting to a New World: English Society in the Seventeenth-Century Chesapeake"

(ms. in progress), chap. 3; and Sydney Webb and Beatrice Webb, *English Poor Law History, Part I: The Old Poor Law* (1927; reprint, Hamden, Conn., 1963), 49–50, 52–53, 56–59, 82–86, 88, 91–92, 215–16. Maryland poor relief was granted by the county courts. In Talbot County from 1662 through 1674, levy accounts survive for nine years. They show one tax exemption and allowances to eight people. In 1670 three people received assistance; otherwise there were never more than two per year. In Charles County from 1658 through 1674, six levy accounts remain. Only the last two, for 1672 and 1674, show public relief allowances, two each year. *Archives* 54:409–10, 428, 445, 481, 544, 578–79 (for Talbot County); 53:274, 522–23, 619, 60:347, 431, 586–87 (for Charles County). If in Charles County in 1675 there were 568 white free males (see table 1.3), those who received a public allowance were less than .2 percent of this population. *Archives* 60:587.

55. If a man or woman left a will, it had to be presented to the probate court (in Maryland, a central agency called the Prerogative Court), which required the executor named in the will to take an inventory of the deceased's property, to pay all debts, and to distribute the remaining estate according to the provisions of the will. If he or she had died intestate, the court would *on request* appoint an administrator to do the same, making distribution according to the laws of intestacy. Few women in this period left wills or inventories because, generally speaking, the property a married woman brought to her marriage belonged to her husband. Such remaining probate records for women are those of widows or spinsters, and in the woman-short seventeenth century, few women remained unmarried for long. In St. Mary's County in the seventeenth century, a very high proportion of male decedents' estates went through probate, since the court's supervision was a protection to both heirs and creditors. However, people of more distant counties were more deterred by the costs of traveling to St. Mary's City. The Maryland assembly did not enact local arrangements for probate until 1692. In the Chesapeake, land and improvements were not inventoried, since these could not be concealed or carried away. For further discussion of the nature of Maryland estate inventories, see Lois Green Carr and Lorena S. Walsh, "Inventories and the Analysis of Wealth and Consumption Patterns in St. Mary's County, Maryland, 1658–1777," *Historical Methods* 13 (1980): 81–104, and Gloria L. Main, *Tobacco Colony: Life in Early Maryland, 1650–1720* (Princeton, N.J., 1982), 282–86.

The documents used in this book report nearly all values in pounds of tobacco, the money of account in Maryland inventories before the early 1680s. We translated these values into local currency via a tobacco price series published in Russell R. Menard, "Farm Prices of Maryland Tobacco, 1659–1710," *MHM* 68 (1973): 80–85. (No information is available to show the sterling value of local currency.) We then reduced figures in local currency to constant value by a commodity price index. The index is discussed and printed in Russell R. Menard, Lois Green Carr, and Lorena S. Walsh, "A Small Planter's Profits: The Cole Estate and the Growth of the Early Chesapeake Economy," *WMQ*, 3d ser., 40

(1983): 176n. An earlier commodity price index and its construction are described in detail in Carr and Walsh, "Inventories and the Analysis of Wealth," 96–97, 100–101.

56. See the discussion of mobility in the text between n. 35 and n. 40.

57. Unfortunately, we cannot determine the size of the various subgroups among nonofficeholding landowners. In the absence of tax lists, the only economic measure available is the amount of land held. In a newly settled region, this is not a useful predictor of status because the size range of acreage for this group is not great and there is no way to know how much land was improved. We need to know ownership of livestock and labor, and for this we must rely on inventories. However, inventories are biased in ways that prevent them from indicating for the living population the size of the groups they describe. Not everyone goes through probate—the proportion that do so is called the reporting rate—and the chances are that more rich than poor take advantage of this service because of the fees entailed. But without tax lists to give us some idea of the wealth of the living, we cannot adjust inventories for differing reporting rates of various groups. Luckily, it is possible to estimate the overall reporting rate and whether or not it changed. If it does not change, we can accept changes in the distribution of inventoried wealth as representing changes that actually occurred in the living population. Even though we still will not know the actual sizes of the groups affected, we will know whether they were increasing or decreasing. For a full discussion of how we have addressed these problems in working with inventories, see Carr and Walsh, "Inventories and the Analysis of Wealth," 97–98. For further discussion of inventory bias, see Alice H. Jones, "Wealth Estimates for the American Middle Colonies, 1774," *Economic Development and Cultural Change* 18 (1970): 109–21; Gloria L. Main, "The Correction of Biases in Colonial American Probate Records," *Historical Methods Newsletter* 8 (1974): 10–28; and Daniel Scott Smith, "Underregistration and Bias in Probate Records: An Analysis of Data from Eighteenth-Century Hingham, Massachusetts," *WMQ*, 3d ser., 32 (1975): 100–110.

58. This median was close to that for landowners in the living population—250 acres—as seen in the quitrent rolls of 1659 for St. Mary's and Charles counties. Rent Roll 0. These records have been analyzed in Russell R. Menard, "Population Growth and Land Distribution in St. Mary's County, 1634–1710" (Unpublished report, St. Mary's City Commission, 1971), and Walsh, "Charles County, Maryland," 388–97. The rent rolls were proprietary records kept to assist in the collection of the quitrent each landowner owed Lord Baltimore. He granted land in fee simple—that is, the grantee could sell it, lease it, give it away, or devise it without interference—but the owner owed the proprietor a small yearly rent. The difference between the median acreage of inventoried decedents and that of living planters suggests that the estate values for ordinary planters in the inventories are slightly, but not substantially, biased upward.

59. The rent roll for 1659 (Rent Roll 0) shows only three holdings each in St. Mary's and Charles counties as small as fifty acres and only one smaller.

60. On the role of tenancy, see Menard, "From Servant to Freeholder," 52–55; Walsh, "Charles County, Maryland," 388–420; and Carr and Menard, "Immigration and Opportunity," in *The Chesapeake in the Seventeenth Century*, ed. Tate and Ammerman, 224–29.

61. On inmates, see Carr and Menard, "Immigration and Opportunity," in *The Chesapeake in the Seventeenth Century*, ed. Tate and Ammerman, 206–42, esp. 212–27.

62. This is the only one available, since the local records for St. Mary's and Calvert counties have not survived.

63. For the construction and results of the census, see Walsh, "Staying Put or Getting Out," 89–103.

64. Possibly record bias accounts to some extent for this very optimistic profile of the social structure. However, independent estimates of the county's free male population show that the prosopography captures most or all of the free men that one can expect to have been in the county. Ibid., 90–91.

65. Bound laborers were perhaps 10 percent of the adult male population in Charles County. Darrett B. Rutman and Anita H. Rutman have estimated that in 1668, bound laborers, male and female, were as much as 45 percent of the total population of Middlesex County, Virginia, after twenty years of settlement. *A Place in Time: Middlesex County*, 71.

66. On various forms of pay for inmates, see Carr and Menard, "Immigration and Opportunity," in *The Chesapeake in the Seventeenth Century*, ed. Tate and Ammerman, 212–14. Contracts found in the records show that inmates could insist on being paid more than the usual crop. A developer like Gerard could afford to do this for a while in order to get land cleared and buildings and fencing constructed quickly, but small planters probably could not. Inmates also often agreed to work only for a full share of the crop, an arrangement that supplied the planter with extra labor for other tasks. However, a small planter could not waste his good tobacco land. The inmate would be using land that was not bringing his master profit and that would soon be out of production for a long time. On the problems of conserving land, see below, chap. 2, text after n. 26. The manor records show that turnover of inmates was very high. See below, chap. 5, text before n. 42.

67. Among lower Western Shore decedents inventoried between 1671 and 1677, mean and median wealth rose for all four groups. However, the mean rose faster than the median, especially for ordinary landowners, indicating that improvement was greater for the better-off than for the poor.

68. Independent estimates for the numbers of various groups within the county population were particularly unsatisfactory for this year, and the reconstitution of free adult men was incomplete, including no more than 82 percent, and perhaps as few as 65 percent, of the free adult male population. The figures in the table include an adjustment for men missing from the reconstitution, all of whom are assumed to be inmates. See Walsh, "Staying Put or Getting Out," 91–92.

69. Slaves were still a small, although increasing, proportion of bound labor.

On the lower Western Shore, slaves found in inventories were about 9 percent of the bound labor force from 1658 to 1661 and 13 percent from 1671 to 1674. Russell R. Menard, "From Servants to Slaves: The Transformation of the Chesapeake Labor System," *Southern Studies* 16 (1977): table 5.

70. Cf. Edmund S. Morgan, *American Slavery, American Freedom: The Ordeal of Colonial Virginia* (New York, 1975), chaps. 11 and 12, on the increasing proportion of inmates and tenants in Virginia between 1660 and 1675. The Rutmans found that male servants and bachelors combined made up over two-thirds of the white male population in Middlesex County, Virginia, in 1668 and that they outnumbered household heads almost five to one. However, Middlesex bachelors were offspring of resident heads of households more often than was the case in Charles County. "'More True and Perfect Lists': The Reconstruction of Censuses for Middlesex County, Virginia, 1668–1704," *Virginia Magazine of History and Biography* (hereafter *VMHB*) 88 (1980): 59–62.

71. From very rough calculations, we estimate that Cole's total outlay, in 1649–52 prices, for moving to Maryland and getting started was in the neighborhood of £135. Costs of passage and freighting of goods (£8) are given in [Lewger and Hawley], *A Relation of Maryland*, in *Narratives of Early Maryland*, ed. Hall, 96. This value is in sterling, but we have no way to convert it to Maryland currency. Equipment and adult maintenance for a year are based on the freedom dues (clothing, tools) for Henry Spinke in 1649, which came to £3.08 (*Archives* 4:471), plus three barrels of corn at the 1652 price, which came to £3.50, and the valuation of a bed and coverings in an inventory of 1649 (ibid., 4:499), which came to £1.25. This was the minimum for the two servants and Cole's wife. For Cole we added household equipment and additional tools based on the inventory of Thomas Allen in 1649 (omitting his beds), which came to about £12.12 (ibid., 4:405–6). The values of the goods were given in tobacco, which we transformed into Maryland currency, using Russell R. Menard, "A Note on Chesapeake Tobacco Prices, 1618–1660," *VMHB* 84 (1976): 401–10. For the four children we allowed £3.0 each for a year's food and supplies (£1 per child is for corn) and £4 for passage, this being what was charged little Mary Cole, who returned to England in 1662 (see below, chap. 2, text before n. 37). For Cole's land purchase, which came to about £20, see below, chap. 2, n. 5. On the basis of the handful of prices found for the late 1640s and early 1650s, we estimate that a cow with calf and a pregnant sow would have cost about £10, for a total outlay of £133.45.

To establish the value of the estate that Cole began with and make it comparable to his later wealth, we must omit the cost of corn (£18 for everyone) and of transportation (£48 at £8 per adult and £4 per child). We must reduce the other values to constant values with a deflator that we have calculated at 2.01, and we must add the constant value of the servants (£20.48), property that Cole could have sold. Then Cole probably started with an investment in land (without a house), labor, livestock, and goods worth about £54.30 (constant value).

Possibly Cole brought more than the minimum in goods, such as a little linen, some dairy equipment, and perhaps his books. These might have been worth £4 (constant value). A better bed, his joint stools, his chair table and chairs, and additional kitchen equipment might add another £5 (constant value). However, we do not believe that Cole began so well equipped. These additional goods we have valued by using their estimated worth in tobacco from Cole's inventory of 1662 and by converting to 1652 constant value currency with the 1652 tobacco price (2.6 pence per pound) and the 1652 deflator (2.01).

The constant value of Cole's movable estate in 1652 (without the above additional goods) was about £44; in 1662 the movable estate was £153.91 (see table 1.4), about 3.5 times larger. Cole's total estate of 1652, including his unimproved land, came to about £54; in 1662, with land improved, it came to £208 (see table 1.4), or 3.85 times the beginning value.

We must emphasize that these results are imprecise. We aim at only a general idea of Cole's expenditures. The deflator for 1652 is very tentative—it may well be too small—and many sources are inadequate. We have few price observations for corn and livestock and none of a standard kind for household goods. Finally, we have found no references to conversion from local currency to sterling, although both the Maryland and Virginia assemblies attempted at various times to legislate rates. See John J. McCusker, *Money and Exchange in Europe and America, 1600–1775: A Handbook* (Chapel Hill, 1978), 189–214. For convenience, we have expressed shillings and pence as parts of pounds.

72. Cole probably called himself "yeoman" rather than "planter" because he had appointed an English executor. Thus he used the word in its English sense, indicating a more narrowly defined status than we have assigned it in describing Chesapeake society. See above, text before n. 34 and annotation.

73. In twenty-eight references, 1658–62, Cole was called "mister" three times and "gentleman" twice. However, when he was called "gentleman"—both references from 1661—it was not as an individual but as a member of a group so identified in a lump: as a provincial court grand juror and as a St. Clement's Manor freeholder. An assignment of the label "gent." to either group was unusual, although particular members might be so identified. *Archives* 10:535, 41:221, 344, 354, 419, 471, 49:3, 53:627, 629, 630, 657. "Mister" as a form of address was often preliminary to a recognition of gentry status. Lois Green Carr, *County Government in Maryland, 1689–1709* (New York, 1987), 600. For Cole's will and inventory, see below, appendix 1.

74. Our first effort came within 8 percent of Cole's total. Values attached to individual items were then adjusted to yield Cole's sum. We are confident that the results of this process are reliable and that the prices assigned particular commodities are reasonably close to their market value. The prices are in tobacco, and we have converted them to constant currency. See n. 55.

75. The data are drawn from projects of the St. Mary's City Commission, funded by the National Science Foundation (GS32272) and the National Endowment for the Humanities (RO 6228–72–468; RO 10585–74–267).

76. Estimating the value of landholdings in early Maryland is problematic. Too few deeds have survived to support an annual series, and these report sharp price

variations according to the degree of improvement. The following table summarizes the available evidence for the years 1652 through 1674:

Area	Improved Tracts		Unimproved Tracts		All Tracts*	
	N	Pence/ Acre	N	Pence/ Acre	N	Pence/ Acre
St. Mary's	22	75.9	8	18.7	38	54.1
Calvert	3	105.6	3	22.0	6	63.8
St. Mary's and Calvert	25	80.1	11	19.6	44	54.2
Charles	74	49.1	37	17.5	122	37.7

*Includes some tracts unknown as to improvements.

Observations in Calvert are too few to use. Since these few prices are high, rather than low, we combined them with those of St. Mary's for use in valuing Calvert land. The destruction of all St. Mary's and Calvert county records for the period accounts for the small number of observations. Only sales recorded by the clerk of the provincial court remain. Luckily, since this clerk functioned in St. Mary's City, some sales for St. Mary's County are in his records.

Since the mean size of tracts that could be identified as improved was about 200 acres, in valuing land, we assumed that each householder's first 200 acres was improved and valued all additional acreage at the price for unimproved land.

The data are based on deeds of sale recorded in the provincial court (printed in *Archives*, vols. 41, 49, 56, and 57) and in the Charles County court (printed in ibid., vols. 53 and 60).

77. The sum of movable wealth for all estates was £6,564.81, and for estates richer than Cole's, £3,176.86. The sum of total wealth for all estates was £10,666.35, and for estates richer than Cole's, £5,192.45. Among the inventoried in St. Mary's County alone, Cole had a lower position. The ratio of his wealth to the mean and median of all estates was little affected, but the decedents richer than he held 56 percent of the wealth. The sum of total wealth was £5,241.59, and for estates richer than Cole's, £2,933.5.

These analyses deal only with Cole's position in the structure of wealth owned by people who had died and left estates that were inventoried. Inventories are biased toward wealth in two ways. Older people have had longer to accumulate wealth than the young and are also more likely to die; and the poor may be less likely than the rich to go through probate. Bias in our data is suggested in table 1.3. Among the probated dead on the lower Western Shore, the gentry group was 17 percent, whereas in the living adult male population of Charles County in 1660, it was 13 percent. Undoubtedly people richer than Cole were overrepresented in the inventoried population and consequently had a smaller share of wealth among the living than among the dead. In the living population, Cole's position in the wealth structure was probably above the middle, but it surely was not very near the top. For further discussion of bias, see n. 57.

78. Of 93 inventoried decedents, 1658–65, 52 had no children of age. Of 31 ex-servants, 10 were still inmates at death and 16 owned land; of 46 free immigrants, only 8 died as inmates at death and 37 owned land. In the 50 St. Mary's County inventories for 1672–75, discussed in chap. 4, text before n. 52, ex-servants did somewhat better. Of the 18 known ex-servants, 61 percent had land; of the 18 known free immigrants, 77 percent had land.

Chapter 2

1. Russell R. Menard, "From Servant to Freeholder: Status Mobility and Property Accumulation in Seventeenth-Century Maryland," *William and Mary Quarterly* (hereafter *WMQ*), 3d ser., 30 (1973): 53. See also William Fitzhugh to Nicholas Hayward, January 30, 1687, in *William Fitzhugh and His Chesapeake World, 1676–1701: The Fitzhugh Letters and Other Documents*, ed. Richard Beale Davis (Chapel Hill, 1963), 202. Tenants, Fitzhugh explained, "may be found that for a seven year's Lease, will build themselves a convenient dwelling & other necessary houses, & be obliged at the expiration of their time, to leave all in good repair."

2. Edwin W. Beitzell, *The Jesuit Missions of St. Mary's County* (n.p., 1959), 27.

3. On the relationship between Gill and Cole, see William Hand Browne et al., eds., *Archives of Maryland* (hereafter *Archives*), 72 vols. (Baltimore, 1883–1972), 41:170–73.

4. Patents Q:20, 205, 20:17–20, Maryland State Archives, Annapolis, Maryland. Unless otherwise noted, all manuscripts cited are at the Maryland State Archives. The proprietor gave rights to land to anyone who paid the way of a settler, but the land was not therefore free. The owner of the right, called a headright, had to pay for a survey and then a fee for a patent the proprietor issued that defined the boundaries and the yearly quitrent owed him. Despite the quitrent, the patentee owned the land in fee simple and could sell or give it away at will. See Elizabeth Hartsook and Gust Skordas, *Land Office and Prerogative Court Records of Colonial Maryland* (1946; reprint, Baltimore, 1967), 16–17, and Robert Brugger, *Maryland: A Middle Temperament, 1634–1980* (Baltimore, 1988), 14–16. Cole used headrights to patent his Charles County land but purchased his plantation from Thomas Gerard, who had patented St. Clement's Manor.

5. In 1652, Luke Gardiner paid Gerard 5,000 pounds of tobacco in cask for 800 acres on the manor, or 6.3 pounds of tobacco per acre. He was to pay three barrels of Indian corn and two capons yearly. *Archives* 41:143–44. Tobacco was selling for about 2.6 pence per pound in 1652, so Gardiner paid about 16 pence per acre. At the same price, Cole's 300 acres came to about £20, or £10 in constant value. On the constant-value deflator for this date, see chap. 1 n. 71. For tobacco prices, see Russell R. Menard, "A Note on Chesapeake Tobacco Prices,

1618–1660," *Virginia Magazine of History and Biography* (hereafter *VMHB*) 84 (1976): 401–10. A freehold lease to Bartholomew Phillips shows a somewhat different arrangement for rent but states that Phillips had to attend the manor court and give Gerard half of any unmarked swine he killed on the manor. Carroll Papers, ms. 219, Maryland Historical Society, Baltimore, Maryland. Cole clearly had these requirements in his lease. See *Archives* 41:480. Phillips also had to pay Gerard one-tenth of any surplus of hogs or cattle he sold, but Luke Gardiner's account shows no such payments for Cole's estate. Phillips's lease allowed his cattle to run on any unfenced, unplanted part of the manor. He could also cut timber for building and could hawk, hunt, fowl, or fish anywhere on the manor. Probably Cole's lease had similar arrangements.

6. William Page, ed., *The Victoria History of the County of Middlesex*, 8 vols. (London, 1911–85), 2:206–7.

7. There is a helpful discussion of the difficulties of small grain production in pioneer communities in Lewis C. Gray, *History of Agriculture in the Southern United States to 1860*, 2 vols. (Washington, D.C., 1933), 1:161–63.

8. On Indian agriculture at contact, see the account of John Smith in *The Generall Historie of Virginia, New England, and the Summer Isles . . .* (1624), in *The Complete Works of Captain John Smith (1580–1631)*, ed. Philip L. Barbour (Chapel Hill, 1986), 2:112–13. On English adaptation in early Virginia, see Lorena S. Walsh, "'To Labour for Profit': Plantation Management in the Chesapeake, 1620–1820" (unpublished manuscript), chap. 1.

9. Nathaniel Shrigley, *A True Relation of Virginia and Maryland* (London, 1669), 5, in *Tracts and Other Papers, Relating Principally to the Origin, Settlement, and Progress of the Colonies in North America*, ed. Peter Force (hereafter *Tracts*), 4 vols. (Washington, D.C., 1836–47), vol. 3, no. 7. Among 165 household inventories probated in St. Mary's County from 1658 through 1677, only 4 percent had plows. St. Mary's County Inventory File, St. Mary's City Commission (hereafter SMCC), Maryland State Archives.

10. On farm size, see Lois Green Carr, "Inheritance in the Colonial Chesapeake," in *Women in the Age of the American Revolution*, ed. Ronald Hoffman and Peter J. Albert (Charlottesville, Va., 1989), table 5; Joan Thirsk, ed., *The Agrarian History of England and Wales, IV: 1500–1640* (Cambridge, 1967), 21–22, 26, 30, 33, 34, 36, 40, 51, 57, 58, 67, 69, 71, 78, 85, 86–87, 92, 106; and idem, *The Agrarian History of England and Wales, V: 1640–1750*, 2 vols. (Cambridge, 1984), 1:22, 36–37, 68, 70, 72, 190–91, 292, 322, 326, 346.

11. For a discussion of Indian populations and their rapid decline from disease at contact, see Francis Jennings, *The Invasion of America: Indians, Colonialism, and the Cant of Conquest* (Chapel Hill, 1975), chap. 1. On the labor-intensive character of tobacco culture, see chap. 3.

12. On orchards, see, for example, *Archives* 49:157, 469, 57:32–34, 69:316, 70:87; Wills 1:283, 484, 4:273; and Thomas Glover, *An Account of Virginia, Its Situation, Temperature, Productions, Inhabitants, and Their Manner of Planting*

and Ordering Tobacco, reprinted from the *Philosophical Transactions of the Royal Society*, June 20, 1676 (Oxford, 1904), 13–14.

13. Robert Beverley, *The History and Present State of Virginia*, ed. Louis B. Wright (Chapel Hill, 1947), 293, 316. Beverley's book was originally published in 1705. Beverley also comments on the absence of malthouses as a discouragement to planting barley and making beer.

14. Estates of 152 householders were inventoried at their deaths over the years 1658–70 in St. Mary's, Charles, and Calvert counties. Of these, 140, or 92 percent, had cattle, hogs, or both. Lower Western Shore Inventory File, SMCC. Many observers commented on the practice of letting livestock roam free to forage in the woods and on the inadequacy of feed in winter. Glover, *Account of Virginia*, 19; "A Letter from Mr. John Clayton, Rector of Crofton at Wakefield in Yorkshire, to the Royal Society, May 12, 1688," 25, in *Tracts*, vol. 3, no. 12; Shrigley, *True Relation of Virginia and Maryland*, 5, in *Tracts*, vol. 3, no. 7; Jaspar Dankers and Peter Sluyter, *Journal of a Voyage to New York and a Tour in Several of the American Colonies in 1679–80 ...* , trans. Henry C. Murphy (Brooklyn, N.Y., 1867), 217; "Report of the Journey of Francis Louis Michel, from Berne, Switzerland, to Virginia, October 2, 1701–December 1, 1702," trans. William J. Hinke, *VMHB* 24 (1916): 36; Gregory A. Stiverson and Patrick H. Butler III, eds., "Virginia in 1732: The Travel Journal of William Hugh Grove," *VMHB* 85 (1977), 33. Two administration accounts of the 1670s suggest that winter feed supplied to animals was about three-quarters of a bushel of corn per head of livestock over a whole winter! Inventories and Accounts 2:233, 6:540–43. On wolves, see, for example, York County Deeds, Orders, and Wills (hereafter York County DOW), 1657–62 (transcript), 34, 90, Virginia State Library, Richmond, Virginia. On miring, see Testamentary Proceedings 13:114–15, 17:69; *Archives* 41:167, 175, 430. Legislation for wolf bounties was in force in Maryland from 1654 until at least 1763, except for a brief time between 1669 and 1671, when the assembly overlooked the act in a bill to revive temporary laws. *Archives* 1:347, 362, 372, 537, 2:150, 215–16, 325, 13:520–21, 22:479, 26:326–27, 29:341–42; Acts 1728, chap. 7, in Thomas Bacon, ed., *The Laws of Maryland at Large, with Proper Indexes ...* (Annapolis, Md., 1765). As late as 1727, sheep were being killed by wolves in one of the older sections of Prince George's County. Inventories 12:467. See also the accounts of livestock practices in Gray, *History of Agriculture* 1:201–2, and Wesley N. Laing, "Cattle in Seventeenth-Century Virginia," *VMHB* 67 (1959): 160–61.

15. John Worlidge, *Systema Agriculturae; or, The Mystery of Husbandry Discovered* (London, 1669), 130–31, calls for planting apple trees at least 20 to 30 feet apart. At 25 feet apart, about 72 trees can be planted per acre. References in Maryland records in 1710, 1714, 1720, and 1739 call for plantings 20, 30, 30, and 35 feet apart, respectively. Charles County Court and Land Records C#2:168; Provincial Court Deeds TP#4:309–12; Wills 16:277; Somerset County Deeds MF#4:63a. See also below, chap. 3 n. 54.

16. *Archives* 1:79, 97, 160–61, 251–52, 349–50, 2:548. The law was theoretically in effect until 1692, when it failed of inclusion in the revised laws of that year, but prosecutions under it had ceased by the 1670s. The last prosecution we have so far found recorded was in 1662. Ibid., 49:85. From the 1660s, evidently sufficient corn was being grown to guard against serious shortages.

17. John Rolfe in 1618 estimated 4 or 5 barrels per acre (at 4 bushels instead of the usual 5 to the barrel), although 6 or more could be obtained on new land. Smith, *Generall Historie of Virginia*, in *Complete Works of Captain John Smith*, ed. Barbour, 2:267. This comes to 16 to 20 bushels, which is similar to the 18 bushels per acre that Darrett B. Rutman has estimated for New England yields. *Husbandmen of Plymouth: Farms and Villages in the Old Colony, 1620–1692* (Boston, 1967), 43. We infer that corn measures referred to shelled corn from the following argument. Corn when shelled comes to half its measurement in ears. *The Diary of Colonel Landon Carter of Sabine Hall, 1752–1778*, ed. Jack P. Greene (hereafter *Carter Diary*), 2 vols. (Charlottesville, Va., 1965), 1:522; Harold B. Gill, Jr., "Cereal Grains in Colonial Virginia" (report prepared for the Colonial Williamsburg Foundation, Inc., October 1974), 22. Fifteen bushels of corn was part of a servant's freedom dues, supposedly enough to feed him or her for a year. Beverley, *State of Virginia*, 274. A peck of cornmeal (the equivalent of a peck of shelled corn, since little is lost in grinding the corn) was the weekly food allowance for an adult slave in eighteenth-century Chesapeake. "Journal of William Grove," *VMHB* 85 (1977): 32. But 15 bushels of corn, or 60 pecks, would shell to only 30 pecks, whereas at a peck a week, 52 pecks of shelled corn would be necessary for a freedman's diet, if he ate as well as a slave did later. Three barrels of shelled corn allows 52 pecks for food and 8 pecks for seed, replanting, spoilage, etc.

18. W. Noel Sainsbury et al., eds., *Calendar of State Papers, Colonial Series, America and West Indies* (hereafter *CSP Col.*), 43 vols. to date (London, 1860–), *1696–1697*, no. 1285, 591; *Archives* 36:267; *Carter Diary*, 1:149; Russell R. Menard, "The Tobacco Industry in the Chesapeake Colonies, 1617–1730: An Interpretation," *Research in Economic History* 5 (1980): 145–46 and table 2. On weight per plant, see below, n. 30.

19. Glover, *Account of Virginia*, 28–29. A proclamation of the governor of Virginia, April 30, 1628, speaks of 4.5 feet. William Waller Hening, ed., *The Statutes at Large, Being a Collection of the Laws of Virginia from the First Session of the Legislature in 1619*, 12 vols. (Richmond, Va., 1809–23), 1:130. However, John Banister in about 1688 spoke of tobacco planted out as "about 3 foot distance." Joseph Ewan and Nesta Ewan, *John Banister and His Natural History of Virginia* (Urbana, Ill., 1970), 345, 361. In 1697 an observer said that 10,000 plants were put on about three acres. *CSP Col., 1696–1697*, no. 1253, 582–83. On three acres, 10,000 plants are nearly 4 feet apart.

20. Martin L. Primack, "Land Clearing under Nineteenth-Century Techniques: Some Preliminary Calculations," *Journal of Economic History* 22 (1962):

484–97. Primack suggests 13.5 man-days to clear an acre by girdling. Jack Larkin, Chief Historian of Sturbridge Village, has calculated a range of 16 to 30 days for full clearance, depending on wage estimates used to make the calculation. If reduced by 40 percent for girdling, this produces a range of 9.6 to 18 days. Letter to Lois Green Carr, May 2, 1983. We have assumed 12 to 13.5 days per acre.

Most varieties of hardwoods must be green when cut, even with the hand tools of today. Of course, the smaller branches that fell from girdled trees could be chopped or sawed. For these points we have relied on Garry W. Stone, formerly Director of Research, Historic St. Mary's City, St. Mary's City, Maryland, and David O. Percy, former Director, National Colonial Farm, Accokeek, Maryland.

21. On the "seasoning" of newcomers, see Edmund S. Morgan, *American Slavery, American Freedom: The Ordeal of Colonial Virginia* (New York, 1975), 158–63, 180–84, and Lorena S. Walsh, "Servitude and Opportunity in Charles County, Maryland, 1658–1705," in *Law, Society, and Politics in Early Maryland*, ed. Aubrey C. Land, Lois Green Carr, and Edward C. Papenfuse (Baltimore, 1977), 115–17.

22. Patents Q:18.

23. In 1624, William Capps counted three boys as one and a half hands. Susan Myra Kingsbury, ed., *The Records of the Virginia Company of London*, 4 vols. (Washington, D.C., 1933–35), 2:524–25. In 1727, the Maryland assembly passed an act limiting production per hand to 7,000 plants per adult laborer and 3,500 plants for those age twelve to sixteen. Gray, *History of Agriculture* 1:271.

24. Robert Cole listed his children's birthdates in his will, printed in appendix 1. On the servants, see Patents Q:18, 5:73. On Mills, see *Archives* 41:242; Wills 1:82. From 1654 until 1661, servant terms for those who came without indenture were for four years unless the servant was under age twenty-one; six years if age sixteen to twenty; seven years if age twelve to sixteen; and to age twenty-one if under age twelve. *Archives* 1:352. From 1661 to 1666, terms were four years if age twenty-two or more; five years if age eighteen through twenty-one; six years if age fifteen through seventeen; and to age twenty-one if under fifteen. Ibid., 1:409, 443, 453, 557. In 1666 these terms were extended by a year, but servants under fifteen still served until age twenty-one. In 1671, this last provision was extended to age twenty-two. Ibid., 2:147, 335. Adult servants who had written indentures commonly served four years; those under age twenty-one served longer terms. David W. Galenson, *White Servitude in Colonial America: An Economic Analysis* (Cambridge, 1981), 101–2. The purchase of Alvey and the arrival of Tinsley in 1657 suggest that Cole's original two servants served five years.

25. On the sex-segregated character of dairying, see Gervase Markham, *The English Housewife, Containing the Inward and Outward Virtues Which Ought to Be in a Complete Woman . . .* , ed. Michael R. Best (Montreal, 1986), 169–70. Markham's book was originally published in 1615. John Lewger wrote Lord Baltimore in 1639 that a dairy "will require a woman." *The Calvert Papers, Number One*, Maryland Historical Society, Fund Publication no. 28 (Baltimore, 1889),

196. All references to milking, butter making, and cheese making that we have found in Maryland records refer to women, e.g., *Archives* 41:14–15, 53, 211, 335, 474, 577, 53:375, 54:583.

26. See Cole's inventory in appendix 1 for the dairying equipment and see chap. 3, text from before n. 59 through n. 63, for a discussion of dairy activity. For Heston's location, see the map in Page, *History of the County of Middlesex* 1:2.

27. Land used only for corn could be used for seven years before beginning the rotation. E. W., *Virginia: More Especially the South Part Thereof, Richly and Truly Valued* . . . (London, 1650), 48, in *Tracts*, vol. 3, no. 11. Carville V. Earle, *The Evolution of a Tidewater Settlement System: All Hallow's Parish, Maryland, 1650–1783*, University of Chicago Department of Geography Research Paper no. 170 (Chicago, 1975), 29 describes the rotation. In a recent article, he argues that rotation was an innovation of the 1680s in response to a serious depression. Until then, planters used manure. "The Myth of the Southern Soil Miner: Macrohistory, Agricultural Innovation, and Environmental Change," in Donald Worster, ed., *The Ends of the Earth: Perspectives on Environmental History* (New York, 1988), 175–210. We find this dating for rotation unlikely. For one thing, evidence in table 2.3 shows far more rapid increase in crop per hand from the 1640s to the 1670s than after 1680. For another, as we will show in chapter 3, planters could not pen their animals for manure because of the difficulties of feeding them. Direct evidence on rotation practice is slight, but Thomas Glover, in a report to the royal society in 1676, was explicit. "When the strength of their ground is worn out they never manure it to bring it in heart, but . . . clear more ground out of the Woods to plant in." *Account of Virginia*, 12.

28. We have estimated the good soils from the soils maps of the area made by the U.S. Department of Agriculture, *Soil Survey of St. Mary's County, Maryland* (Washington, D.C., 1978), sheets 14, 20. Most of the soils good for tobacco were sandy, light soils.

29. Patents Q:18, 48, 5:73, 9:52; Wills 1:82, 185. See also *Archives* 53:627. The timing of the Sheppys' removal from the Coles in 1661 is suggested by the acquisition of the two servant women and the fact that Mary Mills's term would have been up if she had had a four-year indenture (presumably made, despite her probable status as kin, to repay Cole for her transportation). Since Alvey did not appear in Cole's inventory of April 1662, we have assumed that he too served four years, 1657 through 1660.

30. After the 1650s, figures for production per hand are for Maryland only. Figures for Virginia after 1660, collected by Lorena S. Walsh, are somewhat lower, suggesting that Virginia planters were leaving fewer leaves on their plants. On this point, see Darrett B. Rutman and Anita H. Rutman, *A Place in Time: Explicatus* (New York, 1984), chap. 2 and table 2. See chap. 3, text before n. 20, for pruning tobacco plants.

Gloria L. Main, in *Tobacco Colony: Life in Early Maryland, 1650–1720* (Princeton, N.J., 1982), table 1.2, shows lower figures than we do in table 2.3 for oronoco per hand in the period after 1680—in the 1,500–1,600 pound range. Main made her estimates by dividing inventoried crops by the inventoried labor force plus the head of the household. She ignored family members and free inmates, a fact that gives her results an upward bias, but she also ignored variations in planter decisions about how much tobacco to produce, which provides a downward bias. In addition, the crop shown in the inventories may not be the whole crop. Menard's figures are based on reported crop shares, a better record of actual yields per hand. However, he has comparatively few observations. Carville Earle shows 1,914 pounds per hand in All Hallow's Parish in Anne Arundel County for the period 1660–99 (thirty-four observations), based on a method similar to Main's. *Evolution of a Tidewater Settlement System*, 25–27 and table 4.

Note that if 9,000 plants produce 1,500 pounds of tobacco, it takes 6 plants to make a pound. This is close to the ratio for the 10,000 plants that produced about 1,900 pounds of tobacco by the 1690s (see table 2.3). The only figures that contemporary observers give for plants per pound are from 1623 (500 pounds from 2,000 plants), 1648 (5 or 6 plants to the pound from worn land, 1 plant to the pound from fresh land), and 1724 (8 plants to the pound). Kingsbury, *Records of the Virginia Company* 4:38; Edmund Plowden, *A Description of the Province of New Albion . . .* (London, 1648), 25, in *Tracts*, vol. 2, no. 7; Arthur P. Middleton, *Tobacco Coast: A Maritime History of the Chesapeake Bay in the Colonial Era* (Newport News, Va., 1953), chap. 4 n. 33. The 1724 reference, which comes from a report of the governor of Virginia made in connection with efforts to stint tobacco production, clearly cannot apply to Maryland in the seventeenth century and may never have applied to Maryland tobacco, where leaves per plant may always have been greater than in Virginia. See Middleton, *Tobacco Coast*, chap. 4 n. 27, and Ewan and Ewan, *John Banister*, 360.

31. T. C., *An Advice How to Plant Tobacco in England* (London, 1615).

32. There were efforts to grow sweet-scented in Maryland during the 1650s and 1660s, but they proved a failure. *Archives* 41:93, 289–90, 425, 439, 54:221, 559–61, 57:533. For a Virginia experiment, see "Letters Written by Mr. Moray, a Minister, to Sr. R. Moray, From Ware River in Mobjack Bay, Va., Feb. 1, 1665," *WMQ*, 2d ser., 2 (1922): 157–61. For the introduction of sweet-scented tobacco in Virginia, see Rutman and Rutman, *A Place in Time: Explicatus* 4–6.

33. See chap. 3, text before n. 26, for curing. The *Advice* of 1615 recommended stringing the leaves, and a reference of 1624 shows that this method of drying was then in use at Flowerdew Hundred. H. R. McIlwaine, ed., *Minutes of the Council and General Court of Virginia, 1622–32, 1670–76* (Richmond, Va., 1924), 27.

34. See Menard, "Tobacco Industry," 142–55, for a detailed description of these processes and the sources of the renewed expansion after 1715.

35. See the transcripts of the account printed in appendix 1. The account that follows is based on these documents, except as noted. References to the transcripts are not footnoted unless necessary.

36. Lois Green Carr and Lorena S. Walsh, "The Planter's Wife: The Experi-

ence of White Women in Seventeenth-Century Maryland," *WMQ*, 3d ser., 34 (1977): 564–65.

37. Mary's visit to England is inferred from the expenses of her sea voyage shown in the account.

38. On whole and half hands, see n. 23. See appendix 2 for a discussion of the Cole family members' entry into and exit from the plantation labor force.

39. Carr and Walsh, "Planter's Wife," 561; Main, *Tobacco Colony*, 175–77.

40. See table 2.2.

41. On corn in inventories, see Lois Green Carr, "Economic Diversification in the Colonial Chesapeake: Somerset County, Maryland, in Comparative Perspective," in *Colonial Chesapeake Society*, ed. Lois Green Carr, Philip D. Morgan, and Jean B. Russo (Chapel Hill, 1988), table 2. The governor of Maryland issued proclamations to forbid export of corn in years when the crop was short. *Archives* 3:194–95, 293, 443, 452–53. John Hammond comments on occasional opportunities to sell provisions to ships or in the West Indies. *Leah and Rachel; or, The Two Fruitful Sisters, Virginia and Maryland . . .* (London, 1656), 19, in *Tracts*, vol. 3, no. 14. See also *A Perfect Description of Virginia . . .* (London, 1649), 15, in *Tracts*, vol. 2, no. 8. See chap. 3, text between n. 45 and n. 49, for a discussion of why planters did not grow corn for export.

42. Glover, *An Account of Virginia*, 16; Beverley, *State of Virginia*, 292; [John Lewger and Jerome Hawley], *A Relation of Maryland . . .* (London, 1635), in *Narratives of Early Maryland, 1633–1684*, ed. Clayton Colman Hall (1910; reprint, New York, 1967), 76; Durand, of Dauphine, *A Huguenot Exile in Virginia*, ed. Gilbert Chinard (New York, 1934), 115; *Archives* 4:412, 10:58, 499, 509, 17:300–301; Charles County Court and Land Records R#1:228.

43. Lower Norfolk Deed Book A (transcript): 77, microfilm, Virginia State Library; *Archives* 41:252–53, 49:326.

44. On cattle marking, see *Archives* 1:251, 295, 2:140, 277, and Hening, *Statutes at Large* 1:244. For references to the "wild gang," see York County DOW, 1657–62 (transcript), 65, 90, 132, microfilm.

45. On winter feeding of corn and husks, see Glover, *An Account of Virginia*, 19; Inventory and Accounts 2:233, 6:540–43; *Archives* 41:318, 351; and "Letter from Mr. John Clayton," 18, 26, in *Tracts*, vol. 3, no. 12 (the earliest reference [1688] we have found to the use of blades for fodder). On the value of blades and tops, see Gray, *History of Agriculture* 1:200–201. The earliest reference to tops we have found is in 1696 in Deakins v. Ashforth: "to planting and plowing your cornfield and Cutting and housing your Corne and topps." Prince George's County Court Records A:70. On miring, see Testamentary Proceedings 13:114–15, 17:69; *Archives* 41:167, 175, 430; and York County DOW, 1657–62 (transcript), 34, microfilm. On wolves, see above, n. 14.

46. A law passed in 1642 required guardians to "deliver an exact account once everie year" to the county court, which was "required to keep an exact register thereof." Hening, *Statutes at Large* 1:261. In 1656, a second law required that guardians give orphans at age the exact number, kind, and age of cattle taken

into the guardian's custody to begin with, thereby removing the necessity for more than the first recording of the cattle, although the law of 1642 was not repealed until 1705. Ibid., 2:92–94, 3:371–76. In York County, the cattle accounts disappear in the early 1660s.

47. York County DOW, 1657–62 (transcript), 33, 65, 90, 132, 174, 180, and 1645–49 (transcript), 180–83, 400–403, microfilm; Lower Norfolk Deeds A:17–19, 53–57, B:139a–40, microfilm, Virginia State Library, Richmond. The survival calculations are available in Lois Green Carr, "Livestock Increase and Its Implications for Diet in the Seventeenth-Century Chesapeake," *St. Mary's City Research Series* (St. Mary's City, Md., forthcoming), obtainable from Historic St. Mary's City, St. Mary's City, MD, 20686. For sex ratios, see Ivar Johansson and Jan Rendel, *Genetics and Animal Breeding*, trans. Michael Taylor (1963; reprint, San Francisco, 1968), 58. We thank David O. Percy for this reference. Note that Sam B. Hilliard estimates a 50 percent survival rate for calves in the South in the middle decades of the nineteenth century. *Hogmeat and Hoecake: Food Supply in the Old South, 1840–1860* (Carbondale, Ill., 1972), 128.

48. For further discussion of these limits, see chap. 3, text near nn. 45–49.

49. G. E. Fussell, *The English Dairy Farmer, 1500–1900* (London, 1966), 56–57; Robert Trow-Smith, *A History of British Livestock Husbandry* (London, 1957), 238. Leonard Mascal, *The Government of Cattle, Divided into Three Books* ... (London, 1633), 53, suggests that cows could bear until fifteen years old, but cows this age are very rare in Chesapeake inventories, and Trow-Smith's and Fussell's studies of English records bear out the finding that ten to twelve years was the usual age at which cows became barren. Mascal also recommended that heifers not be put to the bull before they were three years old (ibid.), but among the range cattle of Chesapeake, it was doubtless not possible to exercise this control.

50. Glover, *An Account of Virginia*, 19; Shrigley, *True Relation of Virginia and Maryland*, 25, in *Tracts*, vol. 3, no. 7; Dankers and Sluyter, *Journal*, 217. Cattle care had not changed much in the South by the mid-nineteenth century and continued to evoke critical comment. Hilliard, *Hogmeat and Hoecake*, chap. 6.

51. For a comment on the ferocity of boars, see *Archives* 10:243–45, 258. Observers commented on the great numbers of swine, which found mast and other food in the woods. "Letter from Mr. John Clayton," 36, in *Tracts*, vol. 3, no. 12; *Perfect Description of Virginia*, 3, in *Tracts*, vol. 3, no. 8; John Lewger to Lord Baltimore, January 5, 1639, in *Calvert Papers, Number One*, 196; [Lewger and Hawley], *A Relation of Maryland*, in *Narratives of Early Maryland*, ed. Hall, 76; George Alsop, *A Character of the Province of Maryland* ... (London, 1666), in *Narratives of Early Maryland*, ed. Hall, 347.

52. Trow-Smith, *British Livestock Husbandry*, 126–28, 250–52; Gervase Markham, *Cheape and Good Husbandry* ... , 7th ed. (London, 1648), 128; Mascal, *Government of Cattle*, 256, 279. On survival in seventeenth-century Maryland and on hog production on the Cole plantation, see below, appendix 3, and Carr, "Livestock Increase."

53. Ages of cattle and hogs in inventories suggest these conclusions. Animals are very rarely identified as oxen, but the term *steer* may have covered animals trained to haul, and those over age six or seven may have been oxen. When plows began to appear at the end of the century, more steers must in fact have been oxen. On the appearance of plows, see Carr, "Diversification," in *Colonial Chesapeake Society*, ed. Carr, Morgan, and Russo, 353–54. On age at beefing, see Trow-Smith, *British Livestock Husbandry*, 238.

54. It has been estimated that today 5 acres of pinewoods in summer and 15 acres in winter will support one cow but that in deciduous forests, cows require more acreage in winter. Hilliard, *Hogmeat and Hoecake*, 176. Using these estimates, we conclude that the twelve cows and six full-grown steers that Cole had at his death required in winter all or more than the 270 acres he was not using. Supposing young cattle required half as much, the nineteen young cattle needed another 135 acres or more. Ungranted land was adjacent and available, and Cole's lease allowed him the use of it. But more than fifty head of cattle would have required considerably more land and would have driven cattle to range even farther for food. When Cole inventoried his cattle, two animals were at large on or near distant farms, and in 1664 Gardiner had a bull killed which had "got into the wild gange."

55. See appendix 3 and table 4.1.

56. Gray, *History of Agriculture* 1:191. A will of 1693 mentions the use of cuttings to start trees. St. Mary's County Wills PC#1:80.

57. Nurseries are not mentioned until later (see, for 1695, Inventories and Accounts 13b:70), but this seems the most efficient, least time-consuming method.

58. Beverley, *State of Virginia*, 314, reports that apple trees took about seven years to bear and peach trees three years.

59. See chap. 5, text near nn. 49–50.

60. See chap. 4, text before n. 3.

61. Cattle counts were compiled from Testamentary Proceedings, vols. 1–6. On average family size, see Carr, "Inheritance in the Colonial Chesapeake," table 4, in *Women in the Age of the American Revolution*, ed. Hoffman and Albert.

62. See Cole's will and the Cole Plantation Account in appendix 1 and see appendix 3, tables A3.2 and A3.3. The mean value of a cow with calf over the years 1668 to 1673 ranged from 550 to 750 pounds of tobacco. SMCC Price Files, Maryland State Archives.

63. The Reverend Mr. John Clayton commented in 1688 that Virginians "never shoe them [horses], nor stable them in general." "Letter from Mr. John Clayton," 35, in *Tracts*, vol. 3, no. 12.

64. In fact, genetically determined sex ratios for horses slightly favor females at 3.53 females for every 7 foals born. Johansson and Rendel, *Genetics and Animal Breeding*, 58.

65. An illustration of the value put on horses at this time is found in the will of Anne Davis in York County, Virginia, in February 1674. She gave her grandson cows and mares, with elaborate provisions for the disposal of the mares and their

increase should the grandson die before coming of age. These provisions resemble those made later for the distribution of slaves. York County DOW 5:66, microfilm.

66. "Letter from Mr. John Clayton," 15–25, esp. 23, in *Tracts*, vol. 3, no. 12; Glover, *An Account of Virginia*, 19; H. K. Roessingh, "Tobacco Growing in Holland in the Seventeenth and Eighteenth Centuries: A Case Study of the Innovative Spirit of Dutch Peasants," *Low Countries Year Book/Acta Historiae Neerlandicae* 11 (1978): 28–34.

67. Such land shortages did not begin to appear even in the tidewater until late in the eighteenth century, partly because of inheritance practices. See Carr, "Inheritance in the Colonial Chesapeake," in *Women in the Age of the American Revolution*, ed. Hoffman and Albert, 163, 166, and table 3.

See also the comments of Ester Boserup, *Population and Technological Change: A Study of Long-Term Trends* (Chicago, 1981), 134–37. European settlers in frontier countries, she argues, "abandoned labor-consuming practices like fertilization and protection against erosion. Instead, they shifted cultivation to new land when yields declined after a period of cultivation without protective methods. In other words, they shifted backward from a European-type short fallow or annual cropping to a modernized long-fallow system, a sort of bush fallow using European-type equipment. The settlers have been blamed for the devastating methods they used, which exhausted and eroded the land, but their output per man hour was higher than in Europe, where some labor went into soil protection" (p. 135).

It should be noted that in the Chesapeake, the hoes and shallow plows of the colonial period did not much erode the soil. It was the "improving" farmer who began deep plowing after the Revolution who did the damage. See Edward C. Papenfuse, *In Pursuit of Profit: The Annapolis Merchants in the Era of the American Revolution, 1763–1805* (Baltimore, 1975), 220–21; Henry M. Miller, "Transforming a 'Splendid and Delightsome Land': Colonists and Ecological Change in the Chesapeake 1607–1820," *Journal of the Washington Academy of Sciences* 76 (1986): 174–75.

68. From the 1720s, valuations of orphans' estates exist in abundance among the surviving eighteenth-century Maryland court records. The very earliest valuations (1698–1704) show concern about waste from overclearing. See Charles County Court and Land Records V#1:374–75; Prince George's County Judgments B:251, 279; Baltimore County Land Records HW#2:235; Anne Arundel County Judgments G:253; Kent County Marks of Cattell and Other Small Business GL#1:90.

Chapter 3

1. The best accounts of tobacco culture in the seventeenth century are in Thomas Glover, *An Account of Virginia, Its Situation, Temperature, Productions, In-*

habitants, and Their Manner of Planting and Ordering Tobacco, reprinted from the *Philosophical Transactions of the Royal Society,* June 20, 1676 (Oxford, 1904), 28–29; George Alsop, *A Character of the Province of Maryland ...* (London, 1666) in *Narratives of Early Maryland, 1633–1684,* ed. Clayton Colman Hall (1910; reprint, New York, 1967), 363; and John Banister's account, written about 1688, published in Joseph Ewan and Nesta Ewan, *John Banister and His Natural History of Virginia* (Urbana, Ill., 1970), 345, 360–61. However, these are far from complete. We have relied also on later accounts, as noted, taking care not to "read back" practices that we can identify as eighteenth-century innovations. Preparation of tobacco seedbeds could begin as early as mid-January in Virginia (*The Diary of Colonel Landon Carter of Sabine Hall, 1752–1778,* ed. Jack P. Greene [hereafter, *Carter Diary*], 2 vols. [Charlottesville, Va, 1965], 1:140, 200, 252, 333, 346, 357, 536), but the season in Maryland was a little later. A good short summary of seventeenth-century tobacco production is available in Gloria L. Main, *Tobacco Colony: Life in Early Maryland, 1650–1720* (Princeton, N.J., 1982), 31–36.

2. David O. Percy, *The Production of Tobacco along the Colonial Potomac,* National Colonial Farm Research Report no. 1 (Accokeek, Md., 1979), 15.

3. William Tatham, *An Historical and Practical Essay on the Culture and Commerce of Tobacco* (London, 1800), reprinted in facsimile in G. Melvin Herndon, *William Tatham and the Culture of Tobacco* (hereafter *Tatham*) (Coral Gables, Fla., 1969), 1–129; Curtis Carroll Davis, "'A National Property': Richard Claiborne's Tobacco Treatise for Poland" (hereafter "Claiborne"), *William and Mary Quarterly* (hereafter *WMQ*), 3d ser., 21 (1964): 93–117.

4. "Claiborne," 102–3; *Tatham,* 8–9; *Carter Diary* 1:140. Most time requirements for tobacco culture are from estimates for cultivating a crop of 9,000 tobacco hills by one man, estimates offered in a letter—from W. C. Nicholas of Albermarle to Mr. Rodman of North Carolina—sent to the Agricultural Society of Richmond and published in *Agricultural Museum* 2 (1811): 149. We thank David O. Percy, former Director, National Colonial Farm, for this reference. Nicholas offered nine days for preparing and seeding the tobacco beds, but he evidently meant to include the days needed to tend them until transplanting.

5. See Nicholas letter cited in n. 4; "A Letter from Mr. John Clayton, Rector of Crofton at Wakefield in Yorkshire, to the Royal Society, May 12, 1688," 18, in *Tracts and Other Papers, Relating Principally to the Origin, Settlement, and Progress of the Colonies in North America,* ed. Peter Force (hereafter *Tracts*), 4 vols. (Washington, D.C., 1836–47), vol. 3, no. 12; *Carter Diary* 1:160, 224–25, 415, 536. John Banister also comments on the fly at about the same time. Ewan and Ewan, *John Banister,* 345, 361. See below, table 3.1, for our estimate of the time required to care for the beds. We have supposed an average of .5 hours per day for covering and uncovering the beds, increasing to an average of 1 to 1.5 hours per day when watering and weeding were necessary. These estimates bring the total time spent on the beds to more than the 9 days suggested by Nicholas.

6. *Carter Diary* 1:158, 172, 260–61, 2:662, 1012.

7. See the discussion in chap. 2, text before n. 19, and annotation.

8. On varieties, see Robert Beverley, *The History and Present State of Virginia*, ed. Louis B. Wright (Chapel Hill, 1947), 143–44, 180, and Louise Larson, trans., "Peter Kalm's Description of Maize, How It Is Planted and Cultivated in North America, Together with the Many Uses of This Crop Plant," *Agricultural History* 9 (1935): 104. On hills per acre and stalks per hill, evidence is varied and mostly from the eighteenth century, when cornfields were often plowed before hilling. The only seventeenth-century reference is from Banister, who said, "We plant it [corn] in rows three or four grains in a hill about five or six foot distant" (Ewan and Ewan, *John Banister*, 358). According to the Swedish observer Kalm, who traveled in North America from 1748 through 1751, the large corn was planted in hills six to nine feet apart, or at 1,210 to 489 hills to the acre, with three or four stalks per hill; the smaller varieties were planted at half this distance. Or, if the field was fully plowed, the hills for large corn were four to six feet apart, or at 2,722 to 1,210 hills to the acre, and again half the distance apart for the small. He also noted that if the cornfields were tilled only with hoes, hills could be as close as three feet, but here he did not distinguish between the kinds of corn. Larson, "Peter Kalm's Description," 105. John Harrower in the early 1770s observed hills with three to four stalks at six feet apart, or at 1,210 hills per acre, but he mentioned that some planters used the distance of eight feet, or only 680 hills per acre. *The Journal of John Harrower: An Indentured Servant in the Colony of Virginia, 1773–1776*, ed. Edward M. Riley (Williamsburg, Va., 1963), 52–53, 93, 112. George Washington stated that hills six by six, with two stalks per hill, were a usual practice. *The Writings of George Washington from the Original Manuscript Sources 1745–1799*, ed. John C. Fitzpatrick, 39 vols. (Washington, D.C., 1931–44), 29:415. Landon Carter had an unusual method, planting his hills at two feet by seven, or at 3,111 hills per acre, but he described his neighbors as insisting on planting hills at six feet by five, or at 1,452 hills per acre. Carter kept only one stalk to a hill, whereas his neighbors kept two; hence Carter did not obtain higher yields per acre than they. He claimed he saved time in weeding. *Carter Diary* 2:678–80.

For the purposes of this analysis of the Cole plantation, we have selected 1,210 hills of large corn to the acre on the grounds that (1) if tobacco hills could be made at four feet apart, corn hills could be made at six, even when tree stumps were in the way; (2) a space of eight or nine feet was unnecessary if horse-drawn plows were not in use; and (3) 1,210 hills could produce three barrels per acre. A calculation derived from Landon Carter brings two and a half barrels per 1,000 hills, which is the equivalent of three barrels per acre. He estimated 800 ears of shelled corn to a barrel, which comes to two and a half ears per pint, and 800 grains per pint (his minimum estimate), which implies 320 grains per ear. Ibid., 1:296, 2:678–79. If Gardiner planted two stalks to a hill and got one ear to a stalk, he got 640 grains per hill and 640,000 grains per 1,000 hills, which comes to 800 pints and thus two and a half barrels per 1,000 hills. This is a minimum estimate, which implies a seed/yield ratio of 160 to 1, whereas the common estimate was 200 to 1. See Durand, of Dauphine, *A Huguenot Exile in Virginia*, ed. Gilbert Chinard (New York, 1934), 116, and Larson, "Peter Kalm's Description," 109. If there were two ears per stalk and/or if Gardiner planted hills more tightly, the yields would be higher. On the other hand, Carter states that two barrels per 1,000 hills was a "common" reckoning, and William Grove noted a yield of one to two barrels per 1,000. In addition, in very droughty years, the yield could be very small. Carter found in one bad year that his crop was cut nearly in half. *Carter Diary* 2:716, and "Travel Journal of William Grove," 33.

For a general discussion of eighteenth-century practices on a small plantation, see David O. Percy, *Corn: The Production of a Subsistence Crop on Colonial Potomac*, National Colonial Farm Research Report no. 2 (Accokeek, Md., 1977), and idem, "By the Sweat of Their Brows: Field Crop Labor in 18th-Century Southern Maryland" (Paper presented to the Washington Area Seminar in Early American History, April 28, 1982). Percy assumed 2,420 hills per acre, but he supposed these would yield twenty bushels per acre, an estimate based on the supposition that planters measured corn in ears rather than as shelled corn. He has since revised his estimate to forty bushels per acre. He has also found an error in his calculations for weeding time. When these discrepancies are accounted for, his estimates and ours are very close, with the exception of production per acre as opposed to production per 1,000 hills. We think his estimates for hills per acre too high for the seventeenth century, when manuring was not the practice. Gregory Stiverson also assumed that planters measured corn in ears, leading him to suppose that Maryland proprietary tenants of the eighteenth century consumed most of the corn they raised on fifteen acres. *Poverty in a Land of Plenty: Tenancy in Eighteenth-Century Maryland* (Baltimore, 1977), 95; Gregory A. Stiverson, "Early American Farming: A Comment," *Agricultural History* 50 (1976): 37–44. For a demonstration that corn measures were in shelled corn, see above, chap. 2 n. 17.

9. E. W., *Virginia, More Especially the South Part Thereof, Richly and Truely Valued* . . . (London, 1650), 12, in *Tracts*, vol. 3, no. 11.

10. On the time required for planting, see n. 14.

11. *Carter Diary* 2:688. Carter estimated 333 hills per day and thought it slow, but his land may have been plowed. The estimate in *Agricultural Museum* 2 (1811): 149, was twenty days for 9,000 hills, which would come to about 450 hills per day, or 1.33 hills per minute, but this undoubtedly assumed land already plowed. See below, text before n. 48.

12. In the eighteenth century, planters generally planted winter barley, a variety that did not require the best soil, in the fall. David O. Percy, *"English" Grains along the Colonial Potomac*, National Colonial Farm Research Report no. 3 (Accokeek, Md., 1977), 9–10. However, the varieties grown in England in the seventeenth century were planted in March, although a new, fast-ripening kind could be planted in May and still be harvested in July. Joan Thirsk, ed., *The Agrarian History of England and Wales, IV: 1500–1640* (Cambridge, 1967), 170.

We have found no seventeenth-century references to the timing of pruning orchards, but the English handbooks indicate early spring. See Gervase Markham, *The English Husbandman, Drawne into Two Bookes . . . The First Part* (London, 1635), 148–53, and John Worlidge, *Systema Agriculturae; or, The Mystery of Husbandry Discovered* (London, 1669), 132–33. Eighteenth-century diaries indicate January through March.

13. *Carter Diary* 1:216, 2:654. Carter thought corn should be planted, or at least that planting should begin, by April 10.

14. Ibid. 1:558, tells that six slaves planted 160,000 in five days in light land, or 26,666.67 per hand, and 5,333.33 per hand per day; in stiff land an unknown number of slaves planted less than 25,000 per hand in eight days, or 3,125 per hand per day. The question is whether Carter meant grains or hills. If grains, then at four grains per hill and 1,210 hills per acre, eight man-days are needed to plant nine acres in light land, but only two if hills are meant. We have assumed grains. On Cole's soils, see below, chap. 2 n. 28. Larson, "Peter Kalm's Description," 106–7, 115, speaks of the eighteenth-century scourge of crows and squirrels. On squirrels in the seventeenth century, note the report that they greatly reduced the Virginia corn crop after the severe winter of 1674–75. Thomas Holden to Joseph Williamson, Falmouth, May 3, 1675, SP 29/370, no. 88, Public Record Office, London. Maryland laws began to require Maryland courts to pay bounties for killing crows in 1704 and squirrels in 1710. William Hand Browne et al., eds., *Archives of Maryland* (hereafter *Archives*), 72 vols. (Baltimore, 1883–1972), 26:326–27, 29:341–42.

15. Larson, "Peter Kalm's Description," 107; Percy, *Corn*, 14–15; *Carter Diary* 1:415, 575. We have found only one seventeenth-century reference for corn cultivation, that of John Banister, writing about 1688. Ewan and Ewan, *John Banister*, 358. He spoke of two, instead of the three, weedings that eighteenth-century sources reveal. If planters weeded only twice, the second weeding was probably in late June. This would relieve the May schedule a little. John Winthrop, Jr., in Massachusetts also spoke of two weedings, but in a cooler climate with a shorter growing season. Fulmer Mood, "John Winthrop, Jr., on Indian Corn," *New England Quarterly* 10 (1937): 128. There are two eighteenth-century estimates for time needed for weeding corn. Carter twice mentioned about 700 hills per day (*Carter Diary* 1:577, 586), and Thomas Jefferson mentioned 500. Henry A. Wallace, "Thomas Jefferson's Farm Book: A Review Essay," *Agricultural History* 28 (1954): 134. We are indebted to David O. Percy for these references. Since Carter believed that his unique way of planting hills at seven by two made weeding faster, we have selected the 500-hill figure.

16. *Carter Diary* 1:160, 231–32, 268, 272, 415; *Tatham*, 121.

17. *Tatham*, 16, 122; Glover, *An Account of Virginia*, 28–29; Sir Dalby Thomas, *An Historical Account of the Rise and Growth of the West-India Collonies . . .* (London, 1690), quoted in Jerome E. Brooks, ed., *Tobacco: Its History Illustrated by the Books, Manuscripts, and Engravings in the Library of George Arents, Volume*

II, 1615–1698 (New York, 1938), 530–32; *Agricultural Museum* 2 (1811), 149.

18. *Archives* 10:27. The tobacco required three months of maturing before it could be cut. *Tatham,* 121.

19. *Carter Diary* 1:225, 399, 567, 575, 584, 586, 2:587; Larson, "Peter Kalm's Description," 107; Percy, *Corn,* 14–15. In some years, Carter's corn was not laid by until the end of July. *Carter Diary* 1:164, 2:1137. Percy discusses suckering and topping corn later in the season, adding an additional fifteen days of work for an eighteenth-century five-acre field, but suckering was extra care undertaken only if time permitted. Topping was probably not a practice in the 1660s. See above, chap. 2 n. 45.

20. On the barley harvest, see *Carter Diary* 2:756, 833, 1108; Percy, *"English" Grains,* 16. Since Cole's inventory shows no sickle for cutting barley, we must assume that Gardiner lent a tool for the purpose. This also suggests that the barley was one of Gardiner's innovations. On weeding and worming, topping, priming, and suckering tobacco, see *Tatham,* 17, 18 (quote), 19–22, 114–15, 122–24; "Claiborne," 103–4; Percy, *Production of Tobacco,* 22–26. *Agricultural Museum* 2 (1811): 149, gives the time necessary for these tasks as forty-four man-days for 9,000 plants. In the eighteenth century, slaves were taught diligence at these tasks by nasty methods, such as being forced to eat the worms they missed. John Brickell, *The Natural History of North Carolina . . .* (1737; reprint, Murfreesboro, N.C., 1968), 168; Frederick F. Siegal, *The Roots of Southern Distinctiveness: Tobacco and Society in Danville, Virginia, 1780–1865* (Chapel Hill, 1987), 98. When Knott or young Robert was in charge, this kind of discipline may have been lacking. On an eighteenth-century planter's comments on the need for heat, but not drought, see *Carter Diary* 1:164, 277, 278, 279, 449, 450.

21. *Archives* 1:97–98, 372, 446, 2:150, 215, 290, 336, 543, 10:112, 361, 380, 430, 438, 497, 510, 41:192, 280, 537, 541. John Banister about 1688 stated that sweet-scented tobacco was topped to six to eight leaves, oronoco to fourteen to sixteen leaves. Ewan and Ewan, *John Banister,* 360. By the late seventeenth century, Virginia planters who grew sweet-scented tobacco were beginning to market separately the less valuable underleaves, separating them from the better leaf and removing stems and damaged parts. Robert Carter Letterbook, 1723–28, entry for August 1, 1723, Alderman Library, University of Virginia. By the 1740s at least, some Maryland planters were doing the same, but it was not practice to stem oronoco leaf. With the damaged parts left in, such tobacco was worth little, and it was more usual practice among oronoco growers to discard it. Lorena S. Walsh, "'To Labour for Profit': Plantation Management in the Chesapeake, 1620–1920" (unpublished manuscripts), chap. 3.

22. *Tatham,* 23, 24 (quote), 124–25.

23. Ibid., 23–27, 115, 124–26; Glover, *An Account of Virginia,* 28–29 (quote); Alsop, *Province of Maryland,* in *Narratives of Early Maryland,* ed. Hall, 363; *Archives* 49:304–5 (on pegging); "Claiborne," 105–6. On a Virginia plantation in 1770, cutting began September 6 and was not quite finished on October 11. *Carter Diary* 1:481, 511.

24. Ewan and Ewan, *John Banister*, xviii–xxii, 360 (quote); *Archives* 4:455–56, 10:561, 41:330; Charles County Court and Land Records H#1:70, 259. "Thomas Allcocke was gone about a weeke or near a fortnight to get seidge to cover ye tobaccoe houses." On tobacco houses in Holland, see H. K. Roessingh, "Tobacco Growing in Holland in the Seventeenth and Eighteenth Centuries: A Case Study of the Innovative Spirit of Dutch Peasants," *Low Countries Year Book/ Acta Historiae Neerlandicae* 11 (1978): 32. On Dutch merchants, see Philip Alexander Bruce, *Economic History of Virginia in the Seventeenth Century*, 2 vols. (1895; reprint, New York, 1935), 1:351–59. For tobacco houses of the 1770s in Virginia, see *Tatham*, 30–32.

25. *Agricultural Museum* 2 (1911): 149; *Archives* 1:245.

26. Glover, *An Account of Virginia*, 28–29; Thomas, *An Historical Account*, in *Tobacco: Its History*, ed. Brooks, 530–32; *Tatham*, 22–23, 36–37, 115; *Carter Diary* 1:177–78. There is a reference to "house burnt" tobacco in 1642, *Archives* 1:98, suggesting that fires were used to dry the crop.

27. *Archives* 1:98, 10:140, 531, 41:153–55, 166–67, 54:221, 237; *Tatham*, 37–39 (quote), 126–28; *Carter Diary* 1:177–78.

28. T. H. Breen, *Tobacco Culture: The Mentality of the Great Planters on the Eve of Revolution* (Princeton, N.J., 1985), 40–83, emphasizes the skill and judgment required to make a good crop.

29. On bulk shipment, see Arthur P. Middleton, *Tobacco Coast: A Maritime History of the Chesapeake Bay in the Colonial Era* (Newport News, Va., 1953), 132–34; *Archives* 4:359, 10:152. On regulation of hogshead size, see *Archives* 1:371, 537, 2:150, 215, 290, 336, 412, 465, 529; William Waller Hening, ed., *The Statutes at Large, Being a Collection of the Laws of Virginia from the First Session of the Legislature in 1619*, 12 vols. (Richmond, Va., 1809–23), 1:456, 3:51–53, 435–40. On hogshead weights and tobacco freight rates, see Russell R. Menard, "Economy and Society in Early Colonial Maryland" (Ph.D. diss., University of Iowa, 1975), appendix, tables 10, 11; idem, "The Tobacco Industry in the Chesapeake Colonies, 1617–1730: An Interpretation," *Research in Economic History* 5 (1980): figure 9.

30. On "foot packt" hogshead weights, see *Carter Diary* 1:515–16; Inventories 6:223. Unless otherwise indicated, all manuscripts cited are at the Maryland State Archives, Annapolis, Maryland. Literary evidence and hogshead weights suggest that prizes were appearing in Virginia in the 1690s and in Maryland two decades later. Evidently advances made in packing also enabled the tobacco to keep better for longer. When shipping schedules shifted later in the eighteenth century, tobacco no longer deteriorated much when kept around for a year or two. See Walsh, "'To Labour for Profit,'" chaps. 3, 4.

31. *Tatham*, 38–42, 116; *Carter Diary* 1:347; *Agricultural Museum* 2 (1811): 149; Percy, *Production of Tobacco*, 38. Planters could not afford to risk poor cask, and even very poor planters paid a cooper to make the hogsheads. See, for example, the deathbed letter of Walter Gifford to his mate in 1675, quoted in Lois Green Carr and Russell R. Menard, "Immigration and Opportunity: The Freed-

man in Early Colonial Maryland," in Thad W. Tate and David L. Ammerman, eds., *The Chesapeake in the Seventeenth Century: Essays on Anglo-American Society and Politics* (Chapel Hill, 1979), 232.

32. *Archives* 10:278; Gloria L. Main, *Tobacco Colony: Life in Early Maryland, 1650–1720* (Princeton, N.J., 1982), 37.

33. On corn, see Larson, "Peter Kalm's Description," 108–11, and *Carter Diary* 2:638–39. Carter estimated that ten hands gathered and stored 100 barrels in four days. The question is whether in this context his barrels referred to shelled corn or corn in ears. If shelled, then at Carter's estimate of 800 ears of shelled corn to a barrel (*Carter Diary* 2:679), each hand gathered 2,000 ears, which on the Cole plantation would have come from 1,000 hills, or nearly an acre, supposing 2 plants to a hill and 1 ear to a plant. Four hands would take a bit less than 3 full days to gather Cole's corn. If the measure is for ears, the four hands took about 5.5 days. This is the measure selected for table 3.1. We have not found references to corn cribs in the seventeenth-century records, but we have a few references to lofting corn and a reference to a "corn house." *Archives* 4:350, 10:17, 73, 60:252–53. Cole mentioned lofts in his inventory but no outbuilding for corn. On barley, see *Carter Diary* 1:469, 2:613, 625, and Percy, *"English" Grains*, 20. On cider making and meat preserving, see chap. 3, text between n. 53 and n. 58. On transplanting fruit trees in the fall in England, see Worlidge, *Systema*, 130–31.

34. See chap. 2, text near n. 20, and annotation.

35. Laws requiring fencing were passed in 1640, 1654, and 1662. By 1662 a fence around a cornfield had to be five feet high. This law was revived continuously until 1692, when a similar law was passed. Such laws were still in effect when Thomas Bacon published his compendium in 1765. *Archives* 1:96, 344, 413–14, 537, 2:150, 215, 290, 336, 412, 464, 555, 7:82, 214, 245, 314, 327, 400, 435, 13:123, 139, 211, 474; Thomas Bacon, ed., *The Laws of Maryland at Large, with Proper Indexes . . .* (Annapolis, Md., 1765).

36. Markham, *The English Husbandman*, 197–200; idem, *The Second Booke of the English Husbandman, Conteyning the Ordering of the Kitchin Garden . . .* (London, 1635), 5; *Archives* 10:157; Richard B. Davis, ed., *William Fitzhugh and His Chesapeake World* (Chapel Hill, 1963), 175–76.

37. *Tatham*, 11n.

38. Edmund Berkeley and Dorothy S. Berkeley, eds., "Another 'Account of Virginia' by the Reverend John Clayton," *Virginia Magazine of History and Biography* (hereafter *VMHB*), 76 (1968): 425–26; *Archives* 41:27, 65:254; Charles County Court and Land Records L#1:361. We have found one seventeenth-century record of a post-and-rail fence. Westmoreland County Wills, Deeds, Patents, 1653–59, p. 31, microfilm, Virginia State Library, Richmond. By mid-eighteenth century, Landon Carter was considering post and rail after a great March wind blew down much of his fencing. *Carter Diary* 1:151.

39. The calculation for the field crops supposes 522 panels of seven nine-foot rails each, assuming that two panels set at an angle covered 15 feet. If the worm

fence was staked, as described in *Tatham*, 10–11, and as shown in the photograph, 1,044 stakes five to six feet long were also needed. The assumption of planting fruit trees at 25 feet distance is based on data in chap. 2 n. 15, and on calculations made from various eighteenth-century Orphans' Court valuations that show the number of trees and fence panels, assuming, as above, that two nine-foot panels set at an angle take up 15 feet of circumference. See, for example, Prince George's County Deeds T:517, and Somerset County Deeds, 1711–13, p. 143, 1713–17, p. 122, 1730–35, p. 98. Of course, the farther apart the trees, the more fencing is required.

40. Berkeley and Berkeley, "Another 'Account of Virginia,'" 426.

41. Just preparing the rails may sometimes have required as much as eleven to twelve man-days. In 1669, one Simon Serrell was paid 1,000 pounds of tobacco for "cutting and nailing two thousand good sufficient fencing loggs." *Archives* 65:254. Allowing a day's work at 30 pounds of tobacco a day (an upper bound), this man produced 60 rails per day. However, he was working slowly. How fast a man can produce rails depends on the kind of wood and whether it has grown on well-drained ridges or in wetter land. Chestnut, for example, can be rived very quickly, and trees grown on ridges are less resilient and hence easier to rive than those grown on less well-drained soils. Cole's land was level, not hilly, and he probably had no chestnuts.

42. Charles County Court and Land Records H#1:71–72.

43. On the laws, see n. 35. For examples of broken fences, see n. 42 and *Archives* 10:459, 460, 53:634; Charles County Court and Land Records E#1:31; Westmoreland County Deeds, Patents, Wills, 1665–77, p. 167, microfilm, Virginia State Library, Richmond.

44. Alsop, *Province of Maryland*, in *Narratives of Early Maryland*, ed. Hall, 357; John Hammond, *Leah and Rachel; or, The Two Fruitful Sisters, Virginia and Maryland* . . . (London, 1656), 12, in *Tracts*, vol. 3, no. 14. Experiments at the National Colonial Farm, Accokeek, Maryland, show that thirty cords of wood per year were needed for a cooking hearth, less for hearths not used year round. Thirty cords could be got from land cleared each year. Personal communication from David O. Percy, former Director.

45. On the English calendar and diverse activities, see Gervase Markham, *Markham's Farewel to Husbandry* . . . (London, 1676), 121–26; Thirsk, *IV: 1500–1640*, 430–31.

46. Peter Kalm noted that short corn hills could be half the distance required by the large varieties of corn. Larson, "Peter Kalm's Description," 105. If seventeenth-century planters weeded only twice, this additional crop could be more easily managed.

47. Some export of corn can be inferred from proclamations and laws forbidding it. *Archives* 1:96, 161, 2:561, 3:194, 293, 443, 15:44, 194, 17:48, 179–80, 269–70.

48. Banister indicated that as early as the 1680s, a few planters were beginning to hasten the weeding of corn with horse-drawn hoe-harrows, but he does not

mention plows. Inventories indicate that harrows of any consequence were infrequent, and crude brush harrows that might have escaped appraisal would have been ineffective in heavy weeds. However, Banister asserted that "a man & boy & one horse will go over as much ground a day as 8 or 10 hands are able to strike out." Ewan and Ewan, *John Banister*, 358. This suggests that eighteenth-century planters who used plows to hasten weeding saved a lot of time.

49. On eighteenth-century diversification, see Carville V. Earle, *The Evolution of a Tidewater Settlement System: All Hallow's Parish, Maryland, 1650–1783*, University of Chicago Department of Geography Research Paper no. 170 (Chicago, 1975), 128–30; Paul G. E. Clemens, *The Atlantic Economy and Colonial Maryland's Eastern Shore: From Tobacco to Grain* (Ithaca, N.Y., 1980), 168–205; and Lois Green Carr, "Economic Diversification in the Colonial Chesapeake: Somerset County, Maryland, in Comparative Perspective," in *Colonial Chesapeake Society*, ed. Lois Green Carr, Philip D. Morgan, and Jean B. Russo (Chapel Hill, 1988), 342–82. On changes in husbandry, see Walsh, " 'To Labour for Profit,' " chaps. 4–5, and Lois Green Carr and Russell R. Menard, "Land, Labor, and Economies of Scale in Early Maryland: Some Limits to Growth in the Chesapeake System of Husbandry," *Journal of Economic History* 49 (1989): 407–18.

50. Carr and Menard, "Land, Labor, and Economies of Scale." Probate inventories for several Chesapeake regions show that less than half—in some areas less than a quarter—of the eighteenth-century planters worth less than £50 had surplus corn, whereas by the 1770s, 70 to 95 percent of richer planters did so. The proportion of poor planters who showed wheat was much smaller, usually under 10 percent, except on the upper Eastern Shore.

51. The adult male ration is 4.57 cups per day, based on the ration of one peck per week discussed in chap. 2 n. 17. At Colonial Williamsburg a researcher found that she took fifteen minutes to grind a cup. Personal communication from Patricia Gibbs. Harriet Stout, formerly an interpreter at Historic St. Mary's City, has reported that she could do the work somewhat faster. We have estimated ten minutes per cup. For the ration for women and children, see Appendix 2, table A2.4.

52. On washing, see Main, *Tobacco Colony*, 185. On "pickeing" for the twins, see Lorena S. Walsh, "Charles County, Maryland, 1658–1705: A Study of Chesapeake Social and Political Structure" (Ph.D. diss., Michigan State University, 1977), 108.

53. Anthony Fitzherbert, *The Boke of Husbandry* (London, 1534), 60b–61. There was much greater emphasis on scrubbing floors, woodwork, and utensils in Holland. See Simon Schama, *The Embarrassment of Riches: An Interpretation of Dutch Culture in the Golden Age* (New York, 1987), 375–97.

54. The very earliest accounts speak of wild strawberries and raspberries. See, for example, [John Lewger and Jerome Hawley], *A Relation of Maryland . . .* (London, 1635), in *Narratives of Early Maryland*, ed. Hall, 80, which speaks of strawberries in April and raspberries in June. However, May is more likely for strawberries. See *Archives* 10:508. What kinds of fruit trees Cole had is unknown.

The account mentions only cider but shows a "mobby tub." Beverley says peaches make mobby. *State of Virginia*, 315. Glover, *An Account of Virginia*, 13–14, mentioned a variety of apples: "Pear-mains, Pippins, Russetens, Costards, Marigolds, Kings-apples, Magitens, Batchelours, and many others." English experts considered pearmains, pippins, and russets especially good for eating, and the last two kept well. The russets ripened late. Worlidge, *Systema*, 140; J. Mortimer, *The Whole Art of Husbandry; or, The Way of Managing and Improving of Land* (London, 1708), 534, 535, 575; Simon Hayward, *A Most Profitable New Treatise from Approved Experience, of the Art of Propagating Plants*, 115–16, printed with William Lawson, *A New Orchard and Garden . . .* (London, 1618). In Somerset County, Maryland, in 1666, a planter ordered in his will that two hundred trees be planted, half in winter fruit and half in summer fruit. Wills 1:283. In 1711, two Charles County planters leased land with instructions for planting twenty winter apple trees and twenty summer apple trees, but several other leases of the same period specified only winter apples. Charles County Court and Land Records C#2:226, 229, 248, H#2:324, 427; Provincial Court Deeds TD#4:309–12. Richard Surflet, *Maison Rustiques or the Countrie Ferme . . .* (London, 1616), 16, mentioned dried fruits, but we have found no Chesapeake references.

55. The time for preserving meat in any quantity is inferred from English practice and the overall labor demands on planters at other times of year. Markham, *Farewel to Husbandry*, 124–26. Recent historians of English husbandry note that there was no evidence in early modern England of massive fall slaughters and that livestock might have been fattened and killed at various times of the year. Robert Trow-Smith, *A History of British Livestock Husbandry* (London, 1957), 129; B. H. Slicher Von Bath, *The Agrarian History of Western Europe, A.D. 500–1850* (New York, 1963), 182. However, eighteenth-century farm diaries show fall slaughter of hogs and of cattle designed for beef to be a standard practice. Walsh, "'To Labour for Profit,'" chaps. 4, 6. Range-fed cattle were too scrawny to slaughter after early January, and meat from large animals would not keep in summer. Young stock, unless too weak to prosper, was too valuable to kill. Hogs were most efficiently fattened on new corn, available in the fall, including nubbins and soft corn that would not keep. On times for calving and dairying, see *Archives* 4:335, 429, 507, 536, 41:205, 281, 252–53, 335, 53:495; Testamentary Proceedings 5:371. The timing of calf births can to some degree be inferred from the York County guardian accounts in York County Deeds, Orders, and Wills, 1657–62 (transcript), 34, 65, 90, 132, 174, microfilm, Virginia State Library, Richmond.

56. *Archives* 60:231–32.

57. Worlidge, *Systema*, 139–40; Mortimer, *Whole Art of Husbandry*, 577–86 (quotation at 585–86).

58. David O. Percy, *Of Fast Horses, Black Cattle, Woods Hogs, and Rat-Tailed Sheep: Animal Husbandry along the Colonial Potomac*, National Colonial Farm Research Report no. 4 (Accokeek, Md., 1979), 27–28, 49–51, gives more detail

on methods of slaughter and preservation. See also Sam B. Hilliard, *Hogmeat and Hoecake: Food Supply in the Old South, 1840–1860* (Carbondale, Ill., 1972), 43. The Coles may have used a great deal of milk, if available, in the summer, when hot weather made the slaughter of large animals less practical. See the comments of Robert Carter to Benjamin Grayson, July 3, 1731, Letterbook, 1728–31, Alderman Library, University of Virginia. "They [some complaining English miners] have plenty of milk now, & if they had nothing else to live uppon, Good Milk & Honey & milk & mush might very well content them in these Summer months. How many hundred Families in Virginia better men than ever these Fellows will be & work a great deal harder, have no meat at this Time of ye year."

59. Gervase Markham, *The English Housewife, Containing the Inward and Outward Virtues Which Ought to Be in a Complete Woman . . .* , ed. Michael R. Best (Montreal, 1986), 170.

60. Ibid., 143–48; G. E. Fussell, *The English Dairy Farmer, 1500–1900* (London, 1986), 160–65, 204–5; Joan M. Jensen, "Churns and Buttermaking in the Mid-Atlantic Farm Economy, 1750–1850," *Working Papers from the Economic History Research Center* 5, nos. 2 and 3 (1982): 70–72. Churns were tapered wooden casks with plungers for agitating the cream. Jensen suggests that most early churns were only about eighteen inches high and could hold no more than a gallon of cream, which could make about three pounds of butter. However, early pictures of people churning suggest somewhat larger churns. See, for example, Markham, *English Housewife*, 171, and M. E. Seebohm, *The Evolution of the English Farm*, rev. 2d ed. (London, 1952), 186 (figure 54).

61. Trow-Smith, *British Livestock Husbandry*, 119; Markham, *English Housewife*, 141; Mortimer, *Whole Art of Husbandry*, 167. See also n. 62, below.

62. Butter making estimates are hampered by lack of information about what milk production was per day and how long cows remained in milk. What little information we have from the Chesapeake area is from a later period. Richard Parkinson, *A Tour in America in 1798, 1799, and 1800*, 2 vols. (London, 1805), 284–92, comments that even by the late eighteenth century, a milk yield as low as a quart per cow per day was common. Indirect evidence for yields comes from George Washington. He spoke of cows in milk for seven months. His cows produced 5 pounds of butter per month, but how many gallons of milk were represented is unknown. James T. Lemon, "Household Consumption in Eighteenth-Century America and Its Relationship to Production and Trade: The Situation among Farmers in Southeastern Pennsylvania," *Agricultural History* 41 (1967): 63. George Fussell, using early modern English accounts to estimate milk/cream/butter ratios, found that 6 gallons of milk made a gallon of cream, which made 3.2 pounds of butter. By this measure George Washington's cows produced only 1.25 pints of milk per milking, or 1.5 quarts per day. At 2 pounds of butter per gallon of cream—the cream/butter ratio a modern dairymaid reportedly achieved with a churn—the cow produced 1 quart per milking. Fussell, *English Dairy Farmer*, 208; Jensen, "Churns and Buttermaking," 72. Note that George Washington's 35 pounds of butter per cow per year is the same as found for Virginia in

1850 by dividing the pounds of butter produced by the number of cows enumerated, as shown in the census of that year. Hilliard, *Hogmeat and Hoecake*, table 9.

63. Markham, *English Housewife*, 148. As late as 1945, Fannie Merritt Farmer, *The Boston Cooking-School Cook Book*, 7th ed. (New York, 1945), 136, described a similar procedure.

Chapter 4

1. Again, unless otherwise noted, values reported in this book are in local currency adjusted to constant values by a commodity price index. For the figure £54, see chap. 1 n. 71.

2. For the timing of cycles in the tobacco trade, see Russell R. Menard, "The Tobacco Industry in the Chesapeake Colonies, 1617–1730: An Interpretation," *Research in Economic History* 5 (1980): 128–42. In the Cole plantation accounts, income and expenditures for the years 1671 and 1672 are lumped together. We assumed that equal amounts of tobacco were earned and spent in the two years. Differences between those years reported in tables 4.1 through 4.5 therefore reflect only changes in the price of tobacco and the commodity price index as reported in chap. 1 n. 55.

3. The relationships between shifting fortunes in the tobacco industry and other sectors of the economy are described in Menard, "Tobacco Industry," 123–28. Formal statistical tests of the argument advanced in this paragraph are reported in Russell R. Menard, Lois Green Carr, and Lorena S. Walsh, "A Small Planter's Profits: The Cole Estate and the Growth of the Early Chesapeake Economy," *William and Mary Quarterly* (hereafter *WMQ*), 3d ser., 40 (1983): 182n–83n.

4. For the proportions allowed for women and children, see Appendix 2, table A2.4. Although housing could be considered part of farm capital, shelter has a cost, and the use of that housing needs to be part of subsistence income. Our data, in any case, do not separate the cost of room from that of food, washing, and other services. For examples of contracts for room and board, see Charles County Court and Land Records R#1:125, 156, 181, Maryland State Archives, Annapolis, Maryland. Unless otherwise indicated, all manuscripts cited are at the Maryland State Archives. For useful discussions of plantation self-sufficiency, see Carville V. Earle, *The Evolution of a Tidewater Settlement System: All Hallow's Parish, Maryland, 1650–1783* (Chicago, 1975), 101–42, and Gloria L. Main, *Tobacco Colony: Life in Early Maryland, 1650–1720* (Princeton, N.J., 1982), 48–96.

5. Menard, Carr, and Walsh, "A Small Planter's Profits," 186n–87n, offers a statistical assessment of the arguments advanced in this paragraph.

6. The literature on export-led growth in early America is surveyed in John J. McCusker and Russell R. Menard, *The Economy of British America, 1607–1789* (Chapel Hill, 1985), 17–32.

7. Adam Smith, *An Inquiry into the Nature and Causes of the Wealth of*

Nations, ed. Edwin Cannan (New York, 1937), 532. Smith's book was originally published in 1776. Edmund S. Morgan argues that taxes in seventeenth-century Virginia were very high and a major source of popular discontent. *American Slavery, American Freedom: The Ordeal of Colonial Virginia* (New York, 1975), 209, 246–47, 345–46.

8. The evidence permits an estimate of the internal rate of return, a more formal measure of performance, which was roughly 15 percent per year under a conservative set of assumptions. For details of the calculations, see Menard, Carr, and Walsh, "A Small Planter's Profits," 190. The rate of return shown in this article was higher than we show here because of some undetected errors in our tables. For the land patented for Cole's sons, see Patents 11:141, 12:134, WC#2:127–28, B#23:285–88.

9. See, for example, Morgan, *American Slavery, American Freedom,* 180–95. For a contrary view, note Wesley Frank Craven's suggestion that historians "have drawn a darker picture of economic conditions in Virginia through the third quarter of the century than is warranted." *White, Red, and Black: The Seventeenth-Century Virginian* (Charlottesville, Va., 1971), 21.

10. Russell R. Menard, "Comment on Paper by Ball and Walton," *Journal of Economic History* (hereafter *JEH*) 36 (1976): 124–25; Russell R. Menard, P.M.G. Harris, and Lois Green Carr, "Opportunity and Inequality: The Distribution of Wealth on the Lower Western Shore of Maryland, 1658–1705," *Maryland Historical Magazine* 69 (1974): 169–83; P.M.G. Harris, "Integrating Interpretations of Local and Regionwide Change in the Study of Economic Development and Demographic Growth in the Colonial Chesapeake, 1630–1775," Regional Economic History Research Center, *Working Papers* 1 (1978): 35–72; Terry L. Anderson, "Wealth Estimates for the New England Colonies, 1650–1709," *Explorations in Economic History* 12 (1975): 151–76; McCusker and Menard, *Economy of British America,* 267–68.

11. Percy Wells Bidwell and John I. Falconer, *History of Agriculture in the Northern United States, 1620–1860* (Washington, D.C., 1925), 82. Aubrey C. Land emphasizes the importance of this process in capital formation along the bay in "Economic Behavior in a Planting Society: The Eighteenth-Century Chesapeake," *JEH* 33 (1967): 469–85.

12. There are several ways of calculating the rate of savings, but they all point to the same conclusion. A comparison of the total increase in estate value (£150.36) with net income from subsistence and the market plus that increase (£401.27) yields an investment-to-income ratio of 37.5 percent. Alternatively, one could measure the savings rate as the ratio of income devoted to maintaining the work force and plantation to total income, or as the ratio of income devoted to maintaining the operation plus the increase in estate value to total income plus that increase. Such measures also describe a high savings rate.

13. Ester Boserup's discussion of agricultural investment is helpful here. *The Conditions of Agricultural Growth: The Economics of Agrarian Change under Population Pressure* (London, 1965), esp. p. 88.

14. Menard, Carr, and Walsh, "A Small Planter's Profits," 195n, provides a more detailed discussion of wealth-to-income ratios. For the pattern of growth in Chesapeake wealth levels after 1680, see n. 10, above; Allan Kulikoff, "The Economic Growth of the Eighteenth-Century Chesapeake Colonies," *JEH* 39 (1979): 275–88; and Paul G. E. Clemens, *The Atlantic Economy and Colonial Maryland's Eastern Shore: From Tobacco to Grain* (Ithaca, N.Y., 1980), 228–32. Harris, "Integrating Interpretations," 35–72, emphasizes local variations of timing in growth.

15. The argument in this paragraph is elaborated in Lois Green Carr and Russell R. Menard, "Land, Labor, and Economies of Scale in Early Maryland: Some Limits to Growth in the Chesapeake System of Husbandry," *JEH* 49 (1989): 407–18. There is a useful discussion of the size and characteristics of "quarters" in Main, *Tobacco Colony*, 128–35.

16. Cary Carson et al., "Impermanent Architecture in the Southern American Colonies," *Winterthur Portfolio* 16 (1981): 135–96. Except as noted, what follows here on housing is based on this study.

17. Jasper Dankers and Peter Sluyter, *Journal of a Voyage to New York and a Tour in Several of the American Colonies in 1679–80 . . .* , trans. Henry C. Murphy (Brooklyn, N.Y., 1867), 173, 207. Reconstructions at Historic St. Mary's City have proved the vulnerability of clapboard-roofed houses to leaks and the difficulty of sealing them.

18. Testamentary Proceedings 5:152–90; Inventories and Accounts 24:147–50. Main, *Tobacco Colony*, chap. 4, provides an excellent description of housing arrangements. For more details on seventeenth-century Chesapeake house construction, see the reference in n. 16, above.

19. William Fitzhugh to Nicholas Hayward, January 30, 1687, in *William Fitzhugh and His Chesapeake World, 1676–1701: The Fitzhugh Letters and Other Documents*, ed. Richard Beale Davis (Chapel Hill, 1963), 202–3.

20. "Holly Hill" in Anne Arundel County. A second seventeenth-century structure is the Third Haven Meeting House in Easton, Maryland, built in 1683.

21. James P. P. Horn, "Adapting to a New World: A Comparative Study of Local Society in England and Maryland, 1650–1700," in *Colonial Chesapeake Society*, ed. Lois Green Carr, Philip D. Morgan, and Jean B. Russo (Chapel Hill, 1988), 152–54; William Hand Browne et al., eds., *Archives of Maryland* (hereafter *Archives*), 72 vols. (Baltimore, 1883–1972), 5:266 (quote). Slye's inventory was not appraised, but it is apparent that he was exceptionally rich. He had eleven servants and fourteen slaves. Testamentary Proceedings 5:152–90.

22. Andrew B. Appleby, "Grain Prices and Subsistence Crises in England and France, 1590–1740," *JEH* 39 (1979): 865–87.

23. On the preparation of corn, see text before n. 27. For proclamations regarding corn exports, see chap. 3 n. 47.

24. See appendix 3 and tables A3.6 and A3.7. The discussion in Main, *Tobacco Colony*, 202–4, implies less meat per person. However, her first example is from the Cole account and does not consider likely slaughters made during the first

year but only the meat on hand at Cole's departure. Her third example would supply more than the amounts shown here had she given the adult woman a three-quarter ration. Her second example does not give sufficient information about the ages of the people fed to make a comparison. See also an overseer's agreement of 1691, which gave a man and his wife 400 pounds of meat per year, and an elderly couple's lease, which required a yearly food maintenance (among other payments) that included 400 pounds of meat for the two of them. Provincial Court Deeds WRC#1:567–68; Charles County Court and Land Records I#1:35–36.

25. Henry M. Miller, "An Archaeological Perspective on the Evolution of Diet in the Colonial Chesapeake, 1620–1745," in *Colonial Chesapeake Society*, ed. Carr, Morgan, and Russo, 176–99.

26. See chap. 3, text between n. 53 and n. 63, for dairying, orchard, garden, and wild berries. Early observers mentioned the purslanes and other wild greens. See, for example, [John Lewger and Jerome Hawley], *A Relation of Maryland . . .* , in *Narratives of Early Maryland, 1633–1684*, ed. Clayton Colman Hall (1910; reprint, New York, 1967), 80; Father Andrew White, "A Briefe Relation of the Voyage unto Maryland," in ibid., 40; and Thomas Glover, *An Account of Virginia, Its Situation, Temperature, Productions, Inhabitants, and Their Manner of Planting and Ordering Tobacco*, reprinted from the *Philosophical Transactions of the Royal Society*, June 20, 1676 (Oxford, 1904), 16. On the reaction to peas at a later period, see *The Journal of John Harrower: An Indentured Servant in the Colony of Virginia, 1773–1776*, ed. Edward M. Riley (Williamsburg, Va., 1963), 68: "Extream good green Pease they being the second croap this season."

27. Dankers and Sluyter, *Journal*, 217; "Narrative of a Voyage to Maryland," *American Historical Review* 12 (1907): 335–36; *The Voyages and Travels of Captain Nathaniel Uring*, ed. Alfred Dewar (London, 1928), 12–13. We are indebted to Patricia Gibbs, Colonial Williamsburg Foundation, Inc., for the last reference. See also Main, *Tobacco Colony*, 192–93, 196. On grinding corn, see chap. 3, text before n. 51.

28. Father Andrew White called spring water "our best drinke," but George Thorpe, commenting on death in early Virginia, wrote that "more do die here of the disease of their minds than of theire body by haveing this country victuall over-promised vnto them in England & by not knowinge they shall drinke water here." "Briefe Relation," in *Narratives of Early Maryland*, ed. Hall, 45; Susan M. Kingsbury, ed., *The Records of the Virginia Company of London* (Washington, D.C., 1933), 3:417–18. Archaeologists have found that early settlers in Virginia dug wells, whereas in Maryland, settlers depended on springs. Personal communication from Henry M. Miller, Chief Archaeologist and Director of Research, Historic St. Mary's City.

29. J. Mortimer, *The Whole Art of Husbandry; or, The Way of Managing and Improving of Land* (London, 1708), 582; *The Calvert Papers, Number One*, Maryland Historical Society, Fund Publication no. 28 (Baltimore, 1889), 263; Dankers and Sluyter, *Journal*, 218. As late as 1732, William Grove commented that "They

have good Cyder but never keep it, but drink by pailfulls never Workt," although he on occasion met planters who successfully preserved it. One of these, "Colonel Custis," attributed the difficulties to improper storage. Gregory A. Stiverson and Patrick H. Butler III, eds., "Virginia in 1732: The Travel Journal of William Hugh Grove," *Virginia Magazine of History and Biography* 85 (1977): 30.

30. Miller, "Evolution of Diet," in *Colonial Chesapeake Society*, ed. Carr, Morgan, and Russo, 176–99. Main, *Tobacco Colony*, 195–206, 208–11, has an excellent discussion of diet at various social levels, but see comments above, n. 24. Miller finds that better-off planters were more likely than others to eat deer. On heights and nutrition, see Robert W. Fogel et al., "Secular Changes in American and British Stature and Nutrition," *Journal of Interdisciplinary History* 14 (1983): 445–81, and Kenneth L. Sokoloff and Georgia C. Villaflor, "The Early Achievement of Modern Stature in America," *Social Science History* 6 (1982): 453–81. Of course, a diet too dependent on maize brings pellagra, a miserable skin and gastrointestinal disease that may have been appearing in people that the records show being treated for scurvy or yaws. See Main, *Tobacco Colony*, 202. No one in the Cole household was treated for such symptoms.

31. St. Mary's County Inventory File, St. Mary's City Commission, Maryland State Archives.

32. The inventory of William Eltonhead, Esq., who had an estate of £209, nearly all in land, appears to omit furnishings that belonged to his stepson, and hence this inventory is excluded from this analysis.

33. Nine of the thirty-two householders had consumer assets in this range, which represents a modal value among the inventoried estates. In two estates, the household goods were not sufficiently distinguished to be included in this analysis. These nine modal estates ranged in total value from £125 to £41. Only four of the twenty-two householders not part of the top ten had consumer assets worth more than the modal values.

34. When these items are removed, Cole's "other" category drops to £10.16, more in line with the others of his wealth. He also drops in wealth rank from number 7 to number 8. In his inventory, Cole specifically stated that he had left cloth sufficient to clothe his children until Christmas. He probably expected to return in the December shipping. The category "other" usually consists mostly of guns, gunpowder, and containers for storage.

35. Lorena S. Walsh, "Urban Amenities and Rural Sufficiency: Living Standards and Consumer Behavior in the Colonial Chesapeake, 1643–1777," *JEH* 43 (1983): 109–17.

36. Note that Cole's inventory does not describe the servant bedding in detail. We have not included the servant bedding in the bed count, but since Cole called it "sufficient," we have included four accommodations for the servants in the count of total sleeping accommodations. The four beds listed, at two people per bed, were accommodations for eight, the size of the family.

37. Horn, "Adapting to a New World," in *Colonial Chesapeake Society*, ed. Carr, Morgan, and Russo, table 3; Menard, Harris, and Carr, "Opportunity and

Inequality," 172, figure 1. Neither of these articles measures the value of land, and neither standardizes inventory values to account for price changes. Standardization makes little difference to Maryland values from the mid-1660s until the second decade of the eighteenth century. Of the thirty-two inventoried householders who died between 1658 and 1665, sixteen had less than £50 in movables. If we use undeflated values, the number is the same.

We must warn readers that we cannot be certain that the wealth categories for England and Maryland are entirely comparable. £10 in English sterling may not have purchased the same goods in England as £10 in Maryland currency did in Maryland. We have found no exchange rates for Maryland currency on sterling before the early eighteenth century, but there may have been differences in the two currencies, and goods in inventories were not circulating in the same markets. However, we believe that these rough comparisons have value.

38. Notley had a total of eighty-six chairs, but seven were in an old house with three rooms. Inventories and Accounts 6:576–96.

39. Patents 4:13; Testamentary Proceedings 1D:57; Horn, "Adapting to a New World," in *Colonial Chesapeake Society*, ed. Carr, Morgan, and Russo, table 4, 158–59. Only 20 percent of planters with movables worth less than £50 had sheets over the years 1658–99.

40. Horn, "Adapting to a New World," in *Colonial Chesapeake Society*, ed. Carr, Morgan, and Russo, tables 4 and 5, 158–59, 162–63. In the vale of Berkeley, in estates worth less than £10, 19.9 percent had no tables, and 35.1 percent had no seats; but in the £10 to £49 group, only 7.7 percent had no tables, and 6.5 percent no seats. Above £99, seats were universal and tables absent in less than 5 percent of estates. However, tables clearly had less importance than they do in the twentieth century. See, for example, the numerous illustrations in Simon Schama, *The Embarrassment of Riches: An Interpretation of Dutch Culture in the Golden Age* (New York, 1987), 47, 154–55, 156, 200, 205, 210, 213, 376, 385, 387, 392, 416, 471, 482, 485, 494, 560, which show that tables and work surfaces were often very small and in short supply. People made much more use of the floor.

41. Horn found no forks in the vale of Berkeley, 1660–99. "Adapting to a New World," in *Colonial Chesapeake Society*, ed. Carr, Morgan, and Russo, table 5, 162–63. The first fork to appear in a St. Mary's County inventory was in Notley's of 1679—an agate-hafted fork that was clearly a highly prized personal possession. Inventories and Accounts 6:576–96. Main found what may be four table forks in the 1667 inventory of Stephen Yeo of Calvert County. *Tobacco Colony*, 190. On drinking vessels, see ibid., 190, 222–24. Even in middling and affluent households, Main reported, inventories do not show enough drinking vessels for everyone. On candles and table linen, see ibid., table V.1, and Horn, "Adapting to a New World," in *Colonial Chesapeake Society*, ed. Carr, Morgan, and Russo, table 4. For a discussion of the changes in standards of comfort and gentility that took place in the Chesapeake over the colonial period, see Lois Green Carr and Lorena S. Walsh, "Changing Lifestyles and Consumer Behavior in the Colonial

Chesapeake," in *Of Consuming Interests: The Style of Life in the Eighteenth Century*, ed. Cary Carson, Ronald Hoffman, and Peter J. Albert (Charlottesville, Va., forthcoming).

42. Inventories taken room by room and showing outbuildings do not show privies, nor do archaeological investigations of even the most elite sites in seventeenth-century Maryland. Robert M. Keeler, "The Homelot on the Seventeenth-Century Chesapeake Tidewater Frontier" (Ph.D. diss., University of Oregon, 1978), chaps. 3–6. Keeler describes a pit in the backyard of "St. John's," the home of the provincial secretary; the pit was used as a privy but had no structure over it (65, 133). Otherwise, his discussion of structures on various lots excavated in Maryland and Virginia makes no mention of privies. Garry Wheeler Stone, "Society, Housing, and Architecture in Early Maryland: John Lewger's St. John's" (Ph.D. diss., University of Pennsylvania, 1982), chaps. 2–4, discusses seventeenth-century house construction in the Chesapeake but makes no reference to privies. Henry M. Miller, *Discovering Maryland's First City: A Summary Report on the 1981–1984 Archaeological Excavations in St. Mary's City, Maryland*, St. Mary's City Archaeology Series no. 2 (St. Mary's City, Md., 1986), examines the town-center area of St. Mary's City without finding privies. On chamber pots, see Horn, "Adapting to a New World," in *Colonial Chesapeake Society*, ed. Carr, Morgan, and Russo, table 4; Main, *Tobacco Colony*, tables V.2, VII.1; and Carr and Walsh, "Changing Lifestyles," in *Of Consuming Interests*, ed. Carson, Hoffman, and Albert, table 5.

43. On the nature of the materials, see under the names of each in *The Compact Edition of the Oxford English Dictionary*, 2 vols. (New York, 1971). On underwear, see C. Willett Cunnington and Phillis Cunnington, *The History of Underclothes* (London, 1951).

44. Testamentary Proceedings 5:152–90; Carr and Walsh, "Changing Lifestyles," in *Of Consuming Interest*, ed. Carson, Hoffman, and Albert; David W. Jordan, "Maryland's Privy Council, 1637–1715," in *Law, Society, and Politics in Early Maryland*, ed. Aubrey C. Land, Lois Green Carr, and Edward C. Papenfuse (Baltimore, 1977), 71. For a good discussion of clothing generally, see Main, *Tobacco Colony*, 186–89, 206–8.

45. On contracts, see Lois Green Carr and Russell R. Menard, "Immigration and Opportunity: The Freedman in Early Colonial Maryland," in *The Chesapeake in the Seventeenth Century: Essays in Anglo-American Society and Politics*, ed. Thad W. Tate and David L. Ammerman (Chapel Hill, 1979), 215.

46. Lois Green Carr and Lorena S. Walsh, "Economic Diversification and Labor Organization in the Chesapeake, 1650–1820," in *Work and Labor in Early America*, ed. Stephen Innes (Chapel Hill, 1988), 149–57. In 1638 in the assembly "vpon a question moved touching the resting of servants on Sutturdaies in the afternoone, it was declared by the house that no such custome was to be allowed." *Archives* 1:21. We take this to mean that this English custom was not to be enacted into Maryland law. The subject does not appear again in assembly debates, but George Alsop claimed that servants worked only five and a half days a week.

A Character of the Province of Maryland . . . (London, 1666), in *Narratives of Early Maryland*, ed. Hall, 357. There are also references in the court records that imply Saturday half-holidays. Charles County Court and Land Records F# 1:6; *Archives* 53:462. It seems likely that the custom was observed while the labor force was heavily dependent on English servants but that it disappeared when slaves became the dominant source of labor.

47. Lois Green Carr, *County Government in Maryland, 1689–1709* (New York, 1987), text, 315–19, footnotes, 211; *Archives* 53:431, 54:225; Joseph H. Smith and Philip A. Crowl, eds., *Court Records of Prince George's County, Maryland, 1696–1699*, American Legal Records 9 (Washington, D.C., 1964), 590; Prince George's County Court Records B:50a; Cecil County Court Minutes, 1700–1701, p. 6; Main, *Tobacco Colony*, 113–14. Richard Morris, *Government and Labor in Early America* (New York, 1946), 390–512, esp. 490–91, discusses the rights of servants and their petitions for redress, concluding, as we have, that the courts made a real effort to determine the facts.

48. On servants in England, see Ann Kussmaul, *Servants in Husbandry in Early Modern England* (Cambridge, 1981), and Morgan, *American Slavery, American Freedom*, 126–28. In the Chesapeake, see Darrett B. Rutman and Anita H. Rutman, *A Place in Time: Middlesex County, Virginia, 1650–1750* (New York, 1984), 130–34; Main, *Tobacco Colony*, 113–15; Lorena S. Walsh, "Servitude and Opportunity in Charles County, Maryland, 1658–1705," in *Law, Society, and Politics in Early Maryland*, ed. Land, Carr, and Papenfuse, 119–22; and Morgan, *American Slavery, American Freedom*, 217–18. For penalties for running away or bearing a bastard, see *Archives* 1:373, 441, 489, 2:396, 524. Because servants were salable, they were listed as property in estate inventories, something not seen in English inventories.

49. A law regulating procedure in such petitioning was not passed until 1698, but we have found no examples of costs charged for hearings by petition, whether or not the servant was granted a remedy. Carr, *County Government in Maryland*, text, 318–19, footnotes, 210.

50. Main, *Tobacco Colony*, 114–15. On opportunities, see chap. 1, text between n. 33 and n. 40.

51. Barbara Carson, "Artifacts and Cultural Life in the Seventeenth-Century Chesapeake" (Paper presented to the Third Hall of Records Conference in Maryland History, St. Mary's City, Maryland, May 1984); Barbara and Cary Carson, "Styles and Standards of Living in Southern Maryland, 1670–1752" (Paper presented to the Southern Historical Association, Atlanta, Georgia, November 1976); Cary Carson and Lorena S. Walsh, "The Material Life of the Early American Housewife," *Winterthur Portfolio* (forthcoming); Carr and Walsh, "Changing Lifestyles," in *Of Consuming Interests*, ed. Carson, Hoffman, and Albert; *The Journal of John Fountaine: An Irish Huguenot Son in Spain and Virginia, 1710–1719*, ed. Edward Porter Alexander (Williamsburg, Va., 1972), 86.

52. See text between n. 4 and n. 5, and annotation.

53. On the relationship between social status and officeholding, see chap. 1, text after n. 56.

54. On life expectancies in New England, see Philip J. Greven, Jr., *Four Generations: Population, Land, and Family in Colonial Andover, Massachusetts* (Ithaca, N.Y., 1970), 26–27, 108–9, and Kenneth A. Lockridge, *A New England Town: The First Hundred Years* (New York, 1970), 67–68. For rough comparisons of wealth in Massachusetts and the Chesapeake, see Gloria Lund Main, "Personal Wealth in Colonial America: Explorations in the Use of Probate Records from Maryland and Massachusetts, 1650–1720" (Ph.D. diss., Columbia University, 1973), tables V-1, V-2, and V-3. Table V-3 indicates that when wealth is organized by decile groups, the bottom 20 percent of decedents were slightly better off in rural Massachusetts than in Maryland, but we are not told what levels of wealth the deciles represent, nor are they controlled for age or immigrant status. Overall, it is clear that rural Massachusetts farmers were poorer than those of Maryland. However, Boston residents, on the average, were much richer. See also Gloria L. Main, "The Standard of Living in Colonial Massachusetts," *JEH* 43 (1983): 101–8; Jackson T. Main, "Standard of Living and the Life Cycle in Colonial Connecticut," *JEH* 43 (1983): 159–65; and idem, *Society and Economy in Colonial Connecticut* (Princeton, N.J., 1985), 62–114. A summary of the research on the New England economy, as of 1983, is provided in McCusker and Menard, *Economy of British America*, chap. 5.

55. On the economy and society of the Caribbean, see Richard S. Dunn, *Sugar and Slaves: The Rise of the Planter Class in the English West Indies, 1624–1713* (Chapel Hill, 1972), esp. 72, 85, 96–97, 150–51, 165–77, 266, 301–2; Gary A. Puckrein, *Little England: Plantation Society and Anglo-Barbadian Politics, 1626–1700* (New York, 1984), 24–32, 56–87; Riva Berleant-Schiller, "Free Labor and the Economy in Seventeenth-Century Montserrat," *WMQ*, 3d Ser., 46 (1989): 539–64; and Hilary McD. Beckles, *White Servitude and Black Slavery in Barbadoes, 1627–1715* (Knoxville, Tenn., 1989). Both Berleant-Schiller and Beckles (151–67) argue that opportunities at the bottom disappeared with the introduction of sugar and slaves.

56. Puckrein, *Little England*, 63; Dunn, *Sugar and Slaves*, 59, 67, 126, 272. Studies of heights show that southerners were somewhat taller than New Englanders by the 1750s, suggesting that the southern diet was generally somewhat more nutritious. However, New Englanders were taller than Englishmen. Sokoloff and Villaflor, "Modern Stature," 475. Studies of heights of Caribbean whites are not yet available.

57. See text from before n. 16 until after n. 20.

58. Dunn, *Sugar and Slaves*, 54, 76, 85, 120, 125, 138–40, 182–83, 210, 268–70, 287–99.

59. See Gloria L. Main, "The Standard of Living in Southern New England," *WMQ*, 3d ser., 45 (1988): tables I, III, V, and VII, compared with Lois Green Carr and Lorena S. Walsh, "The Standard of Living in the Colonial Chesapeake,"

ibid., tables II and III and figures 1–4, and Jackson Turner Main, "Summary: The Hereafter," ibid., 161. The comparisons offered here are flawed by the fact that the New England evidence is for householders only, whereas that for the Chesapeake is for all decedents. However, the differences are so marked in the lower wealth groups that the conclusion that New Englanders at these levels enjoyed more amenities than did Chesapeake inhabitants seems firm. Much more work is needed, but the message from these preliminary studies is clear.

60. Dunn, *Sugar and Slaves*, 54, 76, 91–92, 96, 97, 125, 139, 267–86.

61. We have found no estimates for the minimum investment required to start a sugar plantation in the mid-seventeenth century. Dunn remarked that as tobacco and cotton planters of Barbados began to shift to sugar, those with less than twenty or thirty acres did not have sufficient land to justify the investment in mills and other equipment. During the 1640s, land prices in Barbados rose from about 10 shillings to about £5 per acre. At that price, Cole would have paid £150 for just thirty acres of land, although that price doubtless included improvements. *Sugar and Slaves*, 66–67. Even in more newly settled islands, land prices were very high, compared with prices in Maryland. In 1669, Samuel Winthrop paid £275 for two hundred acres in Antigua, or 330 pence per acre. Richard B. Sheridan, *Sugar and Slavery: An Economic History of the British West Indies, 1623–1775* (St. Lawrence, Barbados, 1974), 188. Cole paid 16 pence per acre (nondeflated) for his land. Furthermore, returns to scale were very high for sugar. Given the necessary sugar mills and other equipment, large operations were more cost-effective than small ones. In addition, since one laborer was needed for each acre in cane, the minimum investment in labor was very high. Dunn estimated that in 1680, twenty laborers—and hence, presumably, twenty acres of cane field—were the floor for a small sugar plantation. However, he also found planters with ten laborers raising sugar in Barbados in the late 1640s. *Sugar and Slaves*, 76, 92. In 1646, it was estimated that a £200 investment would allow a profitable operation. Sheridan, *Sugar and Slavery*, 264. Perhaps Cole could have obtained credit to establish himself in sugar, but it seems more likely that he would have fallen into Dunn's category of small planter or become a craftsman. What his advancement in these circumstances would have been is not clear.

Chapter 5

1. Russell R. Menard, "Economy and Society in Early Colonial Maryland" (Ph.D. diss., University of Iowa, 1975), chap. 2; Garry Wheeler Stone, "Society, Housing, and Architecture in Early Maryland: John Lewger's St. John's" (Ph.D. diss., University of Pennsylvania, 1982), chap. 1.

2. Gerard's biography is compiled from the Career File of Seventeenth-Century St. Mary's County Residents, St. Mary's City Commission (hereafter Career File), available for public use at the Maryland State Archives, Annapolis, Maryland. Also available there are brief summaries of these careers, in dBASE

IV. The information on Gerard is summarized in appendix 4. For the Mattapany tract, see Patents AB&H:78, 199, 1:62, and William Hand Browne et al., eds., *Archives of Maryland* (hereafter *Archives*), 72 vols. (Baltimore, 1883–1972), 57:157. Unless otherwise indicated, all manuscripts cited are at the Maryland State Archives.

3. Patents AB&H:68; *Archives* 4:352–53, 49:431, 454, 517, 57:18–19, 67:62–63.

4. See map 5.1. Modern soil conditions for the area can be found in U.S. Department of Agriculture, Soil Conservation Service, *Soil Survey of St. Mary's County, Maryland* (Washington, D.C., 1978), sheets 13, 14, 19, 20, and 25, in combination with table 4 and the Guide to the Mapping Units.

5. Tax lists for 1642 are found in *Archives* 1:142–46, 3:120–21, 123. The number of electors choosing burgesses also shows the rise in numbers of freemen. In 1640 only seven freemen ("we being but a small company in number") met to elect Thomas Gerard's attorney as a burgess for St. Clement's Hundred. By 1652, thirty-seven St. Clement's Hundred electors met. *Archives* 1:89, 49:112.

6. Menard has compiled a list of servants recorded as entering the colony by 1642. For Gerard's development of manor farms and quarters, see *Archives* 4:467, 10:213–15, 41:234, 49:517–19, 520, 57:32–36. The Patent records AB&H, 1, 3, 4, 5, 6 document Gerard's headright claims.

7. Patents AB&H:68. Basford Manor was entitled to a separate manor court, but Gerard administered it as a part of St. Clement's and required Basford freeholders to attend the St. Clement's court.

8. *Archives* 3:89–90.

9. Ibid., 3:118–19. Later in 1653 Gerard was directed to raise a force to disarm or secure Indians in Portoback or Chaptico suspected of "intending mischief." Ibid., 3:293–94. Contacts between local Indians and whites must have been frequent during the early years of settlement. Two manor residents, John Shankes and Vincent Mansfield, learned an Indian language and served as interpreters for the Maryland government. Career File.

10. *Archives* 3:138–39.

11. For the role of the large investor in early Maryland, see Stone, "Society, Housing, and Architecture," chaps. 1–3, and Menard, "Early Colonial Maryland," chap. 2.

12. The Roman Catholic community of early Maryland is perceptively described in Michael James Graham, "Lord Baltimore's Pious Enterprise: Toleration and Community in Colonial Maryland, 1634–1724" (Ph.D. diss., University of Michigan, 1983), chap. 3. See also Edwin Warfield Beitzell, *The Jesuit Missions of St. Mary's County, Maryland* (n.p., 1980).

13. *Archives* 49:112, gives a list of free men in St. Clement's Hundred in 1652; only four were tenants to Gerard. For Gerard's economic difficulties, see his long legal battle with Marmaduke Snow in ibid., vols. 41, 49, and 57.

14. Sale of a freehold is recorded in ibid., 61:143. Manor rents are enumerated in several lists in the Carroll-Maccubbin Papers, MS 219, Maryland Historical

Society, Baltimore. This collection also includes a record of a sale of a freehold to Bartholomew Phillips in 1652; the sale gave rights to hunt, to pasture livestock, and to cut timber for building on unplanted, unfenced, or waste parts of the manor. Additional demands recorded in this sale for one hogshead of tobacco every seventh year and one-tenth of the product of livestock raised for sale on ungranted portions of the manor probably proved uncollectible; these provisions do not appear in later deeds. On the other hand, freeholders jealously preserved their timber-cutting rights into the eighteenth century.

15. St. Clement's Manor Court Records, printed in *Archives* 53:627–37; Carroll-Maccubbin Papers; Career File.

16. See n. 15. For examples of leases, see *Archives* 10:36, 41:463, 49:575, 583.

17. *Archives* 57:220–21.

18. Ibid., 49:579, 581–82.

19. The manor court records are in ibid., 53:627–37. Here and throughout this chapter, information on manor residents comes from these records and from the Career File. Biographies of all people on the manor or in the neighborhood who were connected with the Coles are in appendix 4.

20. See Lorena S. Walsh, "Community Networks in the Early Chesapeake," in *Colonial Chesapeake Society*, ed. Lois Green Carr, Philip D. Morgan, and Jean B. Russo (Chapel Hill, 1988), 217–41.

21. See map 5.1, and *Archives* 53:627–37. The first entry for the court is for 1659, by which time it was already organized. In mid-seventeenth-century England, manors varied greatly in strength of organization and influence on the lives of residents. On the most active, manor courts might meet as often as every three weeks. On weaker manors, the court usually met but once a year. Brian M. Short, "The South-East," in *The Agrarian History of England and Wales, V: 1640–1750*, ed. Joan Thirsk, 2 vols. (Cambridge, 1984), 1:296. St. Clement's followed the second pattern, usually holding one meeting a year.

22. *Archives* 61:531.

23. Ibid., 69:19–21; Wills 1:44.

24. *Archives* 53:627–37.

25. Ibid., 41:480, 53:628, 629, 633, 634. The court decided that by the terms of Cole's lease, he could kill wild hogs but had to pay half to the lord of the manor.

26. Ibid., 61:484.

27. Compare the lists of resiants and jury members in ibid., 53:627, 629, 630–31.

28. Deposition of Samuel Williamson, in *Mason* v. *Cheseldyne*, St. Mary's County, Provincial Court Papers.

29. Suits about boundaries on the manor are found in the Provincial Court Papers for St. Mary's County. Additional materials, many not recorded in surviving St. Mary's County records, are in the Carroll-Maccubbin Papers and the McWilliams Papers, Georgetown University, Washington, D.C.

30. The manor court apparently ceased to meet after Gerard's eldest son and

principal heir, Justinian, died childless in 1688. However, it did not simply fade from memory. Charles Carroll, the richest man in Maryland in the first decades of the eighteenth century, bought the manor from Justinian's widow in 1711. When he began to try to collect manorial rents more assiduously than the Gerards had ever done, residents asked in 1729 that the manor court be reconvened to adjudicate titles and sums due. Very probably the court never met again. The fact that manor residents sought to resurrect it after forty years of inactivity—when it was in their interests to do so—suggests that in earlier years the court may have been abandoned partly for reasons of interest as well. Letter of Joshua Doyne to Charles Carroll, February 7, 1728/29, Carroll-Maccubbin Papers.

31. *Archives* 3:354–57. For a discussion of Gerard's politics, see Edwin W. Beitzell, "Thomas Gerrard and His Sons-in-Law," *Chronicles of St. Mary's* 10 (1962): 300–305, 307–11.

32. *Archives* 2:11, 12, 14, 33, 59, 60, 3:396, 407–9, 41:427, 429, 466, 49:260, 279, 286, 401, 415, 431, 454, 459, 506, 511, 517, 520, 555, 558, 57:81–90.

33. Gerard began to appear more often in Westmoreland County, Virginia, in the early 1660s; some of his activities can be traced in that county's records. For his marriage and removal of assets, see ibid., 57:15, 22, 511–12; Testamentary Proceedings 6:163–64; Wills 1:567; and Westmoreland County Wills and Deeds, 1665–77, pp. 142–43, Virginia State Library, Richmond. A younger son's inheritance was deeded upon the condition that the son help pay his father's debts. Provincial Court Deeds WRC#1:12–17. Gerard's removal of most of his slaves and livestock to Virginia served to keep them out of the clutches of his Maryland creditors, forcing the courts to grant executions for future manor rents. After Thomas's death, his son Thomas was granted possession of Basford Manor for ten years, and another creditor obtained temporary possession of St. Clement's. *Archives* 65:486, 67:62–63, 218–20.

34. *Archives* 67:218–20; Provincial Court Deeds WRC#1:12–17.

35. Memorandum and Tenant's Answers, Carroll-Maccubbin Papers. Among reasons offered for nonpayment were uncertain or defective titles, multiple possessors, a three-year statute of limitations for collecting back rent, rents from deeds of gifts to family members not being due until the fourth generation, and an unwillingness to pay unless "all the Rest in the manor pays."

36. The Carroll family continued to collect most manor rents in corn and capons into the 1760s. They were able to charge rents in tobacco or currency for only a few tracts surveyed after 1711. Carroll-Maccubbin Papers.

37. For the jurisdiction of the county court and its evolution as the predominant institution of local government, see Lois Green Carr, "The Foundations of Social Order: Local Government in Colonial Maryland," in *Town and County: Essays on the Structure of Local Government in the American Colonies*, ed. Bruce C. Daniels (Middletown, Conn., 1978), 72–110, and idem, *County Government in Maryland, 1689–1709* (New York, 1987), chaps. 2–6. The decline of the manor court may have mirrored similar developments in parts of England. David Grayson Allen found that in East Anglia, manorial responsibilities were being trans-

ferred to parish and county governments at almost the same time. *In English Ways: The Movement of Societies and the Transferal of English Local Law and Custom to Massachusetts Bay in the Seventeenth Century* (Chapel Hill, 1981), 153.

38. *Archives* 5:534–35, 15:391–92, 41:144–45.

39. Graham, "Lord Baltimore's Pious Enterprise," chaps. 3, 5, 7.

40. On antiproprietary sentiment on the manor, see Lois Green Carr and David William Jordan, *Maryland's Revolution of Government, 1689–1692* (Ithaca, N.Y., 1974), 53–54.

41. For freedmen, see Lois Green Carr and Russell R. Menard, "Immigration and Opportunity: The Freedman in Early Colonial Maryland," in *The Chesapeake in the Seventeenth Century: Essays on Anglo-American Society and Politics*, ed. Thad W. Tate and David L. Ammerman (Chapel Hill, 1979), 206–42, and Edmund S. Morgan, *American Slavery, American Freedom: The Ordeal of Colonial Virginia* (New York, 1975), 215–34.

42. We are aware of no comparable studies of persistence and mobility for small geographic subdivisions of seventeenth-century Chesapeake counties. Since the rate of movement into or out of such restricted units is almost certainly greater than movement into or out of a much larger area such as a county, it is impossible to say whether this degree of local turnover was in any way exceptional. For studies of persistence and migration within entire counties, see Darrett B. and Anita H. Rutman, "'More True and Perfect Lists': A Note on the Reconstruction of Censuses for a Virginia County, 1668–1704," *Virginia Magazine of History and Biography* 88 (1980): 37–74, and Lorena S. Walsh, "Staying Put or Getting Out: Findings for Charles County, Maryland, 1650–1720," *William and Mary Quarterly* (hereafter *WMQ*), 3d ser., 44 (1987): 69–103. For a discussion of different (and much higher) rates of migration between individual parishes and within whole counties in England, see Charles Pythian-Adams, "Little Images of the Great Country: English Rural Communities and English Rural Contexts" (Paper presented at the conference "The Social World of Britain and America, 1600–1820," Williamsburg, Virginia, September 1985).

43. Lorena S. Walsh, "Servitude and Opportunity in Charles County, Maryland," in *Law, Society, and Politics in Early Maryland*, ed. Aubrey C. Land, Lois Green Carr, and Edward C. Papenfuse (Baltimore, 1977), 123.

44. Lois Green Carr and Lorena S. Walsh, "The Planter's Wife: The Experience of White Women in Seventeenth-Century Maryland," *WMQ*, 3d ser., 34 (1977): table II.

45. Walsh, "Staying Put or Getting Out," 69–103.

46. This argument is developed and documented in Walsh, "Community Networks," in *Colonial Chesapeake Society*, ed. Carr, Morgan, and Russo, 200–241.

47. Analysis of geographic networks as part of a community study is discussed in Darrett B. Rutman, "Community Study," *Historical Methods* 13 (1980): 29–41, and idem, "The Social Web: A Prospectus for the Study of Early American Communities," in *Insights and Parallels: Problems and Issues of Social History*,

ed. William L. O'Neill (Minneapolis, 1973), 57–123. On horses, see Carr and Menard, "Immigration and Opportunity," in *Chesapeake in the Seventeenth Century*, ed. Tate and Ammerman, 218, table 3.

48. These ideas are expanded and documented in Walsh's manuscript in preparation, "'To Labour for Profit': Plantation Management in the Chesapeake, 1620–1820," chap. 2.

49. For elaboration and documentation, see Walsh, "Community Networks," in *Colonial Chesapeake Society*, ed. Carr, Morgan, and Russo, 217–29.

50. Laurel Thatcher Ulrich found that New England women traveled most when neither pregnant nor nursing infants but that a mother was more apt to stay home for the first ten months after the birth of a child than she was during pregnancy. *Good Wives: Image and Reality in the Lives of Women in Northern New England, 1650–1750* (New York, 1982), 140–41.

51. Lorena S. Walsh, "Women's Networks in the Colonial Chesapeake" (Paper presented at the annual meeting of the Organization of American Historians, Cincinnati, 1983); Darrett B. Rutman and Anita H. Rutman, *A Place in Time: Middlesex County, Virginia, 1650–1750* (New York, 1984), 103–13.

52. *Maryland Gazette*, February 15, 1759.

53. Fitzhugh's activities are documented in *William Fitzhugh and His Chesapeake World, 1676–1701: The Fitzhugh Letters and Other Documents*, ed. Richard Beale Davis (Chapel Hill, 1963). Generalizations in this and preceding paragraphs are based on maps and biographical files discussed in Walsh, "Community Networks," in *Colonial Chesapeake Society*, ed. Carr, Morgan, and Russo, 219–25. For similar conclusions about the size of the networks of various occupational groups, see James Russell Perry, *The Formation of a Society on Virginia's Eastern Shore, 1615–55* (Chapel Hill, 1990).

54. Walsh, "Community Networks," in *Colonial Chesapeake Society*, ed. Carr, Morgan, and Russo, 230–41.

55. Walsh, "Women's Networks in the Colonial Chesapeake"; Lorena S. Walsh, "Charles County, Maryland, 1658–1705: A Study of Chesapeake Social and Political Structure" (Ph.D. diss., Michigan State University, 1977), chaps. 5, 7.

56. On security, see Lois Green Carr, "Sources of Political Stability and Upheaval in Seventeenth-Century Maryland," *Maryland Historical Magazine* (hereafter *MHM*), 79 (1984): 46–47 and annotation.

57. See, for example, *Archives* 54:42–44, 49–51, 88–89, 582–87.

58. Ibid., 41:221–23, 54:508–10, for examples.

59. Lorena S. Walsh, "Child Custody in the Early Chesapeake: A Case Study" (Paper presented to the Berkshire Conference in Women's History, Poughkeepsie, New York, 1981); idem, "Women's Networks in the Colonial Chesapeake"; idem, "Charles County, Maryland," chap. 5.

60. Lorena S. Walsh and Russell R. Menard, "Death in the Chesapeake: Two Life Tables for Men in Early Colonial Maryland," *MHM* 69 (1974): 211–27.

61. Carr and Walsh, "The Planter's Wife," 552–53; Russell R. Menard, "Immigrants and Their Increase: The Process of Population Growth in Early Colonial Maryland," in *Law, Society, and Politics*, ed. Land, Carr, and Papenfuse, 88–110.

62. Darrett B. and Anita H. Rutman, "'Now-Wives and Sons-in-Law': Parental Death in a Seventeenth-Century Virginia County," in *Chesapeake in the Seventeenth Century*, ed. Tate and Ammerman, 153–82; Lorena S. Walsh, "'Till Death Us Do Part': Marriage and Family in Seventeenth-Century Maryland," in ibid., 152; Carr and Walsh, "Planter's Wife," 555n.

63. Carr and Walsh, "Planter's Wife," 560.

64. Lois Green Carr, "The Development of the Maryland Orphans' Court, 1654–1715," in *Law, Society, and Politics*, ed. Land, Carr, and Papenfuse, 41–62; Testamentary Proceedings 12B:238–54.

65. *Archives* 61:241.

66. Ibid., 41:169, 237–38.

67. Carr and Walsh, "Planter's Wife," 555–57. Lois Green Carr, "Inheritance in the Colonial Chesapeake," in *Women in the Age of the American Revolution*, ed. Ronald Hoffman and Peter J. Albert (Charlottesville, Va., 1989), 155–60.

68. John Bossy, *The English Catholic Community, 1570–1850* (New York, 1976), chaps. 6, 7.

69. Carr, "Inheritance in the Colonial Chesapeake," in *Women in the Age of the American Revolution*, ed. Hoffman and Albert, 158–62; Carole Shammas, Marylynn Salmon, and Michael Dahlin, *Inheritance in America from Colonial Times to the Present* (New Brunswick, N.J., 1987), 28–29, 280.

70. Carr and Walsh, "Planter's Wife," 556–57.

71. Gardiner paid for a certificate, requested by Cole's mother, attesting to the number of Cole's children then living. It is recorded in *Archives* 49:3. On Hanckes, see chap. 1 n. 8.

72. Walsh, "Child Custody"; Robert Cole's will, printed in appendix 1.

73. Cf. Walsh, "'Till Death Us Do Part,'" in *Chesapeake in the Seventeenth Century*, ed. Tate and Ammerman, 135–36, 148.

74. Ibid., 148–50.

75. Wills 1:422, 631, 5:167, 6:113.

76. Walsh, "Charles County, Maryland," chap. 3.

77. Ibid.; Walsh, "Child Custody"; Carr, "Orphans' Court," in *Law, Society, and Politics*, ed. Land, Carr, and Papenfuse, 52.

78. Walsh, "'Till Death Us Do Part,'" in *Chesapeake in the Seventeenth Century*, ed. Tate and Ammerman, 148–49.

79. In St. Mary's County, fathers willed land to a smaller percentage of daughters in the 1650s and 1660s than they did in the 1680s and 1690s. Lois Green Carr and Lorena S. Walsh, "Women's Role in the Eighteenth-Century Chesapeake" (Paper presented to the conference "Women in Early America," Williamsburg, Virginia, November 1981), table 3.

80. Testamentary Proceedings 12B:238–54; Walsh, "Child Custody."

Chapter 6

1. The biographies in this section are based on appendix 4, which is in turn based on the Career File of Seventeenth-Century St. Mary's County Residents, St. Mary's City Commission, housed at the Maryland State Archives, Annapolis, Maryland. Unless otherwise indicated, all manuscripts cited are at the Maryland State Archives.

2. John Medley died intestate, just after inheriting six hundred acres from his father. Inventories and Accounts 3:35; Wills 1:147. Under English and Maryland inheritance law, since his children were minors, Cole controlled the whole property until they came of age. He then controlled the two hundred acres due his wife for her life as her dower. Her third of Medley's personal property became Cole's at their marriage. 22 and 23 Carole 11, chap. 10, in Danby Pickering, ed., *The Statutes at Large*, 24 vols. (Cambridge, 1762), 8:347–50; William Hand Browne et al., eds., *Archives of Maryland* (hereafter *Archives*), 72 vols. (Baltimore, 1883–1972), 7:195–96. By the Common Law of Curtesy, Cole continued to control his wife's dower lands until his death, even though she predeceased him.

3. Guibert's eleven slaves were probably the equivalent of seven full hands (three were identified as "young" in the inventory, four as "old"), more than a plantation the size and quality of Cole's could support over the long term. Guibert may have been tilling the poorer soils, or perhaps he reduced the length of fallow. On the other hand, Guibert owned additional land. He may have taken the plunge and opened a quarter on another tract, although there is no evidence of such an arrangement in his inventory. Inventories and Accounts 35(B):85. See chaps. 2 and 3 for a discussion of the relationships between farm size, the number of workers, and the establishment of quarters.

4. On the demographic characteristics of immigrants, see chap. 1, text at nn. 41–44, and chap. 5, text at nn. 60–63.

5. On Maryland's "demographic transition," see Russell R. Menard, "Immigrants and Their Increase: The Process of Population Growth in Early Colonial Maryland," in *Law, Society, and Politics in Early Maryland*, ed. Aubrey C. Land, Lois Green Carr, and Edward C. Papenfuse (Baltimore, 1977), 88–110, and Allan Kulikoff, *Tobacco and Slaves: The Development of Southern Cultures in the Chesapeake, 1680–1800* (Chapel Hill, 1986), 54–63.

The argument elaborated in this paragraph has been challenged by T. L. Anderson and R. P. Thomas, "The Growth of Population and Labor Force in the 17th-Century Chesapeake," *Explorations in Economic History* 15 (1978): 290–312. See also Menard's response, "The Growth of Population in the Chesapeake Colonies: A Comment," ibid. 18 (1981): 399–410, and Anderson's reply, "From the Parts to the Whole: Modeling Chesapeake Population History," ibid. 18 (1981): 411–14. The Rutmans, based on their findings for Middlesex County, Virginia, doubt that life expectancy rose. See especially Anita H. Rutman, "Still Planting the Seeds of Hope: The Recent Literature of the Early Chesapeake Region," *Virginia Magazine of History and Biography* 95 (1987): 7–9. We think the evidence for such an increase in Maryland is strong, although the immigrant-native contrast drawn in this paragraph needs reexamination. For a recent contribution, see Daniel S. Levy, "The Life Expectancies of Colonial Maryland Legislators," *Historical Methods* 20 (1987): 17–27.

6. Russell R. Menard, "Five Maryland Censuses, 1700 to 1712: A Note on the Quality of the Quantities," *William and Mary Quarterly* (hereafter *WMQ*), 3d ser., 37 (1980): 616–26.

7. The contrast between immigrant and Creole families emerges clearly from the data presented in Russell R. Menard and Lorena S. Walsh, "The Demography of Somerset County, Maryland: A Progress Report," *Newberry Papers in Family and Community History* 81–2 (1981). See also Lorena S. Walsh, "The Experience and Status of Women in the Chesapeake, 1750–1775," in *The Web of Southern Social Relations*, ed. Walter J. Fraser, Jr., R. Frank Saunders, Jr., and Jon L. Wakelyn (Athens, Ga., 1985), 1–18.

8. On kinship and neighborhood, see chap. 5; Darrett B. Rutman and Anita H. Rutman, *A Place in Time: Middlesex County, Virginia, 1650–1750* (New York, 1984), 94–127, and Kulikoff, *Tobacco and Slaves*, 205–60.

9. There is a growing literature on the rise of slavery in the Chesapeake. Notable studies include Edmund S. Morgan, *American Slavery, American Freedom: The Ordeal of Colonial Virginia* (New York, 1975), 295–315; Russell R. Menard, "From Servants to Slaves: The Transformation of the Chesapeake Labor System," *Southern Studies* 16 (1977): 355–90; Paul G. E. Clemens, *The Atlantic Economy and Colonial Maryland's Eastern Shore: From Tobacco to Grain* (Ithaca, N.Y., 1980), 58–63; David W. Galenson, *White Servitude in Colonial America: An Economic Analysis* (Cambridge, 1981); Gloria L. Main, *Tobacco Colony: Life in Early Maryland, 1650–1720* (Princeton, N.J., 1982), 97–139; and Kulikoff, *Tobacco and Slaves*, 37–44.

For the proportions of slaves to servants in the inventoried bound labor force in 1680 and in the living population in 1710, see Menard, "From Servants to Slaves," and idem, "Five Maryland Censuses," table IV. The proportion of slaves in the inventoried bound labor force in about 1710 is taken from the SMCC computer files for St. Mary's, Prince George's, and Somerset counties, 1707–12. All slaves are included in the data from inventories. The proportion of blacks in the living population of 1680 is an estimate based on figures for Virginia and Maryland in John J. McCusker and Russell R. Menard, *The Economy of British America, 1607–1789*, (Chapel Hill, 1985), table 6–4, which shows blacks as 7.2 percent of the population of both colonies.

10. Charles Calvert to Lord Baltimore, April 27, 1664, *The Calvert Papers, Number One*, Maryland Historical Society, Fund Publication no. 28 (Baltimore, 1889), 249.

11. We know little about how the transition to slavery was financed in any of the American colonies, in part because historians have assumed, following Adam Smith's comments on the West Indies, that it was paid for by English capital. Smith, however, drew a sharp distinction between the sugar islands and the to-

bacco coast, and recent work on Jamaica and the lower South stresses the role of farm building and local capital in funding the initial investments in slavery. Smith, *An Inquiry into the Nature and Causes of the Wealth of Nations* (New York, 1937), 531–56; Nuala Zahedieh, "Trade, Plunder, and Economic Development in Early English Jamaica, 1655–89," *Economic History Review*, 2d ser., 39 (1986): 205–22; Russell R. Menard, "Financing the Lowcountry Export Boom, 1700–1740: Sources of Capital in Early Carolina" (Paper presented to the Social Science History Association, November 1988). On the importance of legal safeguards, see David W. Galenson, "Economic Aspects of the Growth of Slavery in the Seventeenth-Century" (unpublished paper, January 1988).

12. The changing demography of slavery and its implications for Afro-American culture is explored in Russell R. Menard, "The Maryland Slave Population, 1658 to 1730: A Demographic Profile of Blacks in Four Counties," *WMQ*, 3d ser., 32 (1975): 29–54, and Kulikoff, *Tobacco and Slaves*, 317–420. Jean B. Lee, "The Problem of Slave Community in the Eighteenth-Century Chesapeake," *WMQ*, 3d ser., 43 (1986): 333–61, suggests that this interpretation is too optimistic and stresses the persistent obstacles to slave community formation.

13. Menard, "Servants to Slaves," 385–88.

14. Russell R. Menard, "British Migration to the Chesapeake Colonies in the Seventeenth Century," in *Colonial Chesapeake Society*, ed. Lois Green Carr, Philip D. Morgan, and Jean B. Russo (Chapel Hill, 1988), 126–32. Indentured servitude as a source of field labor declined severely after the early eighteenth century. David W. Galenson has demonstrated that by that time, servants leaving London with contracts were more likely to be skilled, but Galenson noted that their role in the colonial economy was very different from that of their seventeenth-century predecessors. *White Servitude in Colonial America*, 51–64.

15. Russell R. Menard, "Economy and Society in Early Colonial Maryland," (Ph.D. diss., University of Iowa, 1975), 425–26.

16. On opportunities, see chap. 1, text between n. 33 and n. 40. Biographies of the Cole servants are in appendix 4.

17. Kulikoff, *Tobacco and Slaves*, 338, reports the distribution of slaves in St. Mary's. On plantation size in the low country and the sugar islands, see Philip D. Morgan, "The Development of Slave Culture in Eighteenth-Century Plantation America" (Ph.D. thesis, University College, London, 1977), and Richard S. Dunn, *Sugar and Slaves: The Rise of the Planter Class in the English West Indies, 1624–1713* (Chapel Hill, 1972), 96–97.

18. Changes that did occur in work routines are discussed in Lois Green Carr and Lorena S. Walsh, "Economic Diversification and Labor Organization in the Chesapeake, 1650–1820," in *Work and Labor in Early America*, ed. Stephen Innes (Chapel Hill, 1988). For changes in the Chesapeake system of husbandry, see chap. 3, text from before n. 48 through n. 50, and Lois Green Carr and Russell R. Menard, "Land, Labor, and Economies of Scale in Early Maryland: Some Limits to Growth in the Chesapeake System of Husbandry," *Journal of Economic History* 49 (1989): 407–18.

19. The sweet-scented areas between the James and Rappahannock rivers did not follow quite the same history. There the collapse of tobacco prices was less in the late seventeenth century and more pronounced in the 1720s. Lorena S. Walsh, "'To Labour for Profit': Plantation Management in the Chesapeake, 1620–1820" (unpublished manuscript), chap. 3.

20. The literature on the Chesapeake economy in the eighteenth century is summarized in McCusker and Menard, *Economy of British America*, 117–43. On the progress of diversification, see also Lois Green Carr, "Diversification in the Colonial Chesapeake: Somerset County, Maryland, in Comparative Perspective," in *Colonial Chesapeake Society*, ed. Carr, Morgan, and Russo, 342–82, esp. 351–63, 372–77.

21. The rise of the Chesapeake gentry and accompanying changes in society, culture, and politics are central themes in the recent literature. Especially important contributions include, in addition to the books by Clemens, Kulikoff, Main, Morgan, and Rutman and Rutman cited elsewhere in this chapter, Bernard Bailyn, "Politics and Social Structure in Virginia," in *Seventeenth-Century America: Essays in Colonial History*, ed. James M. Smith (Chapel Hill, 1959), 90–115; T. H. Breen, *Tobacco Culture: The Mentality of the Great Planters on the Eve of Revolution* (Princeton, N.J., 1985); Rhys Isaac, *The Transformation of Virginia, 1740–1790* (Chapel Hill, 1982); David W. Jordan, *Foundations of Representative Government in Maryland, 1632–1715* (New York, 1987); Charles S. Sydnor, *Gentlemen Freeholders: Political Practices in Washington's Virginia* (Chapel Hill, 1952); Aubrey C. Land, *Colonial Maryland: A History* (Millwood, N.Y., 1981); and Warren M. Billings, John E. Selby, and Thad W. Tate, *Colonial Virginia: A History* (White Plains, N.Y., 1986).

On the gentry in local government, see Lois Green Carr, "The Foundations of Social Order: Local Government in Colonial Maryland," in *Town and County: Essays on the Structure of Local Government in the American Colonies*, ed. Bruce C. Daniels (Middletown, Conn., 1978), 72–110, esp. 90–91, 97–99, and Lorena S. Walsh, "The Development of Local Power Structures: Maryland's Lower Western Shore in the Early Colonial Period," in *Power and Status: Officeholding in Colonial America*, ed. Bruce C. Daniels (Middletown, Conn., 1986), 53–91.

22. For documentation of shifts in family structure and the changing distribution of wealth, see Lois Green Carr, "Inheritance in the Colonial Chesapeake," in *Women in the Age of the American Revolution*, ed. Ronald Hoffman and Peter J. Albert (Charlottesville, Va., 1989), tables 7 and 13. Of course, couples also had more children than immigrant couples of the seventeenth century had had and therefore had to divide their estates among more people. Ibid., 166–70. The Rutmans found that in Middlesex County, Virginia, 75 percent of seventeenth-century sons of the men of highest status failed to maintain the position of their fathers, 50 percent failed from 1700 to 1720, and 60 percent failed from 1721 to 1750. Darrett B. Rutman and Anita H. Rutman, *A Place in Time: Explicatus* (New York, 1984), table 41. Once a man had children of age, the more sons he had, the

less likely he was to be able to endow all of them with the estate and power that had been his, hence the increase in failure rate of sons after 1720. But the rate did not reach the seventeenth-century level.

23. This and the next two paragraphs draw on Lois Green Carr and David William Jordan, *Maryland's Revolution of Government, 1689–1692* (Ithaca, N.Y., 1974), esp. chap. 6.

24. *Archives* 25:258 reports Maryland's Catholic population by county. For the impact of the exclusion of Catholics on officeholding and government in St. Mary's County, see Walsh, "Local Power Structures," in *Power and Status*, ed. Daniels, 69. On Catholic connections to power, see Lois Green Carr, *County Government in Maryland, 1689–1709* (New York, 1987), 692–94.

25. In 1740, at age thirteen, Joseph left Maryland to study at St. Omer's; Robert did the same in 1748 at age fifteen. Both trained as Jesuit novices at Watten and Liège, and both were ordained priests—Robert in 1760 and Joseph in 1762. Joseph died the next year in Rome; Robert served in England from 1767 until his death in London in 1812. Henry's birthdate is unknown, but he left Maryland for Valladolid in Spain in 1757 and died of smallpox in 1763 on the way to his novitiate. When their father, Edward Cole, died in 1762, he left these sons small legacies. Geoffrey Holt, S.J., ed., *The English Jesuits, 1650–1829: A Biographical Dictionary*, Catholic Record Society Publications (Record Series), 70 (Southampton, England, 1984), 62–63; Edwin Henson, ed., *Registers of the English College at Valladolid, 1589–1862*, Publications of the Catholic Record Society, 30 (London, 1930), 190; Wills 31:868–70. We thank Thomas Purvis for drawing our attention to these great-grandsons of the Coles'.

Appendix 1

Note: Biographies of all individuals referred to in the account appear in appendix 4.

1. Depositions taken October 29, 1672, establishing Robert's majority were probably submitted in connection with this suit. Testamentary Proceedings 5:348, Maryland State Archives, Annapolis, Maryland. Unless otherwise indicated, all manuscripts cited are at the Maryland State Archives.

2. Warren's complaint is in ibid., 5:472.

3. Gardiner first submitted an account on August 24, 1673, but Robert Cole failed to appear in court. Ibid., 5:542.

4. Philip Calvert, the half brother of Charles Calvert, served as commissary general or judge of probate from April 1673 until his death in 1682. Donnell M. Owings, *His Lordship's Patronage* (Baltimore, 1953), 122.

5. On December 8, 1674, the sheriff of St. Mary's County reported to the provincial court that he had levied by execution out of the stock of horses divided among Robert Cole's orphans one mare with foal by her side awarded to Gardiner

as executor and that the mare was to be delivered to his widow. William Hand Browne et al., eds., *Archives of Maryland* (hereafter *Archives*), 72 vols. (Baltimore, 1883–1972), 65:439.

6. Philip Calvert, in a letter of February 14, 1673, warned Robert Cole not to dispose of the crop until Gardiner's account was settled. Testamentary Proceedings 6:82.

7. The preceding judgment was also recorded in the Chancery Court. *Archives* 51:457.

8. *Steer*: a young ox, especially one that has been castrated. *The Compact Edition of the Oxford English Dictionary* (hereafter *OED*), 2 vols. (New York, 1971). In seventeenth-century Maryland, steers were used primarily for meat rather than as draft animals.

9. *Heifer*: a young cow that has not had a calf. *OED*. For the effects of differing age distributions among female cattle on the reproductive potential of the Cole herd, see appendix 3.

10. *Brambley* (Bramley): a five-hundred-acre tract on St. Clement's Manor located on the Wicomico River between Mill (Miomake) and Bramleigh creeks. The tract was owned by Justinian Gerard. *Archives* 49:579.

11. *Bassfoord Mannor* (Basford Manor): a four-thousand-acre manor, owned by Thomas Gerard, on the Wicomico River bordering on the north of St. Clement's Manor.

12. *Markes.* To facilitate identification of livestock, which often ran wild, owners marked cattle, horses, and hogs with distinctive patterns cut into their ears. Owners registered their individual marks with the county courts. *Underkeeled* refers to the bottom side of the animal's ear and *overkeeled* to the top. Sometimes animals were branded as well as marked.

13. *Mr. Slyes*: Robert Slye.

14. *Potts* (pots) and *Kettles* were both used for boiling. Utensils that grew narrower toward the top were termed *pots*, and those that grew wider were called *kettles*. Lynne Howard Frazer, "Calling the Kettle a Pot: Reviving Eighteenth Century Cooking Equipment Nomenclature," *Petits Propos Culinaires* 26 (1987): 40–44, 48–49; Robert Blair St. George, "'Set Thine House in Order': The Domestication of the Yeomanry in Seventeenth Century New England," *New England Begins: The Seventeenth Century* (Boston, 1982), 224.

15. *Skelletts* (skillets): cooking utensils of brass, copper, or other metal, having high sides and usually three or four feet and a long handle, used for boiling liquids, stewing meat, etc. Frazer, "Calling the Kettle a Pot," 46, 48, 50; St. George, "'Set Thine House in Order,'" 224.

16. *Fryeing panns* (frying pans): broad, shallow pans with sides flaring outward, a flat bottom, and a long handle, usually of iron, in which food is fried. Frazer, "Calling the Kettle a Pot," 46, 48, 50.

17. *Bell mettle* (bell-metal): an alloy of copper and tin, the tin being in larger proportion than in ordinary bronze. *OED*.

18. *Hookes* (hooks): used, in combination with the iron chain, to suspend pots or pans over the fire. For possible arrangements, see Hugh D. Roberts, *Downhearth to Bar Grate: An Illustrated Account of the Evolution in Cooking Due to the Use of Coal Instead of Wood* (Marlborough, Wiltshire, 1981), 21.

19. *Milktrayes* (milk trays): vessels roughly in the shape of an inverted, truncated cone, ten inches or more in diameter, used for cooling milk. Mary C. Beaudry, Janet Long, Henry M. Miller, Frazer D. Neiman, and Garry Wheeler Stone, "A Vessel Typology for Early Chesapeake Ceramics: The Potomac Typological System," *Historical Archaeology* 17 (1983): 28, 35.

20. *Coule & Coule Staffe* (cowl or coul): a tub or similar vessel for water, etc., especially one with two ears that could be borne by two men on a cowlstaff, or stout stick, thrust through the two handles of the cowl. *OED.*

21. *Powdring tubb* (powdering tub): a wooden tub in which the flesh of animals is "powdered," or salted and pickled. *OED.*

22. *Mobby*: the expressed juice of apples and peaches, used in the distillation of apple and peach brandy. *OED.*

23. *Trenchers*: flat pieces of wood, square or circular, on which meat was served or from which diners ate. St. George, "'Set Thine House in Order,'" 237–38.

24. *Dripping panns* (dripping pans): pans used to catch the drippings from meat roasted on a spit. Roberts, *Downhearth to Bar Grate*, 21–23.

25. *Chafeing dish* (chafing dish): a metal or coarse earthenware vessel on a pedestal with supports around the rim. Chafing dishes held coals used to warm food at the table. Beaudry et al., "A Vessel Typology," 36; St. George, "'Set Thine House in Order,'" 242–44.

26. *Scummer* (skimmer): a shallow utensil, usually perforated, employed in skimming liquids. St. George, "'Set Thine House in Order,'" 223–24.

27. *Grid Iron*: a cooking utensil formed of parallel bars of iron or other metal in a frame usually supported on short legs, used for broiling flesh or fish over a fire. J. Seymour Lindsay, *Iron and Brass Implements of the English House* (London, 1927), 29–30.

28. *Porrengers* (porringers): small basins with one or two handles, usually hemispherical in shape and shallower in relation to the diameter than a cup or pot. Used for eating porridge, stew, soup, etc. Beaudry et al., "Vessel Typology," 32; St. George, "'Set Thine House in Order,'" 240–46.

29. *Ancor* (anker): a cask or keg holding the quantity of ten old wine gallons or eight and a half imperial gallons. Ronald Edward Zupke, *A Dictionary of English Weights and Measures* (Madison, 1968), 6.

30. *Rundletts* (runlets): cask or vessels for holding liquids of varying capacity. Large runlets usually varied between twelve and eighteen and a half gallons, small ones between a pint or quart and three or four gallons. *OED*; Zupke, *Dictionary of Weights*, 147.

31. *Sifter*: a sieve with meshes of wire or horsehair for separating finer from coarser meal, including ground maize (hominy). *OED.*

32. *Joynt Stooles*: stools made of parts joined or fitted together and made by a joiner, as distinguished from one of more clumsy workmanship. Benno M. Forman, *American Seating Furniture, 1630–1730* (New York, 1988), 143–45, 180–85.

33. *Chaire table*: an armchair that has a table top as a back. When used as a table, the back is folded down to rest on the arms. For examples, see Wallace Nutting, *Furniture Treasury* (New York, 1928), nos. 1276, 1767–73.

34. *Dresser*: a table or sideboard in a kitchen, on which food is dressed; often surmounted by rows of shelves on which plates, dishes, and kitchen utensils are arranged, sometimes freestanding but often built into the wall. St. George, "'Set Thine House in Order,'" 304. Cf. Donna C. Hole, "The Kitchen Dresser: Architectural Fittings in Eighteenth and Early Nineteenth Century Anglo-American Kitchens," *Petits Propos Culinaires* 9 (1981): 25–37.

35. Pictures appear not infrequently in Maryland inventories of the period. Their small appraisal value when listed by item—one pence to a few shillings—indicates that they were cheap reproductions (perhaps woodcuts) and not original paintings. The fact that groups of six to twenty-four small pictures often appear in the inventories of known Roman Catholic families suggests that these may have been holy pictures.

36. *Stilliard* (steelyard): a portable balance consisting of a lever with unequal arms, which moves on a fulcrum; the article to be weighed is suspended from the shorter arm, and a counterpoise is slid on the longer arm until equilibrium is produced, its place on this arm (which is notched or graduated) showing the weight. St. George, "'Set Thine House in Order,'" 194–96.

37. *Case with Six bottles pewter Screwes*: flat-sided bottles designed to fit in a divided wooden case and fitted with threaded pewter caps. Ibid., 284–85.

38. *Specled Dutch potts*: tin-enameled earthenware drinking vessels speckled with blue or manganese. Examples have been found in archaeological excavations at St. Mary's City, Maryland. Personal communication with Henry Miller, Historic St. Mary's City; Beaudry et al., "Vessel Typology," 30.

39. *Pillow beares*: pillowcases. *OED*.

40. *Dyaper* (diaper): a linen fabric (sometimes part linen, part cotton) woven with a small, simple pattern formed by the different directions of the thread and the different reflections of light from its surface and consisting of lines crossing diamond-wise, with the spaces variously filled up by parallel lines, a central leaf or dot, etc. Florence M. Montgomery, *Textiles in America, 1650–1870* (New York, 1984), 218; Eric Kerridge, *Textile Manufactures in Early Modern England* (Manchester, England, 1985), 121.

41. *My mother*: Joan Cole of Heston, Middlesex.

42. *Say*: a cloth of fine texture, usually of wool in this period, twill weave, resembling serge. Montgomery, *Textiles*, 342–43; Kerridge, *Textile Manufactures*, 6–7, 111–13.

43. *Counterpaine* (counterpane): a coverlet for a bed. *OED*.

44. *Holland*: a linen fabric, originally called from the province in the Netherlands. The term usually implies a fine quality. Linda R. Baumgarten, "The Textile Trade in Boston, 1650–1700," in *Arts of the Anglo-American Community in the Seventeenth Century*, ed. Ian M. G. Quimby (Charlottesville, Va., 1975), 241.

45. *Cross cloths*: linen cloths worn across the forehead. C. Willett Cunnington, Phillis Cunnington, and Charles Beard, *A Dictionary of English Costume* (Philadelphia, 1960), 57.

46. *Thred* (thread): the term meant linen in the seventeenth and eighteenth centuries. Personal communication from Linda Baumgarten, Colonial Williamsburg, Virginia.

47. *Stometcher* (stomacher): a women's ornamental covering for the chest worn under the lacing of the bodice. Cunnington, Cunnington, and Beard, *Dictionary of English Costume*, 206.

48. *Pair of woomans bodies* (bodice): an inner garment for the upper part of the body, stiffened with whalebone or wood; it was sometimes padded, corresponding to a pair of stays. Cunnington, Cunnington, and Beard, *Dictionary of English Costume*, 20.

49. *Woosted* (worsted): a closely twisted yarn made of long-staple wool in which the fibers are arranged to lie parallel to each other. The resulting fabrics are smooth and glossy. Baumgarten, personal communication; Kerridge, *Textile Manufactures*, 42–59.

50. *Broad cloth*: fine, plain-woven, dressed (i.e., fulled, napped, and shorn to give a smooth finish that does not ravel when cut), double-width cloth used chiefly for men's garments. *OED*; Baumgarten, personal communication.

51. *Pennistone* (penistone): a kind of coarse woolen cloth formerly used for garments or linings. Some varieties were napped and were often sold undyed. Montgomery, *Textiles*, 320; Kerridge, *Textile Manufactures*, 20.

52. *Serge*: an extremely durable wool fabric, woven in twill weave and usually woolen weft and worsted warp. Serge was lighter and narrower than broadcloth and of better quality than kersey. Montgomery, *Textiles*, 344; Kerridge, *Textile Manufactures*, 113–20.

53. *Irish Stockins*: probably coarse, knitted stockings, a popular English export to Ireland and the Continent in the late sixteenth and the seventeenth centuries. Joan Thirsk, *Economic Policy and Projects: The Development of a Consumer Society in Early Modern England* (Oxford, 1978), 125–27. In 1662, Irish stockings cost 12 lbs. tobacco per pair, whereas woolen stockings cost 18 lbs. per pair, and fine woolen hose, 24 lbs.

54. *Shagcloth*. A cloth having a long nap on one side, usually of worsted but sometimes of silk. Montgomery, *Textiles*, 345–46; Kerridge, *Textile Manufactures*, 106.

55. *Blew linnen* (blue linen): an inexpensive cloth widely used for clothing in the Chesapeake. Ebenezer Cook wrote in 1708, in "The Sot-Weed Factor," that when he reached Piscattaway (in present Prince Georges County),

Where soon repair'd a numerous Crew,
In Shirts and Drawers of *Scotch-cloth* Blue.
With neither Stockings, Hat, nor Shooe,
These *Sot-weed* Planters Crowd the Shoar,
In Hue as tawny as a Moor.

He added in a note, "The Planters generally wear Blue Linnen." *Works of Ebenezer Cook, Gent.: Laureat of Maryland . . .* , ed. Bernard C. Steiner, Maryland Historical Society, Fund Publication no. 36 (Baltimore, 1900), 12.

56. *Ells*: a measure of length varying in different countries. The English ell is 45 inches. R. D. Connor, *The Weights and Measures of England* (London, 1987), 94–95.

57. *Lockrome* (lockram): a linen fabric of varying quality for wearing apparel and household use. It was first made in Locronan, Brittany, from which the name was derived. Montgomery, *Textiles*, 279–81.

58. *Joseph*: probably Joseph Alvey.

59. *Galume* (galloon): a kind of narrow, close-woven ribbon or braid, of gold, silver, or silk thread, used for trimming articles of apparel and furniture. Baumgarten, personal communication.

60. *Bodkin*: a long pin or pin-shaped ornament used by women to fasten up the hair. Cunnington, Cunnington, and Beard, *Dictionary of English Costume*, 20.

61. *Curvell* (coral): a toy made of polished coral, usually with a silver whistle and bells attached, given to infants to assist them in cutting their teeth. Berenice Ball, "Whistles with Coral and Bells," *Antiques* 80 (1961): 552–55.

62. *Silke*: doubtless sewing silk. For varieties, see Thirsk, *Economic Policy and Projects*, 121.

63. *Tape*: a narrow woven strip of stout linen, cotton, silk, or other textile, used as a string for tying garments, etc. *OED*.

64. *Filleten* (filleting): unbleached tape, sometimes of Holland cloth. Montgomery, *Textiles*, 238.

65. *Bindeing* (binding): a tape or braid, often used as a protective covering for the raw edges of a fabric. Ibid., 168.

66. *Points*: tagged lace or cord of twisted yarn, silk, or leather, used to fasten various parts of clothing, where buttons are now used, or used in bunches as decoration. Cunnington, Cunnington, and Beard, *Dictionary of English Costume*, 168.

67. *Mary*: probably Mary Sheppy, with whom Cole left table linen "for the use of my house."

68. *Rugg*: a heavy, warm covering for a bed, often made of napped or shagged wool. Baumgarten, "Textile Trade," 233; Kerridge, *Textile Manufacture*, 40–41.

69. *Flock beds*: bedtick stuffed with coarse tufts and refuse of wool or cotton or of torn cloth. *OED*.

70. *Mall* (maul): a heavy hammer commonly made of wood and often used with wedges to split wood. R. A. Salaman, *Dictionary of Tools Used in the Woodworking and Allied Trades, c. 1700–1970* (New York, 1975), 524.

71. *Tennent Saw* (tenon saw): a fine handsaw, for making tenons for joints, with a back of iron or a frame to keep it from bending. Randle Holme, *Academy of Armory* (1688; reprint, Menston, England, 1972), book 3, chap. 9, p. 365.

72. *Compasses*: instruments used for measuring surfaces, such as cylinders, not directly accessible to the ordinary rule. Salaman, *Dictionary of Tools*, 108, 152–53.

73. *Weeding howes* (weeding hoes or broad hoes). "This is made use of during the cultivation of the [tobacco] crop, to keep it clean from the weeds. It is wide upon the edge, say from ten inches to a foot, or more; of thinner substance than the hilling hoe, not near so deep in the blade, and the eye is formed more bent and shelving than the latter, so that it can be set upon a more acute angle upon the helve at pleasure; by removing the wedge." G. Melvin Herndon, ed., *William Tatham and the Culture of Tobacco* (hereafter *Tatham*) (Coral Gables, Fla., 1969), 13–14.

74. *Hilling hoes* (or narrow hoes). "It is generally from six to eight inches wide, and ten or twelve in the length of the blade, according to the strength of the person who is to use it; the blade is thin, and by means of a moveable wedge which is driven into the eye of the hoe, it can be set more or less *digging* (as it is termed), that is, on a greater or less angle with the helve, at pleasure. . . . The use of this hoe is to break up the ground and throw it into shape." *Tatham*, 12–13.

75. A hogpen was built in 1663 at a cost of 350 pounds of tobacco. See above, Cole Plantation Account, original page number 134.

76. *Lift the tobacco houses*: to erect new buildings or reerect old ones in a new location. *OED*.

77. *Coopers Howell* (howel): a small adz with a gouge-shaped blade, used for cutting the shallow concave surface on the inside top of the staves of cask. Salaman, *Dictionary of Tools*, 157.

78. *Ads* (adz): a tool like an axe with the blade set at right angles to the handle and curving inward toward it; it is used for cutting or slicing away the surface of wood where axes or planes are inappropriate. Ibid., 23–24.

79. *Goods I carry with me*: probably included two hogsheads of tobacco, for which Cole sent no return, belonging to John Piles. See above, Cole Plantation Account, original page number 136.

80. *Asneck or Ratts bane*: arsenic, used as rat poison.

81. *Middle peeces of bacon*: a side of pork, salted and dried, without the spare-ribs. Holme, *Academy of Armory*, book 3, chap. 3, p. 88.

82. *Colonel Evans*: William Evans.

83. *Captain Gardner*: Luke Gardiner.

84. *Doctor Lumbrozio*: John Lumbrozio.

85. The clerk probably misread the price. At 1 1/4 pounds of tobacco per pound of pork, instead of 1 3/4, the value would be as shown.

86. *Mr. Brittaine*: William Brittaine.

87. *The march*: expedition against Indians at the Susquehanna Fort, April to October 1661. *Archives* 1:406–7, 3:410–11, 417, 420–21, 431–33, 434.

88. *The chappell*: the Roman Catholic chapel across St. Clement's Bay on Newtown Neck built by "divers good and Zealous Roman Catholick Inhabitants of New Towne and St. Clements Bay" on one and one half acres of "Bretton's Outlet" deeded by William Brittaine in November 1661. Ibid. 41:531. Robert Cole witnessed this deed.

89. The version of the account recorded in ibid., 57:206, lists the crop as 7,280 lbs.

90. *Mr. Foxhould*: John Foxhall.

91. *Tunn of casque*: cask, probably tobacco hogsheads, sufficient to hold one ton weight.

92. *A servant that was prest to goe out the march*: the march on the Susquehanna Fort in 1661. The servant was one of three men pressed from Col. William Evans's company. *Archives* 3:410–11.

93. *Mr. Salley*: Benjamin Salley.

94. Betty Cole had died in 1670.

95. Total should be 95,700 lbs.

96. *& the Advantage*: indicates the steer is more than three but less than four years old. *OED*.

97. *Berdle* (beetle): a large maul with metal rings round each end of the wooden head to prevent splitting. Salaman, *Dictionary of Tools*, 71–72.

98. *Sallery* (salary). In Maryland, executors were allowed to keep 10 percent of debts received and paid out for their trouble.

99. *Mr. Barton*: William Barton.

100. *Captain Cooke*: Miles Cooke.

101. *Man servant*: John Rey.

102. *Leavies*. County and provincial taxes were assessed by the head on all white native-born males age sixteen and above, all white immigrant male servants age ten and above, and all blacks, male and female, age ten and above. In 1662 there were three taxable men on the Cole plantation—John Elton, Robert Gates, and John Johnson. The tax lists would have been drawn up in June or July after Cole had left the province, so he would not have been counted.

103. *Due by condition*: in a contract, a provision on which its legal force or effect makes it depend. *OED*.

104. *Fran. Cole* is an error for a Cole boy, probably Robert.

105. *Mary*: possibly Mary Sheppy. The shoes may have been part of her freedom dues.

106. *Bartons*: William Barton, who owned "Barton Hall," a tract south of Cole's plantation.

107. *Monumouth Caps* (Monmouth caps): knitted caps, sometimes made of refuse wool, that followed a head-hugging, helmet-shaped pattern with a tall crown and no brim or turn up. Such caps were made at Monmouth and Bewdley, Worcester County, England. Thirsk, *Economic Policy and Projects*, 115; Kirstie Buckland, "The Monmouth Cap," *Costume* 13 (1979): 5–8.

108. *Broad hoes*: see weeding hoes, n. 73.

109. *Narrow hoes*: see hilling hoes, n. 74.

110. *Kersey*: a cheap, coarse, narrow wool cloth of twill weave, fulled after weaving. Montgomery, *Textiles*, 272–73; Kerridge, *Textile Manufactures*, 5–6, 110–11.

111. *Ozen briggs* (osnaburg): a kind of low-priced coarse linen originally made in Osnabrück, Germany. *OED*.

112. *Cheese clouts* (cloths): pieces of cloth in which curds are pressed. *OED*.

113. *Drames*: cordial, stimulant, or spirituous liquor. *OED*.

114. *Vomitt*: a medicine causing vomiting, a common medical treatment.

115. *Impostune* (impostume): an abscess. *OED*.

116. *Made* (maid): Isabel Jones.

117. *Single tens* and *double tens*: nails costing ten and twenty pennies per hundred, respectively. *OED*.

118. *Taffity* (taffeta): a light thin silk or silk and cotton fabric of decided brightness or luster. *OED*.

119. *Francis Cole*. Francis Knott is meant.

120. *Maide*: Isabel Jones.

121. *Cotten* (cotton): in the seventeenth century, a woolen fabric with a long nap, which gave a soft, fuzzy appearance. Kendal cottons, Manchester cottons, and Welsh cottons, named for the places of manufacture, were well-known woolens. *OED*; Baumgarten, "Textile Trade," 238; Kerridge, *Textile Manufactures*, 19.

122. *Man Servant*: William Felsteed.

123. *Mr. Piles*: John Piles.

124. *John Hilton*: another spelling for John Elton.

125. *Freedom cloths*. When they were freed, servants received by the custom of the country an axe, a hoe, a suit of clothes, and three barrels of corn. These clothes were apparently for Robert Gates.

126. Gardiner did not multiply properly. The total should be 175 1/2.

127. *Drumm* (drum): any of various marine and freshwater fishes, of the family Sciaenidae, that have the power of making a drumming noise. *OED*. In Chesapeake Bay, the species most commonly used for food were the black and the red drum, both bottom-oriented species that frequented waters of high salinity. Henry M. Miller, "Transforming a 'Splendid and Delightsome Land': Colonists and Ecological Change in the Chesapeake, 1607–1820," *Journal of the Washington Academy of Sciences* 76 (1986): 175–82.

128. *Falling axes* (felling axe): an axe with a long and narrow head and a long handle used for cutting trees. Salaman, *Dictionary of Tools*, 46–47, 54–56.

129. *Corne for Rent to Mr. Gerard*. Since Cole had purchased his land from Thomas Gerard, the lord of St. Clement's Manor, he paid land rent to Gerard and not quitrents to the proprietor.

130. *Certificate*. This was recorded in the provincial court records. *Archives* 49:3. "Willm Bretton Deposed sayth That Ensigne Robt Cole late of this Province Deceased hath now Five Children lyving in this Province of Maryland, Begott of his loving & naturall wife Rebecca Cole also deceased, (Viz) Robert Cole his

eldest sonne, Mary Cole, his eldest Daughter, Willm Maria Cole his second sonne, Edward Cole his third sonne, & Elizabeth Cole his youngest Daughter. All these are reputed & acknowledged th^e Children of Ensigne Robt Cole late Deceased as afores^d. The s^d Willm Bretton thereuppon having made oath & subscribed his hand this 29° March 1663.

Willm Bretton."

131. Luke Gardiner and William Turpine made supporting depositions. Ibid., 49:3. Turpine, a servant to Gardiner, was transported in 1661 and free by 1671.

132. *Sheeting*: stout cloth of linen or cotton, such as is used for bed linen, etc. *OED*.

133. *Gimblitt* (gimlet): a tool for boring small holes in wood, with a handle forming a T with the shank and a screw point; a kind of boring tool. Holme, *Academy of Armory*, book 3, chap. 9, pp. 363–64; Salaman, *Dictionary of Tools*, 208.

134. *Match coates* (matchcoats): so termed by area Indians, a mantle for protection in winter; generally made of skins, but as European goods became available, generally of duffel, a heavy woolen cloth with long nap. Baumgarten, "Textile Trade," 239. A matchcoat is illustrated in Robert Beverley, *The History and Present State of Virginia*, ed. Louis B. Wright (Chapel Hill, 1947), 161–62. The coats were doubtless exchanged with local Indians in return for a new canoe (in 1662 Cole's canoe was "none of the best although Shee bee new") and game for food.

135. *Facing*: something with which the edges of a garment are trimmed. *OED*.

136. *Jumpp* (jump): a kind of loose, unboned underbodice worn by women; often used instead of stays. Cunnington, Cunnington, and Beard, *Dictionary of English Costume*, 119.

137. *Bussines between Mr. Gerard & Mr. Cole*: probably a suit brought by Gerard against Cole for killing an unmarked hog. *Archives* 41:480.

138. *Tammy*: a fine light-weight worsted cloth of good quality, woven of plain weave, often with a glazed finish. Montgomery, *Textiles*, 360; Kerridge, *Textile Manufactures*, 53–54.

139. *The French man*: unidentified laborer on the Cole plantation.

140. *Mr. Foxwell*: George Foxwell.

141. *Noel*: unidentified, possibly the Frenchman.

142. *Skinns*: probably deer skins.

143. *Fustian*: a kind of coarse cloth made of cotton or cotton and flax; in this period, also a napped wool. Cotton and linen fustian was first made in Lancashire County, England, about 1601. Montgomery, *Textiles*, 244; Baumgarten, "Textile Trade," 240; Kerridge, *Textile Manufactures*, 49–50.

144. *Mackrill*: mackerel.

145. *By the Surveyor*. Luke Gardiner surveyed "St. Edward's" for Edward Cole, "St. Robert's" for Robert Cole, and "St. William's" for William Cole in this year. Patents 40:142–43.

146. *By the Secretary*: fees paid for recording the survey of the children's land.

147. *By a Servant*: probably John Prentice.

148. *By a Servant*: perhaps the unidentified servant sold by Gardiner for 1,600 pounds of tobacco in the same year.

149. *Fillen Hegoes*: either an unidentified individual or a transcription error for "tobacco lent to fill in H[o]g[sh]e[ad]s," i.e., tobacco lent to fill up partially full hogsheads, a common practice.

150. *By a man Servant*: probably Timothy Maham, actually purchased in 1668 but perhaps paid for in 1669.

151. *By a man servant*. Daniel Pritchard and Samuel Hewson were probably both purchased in 1669. The purchase of one of them must have been omitted from the account.

152. *Roancoake* (roanoke): a kind of wampum made and used by Maryland and Virginia Indians. Roanoke appears in several lower Western Shore inventories of the 1650s and 1660s and was generally valued at five pounds tobacco per arm's length. It was often used in the Indian trade and occasionally instead of tobacco as a medium of exchange among Europeans. For examples, see *Archives* 53:629–30, 41:288.

153. Prentice apparently ran away; the 600-pound payment of tobacco made to John Standley in 1671 or 1672 for taking up a runaway servant in Virginia may relate to this escape attempt or to a later episode.

154. *Windeing Sheete* (winding-sheet): a cloth, either a bed sheet or unfinished yard goods, in which a corpse is wrapped for burial. Clare Gittings, *Death, Burial and the Individual in Early Modern England* (London, 1984), 111–21.

155. Gardiner made various errors of calculation that in fact brought the discharge to 96159. The charge (see n. 95) came to 95700 instead of 95800. Consequently, Gardiner was creditor to the estate for 459 pounds of tobacco, not 1183.

156. *His wife*: Elizabeth Hatton Gardiner, the daughter of Richard and Margaret Hatton, who was brought to Maryland as a child. She married Luke Gardiner by 1654 and survived him. Patents AB&H:422; *Archives* 10:354–56.

Appendix 2

1. For the laws defining taxables, see William Hand Browne et al., eds., *Archives of Maryland*, 72 vols. (Baltimore, 1883–1972), 1:449, 2:399. Blacks, male and female, age ten and above, were also taxable.

Appendix 3

1. The dressed carcass of, say, a steer would be the body with hide, organs, head, and feet removed. The dressed carcass of a pig would have bristles brushed off and the organs removed. Robert Mitchell has calculated from military records of the American Revolution that the live weight of a range steer at that time was

550 pounds. From this he inferred that its carcass weight was 300 pounds—or 54.5 percent of live weight, a standard proportion—and that the usable meat was 180 pounds, or 60 percent of carcass weight and about a third of live weight. "Agricultural Change and the American Revolution," *Agricultural History* 47 (1973): 123–24. However, Henry Miller, Chief Archaeologist of Historic St. Mary's City, has argued that the percentage of edible product should be considerably higher, taking into account the likely use not only of brains and inner organs but also of marrow. The bones found in archaeological excavations are broken up for stewing. Personal communication from Miller, March 24, 1988.

To estimate the weight that the organs would add, we turned to an early twentieth-century study: P. F. Trowbridge, C. R. Moulton, and L. D. Haigh, "The Effect of Limited Food on the Growth of Beef Animals," *Missouri Agriculture Experiment Station Research Bulletin No. 30* (Kansas City, 1919), 59–60. (We thank Henry Miller for this reference.) The authors took an eleven-month and a twelve-month steer—the first fed a low-maintenance diet, the second a maintenance diet—and measured the weights of the various components of the animals. Their live weights were 470 and 585 pounds, respectively. The total weights of the edible organs (tongue, lungs, heart, liver, kidneys, brain, sweet breads, pancreas, and spleen) came to 21 and 27 pounds, respectively, which turns out to be close to 4.5 percent live weight for both. If we assume this proportion exists for later ages of livestock, then a seventeenth-century steer of 550 pounds could have 25 pounds of edible organs. To reach total edible product, we must subtract the carcass bones, minus the marrow. Henry Miller has weighed the bones of a modern full-grown, but small, steer (about 750 pounds live weight) at 34 pounds without marrow. If the bone weight is proportional to the live weight, the 550-pound steer had 25 pounds in bone, once the marrow was gone. As a result, the edible product of the steer equals the carcass weight.

For additional estimates of live weights for steers, see Lois Green Carr, "Livestock Increase and Its Implications for Diet in the Seventeenth-Century Chesapeake," *St. Mary's City Research Series* (St. Mary's City, Md., forthcoming). The 550 weight is higher than some estimates for the South in the nineteenth century but lower than others. It is lower than that implied by estimates of carcass weights collected for the seventeenth and eighteenth centuries in Europe; these suggest a mean carcass weight of 400 pounds for a steer, which implies about 730 pounds live weight. It is also lower than that implied by Miller's estimates for seventeenth-century edible product in the Chesapeake. He suggests a mean of 400 pounds for cattle of a variety of ages. "An Archaeological Perspective on the Evolution of Diet in the Colonial Chesapeake, 1620–1745," in *Colonial Chesapeake Society*, ed. Lois Green Carr, Philip D. Morgan, and Jean B. Russo (Chapel Hill, 1988), 199. We have used Mitchell's estimate of 550 pounds for live weight, partly because it is based on an adequate amount of firm data and partly because it provides less meat and hence strengthens the test for availability.

2. See chap. 2 n. 47.

3. Personal communication from David O. Percy, former Director, National Colonial Farm, Accokeek, Maryland, February 1988.

4. See chap. 2 n. 49.

5. The yearlings and two-year-old females of 1662 are reduced to three of each on the assumption that six female calves were born in the years 1660 and 1661 and half survived.

6. Carr, "Livestock Increase"; Sam B. Hilliard, *Hogmeat and Hoecake: Food Supply in the Old South, 1840–1860* (Carbondale, Ill., 1972), 128.

7. Carr, "Livestock Increase," discusses these studies and provides the annotation.

8. *Hogmeat and Hoecake*, 103–4. Robert Gallman estimated two farrowings and four surviving pigs per year in the mid-nineteenth-century South. "Self-sufficiency in the Cotton Economy of the Antebellum South," in *The Structure of the Cotton Economy of the Antebellum South*, ed. William N. Parker (Washington, D.C., 1970), 14 (notes to table 3).

9. See n. 1 for the method for calculating edible product. A problem arises in calculating live weights, and hence carcass weights and edible product, for cows and young animals. For cows, Carr took 75 percent of the weight for a steer, since data she collected from various sources (see her "Livestock Increase") show this proportion. For young steers, she used data supplied by Henry Miller from J. A. Crichton, J. N. Aitken, and P. W. Boyne, "The Effect of Plane of Nutrition during Rearing on Growth Production, Reproduction, and Health of Dairy Cattle," *Animal Production* 2 (1960). These show, for a low-maintenance diet, that at 44 weeks a calf had reached 28 percent of its mature weight; at 80 weeks, 47 percent; at 104 weeks, 62 percent; at 132 weeks, 70 percent; at 182 weeks, 81 percent; and at 250 weeks, 95 percent. Supposing that these proportions apply to seventeenth-century cattle, Carr has inferred that, given 550 pounds live weight for a steer, a 4-year steer weighed about 450 pounds; a 3-year steer, 400 pounds; a 2-year steer, 340 pounds; and a yearling, 180 pounds. Live weight for a calf at 53 pounds comes from B. H. Slicher Von Bath, *The Agrarian History of Western Europe, A.D. 500–1850* (New York, 1963), table IV.

10. Miller, "Evolution of Diet," in *Colonial Chesapeake Society*, ed. Carr, Morgan, and Russo, 176–90.

11. Miller found that 65 percent of the meat weight was in beef. Ibid., 186. However, he used a higher estimate for the amount of usable meat. See above, n. 1.

Appendix 4

1. Patents Q:21, 447, 5:152–53, Maryland State Archives, Annapolis, Maryland.

Index

· · · · ·

All place names and personal names that appear in the text and notes are indexed with three major exceptions. First, names that appear as part of source citations are not indexed. Second, although names of modern historians are indexed when their work is discussed in the text, references to them in the notes are not indexed. Third, for the biographical appendix, we indexed only the names of the primary entries, omitting associated individuals and place names. Places are in Maryland unless otherwise noted.